CW01646298

Watteau

THE DRAWINGS

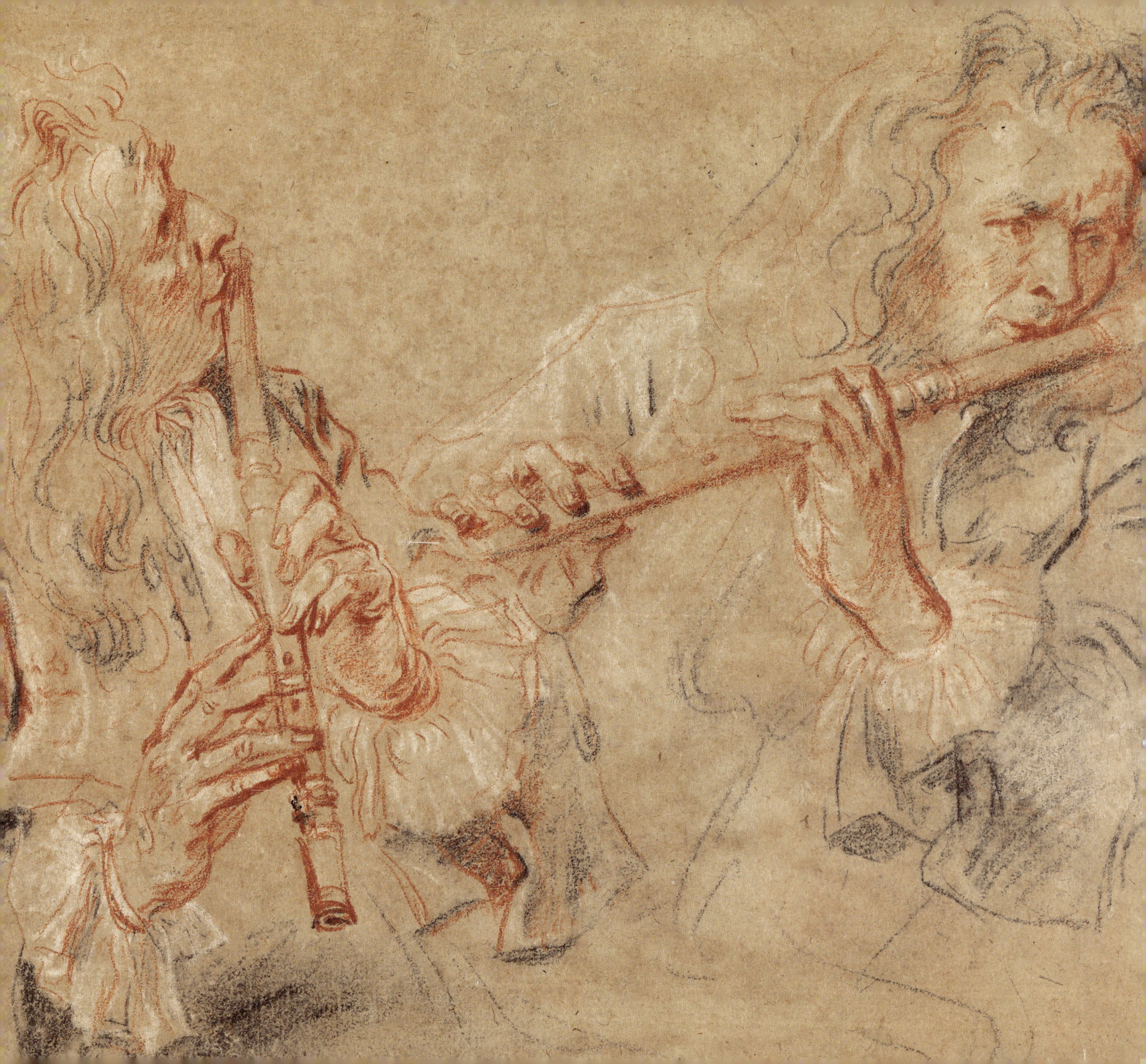

Watteau
THE DRAWINGS

Pierre Rosenberg and Louis-Antoine Prat
with a contribution by Martin Eidelberg

ROYAL ACADEMY OF ARTS

First published on the occasion of the exhibition
'Watteau: The Drawings'

Royal Academy of Arts, London
12 March – 5 June 2011

2009–2013 Season
Supported by JTI

Supported by Region Holdings

The Royal Academy of Arts is grateful to Her Majesty's Government for agreeing to indemnify this exhibition under the National Heritage Act 1980, and to Resource, The Council for Museums, Archives and Libraries, for its help in arranging the indemnity.

EXHIBITION CURATORS
Louis-Antoine Prat
Pierre Rosenberg

Royal Academy of Arts
Katia Pisvin
Cecilia Treves

EXHIBITION ORGANISATION
Idoya Beitia
assisted by Philippa Hemsley

PHOTOGRAPHIC AND COPYRIGHT CO-ORDINATION
Kitty Corbet Milward

CATALOGUE
Royal Academy Publications
David Breuer
Beatrice Gullström
Carola Krueger
Sophie Oliver
Peter Sawbridge
Nick Tite

Translation of texts by Louis-Antoine Prat and Pierre Rosenberg from the French: Caroline Beamish
Design: Myfanwy Vernon-Hunt
Colour origination: DawkinsColour
Printed in Italy by Graphicom

Copyright © 2011 Royal Academy of Arts, London

Any copy of this book issued by the publisher as a paperback is sold subject to the condition that it shall not by way of trade or otherwise be lent, re-sold, hired out or otherwise circulated without the publisher's prior consent in any form of binding or cover other than that in which it is published and without a similar condition including these words being imposed on a subsequent purchaser.

All Rights Reserved. No part of this publication may be reproduced or transmitted in any form or by any means, electronic or mechanical, including photocopy, recording or any other information storage and retrieval system, without prior permission in writing from the publisher.

British Library Cataloguing-in-Publication Data
A catalogue record for this book is available from the British Library

ISBN 978-1-905711-71-0 (paperback)
ISBN 978-1-905711-70-3 (hardback)

Distributed outside the United States and Canada by Thames & Hudson Ltd, London

Distributed in the United States and Canada by Harry N. Abrams, Inc., New York

EDITOR'S NOTE

All works of art illustrated are by Jean-Antoine Watteau (1684–1721) unless otherwise stated.

All dimensions are given height before width, those of works on paper in millimetres and those for paintings in centimetres.

Abbreviations have been used throughout the text to indicate the following three key sources:

DV Emile Dacier and Albert Vuaflart, *Jean de Jullienne et la gravure de Watteau au XVIIIème siècle*, Paris, 1922

PM Karl Theodor Parker and Jacques Mathey, *Antoine Watteau: Catalogue complet de son œuvre dessiné*. Paris, 1957

RP Pierre Rosenberg and Louis-Antoine Prat, *Antoine Watteau, 1684–1721: Catalogue raisonné des dessins*, 3 vols, Milan, 1996

Full details of each work's provenance, exhibition history and bibliographic references can be found in the authors' 1996 catalogue raisonné.

ILLUSTRATIONS
Page 2: detail of cat. 75
Page 7: detail of cat. 38
Page 10: detail of cat. 8
Page 16: detail of cat. 77
Page 20: detail of cat. 48
Page 26: detail of cat. 33
Pages 34–35: detail of cat. 84
Endpapers: cat. 49

Contents

President's Foreword

Jean-Antoine Watteau (1684–1721) was one of the greatest draughtsmen in the history of French art. Active during the last years of the reign of Louis XIV and the Regency, he pioneered a style that favoured spontaneity, lightness and intimacy over the grandiosity and formal rules of academic art. The elegance, charm and immediacy of Watteau's drawings were widely remarked upon by his contemporaries. We are delighted to present the first comprehensive exhibition of the artist's drawings in the United Kingdom.

Watteau drew unceasingly, mostly from life, vividly capturing a gesture or pose, the graceful tilt of a head, the articulation and sheen of drapery, and the subtlety of human expressions. These he conveyed primarily with chalk, his favourite medium, which he handled in an extraordinary variety of ways. He is particularly renowned for his innovative use and mastery of the *trois crayons* technique, the skilful and free juxtaposition of red, black and white chalks for both plastic and expressive effect. The brilliance and development of his draughtsmanship are demonstrated by the wide range of his subject-matter. This encompasses not only *fêtes galantes* and theatre pieces, but also studies after the Old Masters, ornamental designs, portraits, children, nudes, soldiers, musicians, exotic figures and shop interiors.

The idea of mounting this exhibition originated at the Royal Academy. We were delighted when Pierre Rosenberg of the Académie Française, Président-Directeur Honoraire of the Musée du Louvre, Paris, and Louis-Antoine Prat, Professeur at the Ecole du Louvre and Chargé de Mission in the Department of Graphic Arts at the Musée du Louvre, agreed to join us in the enterprise. They are responsible for the careful selection and interpretation of nearly ninety of Watteau's finest sheets. The exhibition and its catalogue benefit immensely from their expertise, which is drawn not least from the extensive research that led to their landmark 1996 catalogue raisonné of Watteau's drawings. Martin Eidelberg's excellent essay charting the growth in appreciation of Watteau's drawings in Britain, where the artist resided in 1719–20, confirms the relevance of this long-overdue exhibition in this country. In addition, 'Watteau: The Drawings' builds on past monographic exhibitions of the work of French artists presented at the Royal Academy, including 'Nicolas Poussin' (1995) and 'Chardin' (1999), both curated by Pierre Rosenberg.

The selection draws on the particularly rich holdings of the Musée du Louvre and of the British Museum, our most generous lenders. We are also very grateful to the many other public and private lenders in Britain and overseas who, together, have made this exhibition possible. We thank them all.

No exhibition can be realised without the assistance of loyal benefactors. We owe a great debt of gratitude to JTI, 2009–2013 Season Supporter of our programme in the Sackler Wing of Galleries, and to Region Holdings, for their support of the exhibition.

Sir Nicholas Grimshaw CBE PRA
President, Royal Academy of Arts

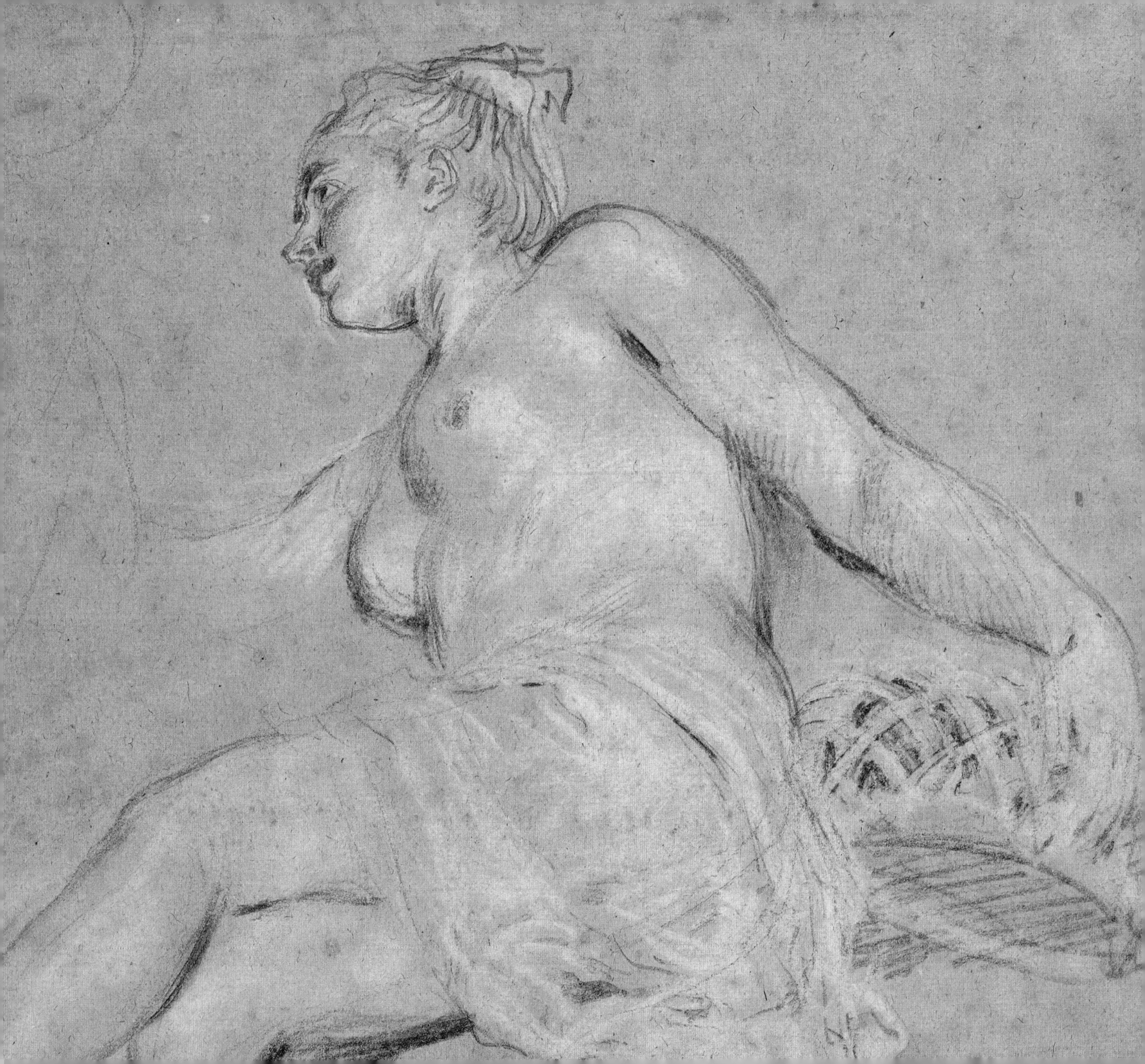

Supporter Statements

As the long-term Season Supporter of exhibitions in the Sackler Wing of Galleries, JTI is delighted to have played a part in bringing this extraordinary exhibition to the Royal Academy. 'Watteau: The Drawings' celebrates an artist whose work has had a profound influence on art over the past three centuries.

Martin Southgate
General Manager UK, JTI

We are delighted to support 'Watteau: The Drawings' at the Royal Academy of Arts. Region Holdings is committed to strengthening economic ties between the West and the East, and to establishing social, urban and physical infrastructures in emerging markets. Contributing to the arts, a universal language across societies and cultures, is a core element of our philosophy. Our partnership with the Royal Academy is a testament to our belief, and we look forward to strengthening it further in the future.

Rehan Atiq
Chairman and CEO, Region Holdings

Acknowledgements

The Royal Academy of Arts would like to thank the following individuals for their generous assistance during the making of this exhibition and its catalogue:

Katharine Baetjer, Aurelia Botella, Sabine Breuer, Stephanie Buck, Linda Cantele, Edmund Capon, Jay A. Clarke, Hélène Couot, Taco Dibbits, Rhoda Eitel-Porter, Christine Ekelhart, Albert J. Elen, James Fairfax, Laurence Garrido, Ann and Gordon Getty, Michel Gierzod, George Goldner, Margaret Morgan Grasselli, Amanda Green, Mechthild Haas, Sophie Harent, Deborah Hatch, Margaret Heck, Lee Hendrix, Thomas Ketelson, Christophe Leribault, Suzanne Folds McCullagh, Hermann Mildenberger, Olaf Molansky, Gabriel Naughton, Peter Raissis, Claudia Rice, Martin Royalton-Kisch, David Scrase, Perrin Stein, Beatrice Stern, Nathalie Strasser, Sandra Tatsakis, Letizia Treves, Carel van Tuyll, Miriam Have Watts, Tim Wilson, and Alan Wintermute.

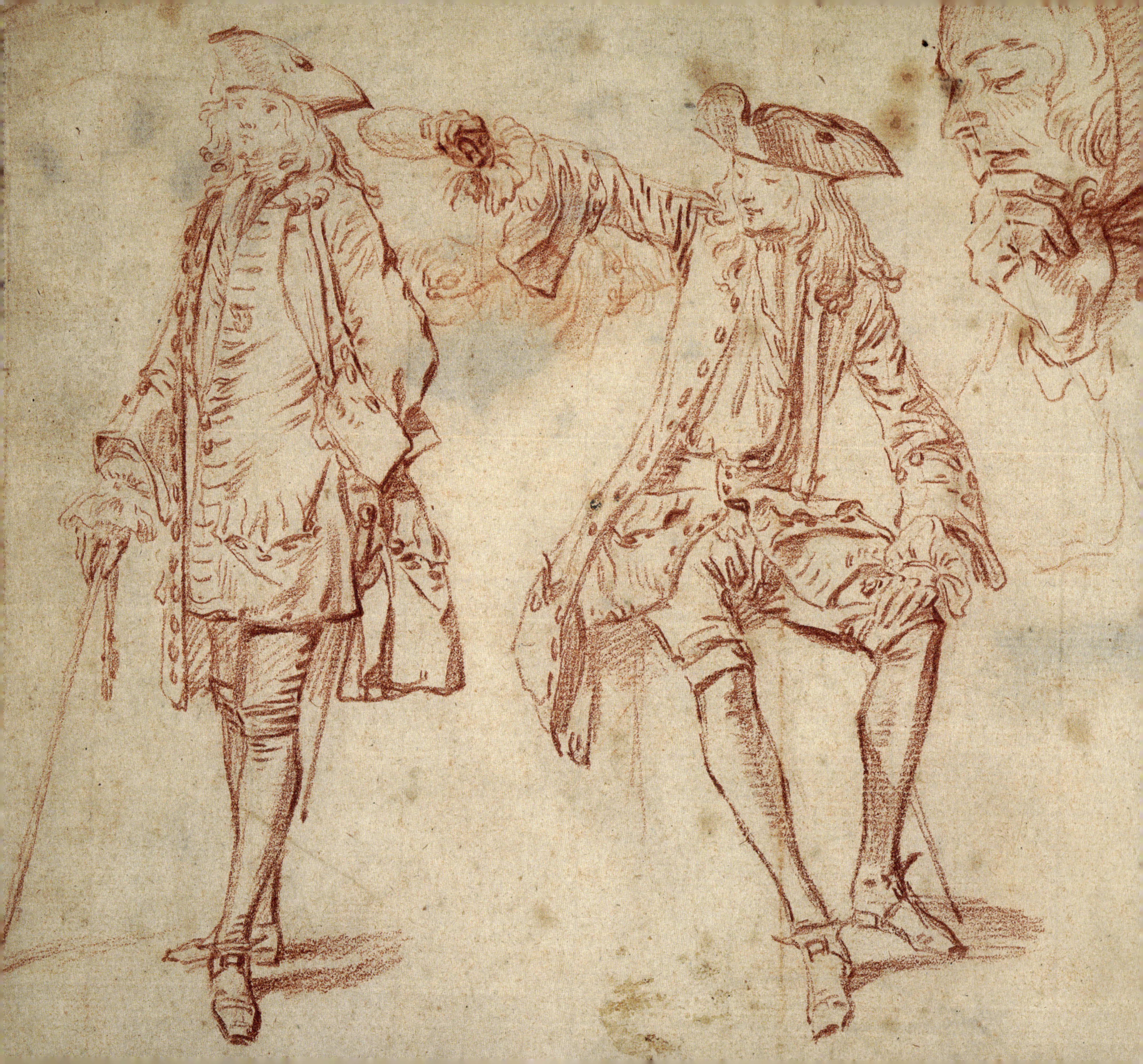

Watteau by His Contemporaries

Pierre Rosenberg

What do we know about the life and career of Watteau?[1] He seems to have been born in Valenciennes on 10 October 1684, although doubt has recently even been cast on the actual date. His background was modest – roofers, carpenters, large families – but is it correct to call him a French artist? Valenciennes was Flemish, then Flemish and Spanish, and did not become French until 1678. To many eighteenth-century authors, Watteau was a Flemish artist. A French painter or a Flemish painter? It is easy to see why the novelty of his art, plus the fact that his paintings and drawings broke with traditional French painting of the reign of Louis XIV, might have shocked certain eighteenth-century critics, encouraging them to relegate his art to another tradition, namely to Flemish genre painting.

Nothing is known about Watteau's earliest apprenticeship in Valenciennes, except that he passed through the studio of a certain Guérin (or Gérin). The Abbé Leclerc, one of his first biographers and also one of the most reliable, informs us that he 'came to Paris in 1702'. He was eighteen. What encouraged him to move to the French capital? Had he had any artistic training? One fact seems certain: in 1703 he was working for a picture dealer named Etienne Desrais in his shop on the Pont Notre-Dame. He spent all day copying the same painting, an old woman wearing spectacles and reading, by Gerard Dou (probably one of the versions of the picture now in the State Hermitage Museum, St Petersburg).

No documentary evidence exists relating to Watteau's life between 1703 and 1707. Around this time he made the acquaintance of Claude Gillot (1673–1722), a painter who had already enjoyed some success. Relations between the two men are shrouded in mystery; we know only that they deteriorated rapidly. Was it jealousy on Gillot's part in the face of Watteau's extraordinary facility? Apart from some lines by Jean de Jullienne, we have no concrete evidence to suggest that Gillot abandoned painting because Watteau's obvious talent so discouraged him.

Soon after this estrangement, Watteau entered the studio of another artist, Claude Audran III (1658–1734), a 'celebrated decorative painter' according to Pierre-Jean Mariette. Audran offered Watteau an added advantage: he was *concierge* (today we would say 'curator') of the Palais du Luxembourg, in which Rubens's series of paintings on the *Life of Marie de Médicis*, now in the Musée du Louvre, could be admired. These canvases were one of Watteau's most important sources of inspiration.

Also in 1709, when he was twenty-five, Watteau was mentioned in the register of the Académie Royale de Peinture et de Sculpture and took second place in the Prix de Rome competition. The subject of his painting is not known. More disturbing is the fact that the prize was awarded to a certain Antoine Grison (or Grisson), an artist who has been completely forgotten. How did Grison beat Watteau to first place? If Watteau had been awarded first place, would he have left for Rome where the French ran an academy that was soon to gain prestige? What would Italy have given him? What influences would he have absorbed? In what way would his style have been altered?

In 1709 Watteau returned to Valenciennes, for reasons we know nothing about. How long did he stay there? According to the Comte de Caylus, 'he did not stay there

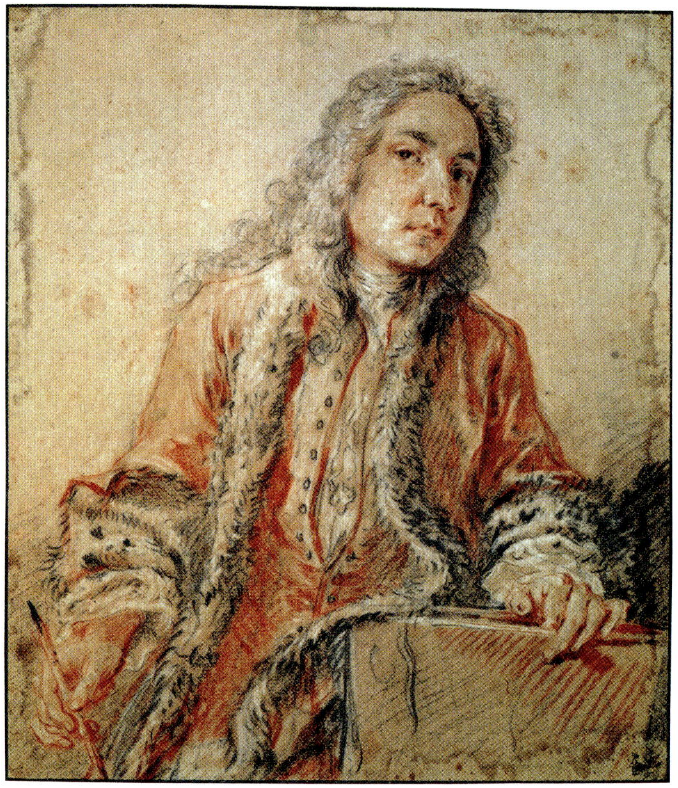

Fig. 1
François Boucher, *Portrait of Watteau*, 1727. Black and red chalk heightened with white, 230 x 200 mm. Musée Condé, Chantilly

long'. At any rate, it was during this trip to Valenciennes that Watteau came into contact with the army – this was the year of the bloody and disastrous Battle of Malplaquet – and while there he painted military scenes for the picture dealer Pierre Sirois. These were not paintings of battles or glorious feats of arms, however; in fact they depicted the anonymity of the troops and the unembellished rigours of the soldiers' daily life.

None of Watteau's early biographers mention his life before 30 July 1712, the date of his acceptance into the Académie Royale de Peinture et de Sculpture, to which he presented several paintings. The Académie requested that he paint what was then called a 'reception piece'. 'The subject of the work has been left to him to decide,' the proceedings of the Académie note. He took a long time to complete his piece. The Académie called him to order on 5 January 1714 and again in 1715, the year of Louis XIV's death.

At this date he was living 'at the Suisse, at the descent from the Pont-neuf'. Count Tessin (1695–1770), the Swedish ambassador to France, paid him a visit. 'Watteau,' he wrote, 'pupil of Gillot, Flemish by birth, succeeds very well in painting grotesques, landscapes, fashions.'

In 1716 Watteau succeeded in postponing submission of his reception piece yet again. The fabulously wealthy banker Pierre Crozat (1665–1740) praised the artist in a letter written to the eminent Venetian pastel painter Rosalba Carriera (1675–1757; fig. 2): 'Among all our painters, I know only Monsieur Watteau to be capable of producing a work suitable to be presented to you.' He adds: 'He is very slow in everything he does.' The reception piece was still awaited. Finally, on 28 August 1717, Watteau was admitted to the Académie Royale de Peinture et de Sculpture thanks to his *Pilgrimage to the Isle of Cythera* (fig. 3). The Académie created a new category of painting for Watteau, the *fête galante*, which a contemporary dictionary (Furetière, edition of 1690) defined as follows: 'Festivities by decent folk' (for the past few years there has been a campaign to class this painting as a 'peinture d'histoire' [history painting]). The title of the piece is (deliberately?) ambiguous. Do pilgrims go to Cythera, the island of Love, full of hope and lust, or do they leave it with melancholy and sadness? Is the painting a hymn to the expectation of love, or is it meant to be nostalgic?

In 1717 Watteau was living with Crozat, and the following year with the painter Nicolas Vleughels (1668–1737). In 1719 he took up residence with Pierre Sirois. At the end of that year he left for London, probably for health reasons. In the grip of 'consumption', or tuberculosis, he wanted to consult the famous doctor Richard Mead (1673–1754), who was also an admirer of his work. It is not impossible also that the artist, ruined by the failure of John Law's economic system in France, might have hoped to make his fortune in England. On 20 August 1720 Watteau was back in Paris: Rosalba Carriera mentions his name in her journal. On 30 September Watteau, a keen music lover, attended a concert in Crozat's house. He was then living in the house of another dealer, Edme-François Gersaint. Seriously ill, he escaped to Nogent-sur-Marne, near

Paris, where he died on 18 July 1721 'of an affliction of the lungs' at the age of thirty-seven, 'a fatal age for painting: the celebrated Raphael of Urbino and Eustache Le Sueur died at that age', commented Antoine de La Roque (see cat. 34). The death of Watteau was announced at the Académie on 26 July. *The Gersaint Shop Sign* (fig. 4), the finest French painting of the eighteenth century, painted in just a few days, was to be his artistic legacy.

* * *

Watteau was 'of medium height and weak constitution' (Jullienne), and 'his health was severely impaired', states Mariette. According to Gersaint, 'his figure was unimposing'. 'His eyes gave no indication of either his talent or the liveliness of his mind' (Caylus). 'He was of a sweet and affable nature' (La Roque), 'cold and indifferent' (Jullienne), 'gloomy of character', with a 'delicate, exhausted temperament', 'indolent and impatient' (Gersaint).

Watteau did not marry. We know of no liaisons, with women or men. He could never settle down and lived first with one person, then with another. 'Unstable', according to Jullienne. 'No sooner was he established in his lodgings than he took against them. He moved hundreds and hundreds of times' (Caylus). According to La Roque, 'he was naturally modest and shy'. 'Boredom dogged him and disgust [...] was his companion' (Mariette). 'Hard work had made him somewhat melancholy' (a word that returns over and over again), 'chilly and awkward to meet, which made those who did not know him treat him as a curiosity. The truth is that he was not very affectionate. He was anxious, always dissatisfied with himself, liking change, never satisfied with where he was – which often made him unbearable to himself and sometimes to his friends as well' (the Abbé Leclerc). To quote Jullienne: 'He had a lively and enquiring mind and noble feelings. He spoke little but well and wrote the same. He was constantly deep in thought, and was a great admirer of nature and of all the painters who copied nature [...] His only defect was indifference and love of change.' Gersaint says: 'His character was anxious and volatile; he stood by his wishes, was a libertine intellectually but was sober of habit, impatient, shy, cold and awkward in manner, discreet and reserved with strangers, a good but difficult friend, misanthropic, a shrewd, biting critic, always dissatisfied with himself and others and slow to forgive. He spoke little but well.'

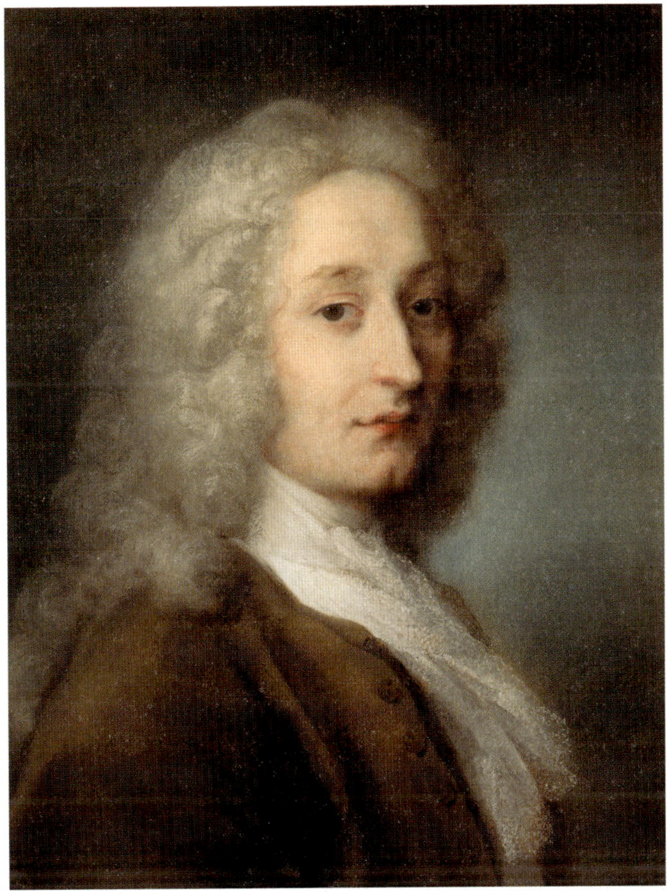

Fig. 2
Rosalba Carriera, *Portrait of Watteau*, 1721.
Pastel, 550 x 430 mm. Museo Civico Luigi Bailo, Treviso

Let us pick out some of the adjectives: La Roque, 'gentle and affable'; the Abbé Leclerc, 'speaking little but well'; Gersaint, 'inconstant'; Caylus, 'caustic and also shy [...] clever'; d'Argenville, 'lively, enquiring mind'; Gersaint, 'melancholy character'; 'sombre', according to Caylus; 'he was constantly deep in thought', according to Leclerc. 'Older than others thanks to the type of mind he had', according to Caylus, who adds 'he had no interest in money'.

Watteau adored music and song. 'He was born at the same time caustic and also shy, two qualities not usually combined by nature. He was bright, and although he had no education, he was shrewd and a delicate judge of music and all works of the mind', according to Caylus, who adds 'reading was his greatest relaxation'.

Watteau, the painter of women, is sometimes seen as an erotic artist – or at least licentious. Caylus explains: 'Watteau had an upright heart and his resignation [the word is an allusion to his impending death] must have been sincere. What is more, he was never carried away by passion, was dominated by no vice and never created anything obscene. He pushed delicacy to the point where, a few days before his death, he recalled various pieces that he believed were insufficiently far from this style, in order to have the satisfaction of burning them, which he did.'

Watteau's working methods were so unusual as to deserve some explanation. Let us take another look at Caylus: 'His custom was to draw his studies in a bound volume, so that he always had a large number to hand. He owned some fancy costumes, some of them from the Commedia dell'Arte, in which he dressed people of either sex, if he found things that would fit, and he drew people in attitudes as nature presented them, much preferring simpler attitudes to any others. When the whim took him to paint a picture he would have recourse to his anthology [in other words, to the "bound volume"]. He chose the figures that best suited his purposes at the time. He formed them into groups, most often according to a landscape background he had designed or prepared. It was rare for him to act otherwise.'

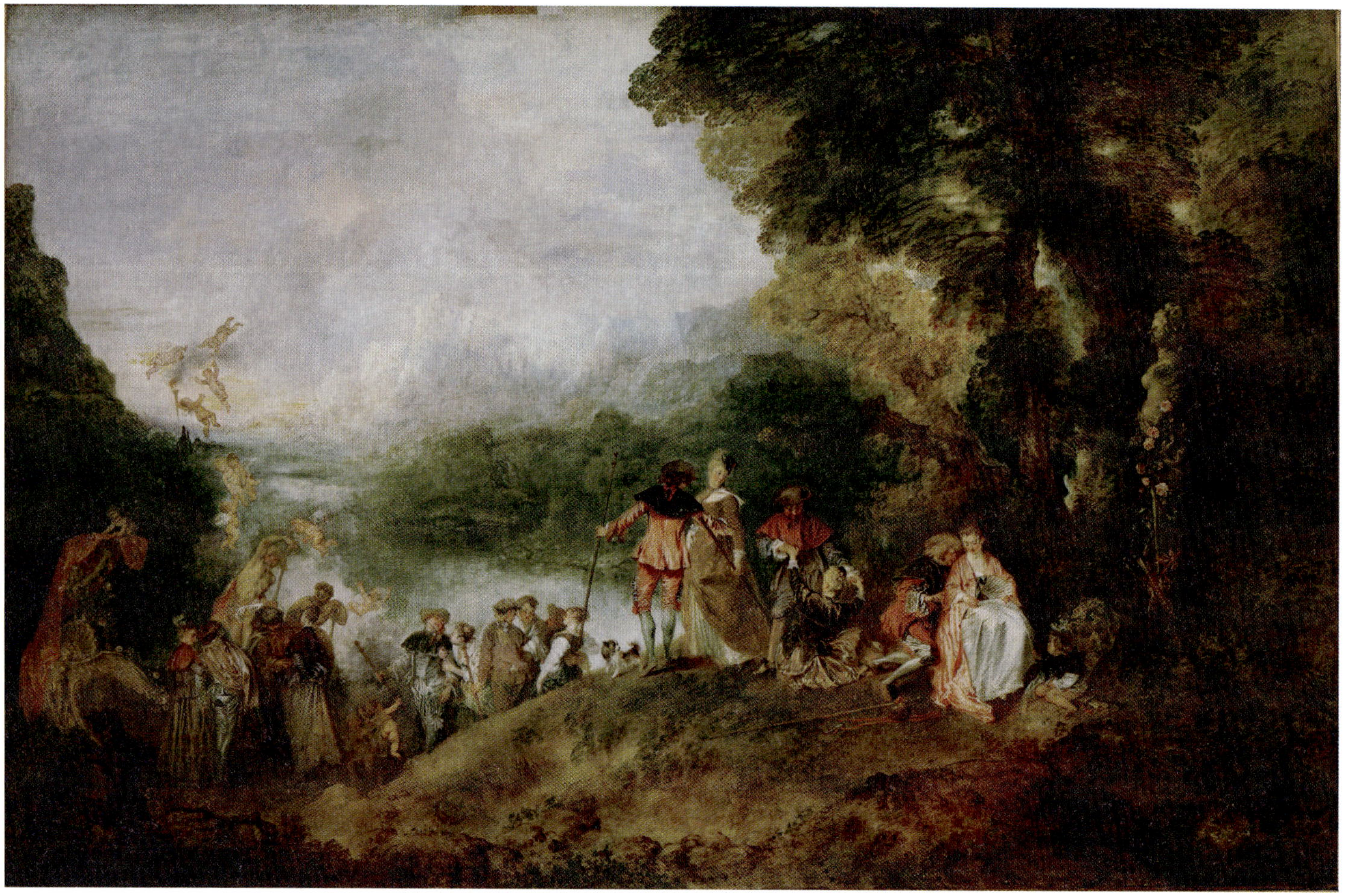

Fig. 3
Pilgrimage to the Isle of Cythera, Watteau's reception piece to the Académie Royale de Peinture et de Sculpture, 1717. Oil on canvas, 129 x 193 cm. Musée du Louvre, Paris

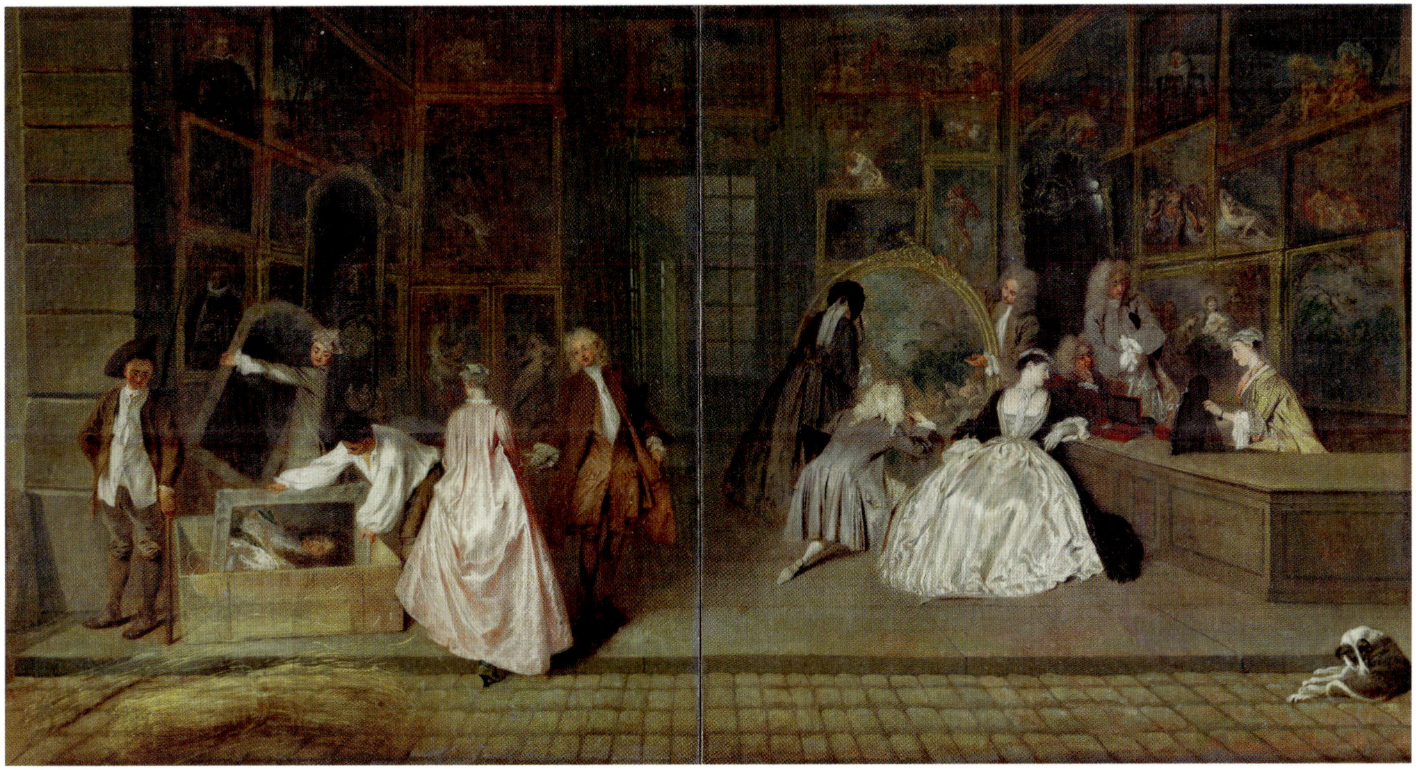

Fig. 4
The Gersaint Shop Sign, 1721.
Oil on canvas, 166 x 308 cm.
Schloss Charlottenburg, Berlin

Although Watteau's paintings were sometimes criticised during his lifetime, as some contemporary texts tell us, his drawings were always greeted with unanimous approval: 'For his drawings, when executed during his great period, in other words since he left the house of M. de Crozat, nothing is finer of its kind: the delicacy, grace, lightness, precision, facility, expression [...] He will always be regarded as one of the greatest and best draughtsmen that France has produced [...] What is more, no-one could reproach me [this is Gersaint] with not having made him a great draughtsman, since I hold his drawings in preference over his paintings. Watteau was of the same mind in this respect. He was more satisfied with his drawings than his paintings and I can assure you that, in that respect, self-esteem hid none of his faults from him. He got more pleasure from drawing than from painting.'

To conclude, let us quote Caylus's fine text: 'Enjoying a good reputation, he had no other enemy than himself, and a certain instability of mind that dominated him [...] Where he settled most easily was in the rooms I had in different *quartiers* of Paris which were used only for sittings with models, for painting and drawing. In these places, which were devoted solely to art, away from interruptions, he and I and a mutual friend [this was Nicolas Hénin, one of Watteau's close friends] of similar tastes experienced the pure joy of youth, combined with liveliness of imagination in the delights of painting. I can state that Watteau, so sombre, melancholy, so shy and critical anywhere else, was here simply the Watteau of the paintings: in other words, the artist they make you imagine – delightful, tender and perhaps a bit of a shepherd.'

ENDNOTE

1 In this text a number of quotations from works by Watteau's contemporaries occur (among them the Abbé Leclerc, Jean de Jullienne, Pierre-Jean Mariette, the Comte de Caylus, Edme-François Gersaint, Antoine de La Roque). These texts can be found in my anthology *Vies anciennes de Watteau*, Paris, 1984; *Le Vite antiche*, Bologna, 1991.

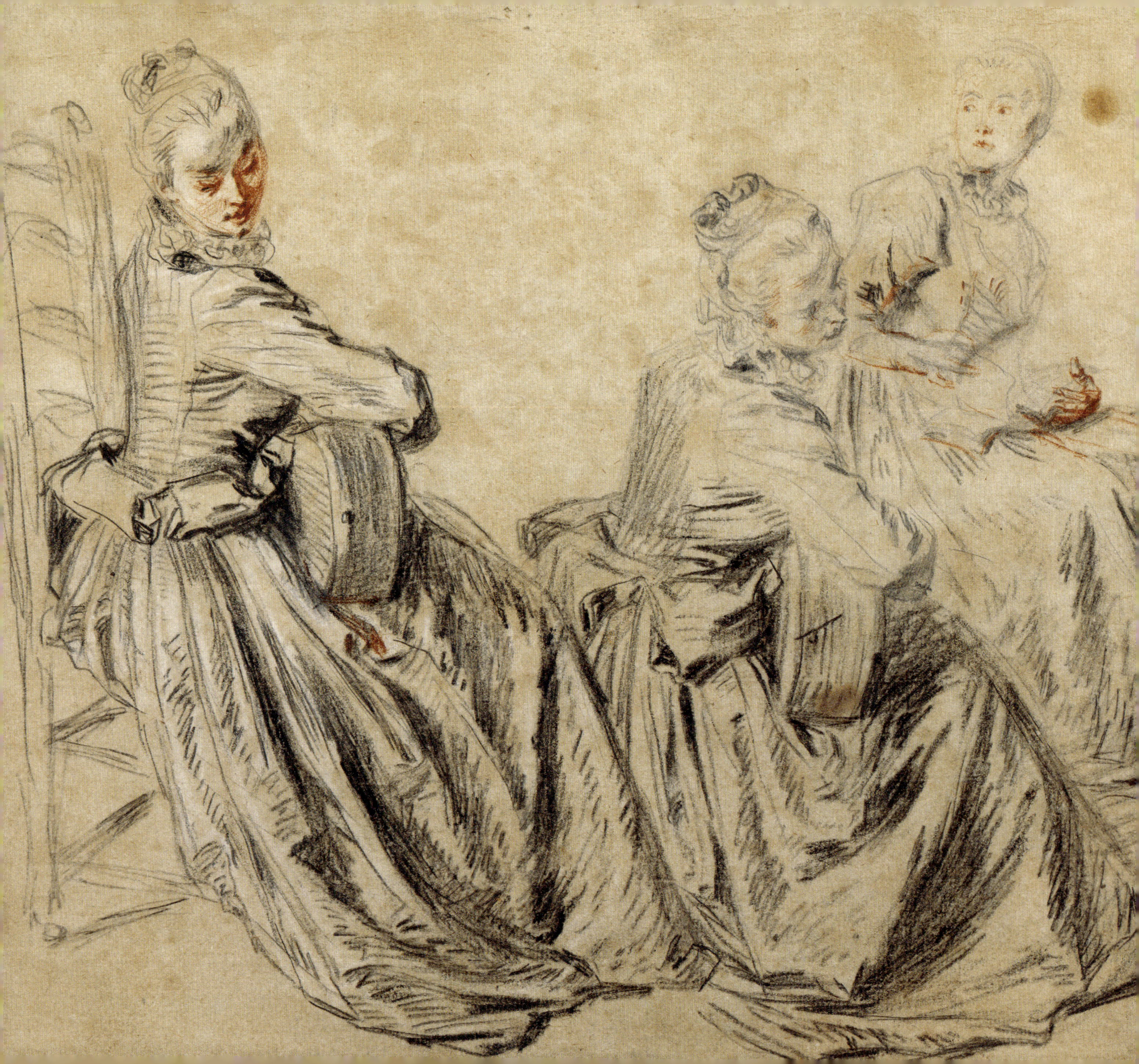

Heady Airs, Festive Airs

Louis-Antoine Prat

According to the *fortune critique* of Watteau, published in Flammarion's *Tout l'œuvre peint...* series, one of the first pieces of writing about Watteau, in *L'abecedario pittorico* by Father Orlandi, published in 1719 during the artist's lifetime, praises his 'accurate drawing' and his '*airs de têtes*' ('heady airs'), which were considered by the author to be 'very fine'. Six years after Watteau's death (fig. 5), in a description of the paintings in the Palais-Royal, Dubois de Saint-Gelais copies Orlandi's description of his 'accurate drawing' word for word, but seems to have added 'his expressions are piquant, his *airs de fêtes* [festive airs] have marvellous grace, his dancing figures are admirable in their lightness, the perfection of their movements and the beauty of their attitudes'. *Airs de têtes, airs de fêtes...* Is the repetition avoided by a welcome printer's error, or by accidental insistence on the idea of a *fête galante* (so novel an idea that we know that the Académie Royale de Peinture et de Sculpture was obliged to create a new genre when Watteau joined its ranks)?

Watteau's heads alone contribute to the lively festivities, provoked here by the reuniting of nearly 90 of his finest drawings. Such an enterprise has not been attempted since the first Watteau exhibition of 1984–85 in Washington, Paris and Berlin, which brought together a total of 143 drawings, some only exhibited in one or two of the venues of this monographic retrospective.

Almost half way between the 1984–85 exhibition, which included a number of less important drawings, and the present one, our catalogue raisonné of Watteau's drawings appeared in three volumes in 1996 with the encouragement and sustained support of the late Leonardo Mondadori, himself a passionate collector and owner at one time of *Three Studies of Female Heads* (Collection Jean Bonna, Geneva; RP 635). This work was the second in an immense enterprise, spread over more than a decade, which allowed us to publish the catalogues raisonnés of the drawings of Poussin (1994) and David (2002). Although a number of important landscapes by Poussin have reappeared since then,[1] and very large numbers of pages by David have also re-surfaced,[2] the same cannot be said for Watteau: very few genuine drawings by Watteau unknown in 1996 have reappeared since then; in fact, not a single one exists that is regarded as important enough to appear here.[3]

Our catalogue raisonné had one particular attribute: it succeeded another volume with the same ambition, entitled *Antoine Watteau: Catalogue complet de son œuvre dessiné*, which was published in 1957 by Sir Karl Theodor Parker and Jacques Mathey (like the present exhibition, a Franco-British collaboration). Despite its mythical status, in our opinion that catalogue required a fundamental overhaul, less on account of its deficiencies than for its excessive generosity. Almost a third of the drawings included by the two experts seemed to us not to be by Watteau; this is why the catalogue raisonné of his drawings, like a *peau de chagrin*, was reduced from 961 numbers to 669. We tried to place each sheet of drawings within its context, comparing it with photographs of Watteau's paintings (or more frequently engravings from the painted works, as these are easier to read). We also attempted to augment the documentary approach by re-examining historical records, by very thorough bibliographical checks (books, articles, exhibition catalogues), and by systematic references to engravings made from the drawings,[4] counter-proofs that might have been taken from them, or copies inspired by counter-proofs. Our system of classification, unlike that of Parker and Mathey, who classified the drawings by subject, was chronological, and this is certainly the area in which reviewers of our work have found the most to criticise.[5]

Watteau's life remains something of a mystery. Written contracts for his work are scarce and are not dated, and he never signed or dated any of his paintings, nor unfortunately his drawings. It is thus difficult to assign his paintings to a particular date; from this a large part of his later chronological development would flow quite logically. In the introduction to our catalogue raisonné, we were at pains to draw attention to the important differences encountered in the essential reading on the subject: the book by Marianne Roland Michel and Margaret Morgan Grasselli's thesis. Roland Michel was of the view that the authentic Watteau, independent of exterior influences, 'was born' about four years earlier than he was for Grasselli. Our catalogue entries here make it clear that these thorny problems of chronology continue to dog us, the more so because Watteau was in the habit of picking up a page of studies some years after he had begun it – making the art historian's task a great deal more complicated – completing it here and there and filling spaces previously left empty.

Links with the painted works, which can be of such assistance to cataloguers of other artists' work, here require caution since another of Watteau's habits was that of reusing figure drawings in paintings of different periods, arranging the figures in different ways, associating a man and woman in one way in one painting, for example, and then in a completely different way in another. Each figure must therefore be traced through various paintings, sometimes far apart in date (when the date is known), and without the result being any help towards the dating of the corresponding drawing. This is the consequence of the artist's habit, which Caylus denounced, complaining that Watteau drew 'without any object'.

One fixed point was to make its mark, about half way through the artist's career. This is supplied by the celebrated series of portraits of Persians: we know that a delegation of Persians arrived in Paris in 1715. The technical maturity of this series of drawings (see cats 23–26), whose obvious similarities make comparison with the ten almost contemporary drawings of Savoyards (see cats 27–32) possible, is made apparent by the use of three colours, black and red chalk with highlights of white chalk. Some authors, however, date this technical advance to at least two or three years earlier; what is more, it is not absolutely sure that the 'Persians' who posed for Watteau were genuinely oriental: their faces look strangely European, arousing the suspicion that they might be Watteau's friends dressed up… as Persians. Nothing about Watteau is ever straightforward.

Even the question of the numerical extent of his graphic work is the subject of debate: according to early sources, which all seem equally reliable, he either bequeathed all his drawings to one of his friends, the Abbé Haranger, canon of St-Germain l'Auxerrois (see cat. 86), or he divided the portfolios between Haranger and three other friends. When Haranger died, more than 1,000 drawings by Watteau were inventoried. Was this a very large proportion of his whole production, or only a quarter of it? Similarly, it is impossible to infer, from the proportion of drawings engraved at the behest of Jean de Jullienne (see fig. 6) for his *Figures de différents caractères* (1726–28), and those extant today (about two out of three), what the totality of the production was – Jullienne evidently only being familiar with part of it.

* * *

That Watteau was always considered a greater draughtsman than a painter is evidence in itself: he knew it, and was disappointed not to attain the same high standard in his paintings as he did in his drawings. The Goncourt brothers and many others wrote about this after his death. Watteau's paintings are often executed with high-risk techniques: he used glazes that are too fragile, did not leave areas of paint to dry before over-painting, and used varnishes that have transformed the appearance of the work and destroyed the light by turning yellow over the years; the paintings have weathered the passage of time far less well than the drawings. It is true that some of the sheets bearing his drawings have been trimmed at the edges, or, worse, have had pieces cut out. It is also true that the rubbing together of pages, from the moment they were bound tightly together in the sketchbooks the artist carried around with him, has caused losses, a process that was aggravated by the making of counter-proofs that was a

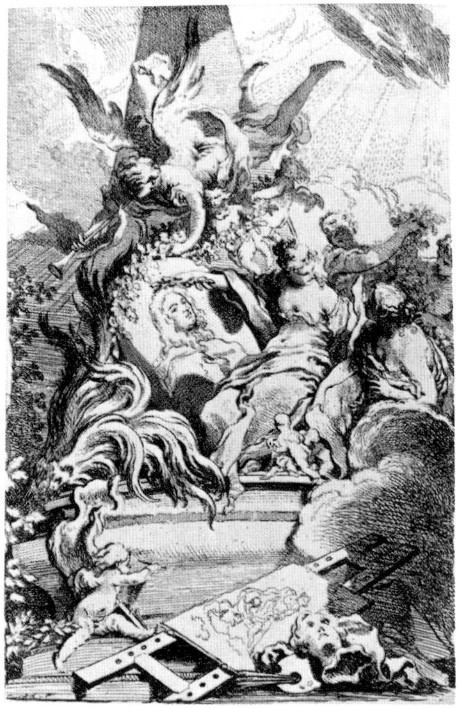

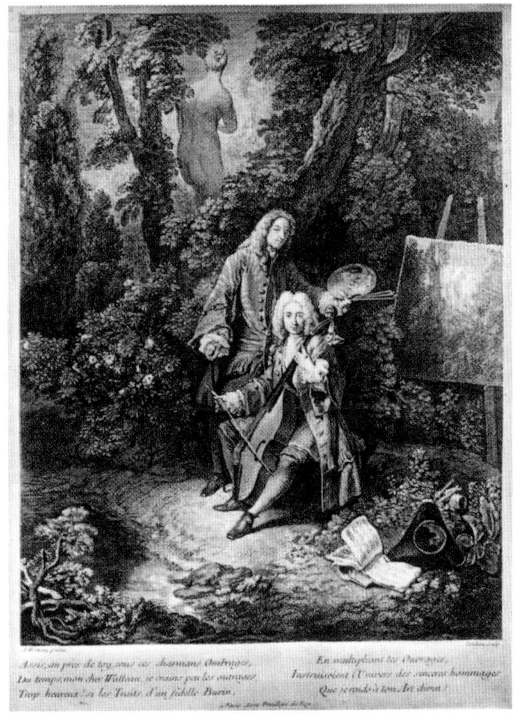

ABOVE
Fig. 5
François Boucher,
The Graces at the Tomb of Watteau,
1728. Engraving

ABOVE RIGHT
Fig. 6
Nicolas-Henri Tardieu, after a lost painting by Watteau, *Seated Beside Thee*, showing Watteau and Jean de Jullienne, 1731. Engraving

commonplace at the period. On the other hand, restorers have had little work to do on the relatively strong papers (stronger at any rate than the papers used for graphic work during the second half of the nineteenth century), and most of Watteau's beautiful drawings have lost none of their radiance and charm.

Among these works, the choice of which ones to present to the British public seemed to us almost to make itself. Aware that a catalogue raisonné and an exhibition, even if their authors are the same, are only very distantly related, we have attempted (while ignoring a number of specific problems) to present an anthology to illustrate Watteau's contribution to the art of drawing in his time – and indeed at any time. The most elaborate pages from his early years, some of which have interesting – even fascinating – versos (which it is becoming more and more difficult to exhibit at the same time as the rectos) are basically given over to people of small stature, described with extraordinary precision and a marvellous feeling for attitude. Of the large series from *c.* 1715–16, we have been able to include more examples than ever next to each other: four Persians, six Savoyards, four preparatory drawings for Crozat's *Seasons*. Following these are about a dozen composite studies of heads, female, male or mixed, some copies from the Old Masters, several studies of musicians, intense family portraits and at least one of Watteau's very rare drawings for a composition, which he only produced occasionally (see cat. 82). Our selection, covering such a short space of time, and which drastic changes to the loans policy of some large institutions will make almost impossible to stage in decades to come, will delight everyone who visits; their faces, we hope, will wear a festive air…

ENDNOTES

1 See most recently Pierre Rosenberg and Keith Christiansen (eds), *Poussin and Nature: Arcadian Visions*, exh. cat., Museo de Bellas Artes de Bilbao and the Metropolitan Museum of Art, New York, 2007–08.

2 See Louis-Antoine Prat and Pierre Rosenberg, 'Dessins de David nouvellement réapparus, I et II', *Colloque en l'honneur d'Antoine Schnapper, Paris, 2009*, forthcoming.

3 A charming *Study of a Female Head* in three colours (119 x 76 mm), engraved in reverse by Jean Audran in *Figures de différents caractères*, no. 141 (RP G57), recently reappeared for sale at the Galerie Arnoldi-Livie, Munich, and was acquired by a French collector. Another drawing, known from the engraving by Jean-Charles François, *Couple Walking to the Right, Woman from the Back* (red chalk, 171 x 295 mm), appeared at Christie's, London, 10 July 2001, lot 106, col. (RP G194). On 9 December 2001 a mount containing four sketches was presented in Lyons; three of these corresponded to the *Figures de différents caractères* (RP G23, RP G60 and RP G119). The fourth, not engraved, a *Mezzetin Playing the Guitar*, was evidently reused in the painting of the same name in the Metropolitan Museum of Art, New York. Another composite page was sold in Paris (Hôtel Drouot, 20 June 2005) from the Groult album; it presented five counter-proofs in a circle around a small drawing in red chalk (107 x 57 mm), depicting a *Man Seen from the Back Playing a Guitar* (lot 26 in the sale catalogue). Two other pages have appeared on the art market in Paris: one was *Study for a Seated Woman, Three-quarter View from the Right and Study of a Left Hand*, which appeared in an advertisement for the De Bayser Gallery. This was a drawing in three chalks (235 x 193 mm), bearing at lower left the mark of the Houbigant collection (L. 1266E); the page seems to have recently entered a private collection in New York. In 2007, a *Study of Two Heads of Old Men* in red chalk (226 x 173 mm), probably after Rubens, appeared at the Galerie Gombert, Paris. Interesting also is that another version of the drawing depicting the *Young Woman Sewing* in *Pastimes According to Age* (whereabouts unknown) surfaced in an auction at La Roche-sur-Yon on 17 November 2010. It bore the stamp of the Schwiter collection, unlike the version from a private collection in Geneva listed in our catalogue raisonné of 1996, no. 306. Although the two pages are very similar, they nevertheless presented a number of differences; each has features scattered here and there that seemed to us to be typical of Watteau, although we were not able to compare the drawings one next to the other.

4 We omitted to mention in the catalogue raisonné, in relation to engravings from Watteau's drawings, the *Livre nouveau de différents trophées*, a rare collection devised by Watteau and engraved by Gabriel Huquier. This error was corrected in Louis-Antoine Prat, 'Le R 847 du R.P.P.II: Caca?', *Mélanges en hommage à Pierre Rosenberg: Peintures et dessins en France et en Italie, XVIIe–XVIIIe siècles*, Paris, 2001, p. 377, note 11.

5 The most targeted reviews in this respect were Bailey 1997, Wine 1997, Roland Michel 1998 and Grasselli 2001.

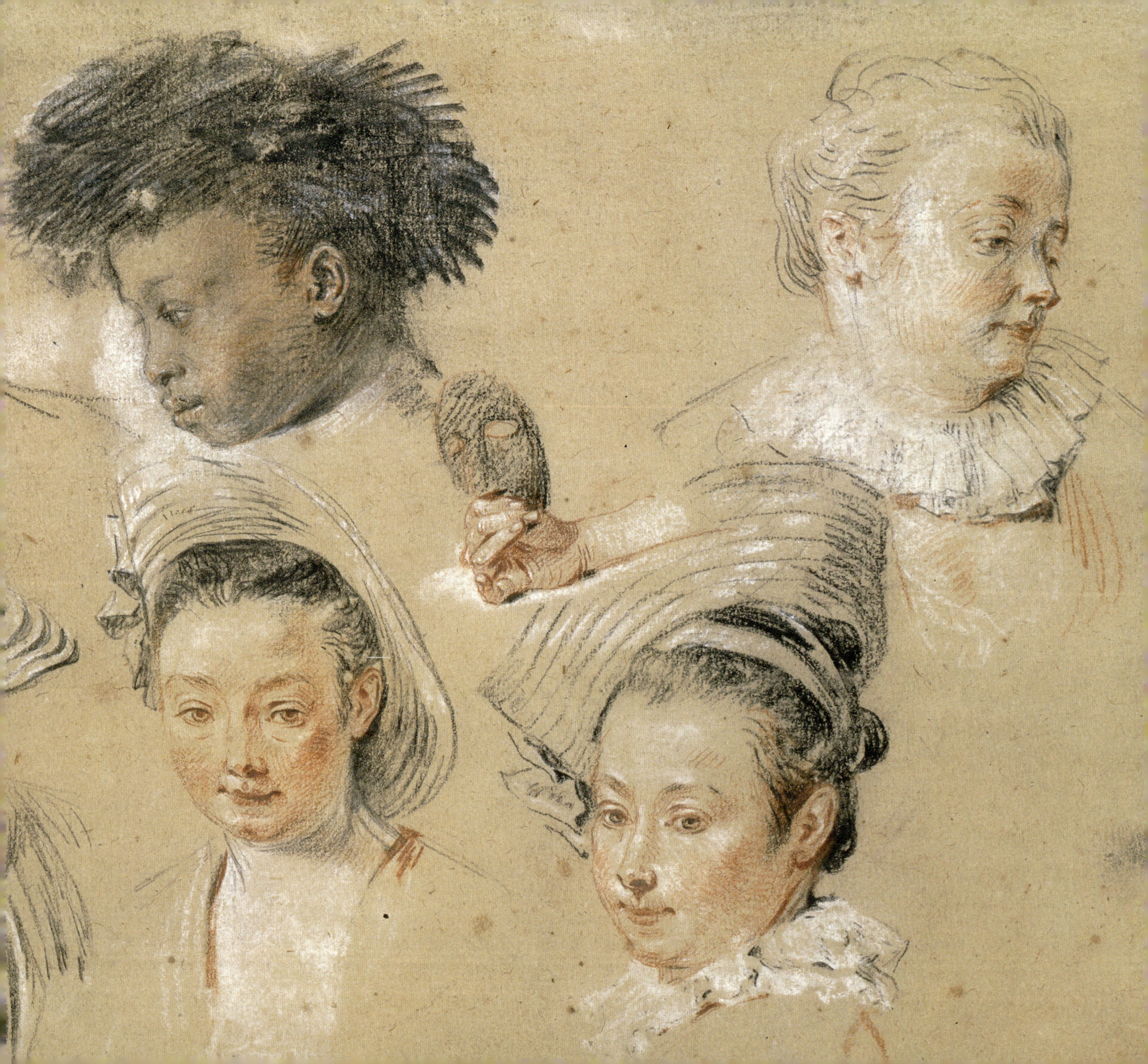

'Resounding Blows': Notes on Watteau's Drawing Technique

Louis-Antoine Prat

'Les Habits sont italiens.' Twenty-four years ago I dared to borrow this title of a Watteau painting for a short story I published at the time:[1] the artist is seen hurrying to catch a pose 'with red chalk, so red that it always stained the inside of his fingers'. Sharpened almost to nothing, the tip of a stiletto, or squashed flat by pressing hard on the page with the pencil-holder, modulated in parallel hatching and controlled in elegant scrolls, this 'blood red chalk' seemed in the early eighteenth century to be the trademark of Watteau's genius as a draughtsman, even though it had already returned to favour in other hands, for example those of his teacher Claude Gillot.

It is hard to imagine Watteau's drawings executed in black chalk alone, and the ones in which black is dominant are instantly disappointing – they look sad (although the female figure possibly in mourning [cat. 81] definitely required this different treatment). Red chalk was seldom used in the seventeenth century, apart from by a few baroque or provincial artists such as Jacques Bellange or Claude Vignon; it returned in full force at the period of the debates on colour, when it was sometimes used by Charles Le Brun, or his rival Pierre Mignard or Mignard's imitator Michel Corneille II. The French followers of Rubens, Antoine Coypel or Charles de La Fosse, restored it to glory, using it with other materials or on its own. Gillot employed it frequently, diluting it in a wash to obtain his distinctive light effects.

As many commentators on the century of Louis XV have observed, the eighteenth century was the golden age of red chalk, and it seems that the technique used by Watteau influenced numbers of his brilliant successors, from François Boucher, who engraved more than 100 of his drawings, to Michel-François Dandré-Bardon, from Hubert Robert to Honoré Fragonard. This compact, ferruginous clay, which Cennino Cennini considered 'very strong and solid, dense and perfect', is supplied to artists in short sticks that they can sharpen as they wish. Its shade varies widely, from light red to purplish or brown, according to the amount of iron oxide or manganese it contains. There is also a distinctly yellow red chalk, called 'sanguine brulée' (burnt red chalk), which was not used by Watteau but later by Boucher and Carl Van Loo.

The *Almanach des Voyageurs à Paris*, published in 1740, gives a complete list of the different shades of red chalk; some of its descriptive adjectives are highly evocative: 'fine carmine, brown, nigger, moorish'.[2] The terms employed transport us to some exotic, oriental place where the warmth of the red chalk can already be imagined. In general, red chalk is a handsome crimson in appearance, or an orange-red particularly suitable for rendering flesh tones. When it is moistened with water it produces darker, colder effects, such as those seen particularly in the work of Watteau's successors, for example Jean-Baptiste Greuze.

It is the extraordinary fineness of the grain, as well as the impression of warmth that emanates from its various shades, that distinguishes Watteau's use of red chalk from that of other users of the medium. His perfect alliance of its two elements, line and tone, can already be seen in the earliest drawings in this exhibition: in *A Barber's Shop* from the Louvre (cat. 2), the perceptible differences in pressure, the variations in the strength used for each stroke, help to emphasise the foreground and to establish a kind of depth of field, creating a perfect illusion. The *Interior of a Draper's Shop* (cat. 6), also from the Louvre, probably slightly later, is exactly the same.

On the other hand, in the page of studies which belonged to Philippe de Chennevières, now in the Musée Jacquemart-André, Paris (cat. 5), it is the use of a stick of red chalk sharpened to a greater or lesser extent that distinguishes the two registers of the page, studies of hands and feet (these are probably copies from an Old Master) and items of clothing on a headless figure.

Deliberately different shades of red chalk can also be used to great effect; this is very evident (and for good reason) in two drawings containing figures, executed by Watteau several years apart, the artist returning to a page he has already used, with chalk of a different shade. One of the two such drawings is in the Metropolitan Museum of Art, New York (cat. 18), the other in a famous private collection (cat. 19). Sometimes, however, two shades of chalk are used on the same page at the same moment, as in *A Man Embracing a Woman* in the Musée Jacquemart-André, Paris (RP 155; fig. 7); this drawing seems to cry out for further emphasis, which can only be provided by the addition of black chalk.

When did Watteau decide to combine red and black chalk? Opinions differ, naturally: anyone leafing through our 1996 catalogue raisonné will have realised that the artist's recourse to two, then three chalks, when the need to express light by using highlights of white chalk became pressing,

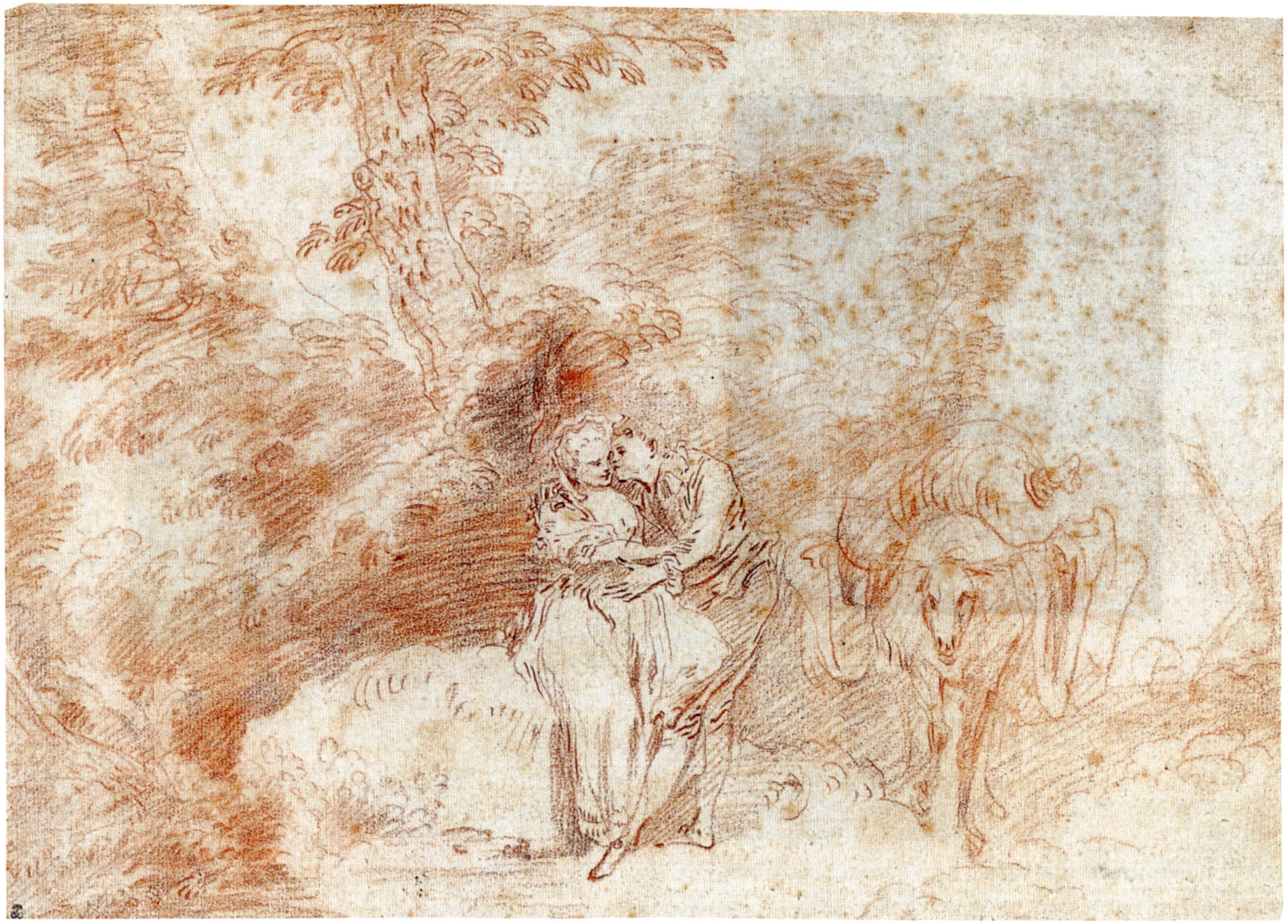

Fig. 7
A Man Embracing a Woman, *c.* 1712.
Two chalks, 218 x 300 mm.
Musée Jacquemart-André,
Paris, inv. 1594

occurred in about 1715, at the time of the first large pages of studies in which various heads are juxtaposed, especially the powerful studies of Persians and Savoyards. Suddenly a kind of harmony was established between the two media, and it was now that black chalk was finally introduced as an indispensable element in the construction of monumental figures; in comparison with the sketches of earlier years, these began to take up considerable space on the page, producing an immediate rise in pictorial quality.

Is the marvellous *Seated Persian Wearing a Turban* in the Louvre (cat. 23), earlier or slightly later than the fabulous Chicago *Standing Savoyard* (cat. 27)? These two celebrated drawings, generally dated 1715, differ in any case in a number of ways: in the drawing of the Persian, the use of black chalk over red chalk in the right half is critical, with its elaborate accents, the kind of 'resounding blows' Antoine-Joseph Dezallier d'Argenville was soon to describe: 'The hatching in his drawings was almost perpendicular, or sometimes leaned slightly to left or right; in others it was blurred with light washes or resounding blows: the freedom of hand, lightness of touch, delicacy in the profiles of his heads, his interest in their headwear, the character in the faces, in the compositions, plus the spirit reigning over all – all this will certainly acquaint the curious with the name of Watteau.'[3]

The opportunity to use red chalk in different ways is dazzlingly illustrated here. The right hand of the Persian, the hand nearest the spectator, is drawn in fine detail, whereas the other is crudely suggested rather than described, with heavy, concentrated rectilinear strokes giving it a massive shape: as an isolated detail this would probably be incomprehensible but here, in its place, it gives the drawing an extraordinary immediacy, a real presence. In the Chicago *Standing Savoyard*, by contrast, both hands are rendered with the same precision, although one is strangely bigger than the other. The energy of the black chalk is expressed around the face, in the circle of beard, as well as in the shadow of the hat, marked by a strong, almost symmetrical curve. Touches of wash and some shaded areas serve to soften the relief of an incredibly life-like figure. The relationship between the red and black chalk is exploited in all its gradations throughout the whole series of Savoyards and Persians. A touch of black chalk can just be detected in the hair of the *Young Savoyard Holding an Oboe, with a Marmot Case Slung across His Shoulder* from Copenhagen (cat. 29), while the *Seated Persian Wearing a Fur Hat* from Haarlem (cat. 24) is covered all over with dark shadows that emphasise the solidity of the model's physical form. Watteau also uses black chalk to create a spatial background for his figures; this is also the way, using a series of bold hatching lines which he links together with some judicious shading, in which he suggests a wall, a floor or the shadow on the face of the *Seated Savoyard Woman* in the British Museum (cat. 31) or in *An Old Woman Seated Beside an Infant in a Cradle* (cat. 32). In the same two drawings, black chalk is applied to the folds of the garments like flames ('resounding blows' perhaps), running up the pleats and folds of the fabrics.

Although he did continue to use red chalk on its own, Watteau seems thenceforward to have reserved it for copies from Old Masters, landscapes or a few isolated figures. The white highlights that appeared on various occasions in studies in red chalk were now joined with the two other coloured chalks to produce the technique known as 'trois crayons' (three chalks). Most of the time, the highlights are applied with extreme delicacy to the inside of the figures. White highlights are also used, however, to isolate an object and make it stand out, for example around the three heads of black men in the Louvre drawing (cat. 48). The alchemy of the three media, their combination on paper whose shade often borders on yellow, beige or almost brown, makes total sense.

Henceforward, Watteau enhanced this technique in two ways that enriched it and perfected it. In some drawings, he added a pale wash, sparingly applied, to the three coloured chalks. This was during his last years (see, for example, the *Three Bust-length Studies of Women; Study of a Left Forearm* in the Teylers Museum, Haarlem; cat. 84). He also took to adding finer, sharper lines – for support or detail – in what has always been called *mine de plomb* (black lead, graphite). A recent, learned article exposes the impropriety of this name, as the graphite pencil used in fact contains no lead.[4] The inaccuracy of this name persisted for two centuries and was used equally for the pencil portraits of Ingres and the landscape sketches of the youthful Corot. In fact Watteau often combines graphite with the greasiest black chalk; this allows him to incise a subject and reveal its full delicacy as in the exquisite *Woman on a Swing, Seen from the Back* (cat. 33) in a private collection or, a little later, as in the intelligently expressive face of the *Young Woman Seated on the Ground* in the Musée Cognacq-Jay, Paris (cat. 73).

In short, as a draughtsman, Watteau could almost be defined by the restrictive nature of his technique: he practically never used anything but 'dry' techniques (chalks), ignoring almost entirely those defined as 'wet'. He occasionally has recourse to pale washes as noted above, or to watercolour (on the reverse side of some pages) to depict plants or landscape or, once only, to design a fan. But these are very rare cases. Dezallier d'Argenville notes that 'everything suited him, apart from the pen', and this almost direct evidence seems to inspire confidence. Also noteworthy is the absence of squaring, useful and frequently employed at the period, which we might have expected from an artist whose avowed aim in his drawings of isolated figures was to reuse their postures in his paintings. Also absent is the bluish paper so frequently employed in the early eighteenth century, when most draughtsmen used it to their advantage, from Antoine Coypel to Louis de Boullogne the Younger, from Jean-Baptiste Oudry to Jean Restout. Some of his successful three-coloured chalk drawings would perhaps gain added relief from this type of paper, for example the extraordinary *Nude Man Kneeling, Holding Fabric in His Right Hand* (cat. 42), related to the Crozat *Seasons*, which fascinates us because of its deliberate, individual yet unexpected use of three chalks, flesh sliding from red to black by a kind of osmosis, the transition achieved with extraordinary ease. Or the interior of the figure's right thigh, where the red chalk is brilliantly lined with darkest black, each of the two lines growing stronger on contact with the other.

Sometimes it is difficult to say which coloured chalk has been applied first and which added later. Often it is obvious, as in *Three Studies of a Young Girl Wearing a Hat* (cat. 53), in which the black bonnets have obviously been added later. By contrast, in a study like *Standing Man Wearing a Cape, His Right Arm Extended* in Rotterdam (cat. 61), although Watteau almost certainly began by drawing the cape in red chalk, the black chalk plays much more than a secondary role, occupying the whole of the lower part of the page. In the *Study of a Young Man Seen from the Back, and another Study of His Right Arm* in the Thaw Collection (promised to the Pierpont Morgan Library, New York, RP 503; fig. 8) the opposite is true: here the red chalk takes over in the lower part of the body. The variety of uses is almost endless, adapting readily to each new encounter. As the late Marianne Roland Michel observed: '…on the forehead and at the nape of the neck there are locks of hair and curls, and it is impossible to discern whether these were sketched in red chalk and completed in black, or exactly the other way round.'[5]

In less than ten years, Watteau enriched his style consistently and almost seamlessly, moving from the precise, restrained use of red chalk on its own to the use of a series of coloured chalks, each employed in all its subtle shades, from carmine to crimson, from grey to jet black, from creamy white to the lightest of highlights. We have observed the figures

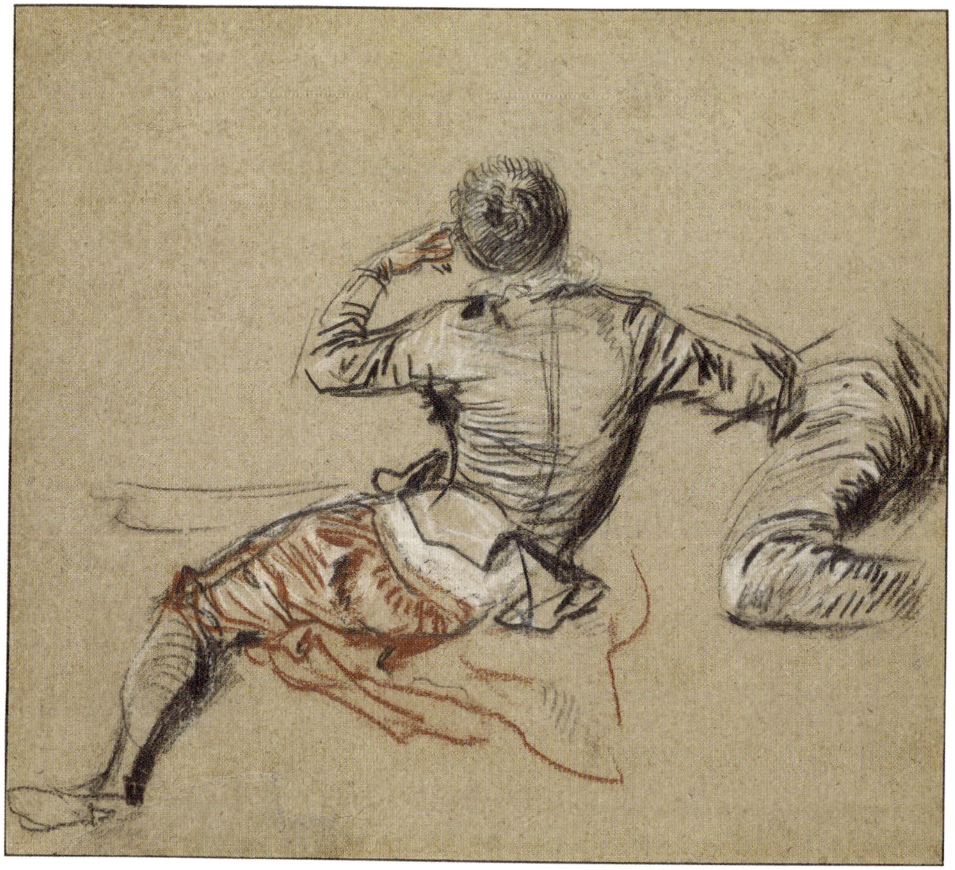

Fig. 8
Study of a Young Man Seen from the Back, and another Study of His Right Arm, 1716–17. Three chalks, 208 x 227 mm. Thaw Collection, The Pierpont Morgan Library, New York, 2000.56

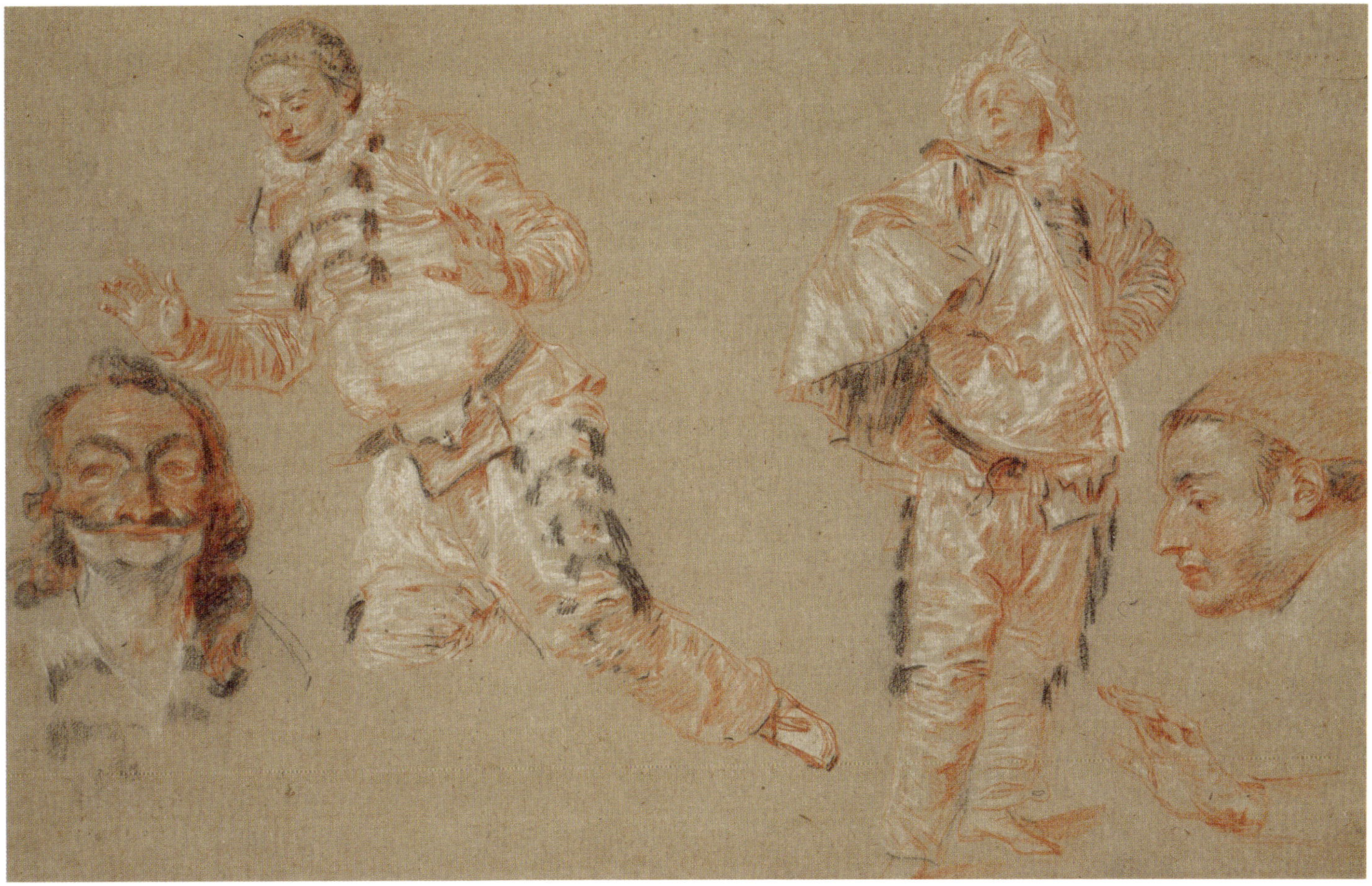

Fig. 9
Italian Comedians, *c.* 1719.
Three chalks, 261 x 403 mm.
Margaret Day Blake Collection,
The Art Institute of Chicago,
inv. 1954.1

growing larger as the years pass, the faces coming closer, the rendering of flesh or the vibration of hands growing more and more subtle in their evocation. Some of the contrasts may surprise us, for example the red mask on the black-ringed face of an actor at lower left on the celebrated page in the Art Institute of Chicago (RP 643; fig. 9). We can assume that, in reality, the model's flesh looked pink behind the mask, itself a shiny black. Watteau's power is to surpass reality in his drawings, relying on a technical skill that has never been equalled (think for example of the efforts of Paul Helleu, termed by Degas the 'steam Watteau', to integrate red and black chalk in his many studies of heads and figures). Watteau gradually acquired this unusual gift for seeing life in three colours and depicting it thus, on pages where the spectator's eye effortlessly rises above illusion, reconstituting objects in their true form, reviving the presence of the departed.

ENDNOTES

1 Louis-Antoine Prat, *Le Tombeau du nouvelliste*, Paris, 1988, p. 66.
2 Quoted by Arlette Serullaz, 'Sanguines des XVIIe et XVIIIe siècles', in *Sanguines du XIXe siècle, de Delacroix à Maurice Denis*, exh. cat., Musée d'Orsay, Paris, 1994, p. 16.
3 Antoine-Joseph Dezallier d'Argenville, *Abrégé de la vie des plus fameux peintres*, Paris, 1762, 4, p. 408.
4 Hélène Guicharnaud and Alain Duval, 'Une Technique graphique au nom ambigu: la "mine de plomb"', *Revue des Musées de France. Revue du Louvre*, Paris, 2010, 3, pp. 41–47.
5 Marianne Roland Michel, *Watteau: Un Artiste au XVIIIe siècle*, Paris, 1984, p. 80.

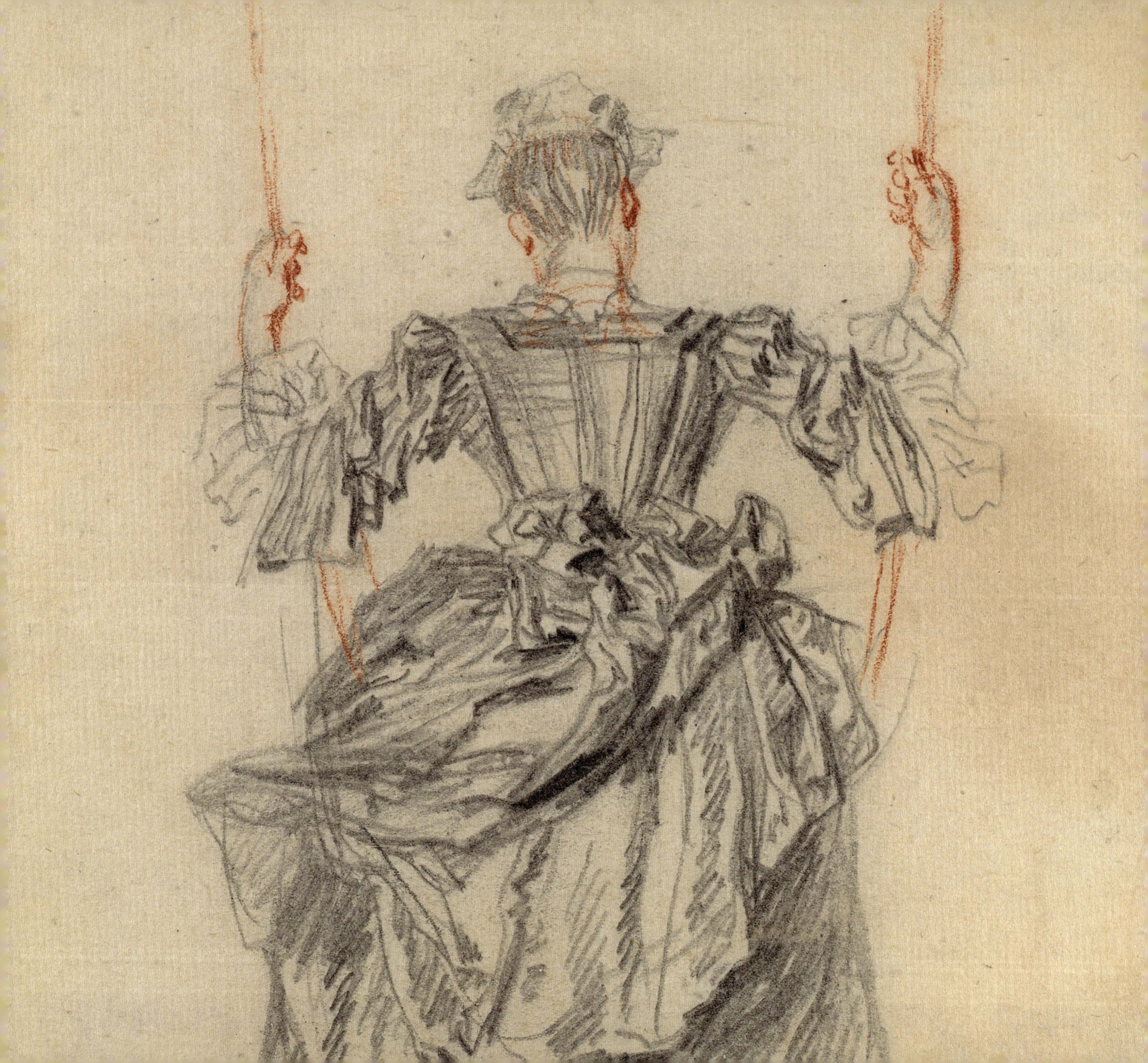

The First Watteau Drawings in England

Martin Eidelberg

The history of Watteau's fame in England is well known, but that narrative largely centres on the appreciation of the artist's paintings. Rarely has anyone considered the issue of his drawings there. The fervent nineteenth-century collecting of his drawings in Britain marks the culmination of a fascinating history whose first moments will be explored here.

The story begins with Watteau's arrival in England, for it was the artist himself who brought the first examples of his draughtsmanship into the country. Remarkably little is recorded about Watteau's stay in England. Although we know approximately when it happened, we have no exact dates. There are suggestions as to why he made the trip but these are only assumptions. We have an idea of some of the people with whom he may have been in contact but this is largely conjecture. Not least, we do not really know how he occupied his time in the English capital. In short, the history of Watteau's trip to England is uncharted. Three major questions should be asked apropos of his drawings in relation to this voyage: did he bring his old sketches with him, did he make new ones while in London, and did he leave any behind or did he take them back to France? These questions, of course, are much easier to pose than answer.

Watteau was still in Paris in September 1719, but must have left within the next few months because the 1720 *Almanach Royal*, prepared in late 1719, already lists him in the English capital.[1] He was back in Paris by August 1720, since his presence there was noted by the Venetian artist Rosalba Carriera.[2] Thus he may have been in London for almost a full year, which accords with the comment by Jean de Jullienne, Watteau's knowledgeable and close friend, that Watteau's absence from Paris lasted about a year.[3] This is a considerable length of time in the artist's extremely short career. Watteau's reasons for this journey are similarly uncertain. Pierre Jean Mariette reported that 'ideas of [gaining a] fortune made him go to London'.[4]

Watteau unquestionably intended to practise his art in England, and thus he would have brought with him his drawings, along with his brushes and other painting paraphernalia.[5] According to Jullienne and other contemporary biographers, despite Watteau suffering from the English climate and illness, 'He did not refrain from making some paintings there…'[6] Edme François Gersaint was even more emphatic: 'he was very busy during his visit to England; his works were sought after and well rewarded.'[7]

The fact that Watteau brought some of his drawings to London can be demonstrated via several paintings that he executed during his London sojourn. Best known are the two paintings that were executed for Dr Richard Mead, *The Italian Players*, now in the National Gallery of Art, Washington, and *Peaceful Love*, a composition known today only through an engraving. Our understanding that they were executed in London is supported by the testimony of George Vertue who, in 1724, wrote that Dr Mead's two paintings were 'Conversations, painted in England'.[8] The announcement in the *Mercure de France* in March 1733, announcing the engraving of *The Italian Players*, reaffirms this: 'newly engraved in England by Mr Baron after a painting by the late Watteau, which is in the collection of Mr Mead … He had it made by Watteau during his trip to London.'[9] Not to be overlooked is a catalogue of Mead's collection published posthumously by his family in 1755; it confirms that Mead specifically commissioned the two paintings when Watteau was in England.[10]

A third painting to be considered is the ravishingly beautiful *The Two Cousins*, now in the Musée du Louvre. The evidence suggests that it too was executed in London. It was originally owned by the French engraver Bernard Baron (1696–1762), who was called to England around 1714 and resided there for most of his career, except for a brief return to Paris from 1729 to 1734.[11] Some scholars date the painting to 1717 in the mistaken belief that Baron was still in Paris then and that he obtained it in the French capital before leaving for England. However, Baron left Paris in *c.* 1714, a date well before the painting was executed. It is improbable that Baron bought the painting after he returned to the French capital in 1729, especially since he was not an art collector of any note. Both men were French artists in a foreign country, both were in Dr Mead's circle, and they would undoubtedly have come together at various times. The logical conclusion, one that curiously has not been considered, is that Watteau gave his painting to Baron in London.

To execute these three paintings, Watteau would have depended on his drawings for each of the twenty-six figures in the three paintings. For example, the woman at the centre of *Peaceful Love* was taken from a sheet with two studies of a model (RP 527; fig. 10). At least fifteen such figural studies, plus a study of a dog and several compositional studies, are extant today. Originally, there would have been at least ten more.[12]

Some of the drawings Watteau used for his London paintings were clearly made prior to his trip. A compositional study for *The Italian Players* is on the verso of a drawing of soldiers dating from *c.* 1710. A sheet with the seated musician used for *Peaceful Love* must have been drawn in Paris because this figure was copied from Adriaan van de Venne's *Feast after the Treaty of Treves*, a painting in the French royal collection that Watteau could only have studied before he left for London.[13] The drawing used for the guitarist at the left of *The Italian Players* is generally dated several years earlier than the painting, and it was used for an earlier painting, *The Rendez-vous* (Private collection). These examples demonstrate that Watteau must have brought a portfolio of studies to London.

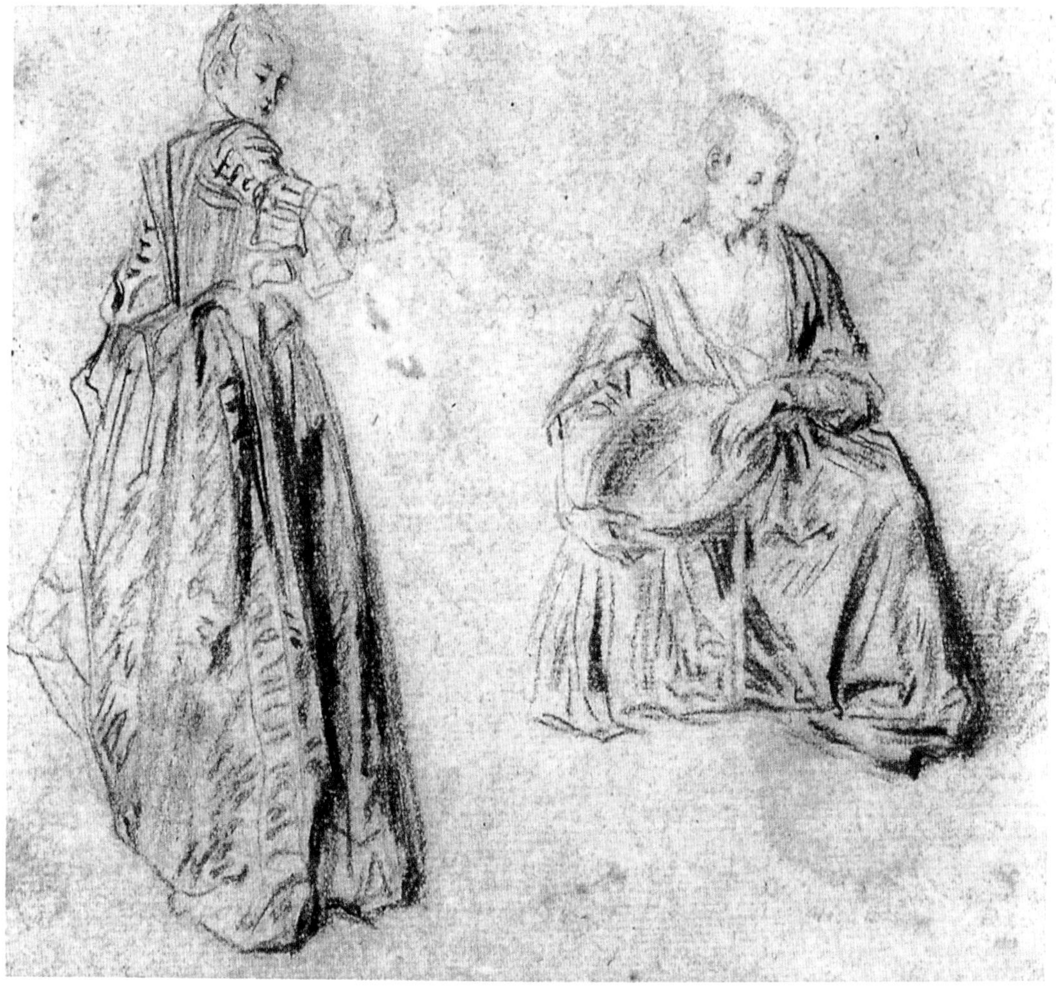

Fig. 10
Two Studies of a Woman, *c.* 1717–19.
Red chalk and graphite, 128 x 139 mm.
Private collection

It is less easy to determine if some of the remaining drawings used for the three London paintings were brought from France, or were drawn in London. This is because the dating of the drawings varies from one scholar to another. For example, does the drawing with two studies of a woman (fig. 10), one of which was used for *Peaceful Love*, date to 1717 as Pierre Rosenberg and Louis-Antoine Prat believe, or does it date from 1717–19 as Margaret Morgan Grasselli maintains? These conundrums, however they are resolved, suggest the intricacies involved in understanding Watteau's *œuvre*.

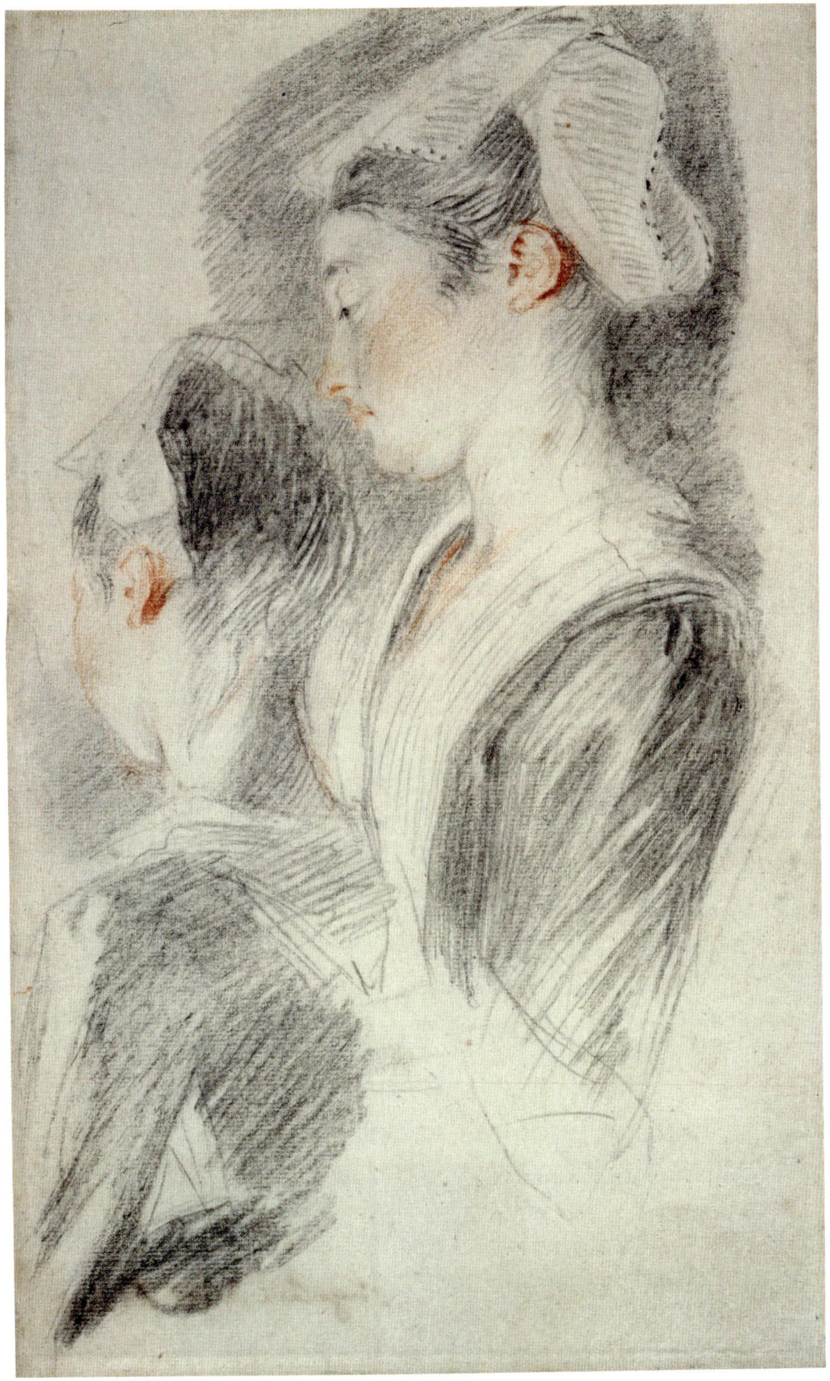

Fig. 11
Two Studies of a Woman, *c.* 1720–21. Black and red chalk, 288 x 172 mm. British Museum, London

Other evidence demonstrates that Watteau drew while he was in London. Indeed, it would have been only natural for him to do so since this discipline was an ingrained part of his daily routine. One of his drawings, a double study of the bust of a woman (RP 645; fig. 11), is on paper with a London watermark, which suggests that it was made while he was in England. There may well be other such examples but, unfortunately, there has been no study of the watermarks on Watteau's drawings. Another drawing that must have been made in London shows an engraver at work in his studio (RP 638; fig. 12).[14] This sheet once had an identifying label, which declared that it represented 'M. Baron the Graver', that is to say, Bernard Baron. Although the identity of the sitter has occasionally been doubted, the image bears a plausible resemblance to Baron and should be understood, accordingly, as a drawing made in England. Another drawing, a caricature of Dr John Misaubin, a Huguenot doctor in London, is no longer extant but it was recorded in a soft-ground etching by Arthur Pond (1701–1758). According to Edmond de Goncourt, Mariette had annotated a copy of the print with a statement that the original had been drawn in a coffee house by Watteau during his sojourn in London.[15] These scattered examples show that Watteau drew during the year he was in England.

It is only natural to presume that Watteau took his drawings back to Paris when he returned there in 1720. Were we assured of the exact chronology of his works, we might be able to show that drawings used for the three London paintings were reused for later canvases. But there is other evidence. For example, the study of the busts of two women (fig. 11) must have been taken back to Paris because, after Watteau's death, it was owned by Mariette who, in turn, gave it to Niccolò Gaburri. The sheet with studies of a standing and seated women (fig. 10) was subsequently engraved for the *Figures de différents caractères* and it must therefore have been in Paris. These admittedly minor features assure us that Watteau took his drawings back to France, which is only natural for a painter still practising his craft.

Watteau undoubtedly gave or sold some of his studies to friends and patrons while he was still in London. The instances of Dr Mead and Bernard Baron come to the fore. In addition to the two paintings he owned, Mead possessed some Watteau drawings, something that seems to have eluded scholars until now. The 1755 posthumous sale of his collection included a lot of three undescribed drawings by Watteau and Jan de Bisschop.[16] Regardless of whether Mead owned one or two examples, Watteau evidently left examples of his draughtsmanship behind.

Similarly, one might presume that Baron had some of Watteau's drawings, especially the portrait of him at work. In fact, that drawing subsequently entered the collection of the portraitist Hugh Howard (1675–1737) and has remained in the British Isles ever since. Also, the caricature of Dr Misaubin must have remained in a London collection since Pond did not etch it until 1739. Other Englishmen might have owned examples of Watteau's drawings, particularly London artists whom he befriended. Philippe Mercier is a prime example of someone who might well have been given drawings, but the records fail us.

We have only occasional insights regarding English collectors of drawings in this period, several of whom were artists. A prime example is the portrait painter Jonathan Richardson (1665–1745), and also his son (1694–1771), who bore the same name. The elder Richardson was an avid collector. As we can tell from the auction catalogue for the sale after his death, he owned one or more studies by Watteau, although they were not enumerated or described.[17] Richardson the Younger had a fabled collection of almost 5,000 drawings; some or perhaps many of these may have come from his father's collection. This magnificent collection was sold soon after his death, and in the sale were at least nine and perhaps as many as thirty drawings classified under Watteau's name.[18]

Also to be mentioned is the marine painter Samuel Scott (1701/02–1772) or perhaps an unnamed collector whose works were mixed with his. Scott seems to have owned two drawings by Watteau that were sold when he retired in 1765.[19] These two drawings were evidently of quality and prized, because they were framed and glazed. It is not without significance that there was also a framed and glazed drawing of a woman's head by Mercier, suggesting something of Scott's circle of acquaintances.

A small number of English art collectors owned Watteau drawings. Anne Donnellan (*c.* 1700–1762), a noted bluestocking, a close friend of the authors Samuel Richardson and Jonathan Swift, and a friend and supporter of George Frideric Handel, led a fascinating life among the leading London intellectuals.[20] She had a modest collection of Italian and Flemish paintings; quite exceptionally, she owned a Watteau study described as 'An historical Drawing'.[21]

Another early eighteenth-century collector of note is Richard Houlditch Jr (d. 1760). His activity as an art collector is often mistakenly assigned to his father (d. 1736), who bore the same name but who is perhaps best remembered for his involvement in the South Sea scandal.[22] There is no indication that the father had much interest in art, but his son did, both as a collector and as something of an historian. The sale after Richard Houlditch Jr's death shows that he had owned a number of drawings ascribed to Watteau.[23] Because the drawings were not enumerated precisely or described, we cannot be certain whether he owned two or three.

The gentry and aristocrats who were building drawing collections in the early eighteenth century would undoubtedly have been attracted to Watteau's work. The Hon. John Spencer (1708–1746), a politician, built up a considerable collection of French drawings and among them were at least fifteen by Watteau.[24] Nine are extant today. They all are splendid examples of his art, mature studies of the sort that Watteau might have brought to London or made while there, although this cannot be proven.

William Cavendish, 3rd Duke of Devonshire (1698–1755), also expressed an interest in adding Watteau drawings to his collection. Because his descendants used the same collector's marks as he did, it is difficult to prove that it was he who purchased the five drawings attributed to Watteau that remain at Chatsworth, but this scenario seems likely.[25]

It is one thing to know that there were indeed English collectors of Watteau drawings in the early eighteenth century. A greater challenge is to determine which drawings they owned and, more to the point, whether these works were actually by the master. As is now well established, many of the so-called Watteau paintings that crossed the Channel in these early years were copies, works by Watteau's pupils and satellites, or pastiches and outright fakes. Alas, it seems that the same held true for Watteau's drawings.

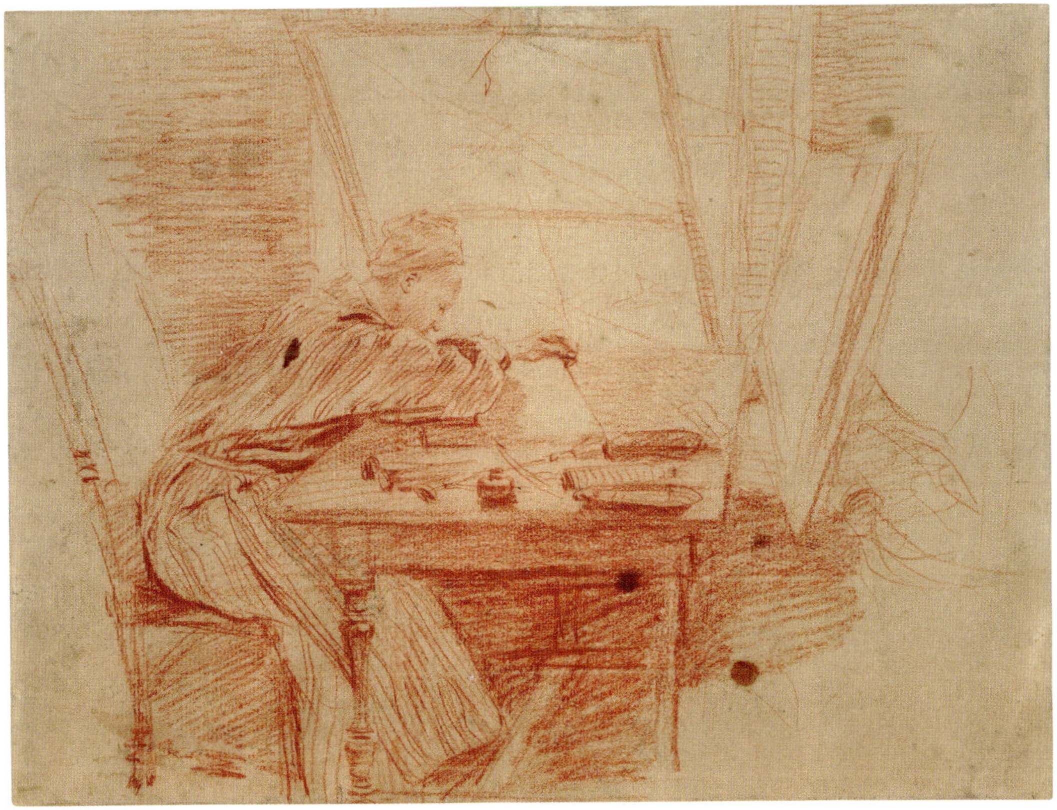

Fig. 12
An Engraver at Work, Sitting at His Table, *c.* 1719–20.
Red chalk, 235 x 304 mm.
British Museum, London, inv. 1874-8-8-227

Three ex-Houlditch 'Watteau' drawings, each stamped with the family's mark, reveal a range of problems.[26] The first is a lovely but rubbed landscape study now in the Pierpont Morgan Library, New York. Although its authorship has recently been challenged, the attribution to Watteau seems reasonable. On the other hand, the second ex-Houlditch drawing, a study of a seated woman, is only in the generic mode of Watteau and is definitely not from his hand. The third drawing, also a landscape study, is not by Watteau but we cannot even be sure it was attributed to him in Houlditch's era.

The only extant example of a drawing that can be traced back to Richardson's collection is a compositional study in red chalk of five figures in a landscape (RP R177; fig. 13). Rather than it being by Watteau, I have proposed it is by Watteau's pupil Pierre Antoine Quillard (*c.* 1704–1733). Similarly, the five sheets of drawings that were in the 3rd Duke of Devonshire's collection – all compositional studies or groups of figures – are quite atypical of Watteau's manner and prove also to be by Quillard, although some scholars maintain that one is by Watteau himself. The Duke's gullibility regarding authentic works by Watteau is also suggested by pendant paintings, supposedly by Watteau, that he bought around this time; one is an intriguing pastiche of the master's figures while the pendant is by Watteau's pupil Jean Baptiste Pater.[27] Although Spencer had a magnificent collection of real Watteau drawings, one quite close to the master's style is by his English disciple Philippe Mercier.[28]

In short, many so-called Watteau drawings that were being collected in the early eighteenth century were not by him, although they were in his manner. Indeed English amateurs had few guidelines by which to make discerning judgements. One of the most telling insights into the situation is offered by a text, *Notices Illustrative of the Drawings and Sketches of Some of the Most Distinguished Masters in All the Principal Schools of Design*, written in the late eighteenth century by the Revd Henry Reveley (1737–1798). This book, supposedly the first in English devoted solely to Old Master drawings, has a section devoted to Watteau. Reveley, like many of his countrymen, was openly hostile to aspects of Watteau's paintings because of what he termed 'the *falsetto* of French style and manners', something which is 'utterly offensive to good taste'. Yet he appreciated Watteau's drawings, even if what he wrote reveals how little he (and much of England) knew of them: 'His drawings are numerous in France, though in England we seldom see any. Those we meet with, are slight and spirited: the figures usually outlined with a pen, and washed with red. I have a Pero [Pierrot] and Columbine, in this style, very pleasingly executed.' Clearly the drawing that Reveley owned, its figures outlined in pen, was not by Watteau.

Reveley aside, the situation improved in the late eighteenth and early nineteenth centuries. The burgeoning appreciation of French art, the growing number of drawings on the French market, the political upheavals in France, and the brisk trade across the Channel were all factors that contributed to the greater availability of better drawings. The English were able to purchase Watteau drawings with increasingly good provenance and authenticity. By the mid-

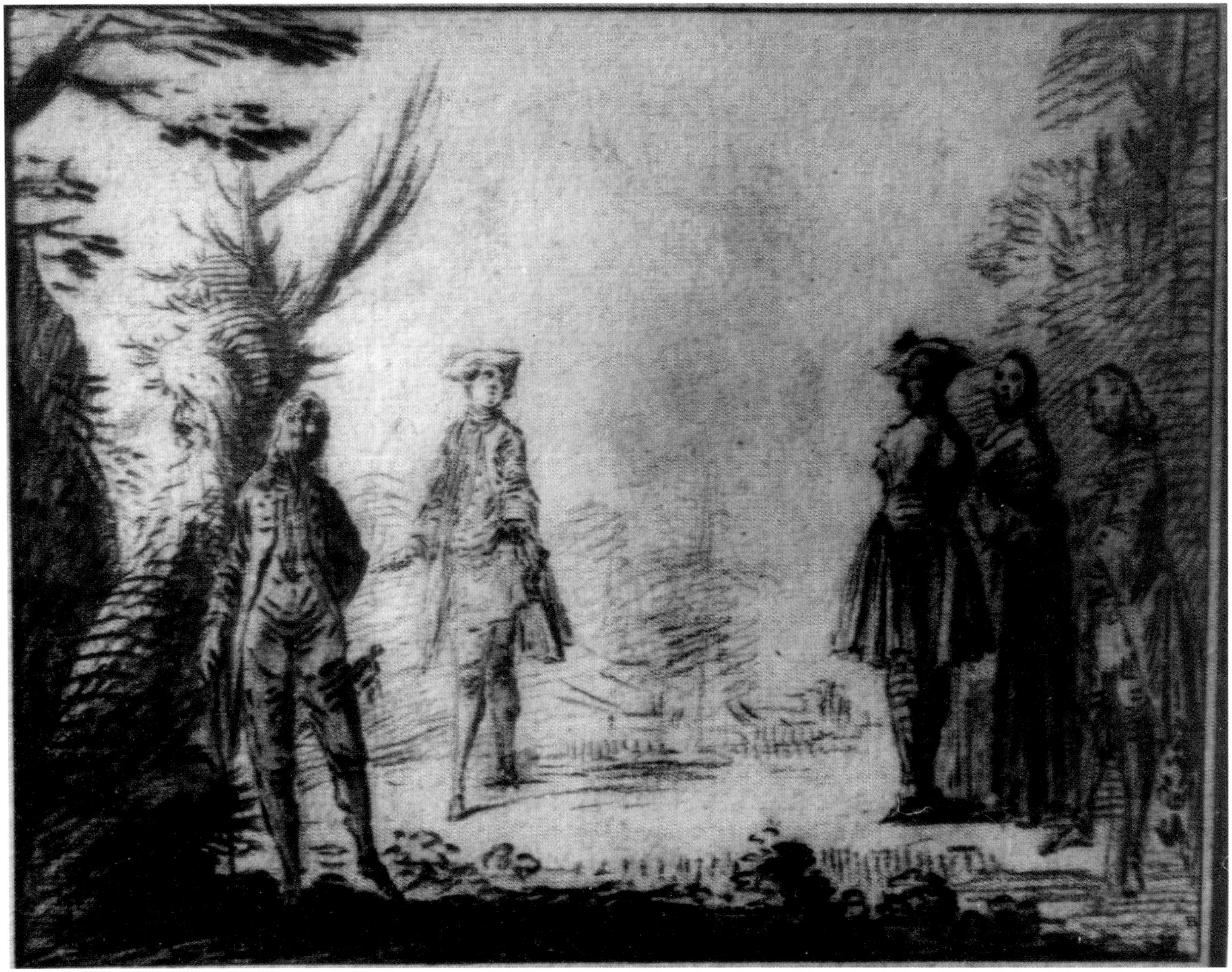

Fig. 13
Pierre Antoine Quillard
(previously attributed to Watteau),
Figures in a Clearing, *c.* 1715–20.
Red chalk, 151 x 261 mm.
Whereabouts unknown

nineteenth century, Andrew James, a London grain merchant, had a superb collection of almost seventy Watteau drawings and was so devoted to the artist and his work that he was known as 'Mr Watteau'. By then, little more than a century after the artist himself had visited London, the collecting of Watteau's drawings in England was on a firm footing.

ENDNOTES

1 *Almanach Royal*, Paris, 1720, p. 241.
2 Bernardina Sani, *Rosalba Carriera: Lettere, Diari, Frammenti*, 2 vols, Florence, 1985, vol. 2, p. 765. See the diary entry for 21 August 1720: 'Veduto M.r Vato, un Inglese…' Perhaps Watteau returned from London with an English travelling companion.
3 Rosenberg 1984, p. 16.
4 Rosenberg 1984, p. 4. (Throughout this text I have avoided the use of hyphens between eighteenth-century French compound forenames in accordance with the practice at that time.) Horace Walpole (*Anecdotes of Painting in England*, 4 vols, London, 1782, vol. 4, p. 73) wrote that Watteau went to England to consult Dr Richard Mead about his worsening health, but this seems to be a later, English perspective.
5 Rosenberg and Prat (1996, vol. 1, p. 568) specifically doubt that Watteau brought his drawings to England, although that assumption is embedded in their explanation of why *Peaceful Love* must have been painted before his trip to England.
6 Rosenberg 1984, p. 16.
7 Rosenberg 1984, p. 36.
8 George Vertue, 'Notebooks: III,' *Walpole Society Journal*, 22, 1933–34, p. 23.
9 *Mercure de France*, March 1733, p. 554.
10 William T. Whitley, *Artists and Their Friends in England, 1700–1799*, 2 vols, London and Boston, 1923, vol. 1, p. 28.
11 Baron was called to England by the engraver Claude du Bosc (1682–*c.* 1745), who needed assistance in engraving a series of the Duke of Marlborough's battles. Du Bosc and Baron had previously worked together in Paris as part of the team of engravers on the *Cent Figures de Levant*, a publication finished only in early 1712. The Marlborough project was finished in 1717. Thus Baron must have arrived in England between 1712 and 1717. Pierre Rosenberg wrongly believed that Baron went to England around 1717 and proposed that *The Two Cousins* had been painted around 1716, before Baron left; see Washington 1984, pp. 356–57, no. 47, and Rosenberg 1990.
12 The drawings for *The Italian Players* include RP 179, RP 219, RP 481, RP 507, RP 621–24, RP 647 and RP 649. For *Peaceful Love* see RP 333, RP 353, RP 527, RP 553, RP 559 and RP 636. For *The Two Cousins* see RP 398, RP 519 and RP 528.
13 Rosenberg and Prat, challenging the notion that Watteau would have brought his drawings with him to London (1996, no. 353), hypothesise that the painting had been executed in Paris and that Watteau brought it with him to London. Why is it easier to imagine that Watteau transported cumbersome paintings rather than loose drawings to London?
14 Although Rosenberg and Prat believe the age of the sitter to be too young to be Baron (then approximately 24 years old), this objection does not hold when one considers Baron's appearance fifteen years later in Gawen Hamilton's 1735 group portrait, *A Conversation of Virtuosi at the Kings Arms* (National Portrait Gallery, London, inv. 1384). Rosenberg and Prat claim that the sitter's bonnet is French, yet such bonnets were worn by the English too, as in Jonathan Richardson's *c.* 1717 portrait of Richard Boyle, 3rd Earl of Burlington (National Portrait Gallery, London, inv. 4818), and in Godfrey Kneller's portraits of the members of the Kit Kat Club.
15 RP G193.
16 Langford, London, 13–26 January 1755, first night's sale, lot 43. To his credit, the drawing is cited by Whitley, *Artists and Their Friends in England*, vol. 1, p. 28.
17 Cock, London, 22 January – 10 February 1747, fifth day, lot 2.
18 Langford, London, 5–12 February 1772, second day, lot 62; third day, lots 23, 39; fourth day, lot 23.
19 Langford, London, 1–4 April 1765, third night's sale, lot 57.
20 For an important study of her life, see Patrick Kelly, 'Anne Donnellan: Irish Proto-Blue Stocking,' *Hermathena*, 154, 1993, pp. 39–68.
21 Langford, London, 10–11 February 1763, second day, lot 41.
22 See Frits Lugt, *Les Marques de collections de dessins et d'estampes*, 2 vols, Amsterdam, 1921, and *Supplément*, The Hague, 1956, vol. 1, p. 415, nos 2214–15; vol. 2, p. 326. Lugt confused the two men and wrongly associated the 1760 sale with Houlditch Sr. Similarly *Sale Catalogues of the Principal Collections of Pictures Sold by Auction in England within the Years 1711–1759*, a manuscript in the British Art Library generally assigned to both the father and the son, appears to be the work of just the son.
23 Langford, London, 12–14 February 1760, lots 8 and 17.
24 Alastair Laing (in *The Drawings of François Boucher*, exh. cat., American Federation of Arts, New York, 2003, pp. 222, 252, no. 87) has cleverly distinguished the Hon. John Spencer's collector's mark (Lugt no. 1530) from those used by his successors, and has hypothesised with good reason that the sale of 10–17 June 1811 of the Spencer collection of drawings comprised those from John Spencer's collection. For the extant ex-Spencer Watteau drawings, see RP 228, RP 310, RP 419, RP 479, RP 532, RP 538, RP 569, RP 574 and RP 617. All these sheets bear the cipher of John Spencer (Lugt no. 1530).
25 For the 3rd Duke of Devonshire, see RP 143 and RP R112–15.
26 RP R392, RP R216 and RP R393.
27 See *The English Connoisseur: Containing an Account of Whatever is Curious in Painting, Sculpture, &c. in the Palaces and Seats of the Nobility and Principal Gentry of England, both in Town and Country*, 2 vols, Dublin, 1767, vol. 1, p. 29. The paintings are still at Chatsworth.
28 RP R735. See Martin Eidelberg, 'Philippe Mercier as a Draftsman', *Master Drawings*, 44, Winter 2006, pp. 423–24.

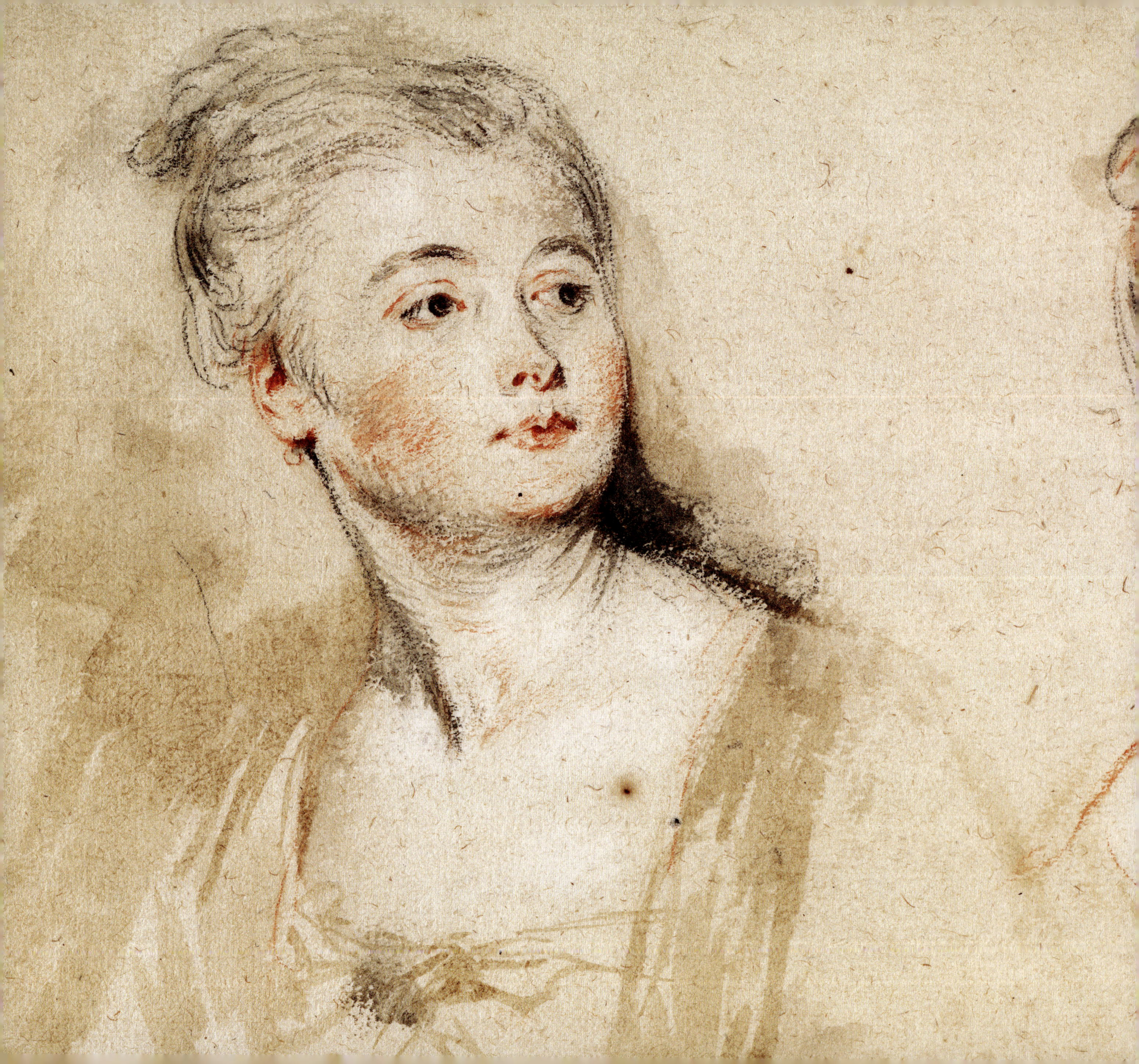

Catalogue

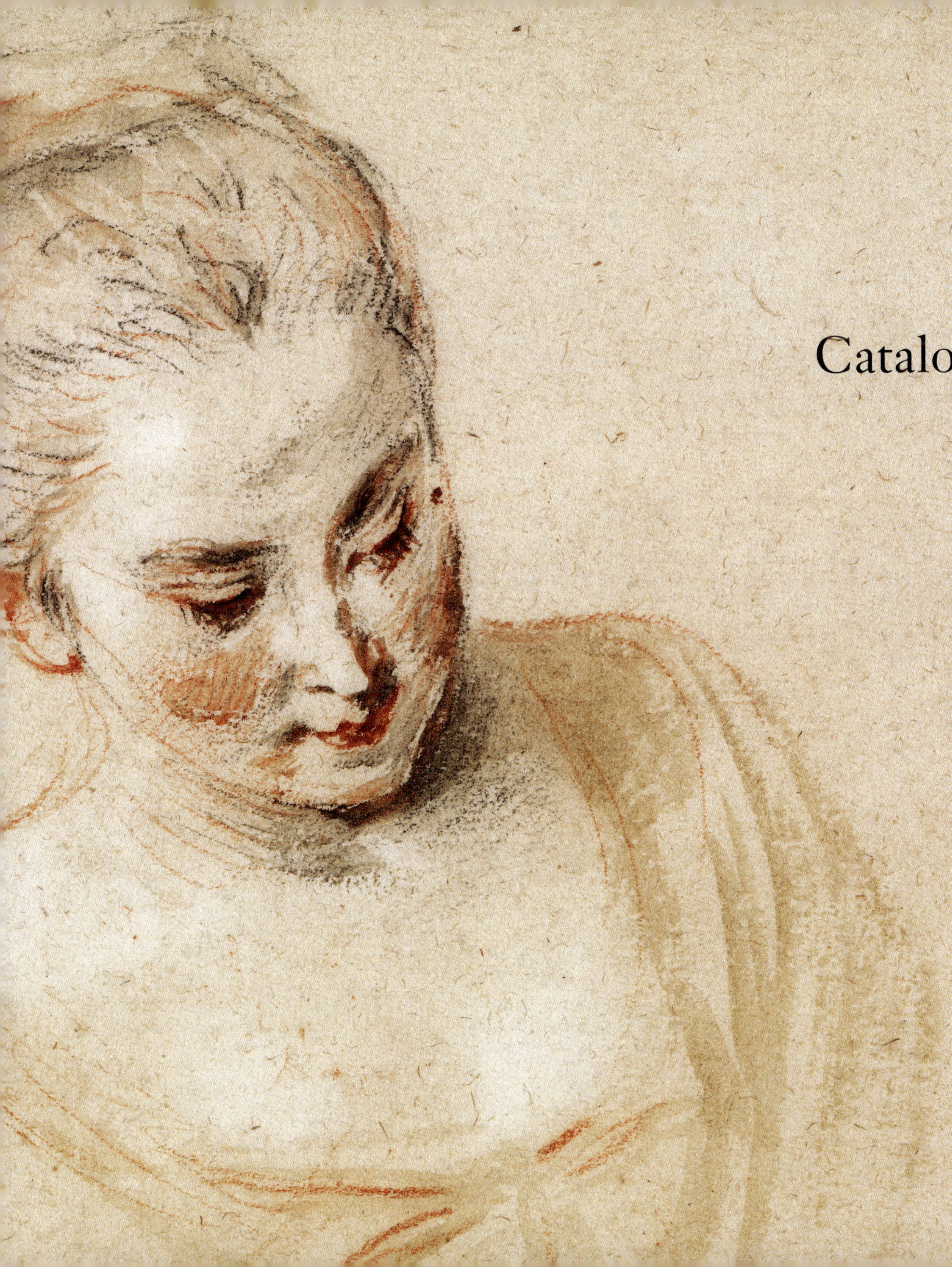

I

Red chalk on paper, 165 x 205 mm; frame line drawn in pen and brown ink
Inscription in graphite at lower right *Watteau* (or *Wateau*?)

The Pierpont Morgan Library, New York, inv. I.275

PROVENANCE, EXHIBITED: PM 25; RP 23; New York 1999, no. 2 (Alan Wintermute); New York 2009A, no. 25 (Perrin Stein)
LITERATURE: PM 25; RP 23; Bailey 1997, p. 47, and fig. 2; Grasselli 2001, pp. 332–33, note 14

Studies of Theatrical Figures (?), and Two Men Seated on the Ground

Although Watteau specialists are divided by controversy, all agree that the present drawing is by Watteau, but were the drawings in the upper register and the two recumbent men in the lower part of the page executed by the artist at the same date (and what is that date)? Parker and Mathey (1957) tend to favour a single date, 1712, as does Margaret Morgan Grasselli, who has quite recently (2001) valiantly defended her point of view. Alan Wintermute, Colin B. Bailey and Perrin Stein concur with a second hypothesis, upheld by us in 1996. All observe the differences in the treatment of the hands, arms and legs of the figures at the top and the figures in the lower register. One detail is worth noting: the hair of the recumbent man in the centre covers the hem of the gown of the woman in the upper register. In our opinion, the upper row dates from about 1709. The two men on the lower part of the page were drawn by Watteau two or three years later.

All the drawings on this sheet, apart from the woman in the upper register, can be compared with figures in paintings – a process dear to Watteau. The two men lying on the ground appear in *The Gathering near the Fountain of Neptune* (Museo del Prado, Madrid). Watteau has reversed their position, placing the one turning to the right here on the left of the painting. PR

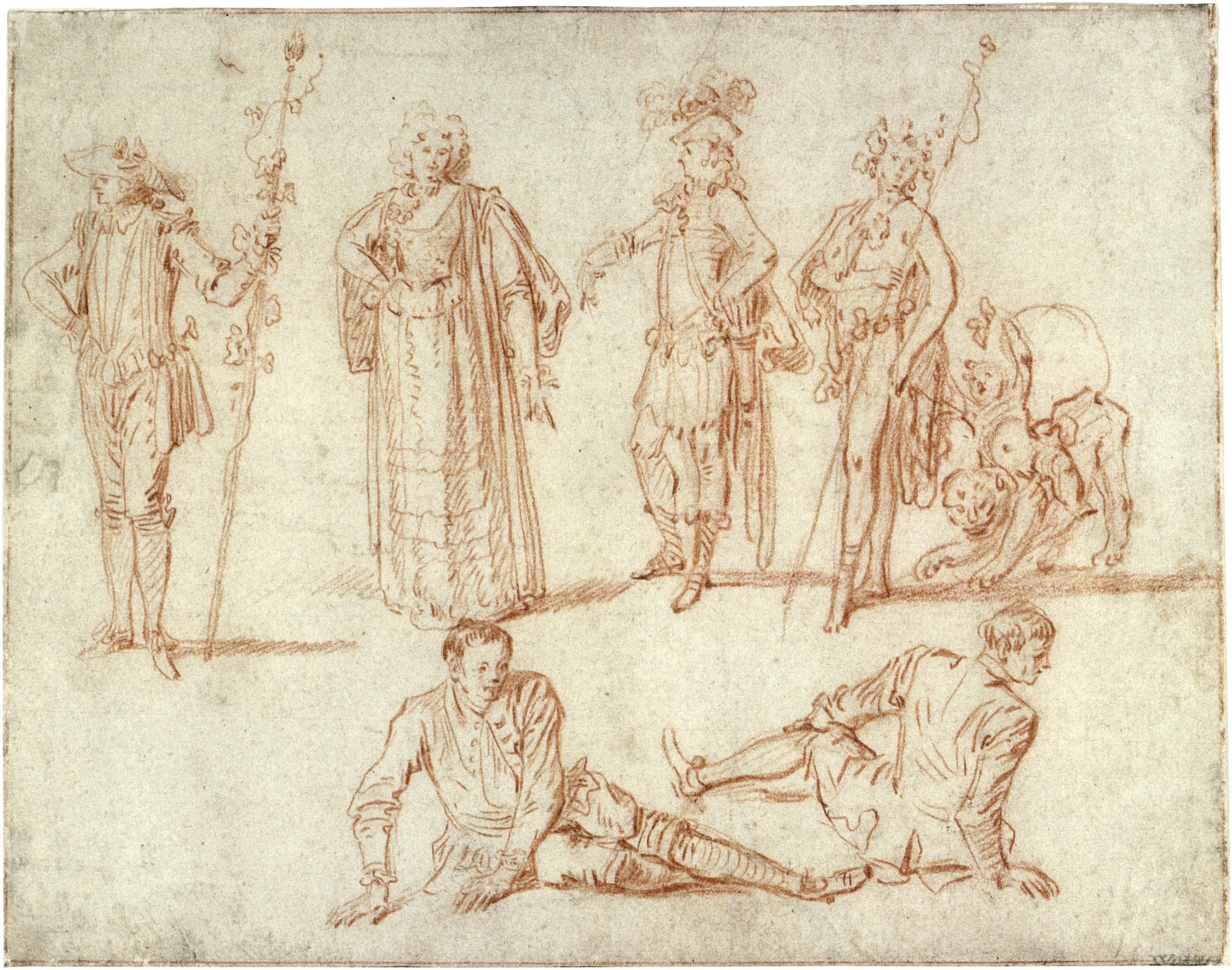

2

A Barber's Shop

Red chalk on paper, 122 x 334 mm; frame line drawn in pen and brown ink
Inscription in red chalk, at lower right *Watteau*

Musée du Louvre, Paris, Département des Arts graphiques, inv. 33362 bis

PROVENANCE, EXHIBITED: PM 139; RP 24; Milan 2003, no. 24
LITERATURE: PM 139; RP 24; Wine 1997, p. 60; Plax 2000, p. 169, fig. 67

This drawing entered the Louvre during the Revolution. Watteau specialists have unanimously compared it with *The Gersaint Shop Sign* (fig. 4), in our opinion among the most beautiful French paintings of the eighteenth century. The comparison relates mainly to the subject, a shop, in this case a barber's shop, seen from outside from the spectator's point of view. Several men, one wearing a sword, are standing examining wigs. As Humphrey Wine observed in 1997, these appear to be in the latest fashion, and should therefore make it possible to give the drawing an accurate date, in our opinion no earlier than 1709.

Not enough attention perhaps has been paid to the two curtains, which, on either side of the composition, frame the scene; they are more reminiscent of the theatre than of the sign for a barber's shop (which we see here in full swing). The male figure on the left, seen from behind, has been queried: he seems to be looking at a painting – although it is difficult to imagine what a painting could be doing here. In fact the man is adjusting his wig in front of a mirror.

For the second Louvre drawing, which is often compared to *A Barber's Shop*, see cat. 6. PR

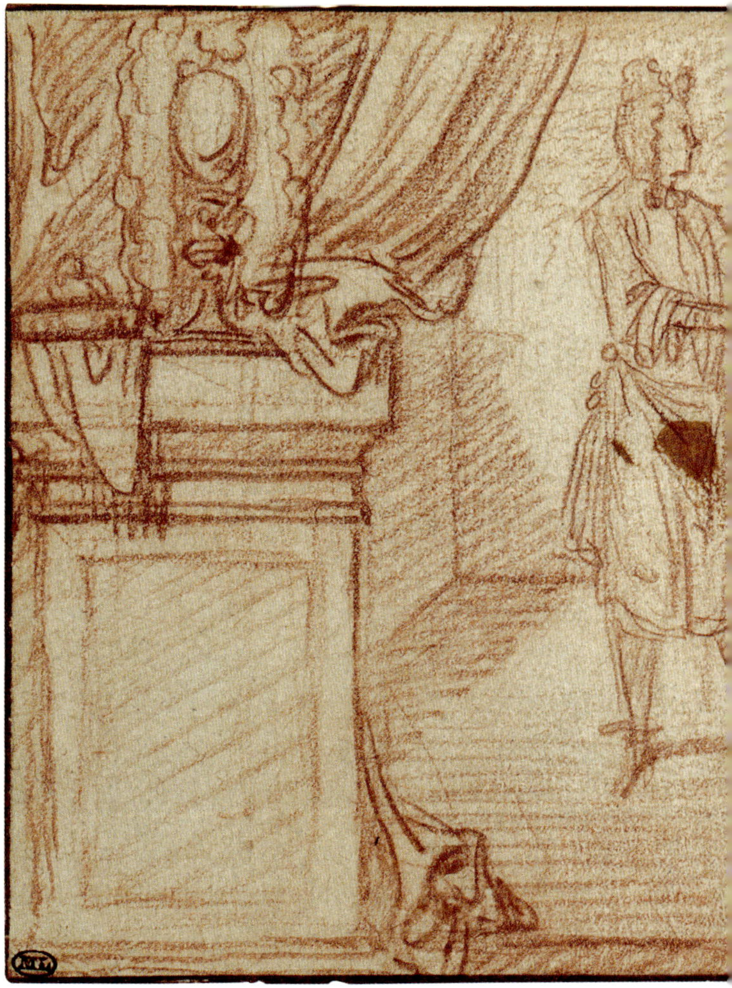

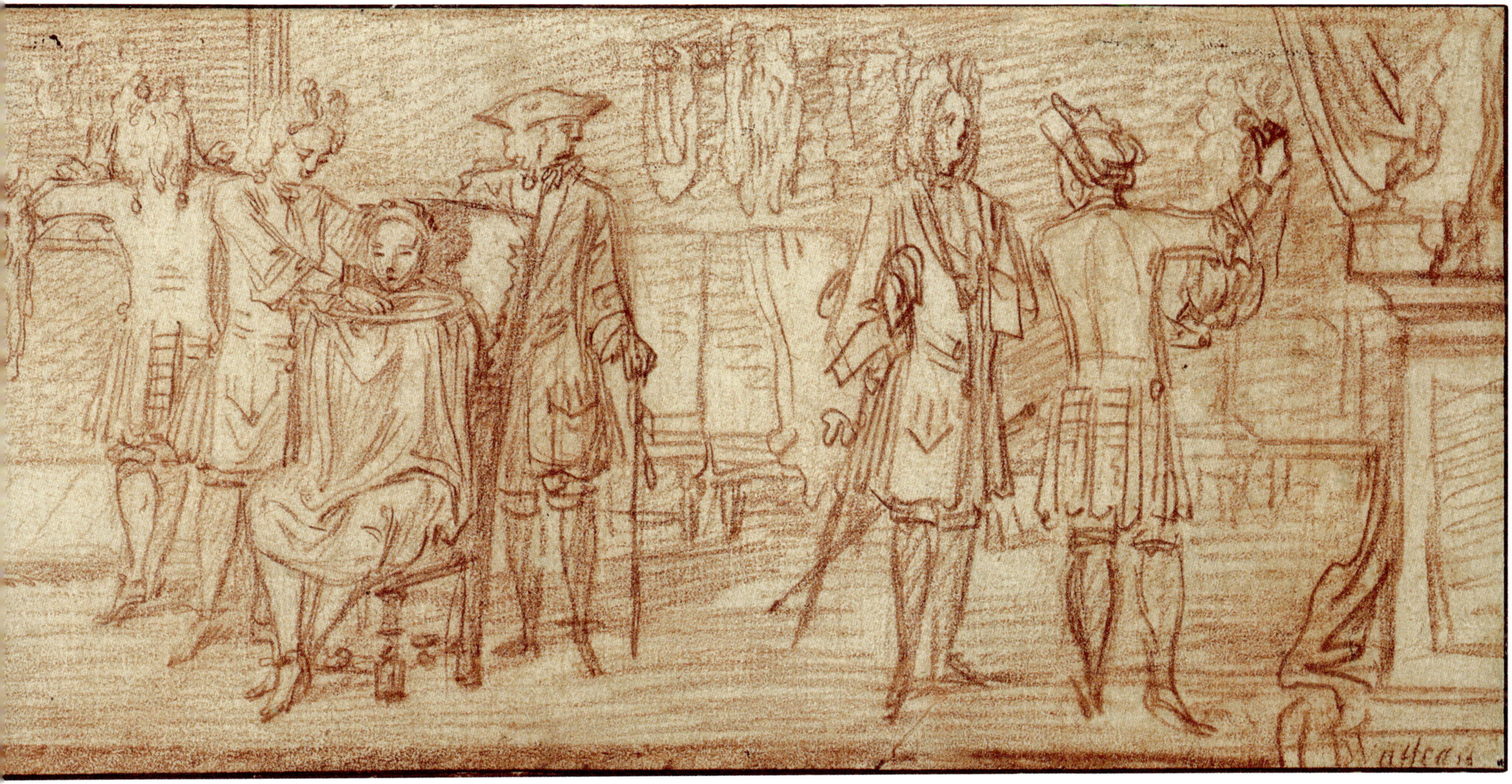

Red chalk on paper, 235 x 169 mm; trimmed at base; frame line drawn in pen and brown ink

The Ashmolean Museum, Oxford. Bequeathed by Francis Douce, 1834, inv. 1863.126

PROVENANCE: PM 175; RP 52
LITERATURE: PM 175; RP 52; Whiteley 2000, no. 835 (with related literature)

3

Sheet of Studies of Six Male Figures

The upper register of figures in this drawing contains two 'doctors' in the costume of the Commedia dell'Arte. They are accompanied by officers, all four of them wearing swords. Jon Whiteley, who catalogued the page recently, seems to prefer the date 1712 to 1709–10 as suggested by us in 1996. Following Parker and Mathey (1957, no. 175), he compares the Oxford drawing to a page of similar format in the Teylers Museum, Haarlem (RP 102), which is also slightly trimmed at the lower edge; this also depicts a number of theatrical doctors wearing their traditional large floppy hats.

Drawn from life, elegantly laid out on the white page, these six figures in Watteau's favourite medium, red chalk – he seldom if ever used pen and ink – belong to the studies he made so frequently, and regularly used in his paintings. Contemporary printmakers seized upon them and reproduced them, ensuring Watteau's rapid fame. PR

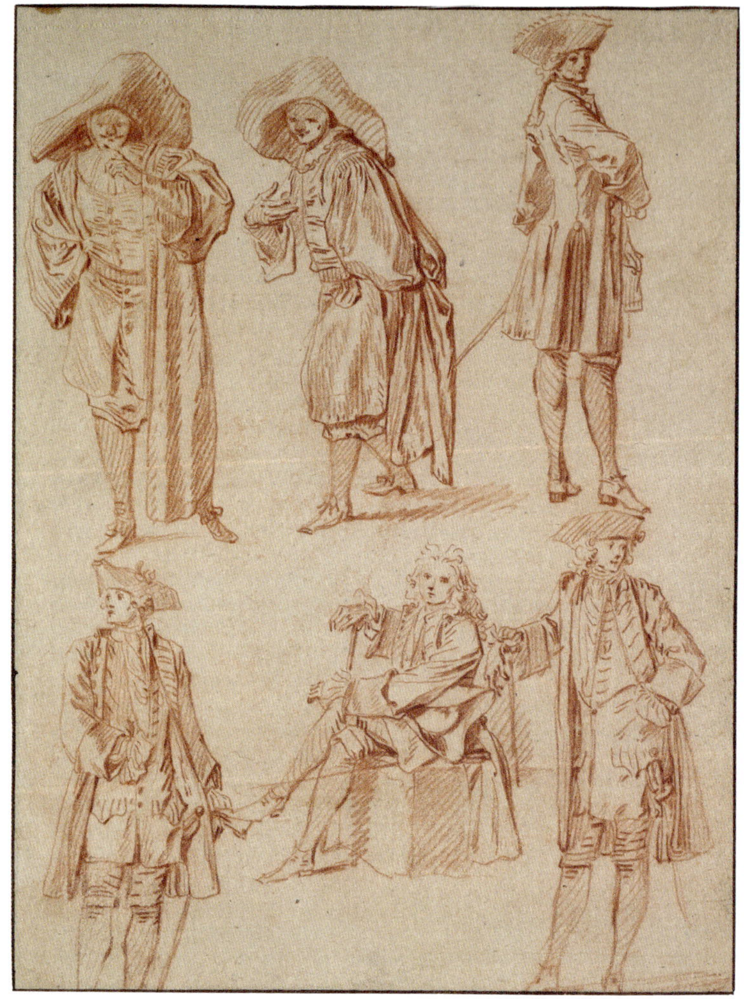

Red chalk on paper, 122 x 195 mm; frame line drawn in pen and brown ink

Ecole nationale supérieure des Beaux-Arts, Paris, inv. 1605

PROVENANCE, EXHIBITED: PM 297; RP 67; Ecole nationale supérieure des Beaux-Arts, Paris, in 1908, L. 829 at lower right; Sydney 2005, no. 3
LITERATURE: PM 297; RP 67; Grasselli 2001, p. 314

4

Three Studies of Soldiers and One Man Kneeling Seen from the Back

Watteau enjoyed drawing soldiers in a wide variety of postures, among them resting, sleeping, seated and exercising. His finest studies on this subject date from 1712–13. Watteau used these figures individually in his military paintings and they were regularly engraved, particularly in the *Figures de différents caractères*, a two-volume collection of 351 drawings engraved between 1726 and 1728 at the request of Jean de Jullienne (1686–1766) by some of the finest engravers of the period, including François Boucher. The collection is a bible for Watteau specialists.

The present sheet has unfortunately been trimmed at the top edge and sides. As in most of Watteau's military studies, the three infantrymen are still wearing their hats – a sort of tricorn – and carrying their muskets. Unusually, however, the three soldiers and the man kneeling seen from the back were all reused by Watteau in the same painting, *Alte* (*The Rest*; Thyssen-Bornemisza Museum, Madrid) – to borrow the title given to the engraving by Jean Moyreau. The date of the drawing – 1710 in our 1996 catalogue raisonné – was slightly modified by Margaret Morgan Grasselli in 2001 to 1708–09. PR

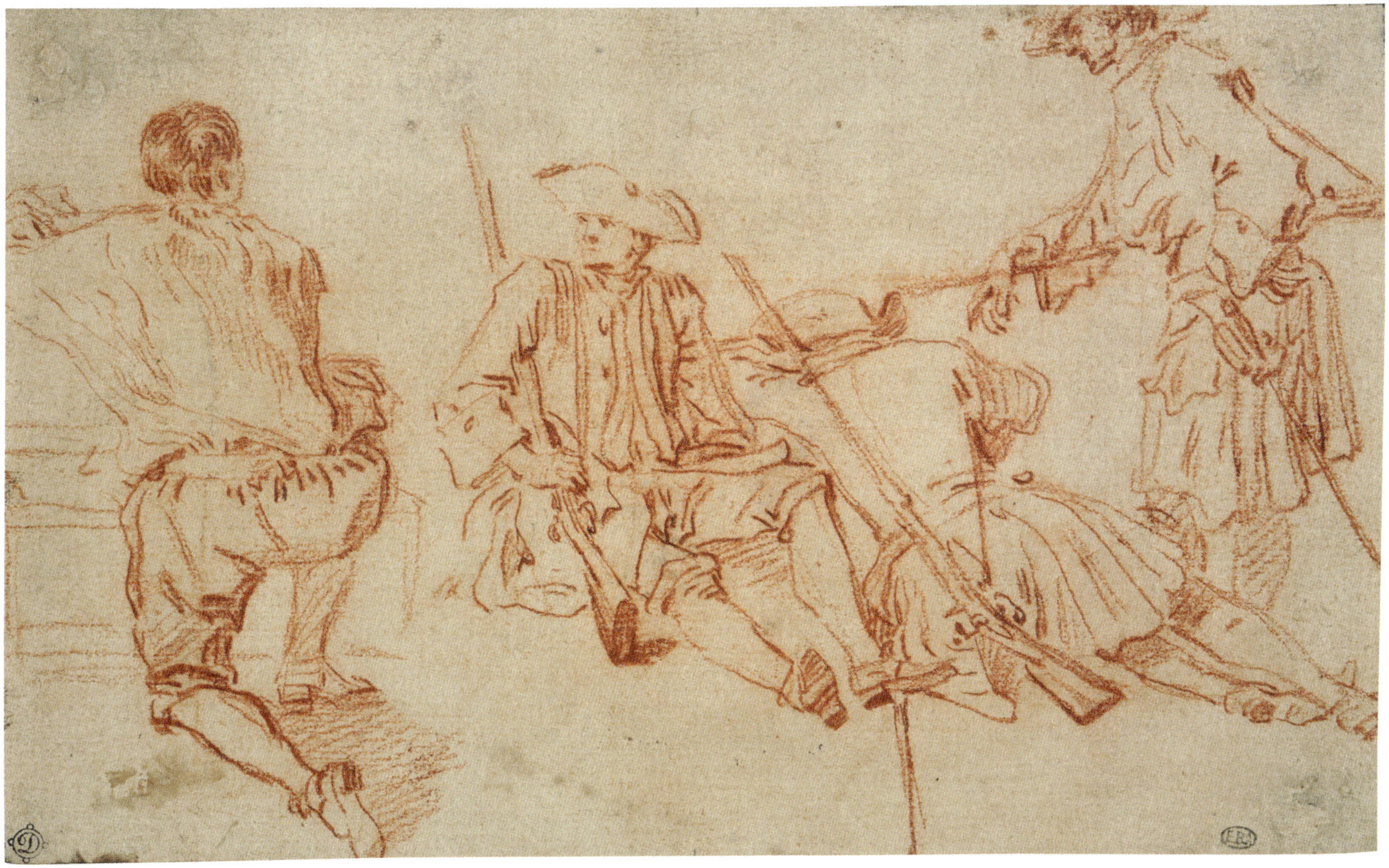

227 x 352 mm

VERSO: Red chalk; oil stains; frame line drawn in pen and black ink

RECTO: Red chalk; the composition is inscribed inside a red chalk frame, arched above, with a second frame line in pen and black ink around three sides

Institut de France,
Musée Jacquemart-André,
Paris, inv. 1595

PROVENANCE, EXHIBITED: PM 803; RP 82; Marquis Philippe de Chennevières-Pointel's mark L. 2072 or 2073 at lower left; Chantilly 1996, no. 5
LITERATURE: PM 803; RP 82; Wine 1997, p. 60; Prat 2003, pp. 29 and 30, fig. 12, recto

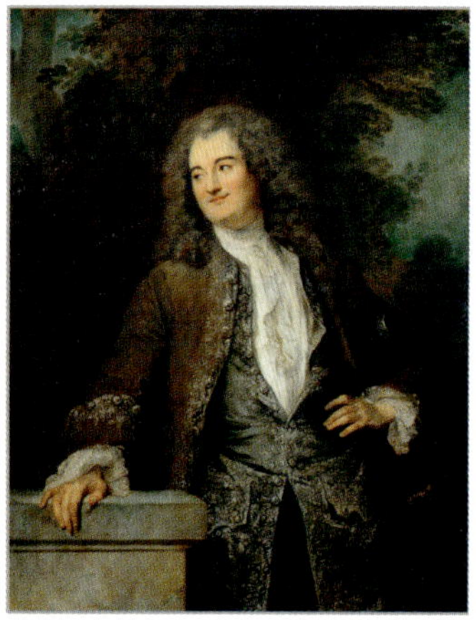

Fig. 14
Portrait of a Gentleman, c. 1720.
Oil on canvas, 130 x 97 cm.
Musée du Louvre, Paris

5

Studies of Eight Hands, the Feet of a Kneeling Figure, and Bust of a Man, verso

The Adoration of the Magi, recto, transversely

The verso and recto of this page require separate study. The drawing belonged to Marquis Philippe de Chennevières-Pointel (1820–1899), one of the most celebrated collectors of the nineteenth century; it is not known where he acquired it. At his sale in 1898 the page was bought for 9,000 francs, no negligible sum at the time, by Nélie Jacquemart (1841–1912), wife of Edouard André. At her death, she bequeathed her entire collection to the Institut de France.

The drawing on the back, an *Adoration of the Magi*, is obviously earlier in date than the one on the front. In 1996 we chose to catalogue the page by this date (1710–11). Seldom reproduced, it must be a copy of a Flemish composition in the manner of Rubens. It has been compared with a painting of the same subject by Jan Lievens (1607–1674), now in the collection of the Queen's University, Kingston, Canada, although it diverges from that work in a number of details. Humphrey Wine has recently cast doubt on the attribution to Watteau of this recto: if the drawing is not by Claude Gillot (1673–1722), which he does not rule out, then it must date from the years that Watteau spent in his studio.

The drawing on the front is much more famous: it contains female hands, feet and, on the right, a half-portrait of a man with his right hand at his waist. The female hands seem to have been drawn from a model, whereas the more energetically drawn bare feet, perhaps belonging to a man kneeling, appear to have been copied from an Old Master. The male half-figure elicits the most questions. He can in fact be compared with the *Portrait of a Gentleman* in the Louvre (fig. 14). The way the jerkin is worn open over the shirt, the man's right hand so similar to the hand in the drawing, the tricorn hat under the arm all inescapably remind one of the painting bought by the Louvre in 1973. These similarities provide a strong argument in favour of attribution of the painting to Watteau, although doubt has recently been cast on this attribution too; the painting is undoubtedly later than the drawing (1714?). It is not yet certain that the drawings on the page were all executed at the same time. PR

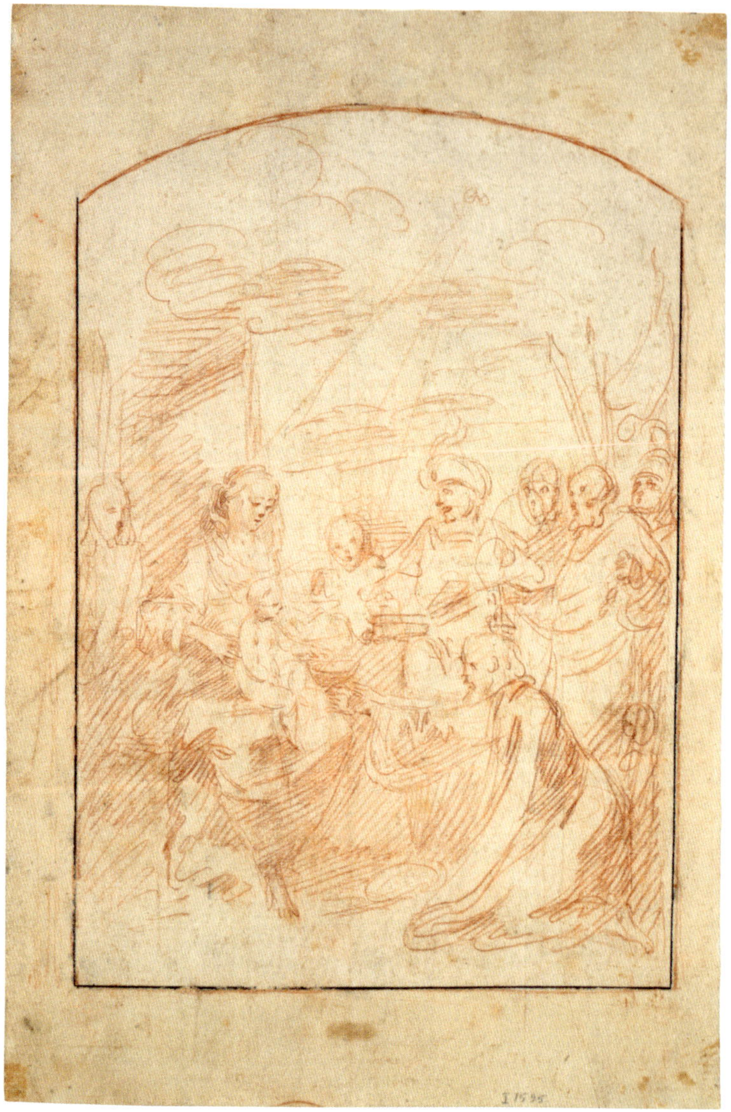

RECTO

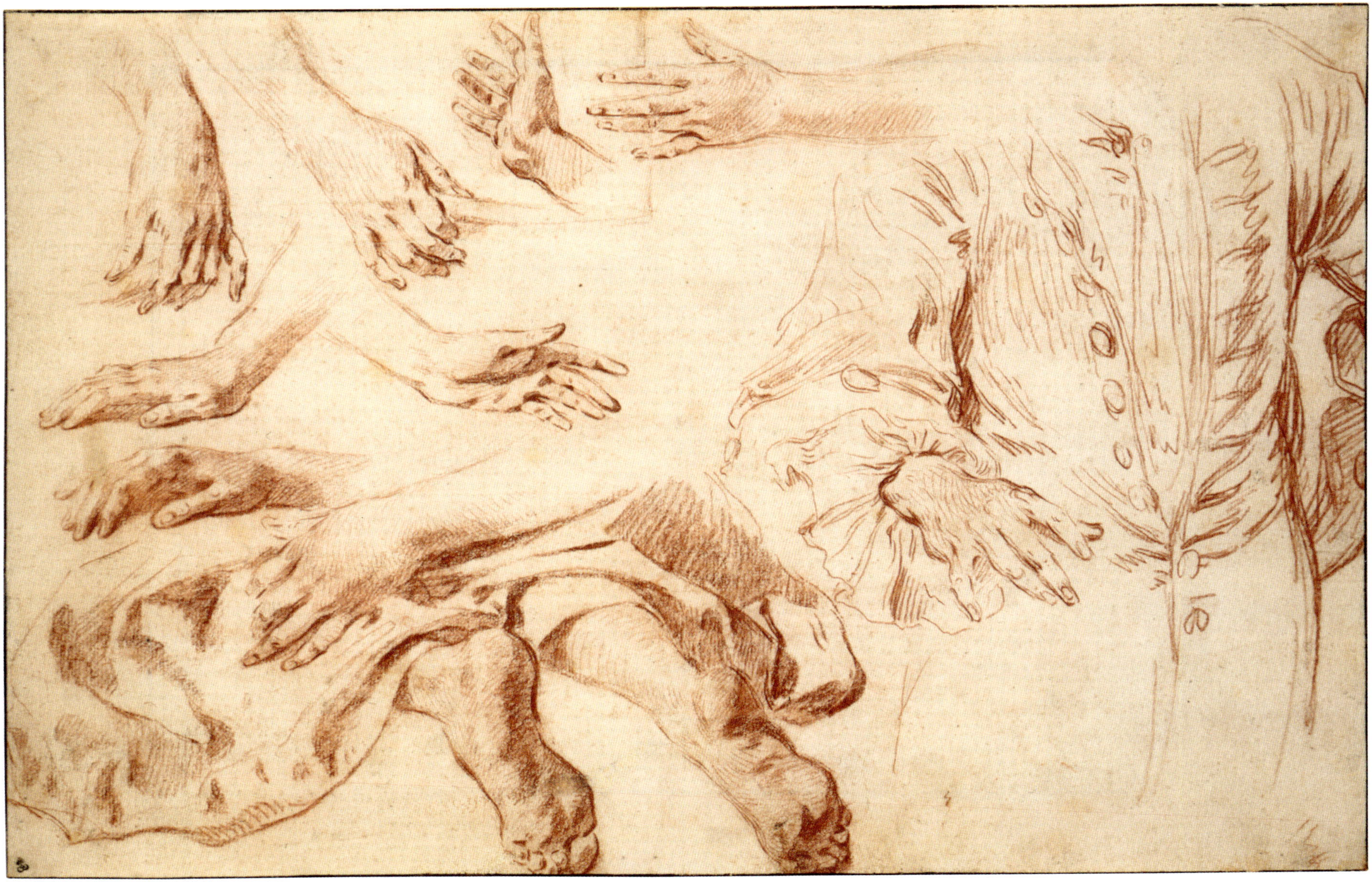

VERSO

Red chalk on paper, 152 x 221 mm; frame line drawn in pen and brown ink
Inscription in red chalk at lower left *Watteau*[*x*] (barely visible)

Musée du Louvre, Paris, Département des Arts graphiques, inv. 33362

PROVENANCE, EXHIBITED: PM 140; RP 87; Musée du Louvre mark L. 1886 at lower left
LITERATURE: PM 140; RP 87; Roland Michel 1998, p. 751; Plax 2000, pp. 169 and 168, fig. 66; Edwards 2006, pp. 43–44, 57–58, fig. 4

6

Interior of a Draper's Shop

This drawing has regularly been compared with the painting *The Gersaint Shop Sign* (Schloss Charlottenburg, Berlin; fig. 4), and also with *A Barber's Shop* (cat. 2) in the Musée du Louvre, a drawing similar in technique but very different in format (the present sheet has obviously been cut down on the right-hand side). Are we looking at a design for a shop sign (a dress shop or a draper's, according to Julie-Anne Plax), and if we are, do the two drawings in the Louvre belong to the same date? Finally, how are we to interpret the curious edifice visible on the left of the composition, behind the small boy? Does the gap reveal a view of the dome of a church or a sideboard?

The dynamism of the composition, with on the right a man striding purposefully into the shop as if he were mounting a step, inclines us to date the page somewhat later than the other page in the Louvre, to perhaps 1711. (Julie-Anne Plax suggests 1705–06.)

The power and energy of the hatching is to be admired, as are the boldness of the perspective, the speed of execution, and the liveliness of the facial expressions, so lightly sketched in with each eye represented by a dot. What impresses most of all about this vigorous drawing is its narrative thrust, always one of Watteau's main preoccupations. PR

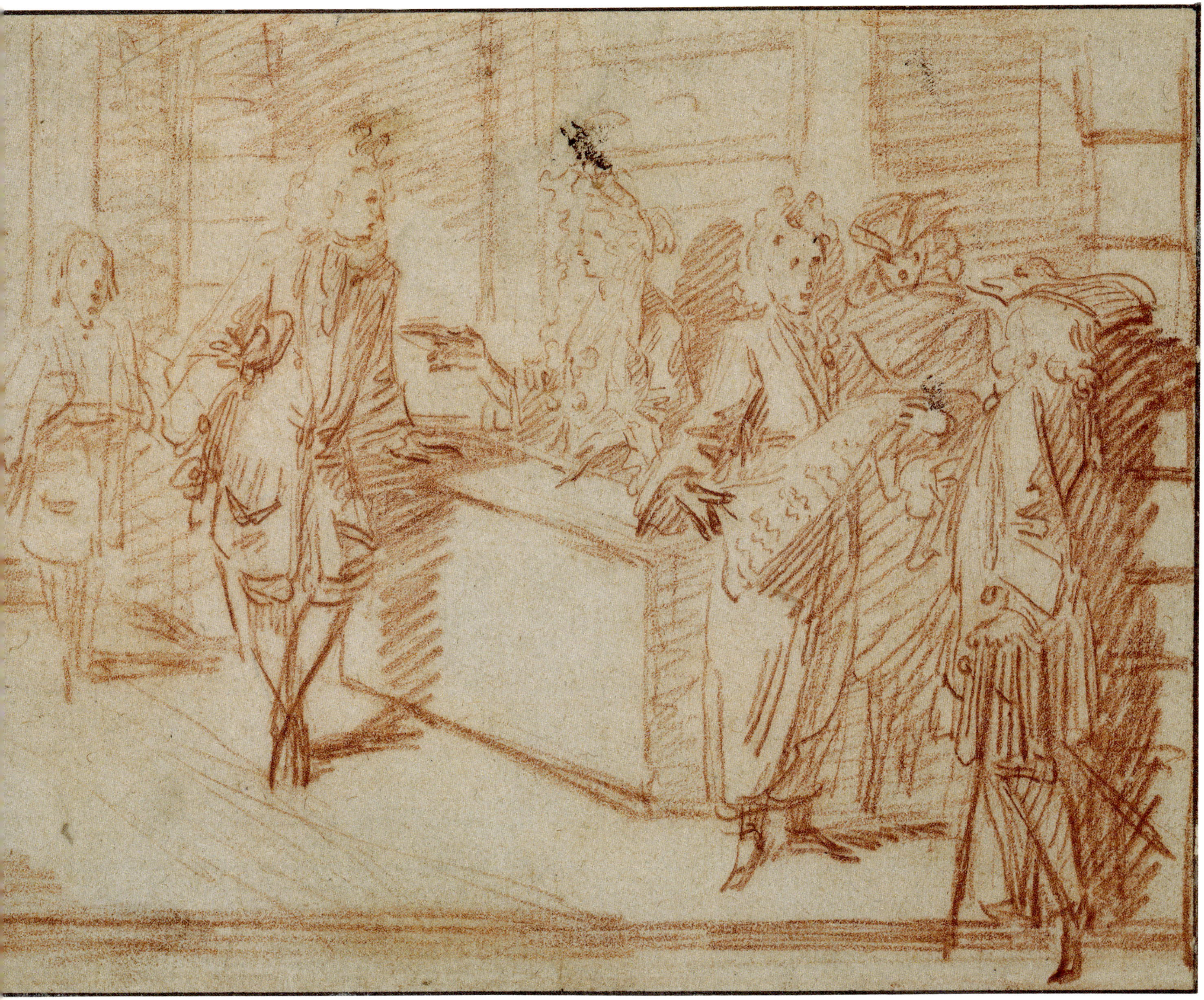

Red chalk on paper, 160 x 190 mm
Inscription in red chalk at lower right *Watteau* (almost invisible)

Collection Jean Bonna, Geneva

PROVENANCE, EXHIBITED: PM 42; RP 100; acquired by Jean Bonna in New York in 2000, L. 3600; Paris 2006, no. 21; Geneva 2006, no. 7a; New York 2009A, no. 67 (Emmanuelle Brugerolles)
LITERATURE: PM 42; RP 100

7

Three Male Figures: One Seated Seen in Three-quarter View, One Standing with Arms Raised, the Third Playing the Violin

The three studies laid on this page by Watteau have nothing in common with one another. They are completely independent, juxtaposed randomly according to which model the artist had by him. He seizes the attitude of each individual, stopping them in their tracks, not even bothering to draw the chair on which the violinist sits. The alteration to the right leg of the central figure suggests that the model had suddenly changed position.

Watteau was to use each of the figures in this drawing – whose date of 1710–11 seems to have been accepted unanimously – in three different paintings: *Jealous Fellows* (lost), *Happy Pierrot* (Thyssen-Bornemisza Collection, Madrid) and *Country Dance* (private collection).

No-one has described this drawing better than the Comte de Caylus (1692–1765): 'His habit was to draw his studies in a bound sketchbook; he thus always had a great many of them to hand. He owned some stylish costumes, some of them clothes from the Commedia dell'Arte, and used to dress people of either sex up in these [...] he caught them in attitudes as nature presented them, preferring the simpler attitudes to any others' (Rosenberg 1984, pp. 78–79). PR

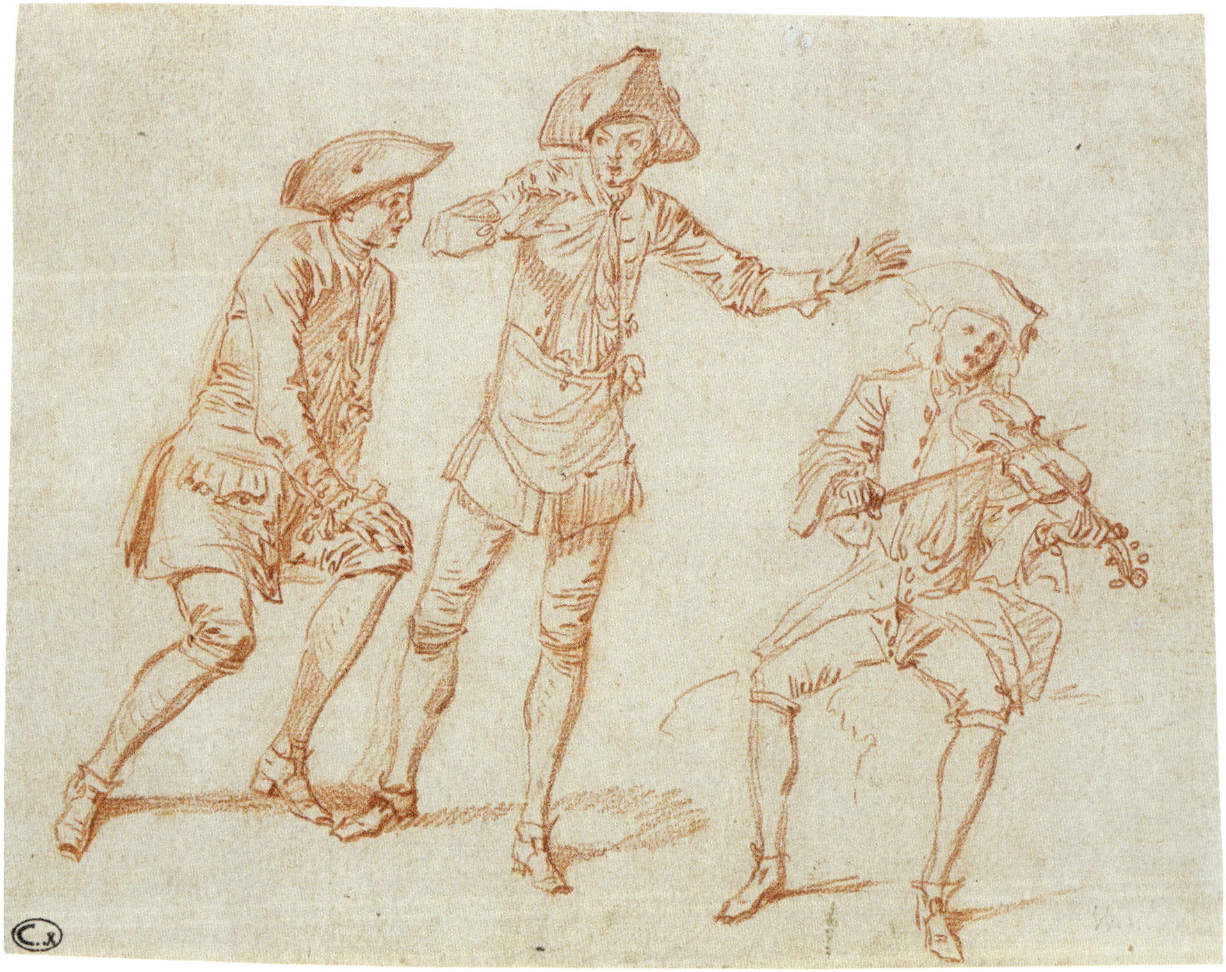

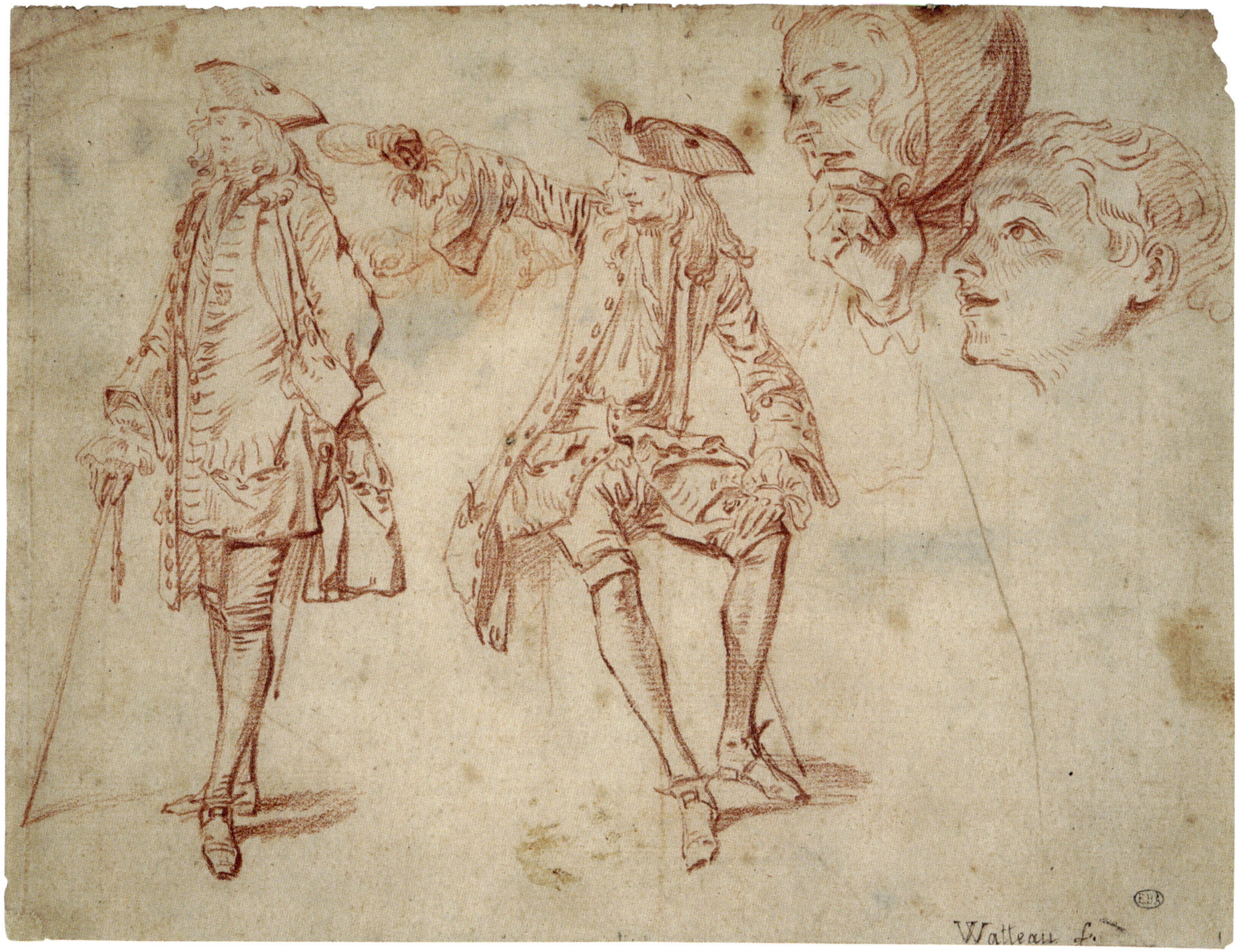

Red chalk on paper, 160 x 204 mm
Inscription written in pen and brown ink at lower right *Watteau f.*

Ecole nationale supérieure des Beaux-Arts, Paris, inv. 1607

PROVENANCE, EXHIBITED: PM 60; RP 101; Prosper Valton mark L. 829 at lower right; Brugerolles 1984, no. 487, rep.; Sydney 2005, no. 4
LITERATURE: PM 60; RP 101

8

Two Male Figures: One Seated, the Other Standing; Two Heads Turned to the Left

The inscription in pen and brown ink was clearly not written by the artist, who never signed his work. The fine alteration to the right hand of the man pouring a drink in the centre of the composition is worth noting; and specialists in Watteau's drawings have long wondered about the two heads seen in profile, appearing to be lit from below, in the upper right-hand corner of the page. They evoke the theatrical world so dear to Watteau's heart. Are they both actresses, or an actor and an actress? Sketched from life, one is listening and the other looking. The very unusual production of two counter-proofs from this drawing, both reproduced in our 1996 catalogue raisonné (RP 101a and RP 101b), has left the page somewhat faded. The drawings are generally agreed to date from 1710–11. PR

9

Studies of Actors, a Pair of Hands and a Fragment of an Arabesque

Red chalk on paper, 168 x 221 mm

Hessisches Landesmuseum, Darmstadt, inv. A.E. 2400

PROVENANCE, EXHIBITED: not mentioned in PM; RP 113; Marquis de Lagoy mark L. 1710 at lower right; Cordellier, Rosenberg and Märker 2007, no. 411 (Peter Märker)
LITERATURE: not mentioned in PM; RP 113; Grasselli 2000, p. 164, fig. 8; Rosenberg 2001 (French edition), pp. 197 and 198, fig. 249; Eidelberg 2003, p. 72, fig. 77; Temperini 2005, p. 9, rep.

The Hessisches Landesmuseum in Darmstadt possesses three drawings by Watteau of similar format and on comparable subjects, all depicting groups of actors and characters from the Commedia dell'Arte. The subject of a recent study by Peter Märker (2007), the drawings all come from the collection of the Marquis de Lagoy, who sold them to the Duke of Dalberg, the latter in his turn presenting his whole collection to the Grand-Duke of Hessen, Ludwig I. The three pages were for a long time thought to be by Claude Gillot (1673–1722) and their attribution to Watteau, which was established only very slowly, was contested by two leading Watteau specialists, Margaret Morgan Grasselli and Martin Eidelberg; we believe today that a date of 1711 is unanimously accepted. Although the figures of actors and actresses are clearly inspired by Gillot and probably copied by Watteau, the crossed hands at the top of the page, powerfully and sensitively drawn, as well as the gnome with bird's feet playing the bagpipes, could only belong to Watteau.

The first Darmstadt drawing (RP 112; Cordellier, Rosenberg and Märker 2007, no. 409 [Peter Märker]), which shows us a group of actors parodying the departure of a troop of soldiers, represents a theatrical scene, in a coherent composition. The other two, by contrast (besides the present drawing, RP 114; Cordellier, Rosenberg and Märker 2007, no. 410 [Peter Märker]), show rows of characters from the Commedia dell'Arte with no connection between them. Among them can be seen the Sorceress, Pierrot, the Fool and other figures from the Italian repertory. The subtle characterisation of each face, the rapidity of line and the joyful humour attached to each model betray the hand of Watteau. PR

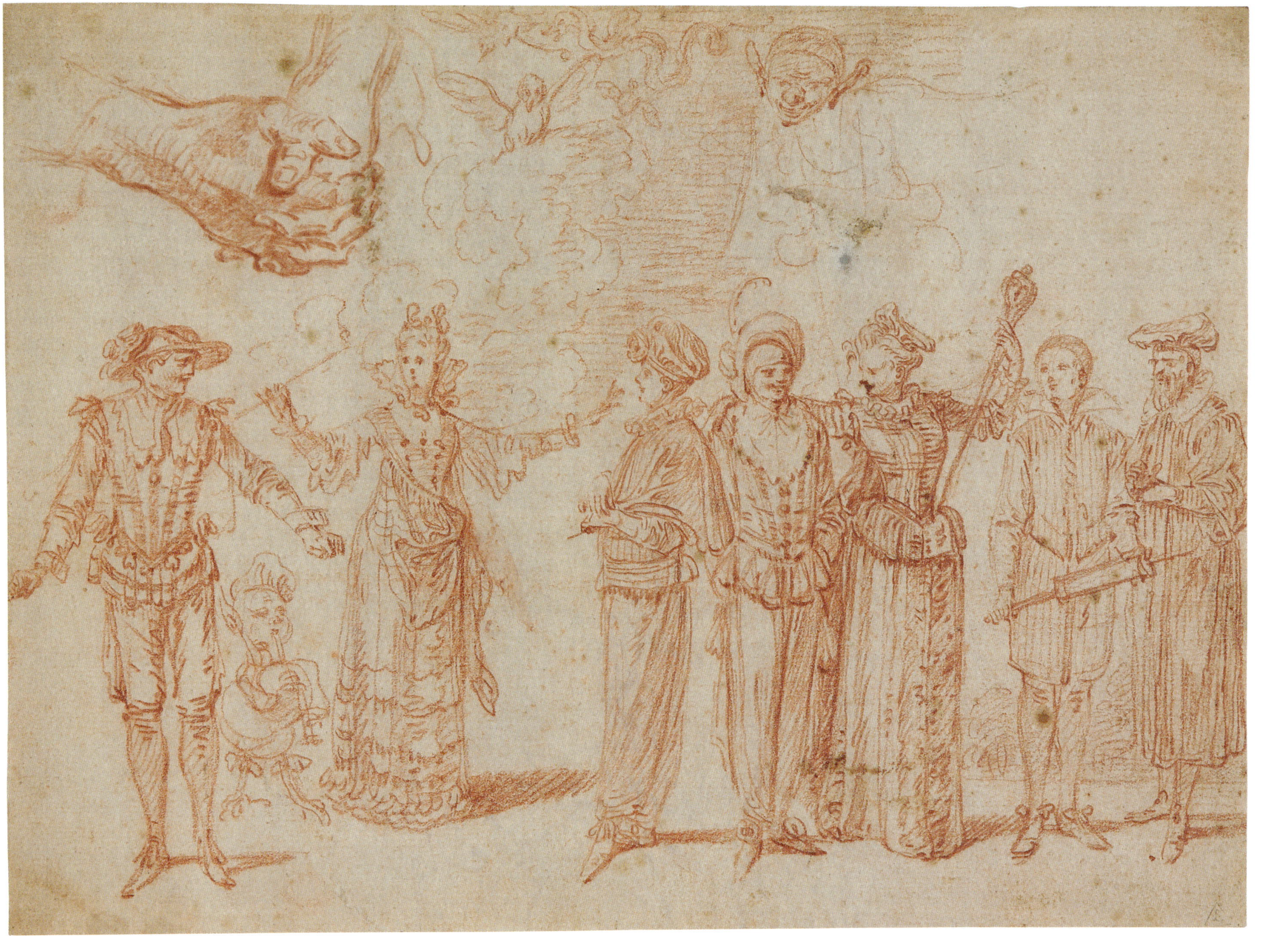

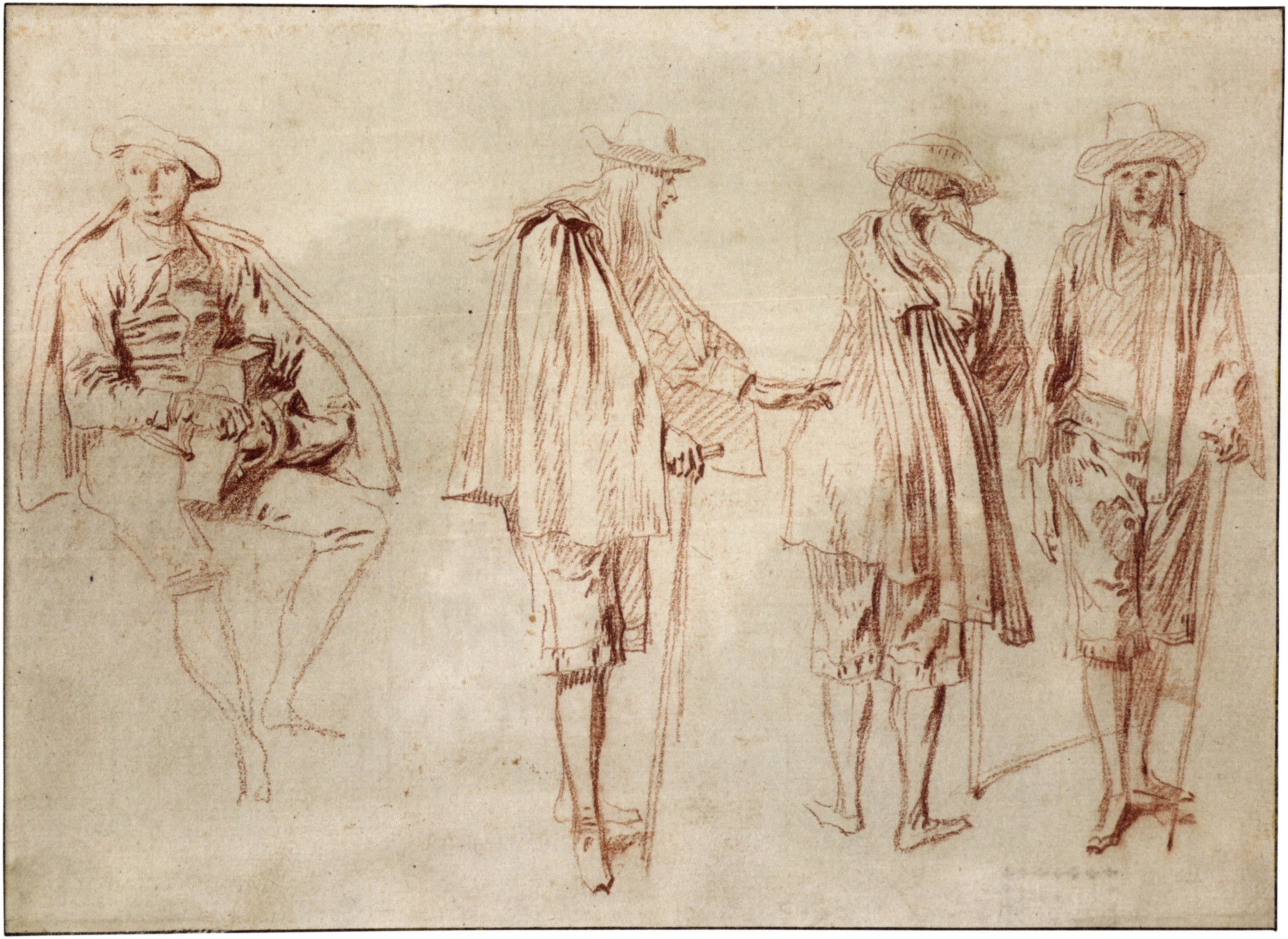

RECTO

10

A Hurdy-gurdy Player and Three Studies of a Long-haired Comedian, recto

Landscape with View of a Church, verso

162 x 220 mm

RECTO: Red chalk on paper; frame line drawn in pen and brown ink

VERSO: Watercolour and red chalk on paper
Inscription (in Watteau's hand?) in red chalk in the upper centre of the drawing *demi teinte Grise / Et Generalement Les ombres / Grise*

Teylers Museum, Haarlem, inv. M15

PROVENANCE, EXHIBITED: PM 53 and PM 472; RP 135
LITERATURE: PM 53 and PM 472; RP 135; Wine 1997, p. 60; Roland Michel 1998, p. 751; Grasselli 2001, pp. 315, 317, 333, note 15 and fig. 3, p. 316 (verso); Rosenberg 2001, p. 179, fig. 225 (verso); Edwards 2006, p. 46; Burollet 2008, p. 172, under no. 106

The attribution to Watteau of the front side of this drawing has been accepted unreservedly by successive specialists in the artist's drawn *œuvre*. Only the date has met with reservations. The date 1711–12 seems today to win the most acceptance. The fine copy in the Musée Cognacq-Jay in Paris should be mentioned; this depicts, in a different order, the hurdy-gurdy player and the long-haired actor from in front and behind, but not in profile. Worth remembering is that in 1931, Parker (p. 27) classed the drawing in the Musée Cognacq-Jay as 'almost equal in quality to the drawing in Haarlem'.

It is the drawing on the back of this sheet – a wooded landscape with a church belfry in the centre and a group of houses – that has caused a great deal of spilled ink. In 1996 we wondered whether 'the drawing would be attributed to Watteau if it were discovered today without its recto'.

The debate can be resumed as follows: (1) Is the verso by Watteau? (2) It is by Watteau, but the heightening in watercolour is a later addition by another hand. (3) Is the inscription in red chalk by Watteau? (4) If the drawing is by Watteau, is its date the same as that of the drawing recto, i.e. *c.* 1711? (5) Finally, can the bell tower be convincingly identified?

Without wishing to reopen the debate that followed the publication of our catalogue raisonné in 1996, when Watteau specialists argued the matter in their reviews, let us say that the attribution to Watteau of the verso is given the benefit of the doubt (Wine 1997) and generally accepted; this was already our view in 1996. Answers to the other questions raised above are 'yes' in favour of the authorship of the drawing, the watercolour heightening and the inscription.

The church tower remains a mystery: people have in general ceased to claim it as Gentilly church, as seen in the background of *The Marmot* (State Hermitage Museum, St Petersburg). In 1984, in the catalogue to the exhibition in Paris, Washington and Berlin (Washington 1984), we compared it with the church tower visible in the background of the Courtauld Institute's *Standing Friar* (cat. 36). To sum up, our prudence (not to say scepticism) in 1996 stimulated research. The presentation in London of the recto and verso of the Haarlem drawing will provide another opportunity to ponder Watteau's working methods, his interests, and his investigations along lines he pursued only occasionally. PR

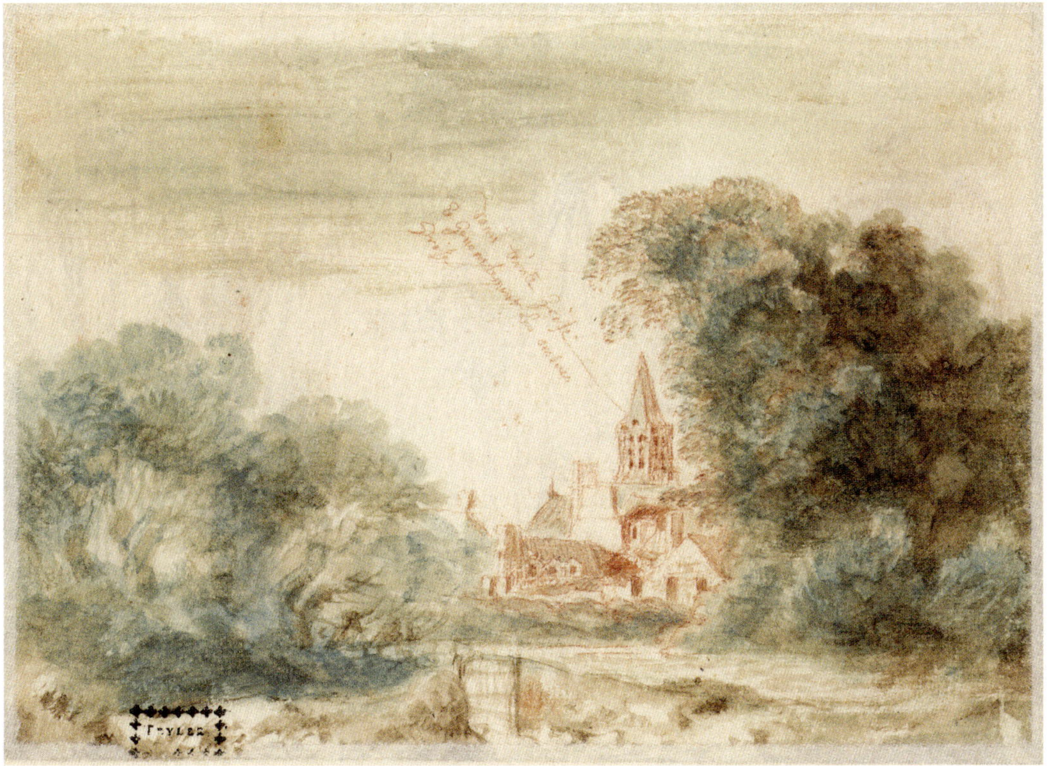

VERSO

11

Three Studies of Pilgrims, One with a Cupid; a Male Figure Raising an Arm

Red chalk on paper, 159 x 211 mm; oil and ink stains; fully glued to backing

Kupferstich-Kabinett, Staatliche Kunstsammlungen, Dresden, inv. C.734

PROVENANCE: PM 22; RP 139; Dresden Kupferstich-Kabinett mark L. 1647 at lower right
LITERATURE: PM 22; RP 139; Roland Michel 1998, p. 751

This drawing, which dates from 1711–12 at the latest (for a different opinion see Roland Michel 1998), has had a considerable afterlife. The pilgrim seen standing on the left, holding a staff, inspired the pilgrim in *The Embarkation for Cythera*, a painting acquired in 1982 by the Städel Kunstinstitut, Frankfurt. The kneeling pilgrim on the right can also be found in a lost painting, *Bon Voyage*, engraved by Benoît Audran (DV 35), as well as in both versions of *Pilgrimage to the Isle of Cythera*, in the Musée du Louvre (fig. 3) and the Schloss Charlottenburg, Berlin (in all three cases without the cupid leaning over his shoulder). The woman in the centre of the page does not appear in any known painting.

The Bibliothèque Municipale in Besançon owns an unpublished counter-proof depicting two pilgrims (fig. 15). On the left of this counter-proof the kneeling pilgrim from the present sheet appears, and on the right the standing pilgrim holding a staff, seen from behind. Watteau's drawing from which this counter-proof was taken is in a private collection in New York (RP 51). This makes one wonder whether the New York drawing originally occupied the right-hand side of the Dresden page, and was it detached from the page? PR

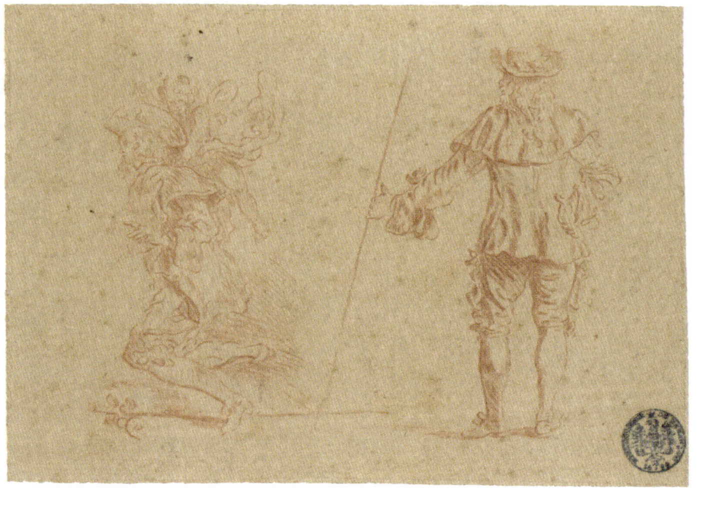

Fig. 15
Two Pilgrims, counter-proof.
Red chalk, 167 x 238 mm.
Bibliothèque Municipale, Besançon

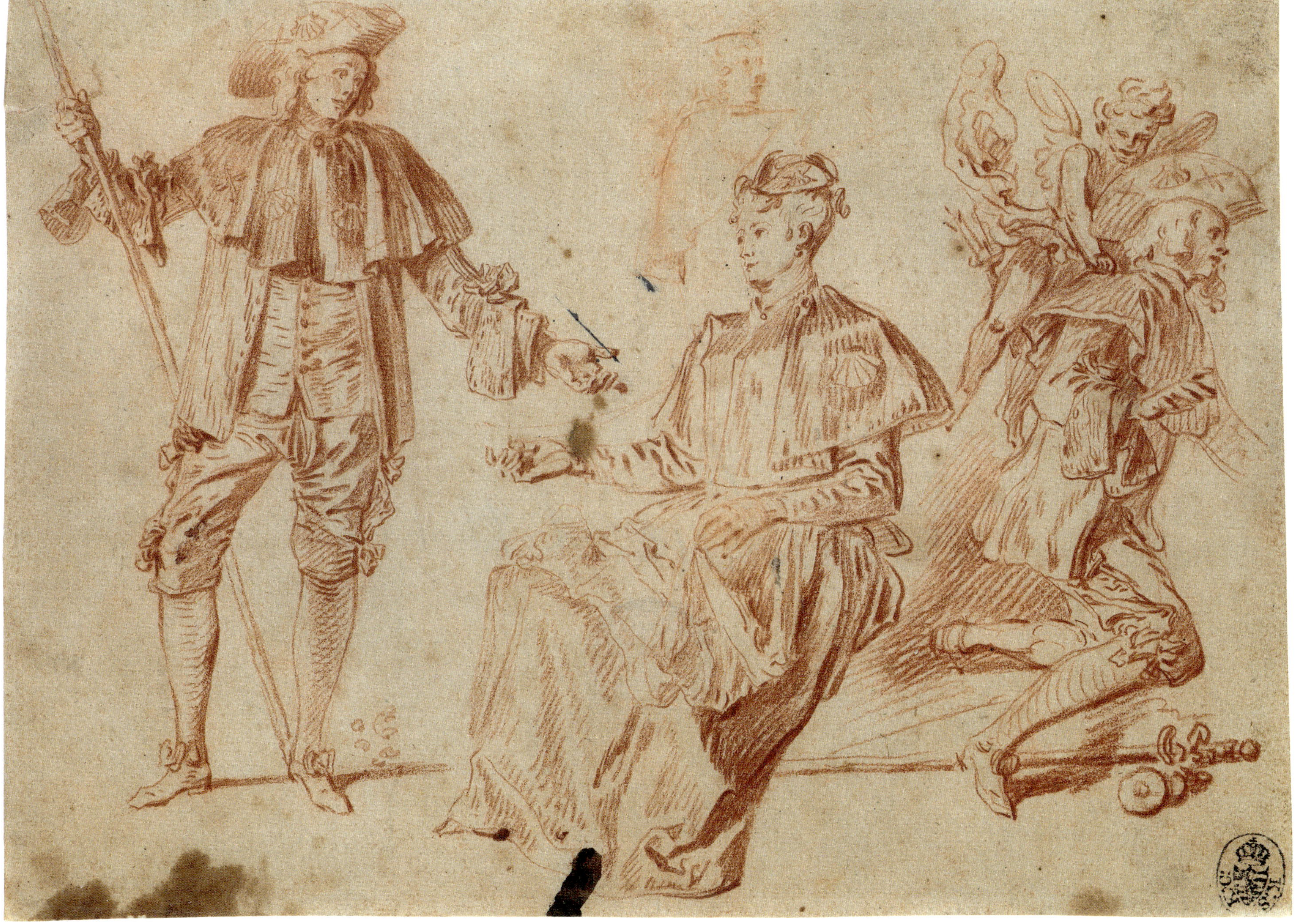

Red chalk on paper, 223 x 340 mm; trimmed at base; fold in centre of page
Illegible inscription, perceptible against the light, upper left

The Ashmolean Museum, Oxford. Bequeathed by Francis Douce, 1834, inv. 1863.127

PROVENANCE, EXHIBITED: PM 853; RP 145
LITERATURE: PM 853; RP 145; Bailey 1997, p. 47; Whiteley 2000, no. 834; Edwards 2001, p. 59, fig. 2; Rosenberg 2001, p. 141, fig. 183; Braunschweig 2005, under no. 11

12

The Shipwreck

This drawing has for many years been viewed in conjunction with lines from *La Vie de Watteau* by Edme-François Gersaint (1694–1750; see Rosenberg 1984, p. 38). Jean de Jullienne (1686–1766), whose friendship with the artist is well documented, as is the vital role he played in having Watteau's principal compositions engraved (thus ensuring unique exposure for Watteau, something few artists of the period enjoyed), is said to have rescued Watteau from difficulties by helping him to avoid losing his savings in the financial collapse in France caused by John Law (1671–1729): '6,000 livres which Jean de Jullienne saved for him from shipwreck at the time when he left for England'. (Law's failure happened in May 1720, the year that Watteau sailed for England, a year before his death.) *Shipwreck* is the title of the engraving made by Caylus after the Oxford drawing, which it is tempting to date to 1720. All the evidence is against this, however: the execution of the drawing, still minuscule with small, sharp lines, and also its subject. In 1996 we felt we had to date it to 1710; Jon Whiteley dated it to between 1710 and 1714 in 2000; for us *c.* 1712 in 2001.

It should be stated at once that so far none of the attempts at interpreting the subject has been convincing. Why the castle and palm trees in the background? Why does Neptune, armed with his trident and riding a conch to which a man who has escaped the shipwreck clings, wreak his vengeance on the four terrified passengers from the ship? Is this an illustration for an opera, a play – it would be pleasing to think that Watteau had read Shakespeare's *The Tempest* – or a novel? Perhaps readers will be able to help us to solve this mystery. PR

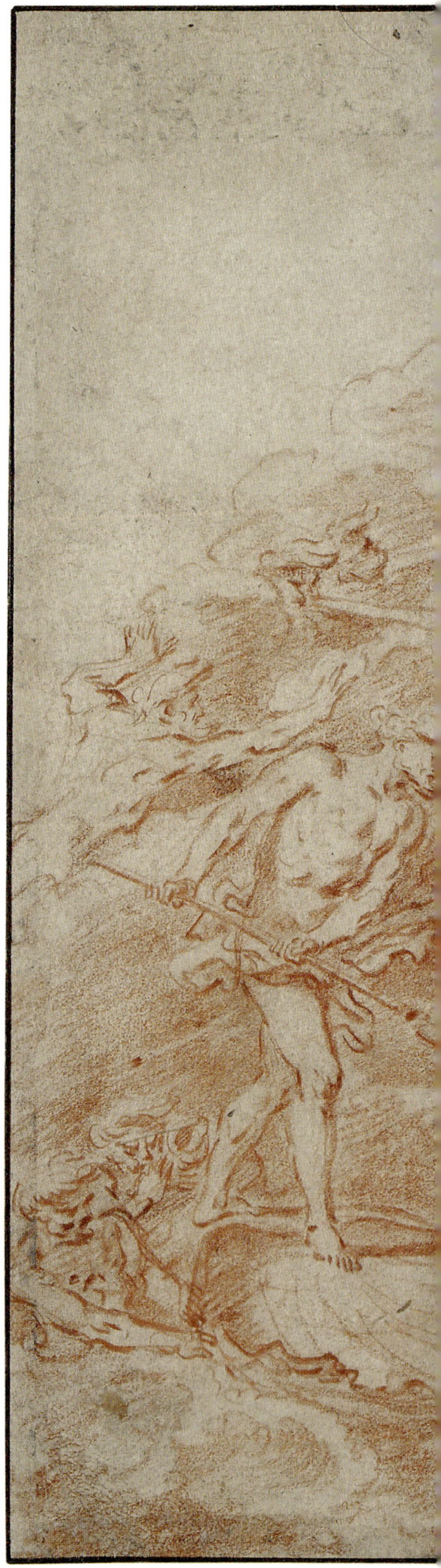

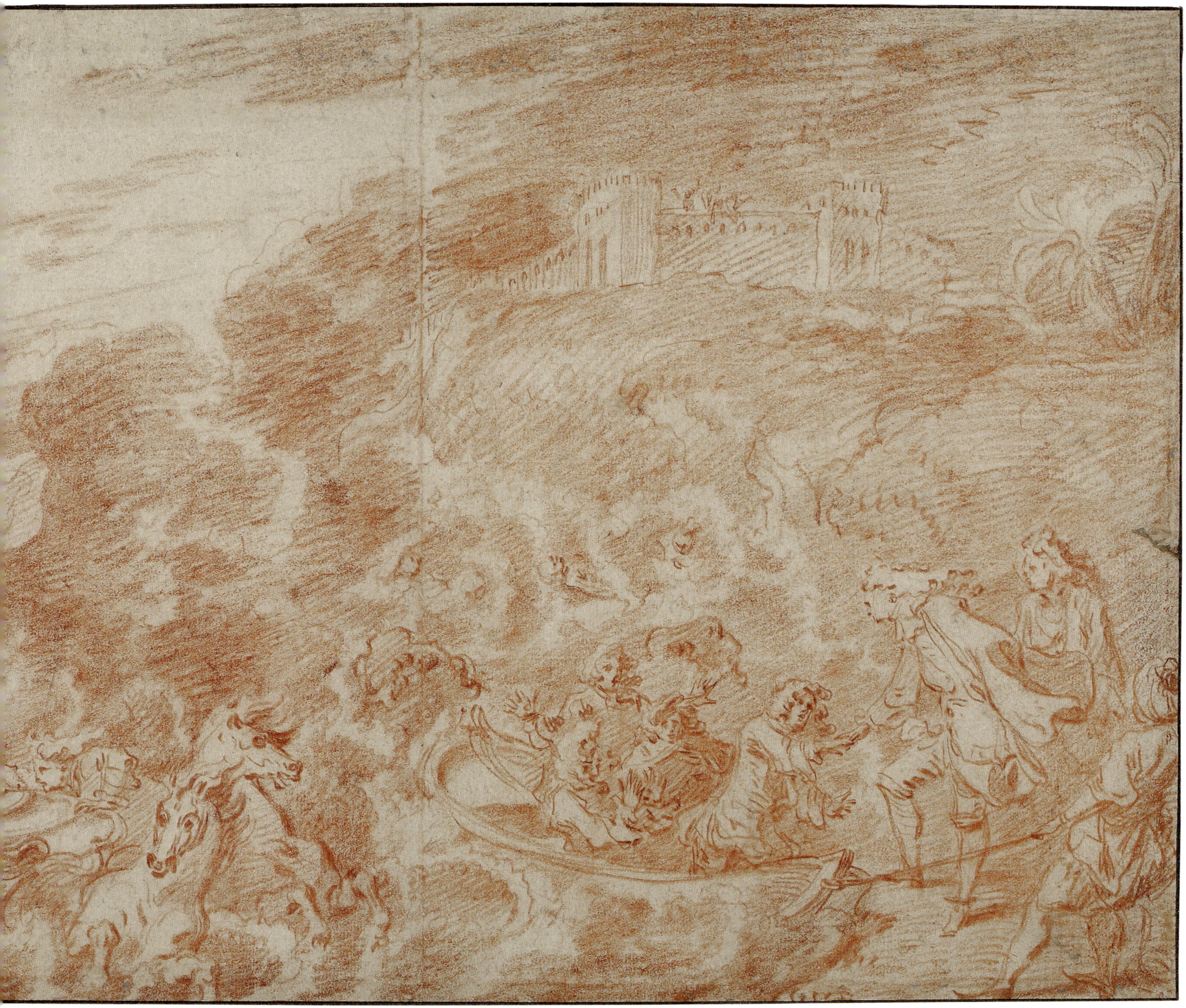

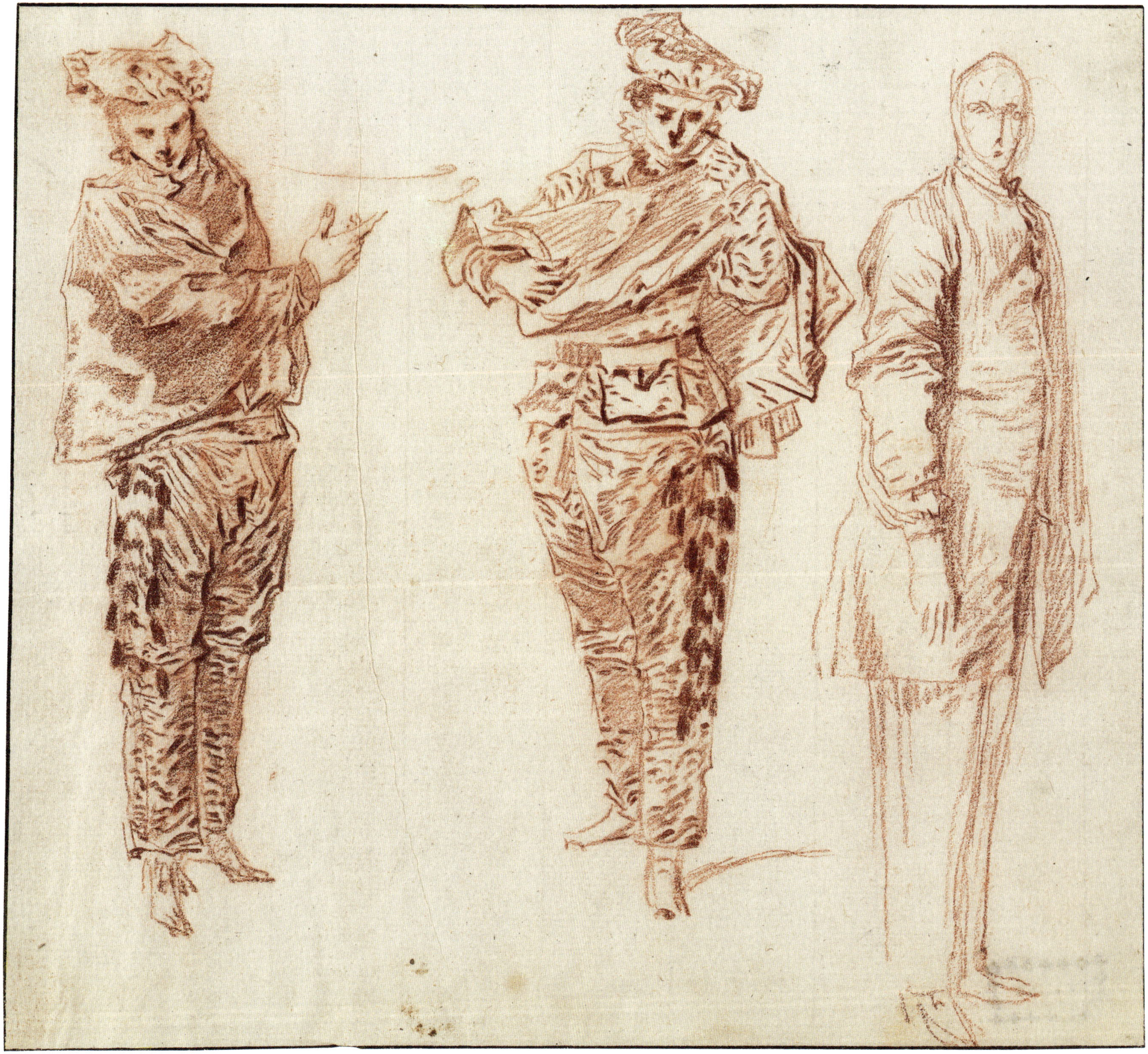

Red chalk on paper, 176 x 190 mm; frame line drawn in pen and brown ink

Teylers Museum, Haarlem, inv. M18

PROVENANCE, EXHIBITED: PM 57; RP 159
LITERATURE: PM 57; RP 159

13

Two Studies of Mezzetin and a Pierrot

The Teylers Museum, Haarlem, has owned a fine collection of drawings by Watteau since the 1820s; with the holdings of the museums of Amsterdam and Rotterdam, this places the Netherlands among the richest in these drawings, along with Great Britain and the United States, and before Russia and Germany.

The drawings of the Mezzetin drawn in two different positions were engraved by Louis Desplaces in *Figures de différents caractères* (on this see cat. 5). As far as the Pierrot is concerned (but is it really a Pierrot?), this was evidently drawn during a different sitting, but also in *c.* 1712: it is more sketchily drawn, yet just as lively as the Mezzetin. In our 1996 catalogue raisonné we drew attention to the existence 'in a private collection in Paris', of two counter-proofs of the left-hand Mezzetin and of the possible Pierrot. These came from the Groult album, a fake containing some 500 drawings and bearing the name of one of its former owners, Camille Groult (1837–1908). This album, which was unfortunately dismantled several times, entered the Musée du Louvre in 1908 thanks to the generosity of M. and Mme Robert-Lepeltier. The two counter-proofs bear the inventory numbers R.F. 51797 and 51803 bis (on the Groult album, see Méjanès 1999 and Rosenberg 2003). PR

14

Four Studies of Soldiers at Rest and One of a Standing Woman

Red chalk on paper, 179 x 198 mm
On the verso, at lower right, the soldier leaning on his elbows on the recto has been traced in red chalk

Museum Boijmans Van Beuningen, Rotterdam, Koenigs Collection, inv. F.I. 150

PROVENANCE, EXHIBITED: PM 249; RP 180; Pierre-Jean Mariette mark L. 1852 at lower right
LITERATURE: PM 249; RP 180; Grasselli 2001, p. 314; Edwards 2006, pp. 46–47, fig. 6; Christie's, New York, auction catalogue, 28 January 2009, under no. 89; Rosenberg and Barthélémy 2011

Watteau does not seem to have introduced the woman standing on the left of this page into any of his paintings. She appears to have been drawn slightly later (1713–14?) than the four soldiers – who may be a single model represented in four different poses – who can be found, grouped in a different way, in *The Diversions of War* (whereabouts unknown; DV 216). The infantryman leaning on his elbows can also be found in *Equipment Convoy*, a painting that belonged to Jean de Jullienne then to Cardinal Valenti Gonzaga; it was regarded as lost for many years, but was recently found. It appeared at Christie's in 2009 (see the excellent entry in their sale catalogue) but was unsold. Six drawings are connected with this painting, which was probably executed in 1715; these include the handsome page from the Prat Collection exhibited here (cat. 32).

The Rotterdam drawing has another interesting feature, in that it belonged to one of the greatest, if not the greatest, of eighteenth-century collectors of drawings, Pierre-Jean Mariette (1694–1774), and bears his celebrated stamp at the lower right-hand edge, a capital 'M' inside a circle. Anyone comparing the Rotterdam drawing with the page on a similar subject in the Ecole des Beaux-Arts, Paris (cat. 4), from some years earlier will notice the development of Watteau's graphic style, which became increasingly confident and assertive.

In 1996 we gave the present drawing the date 1712–13. Margaret Morgan Grasselli in 2001 opted for 1714–15. PR

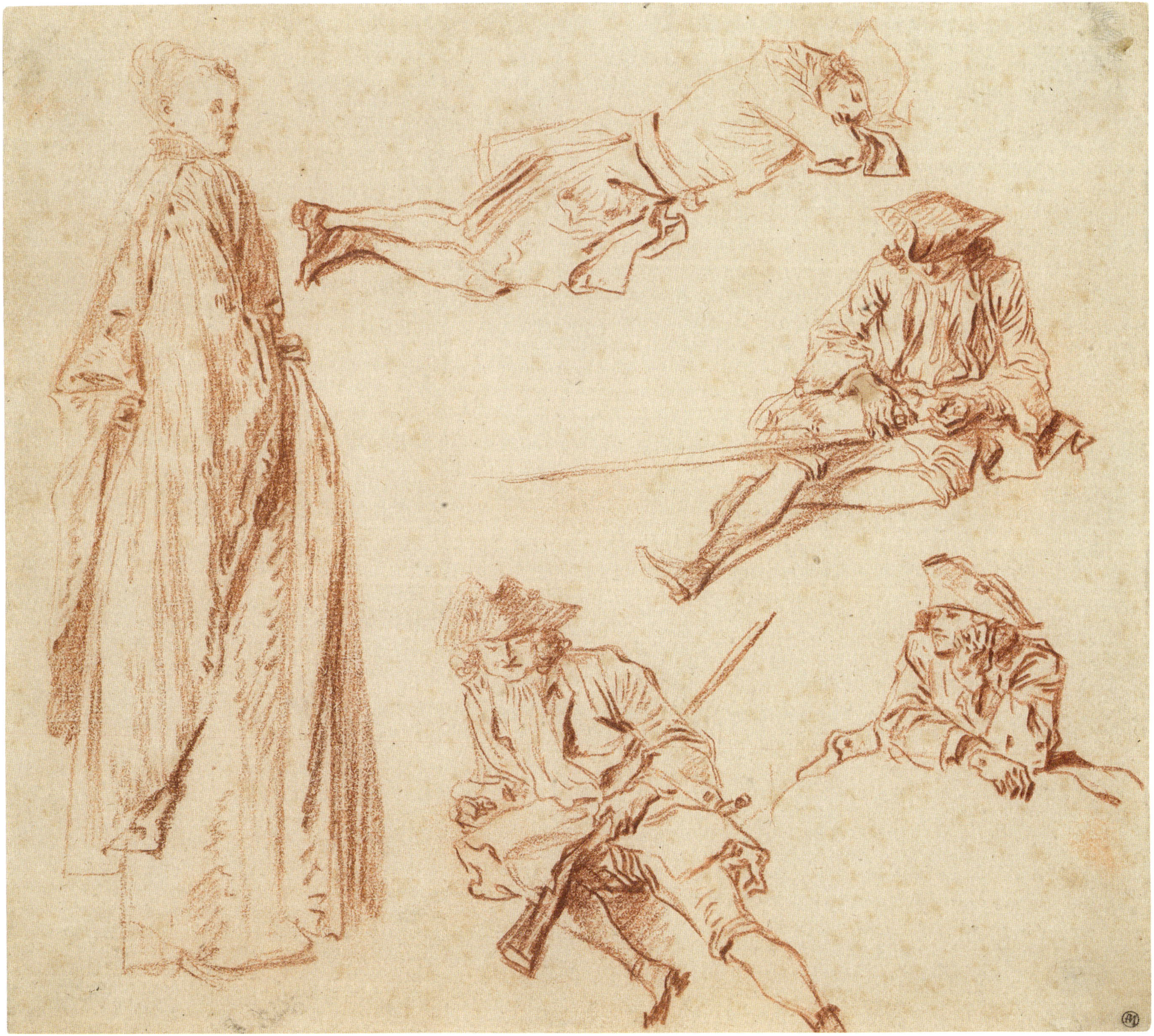

15

Three Figures: One Holding a Staff, One a Bagpiper, the Third Seated on the Ground

Red chalk on cream paper, 197 x 158 mm

Art Gallery of New South Wales, Sydney. Gift of James Fairfax, inv. 487.1993

PROVENANCE, EXHIBITED: PM 88; RP 195; Sydney 2003, no. 59 (Peter Raissis)
LITERATURE: PM 88; RP 195

Watteau places his composition on the page here with admirable skill and confidence. The same model is drawn reclining on the ground, sitting on a leopard skin, and finally playing the bagpipes. Directly or indirectly, each of the three figures is used in *Love in the French Theatre* (Gemäldegalerie, Berlin). The man reclining occupies the centre of the composition. In the painting, Bacchus (its subject) holds a glass and proposes a toast. The bagpiper is relegated to the extreme left of the painting, while the man with the staff, the most detailed, successful and professional drawing on the page, is used only indirectly: Watteau transfers the leopard skin on which he sits to beneath Bacchus's thigh. PR

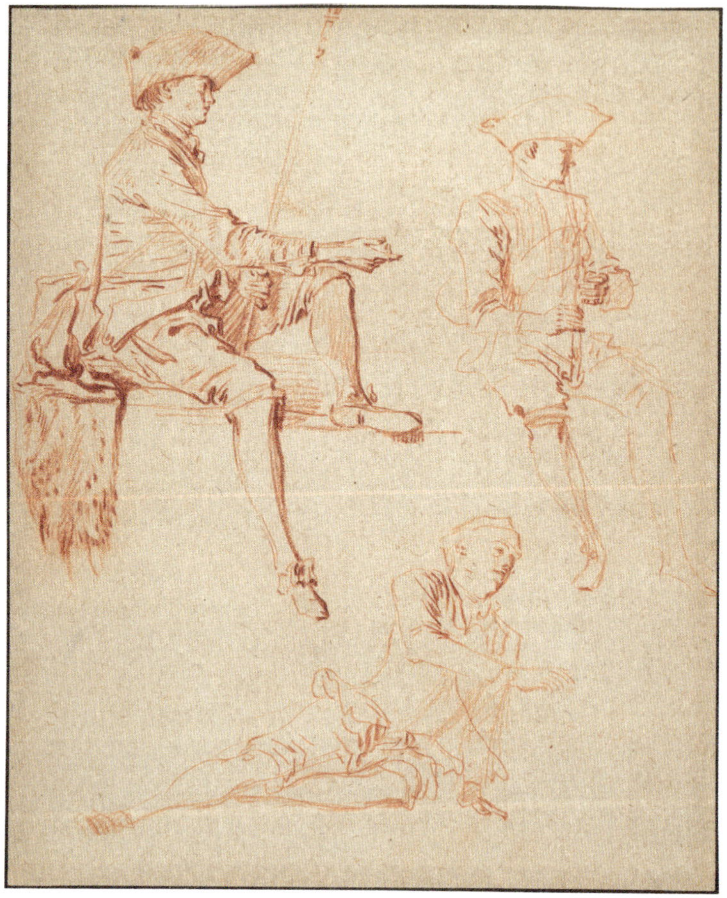

16

Seated Male Figure Holding a Staff

Red chalk on cream paper, 135 x 92 mm

Private collection, Paris

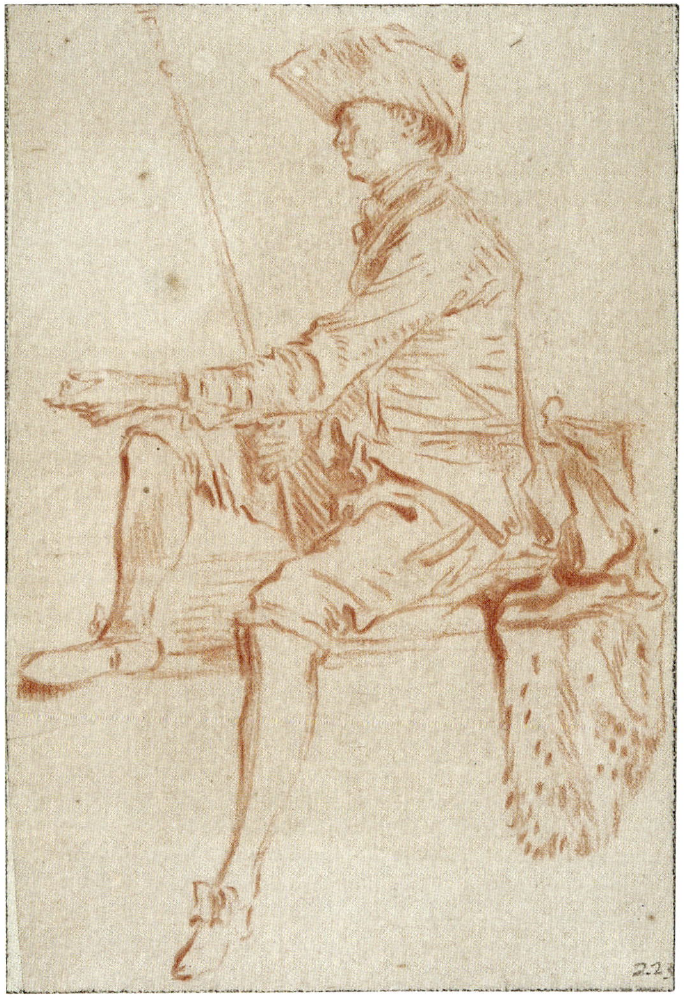

Next to the admirable drawing from Sydney (cat. 15) we wished to display one of the latest (by date) of Watteau's drawings in which he used only red chalk – the hour of the black and white chalk is fast approaching – its counter-proof.

Watteau made many drawings the subject of one or several counter-proofs; this already well-established practice was to reach its apogee in the eighteenth century. Made in a damp press, the counter-proofs, whose date is usually unknown but which must be shortly after the execution of the drawing, were a great commercial success with art-lovers and collectors. We should remember that Mariette preferred the counter-proofs of Edme Bouchardon's drawings to the originals.

Did Watteau take the counter-proofs from these drawings himself? The hypothesis is not entirely without foundation. In his paintings he sometimes copies one of his drawings backwards, which would be comprehensible only if the artist were using reverse proofs.

Counter-proofs in general, and Watteau's counter-proofs in particular, are unreasonably despised nowadays. PR

Red chalk on paper, 151 x 199 mm; frame line drawn in pen and black ink

Fondation Custodia, Paris, Collection Frits Lugt, inv. I. 7208

PROVENANCE, EXHIBITED: RP 209; New York 2009B, no. 1 (Colin B. Bailey)
LITERATURE: not mentioned in PM; RP 209; Grasselli 2001, p. 314; Sarasota 2006, pp. 188–89, under no. 62

17

Three Studies of Soldiers Holding Guns

In our 1996 catalogue raisonné (vol. 1, p. 36) we reproduced a rare photograph undoubtedly taken after the Second World War. This showed a wall in the apartment of the Marquise de Bryas in Orange. On the wall, hanging close together, were seven drawings by Watteau, including the present sheet, which was then framed in the same mount as *Two Soldiers Seen from Behind* (Yale University, New Haven; RP 277). As with the majority of the Watteau drawings from the Groult collection, very few of the seven have remained in France.

The present drawing, unanimously dated 1715, including recently by Margaret Morgan Grasselli and Colin B. Bailey, is one of Watteau's finest military pages. The same foot soldier is depicted in three different positions. Almost without exception Watteau's soldiers wear a tricorn hat and are usually armed with a musket. Their swords were reserved for hand-to-hand combat. Note the turned-back sleeves and the gaiters worn to protect the calves. As Colin B. Bailey reminded us recently, Watteau has emphasised the weight of the cartridge belt bumping against the back of the soldier on the right.

It appears that Watteau made his soldier strike three poses. Rather than drawing him from life without his knowing he was observed, he made a detailed study (without being too precise) of his costume and weapons. What was his aim? None of the three studies is repeated in any of his paintings. On the other hand, each has been engraved facing the same way by Louis Desplaces for *Figures de différents caractères* (see cat. 4). Was Watteau thinking about the use to which his drawings would soon be put, even while he was making them?
PR

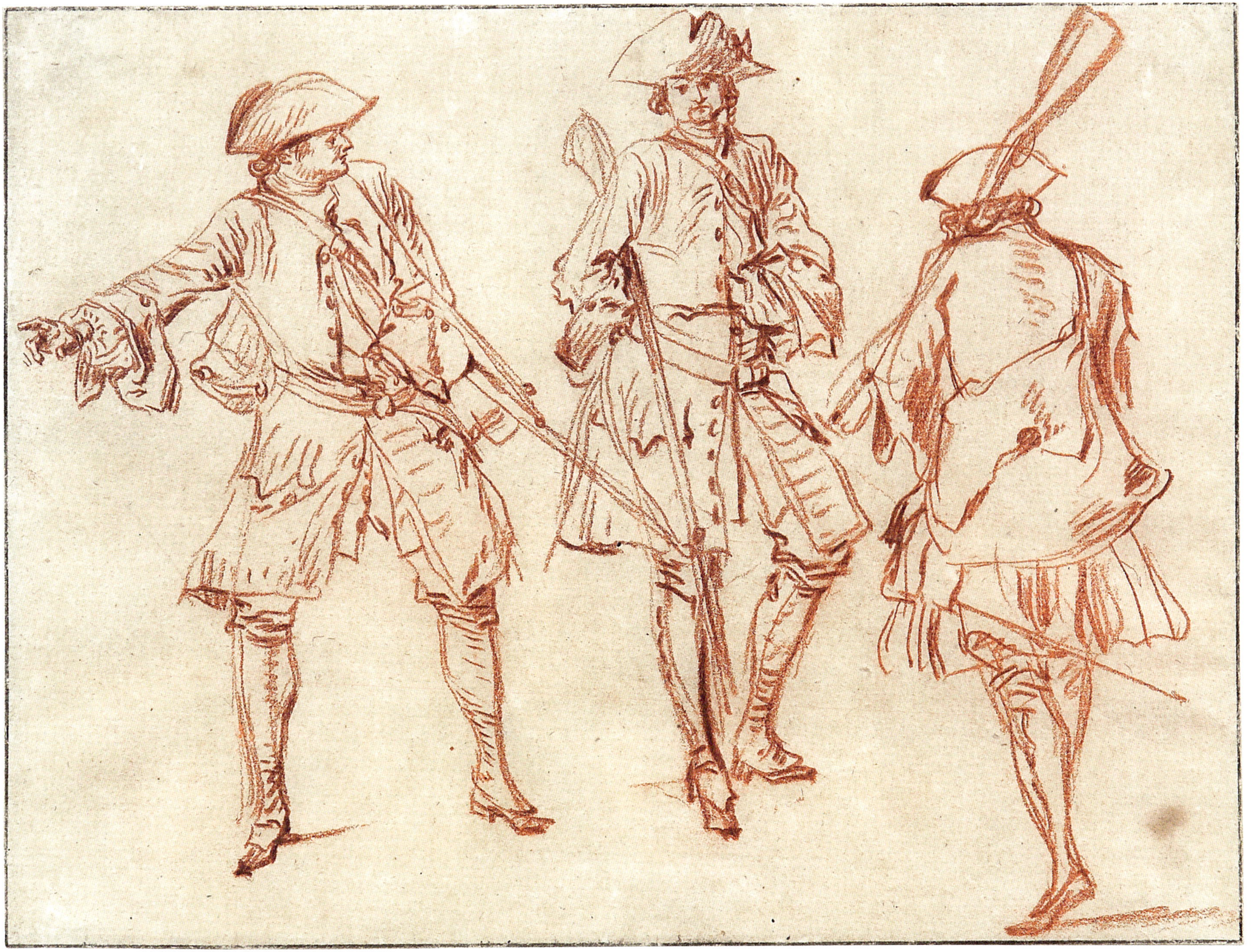

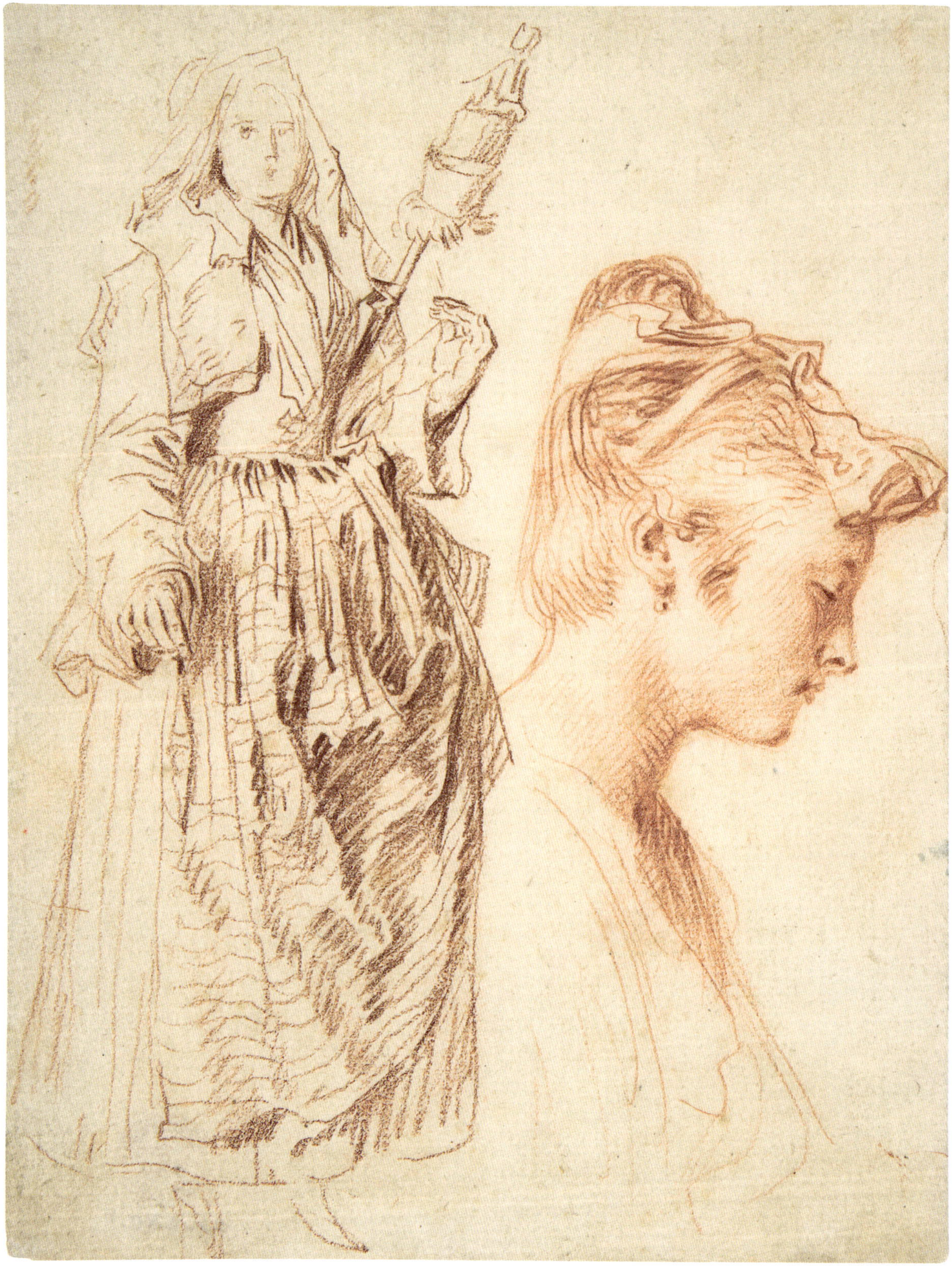

Two shades of red chalk on cream paper, 164 x 122 mm

The Metropolitan Museum of Art, New York. Bequest of Anne D. Thomson, 1923, inv. 23.280.5

PROVENANCE, EXHIBITED: PM 500; RP 226; New York 1999, no. 6 (Alan Wintermute)
LITERATURE: PM 500; RP 226; Rosenberg 2001, p. 142, fig. 184; Temperini 2005, p. 11, rep.

18

Standing Woman Holding a Spindle and Bust of a Woman in Profile

This fine drawing is a perfect example of the practice that was so particular to Watteau. Contrary to what was believed for many years, these two figures were not drawn at the same date (the two different shades of red chalk used by the artist also confirm this).

The spinning woman on the left of the page, drawn again by Watteau seated (RP 227), must date from 1713–14. She was engraved by Benoît Audran for the *Recueil Jullienne* (from the name of its patron Jean de Jullienne [1686–1766]; the *Recueil Jullienne* reproduces Watteau's principal paintings); the engraving was repeated by François Boucher in the *Figures de différents caractères* (on this, see cat. 4). The painting for which she prepares the way, however, has never been located.

On the other hand, the elegant head of a young woman seen in profile very probably dates from 1717–18. She can be found in several mature drawings by Watteau, two of them here (cats 68, 69).

The juxtaposition of these two figures so radically different in scale does no harm to the page – in fact it gives it its charm. In addition, it allows us to appreciate the development of Watteau's style to the full: the drawing of the spinner is slightly hesitant and piecemeal, whereas the young woman with lowered eyes, seen in profile, the nape of whose graceful neck we so admire, bears witness to the mastery gained by Watteau in the space of a few years. PR

Red, black and white chalks on paper, 253 x 215 mm

Private collection, New York

PROVENANCE, EXHIBITED:
PM 714; RP 228;
New York 1999, no. 8
(Alan Wintermute)
LITERATURE: PM 714; RP 228;
Rosenberg 2001, pp. 179–80, fig. 226;
New York 2007, rep. at no. 2

19

Studies of a Standing Woman and a Seated Boy Holding a Key

The drawings on this page were made in two stages: the young woman standing on the left is significantly earlier in date than the boy. In order not to cover the woman's long dress, Watteau cuts off the boy's right arm. The boy holds a key in his left hand, which suggests that Watteau drew him for a particular purpose, but he is not to be found in any of Watteau's paintings. The artist drew him several times (see cats 74, 75). Here he studies the head with particular attention, going over the hair and the shirt collar vigorously with black chalk.

The adolescent's amused expression is admirable, with his big wide eyes, lively face and interested gaze. PR

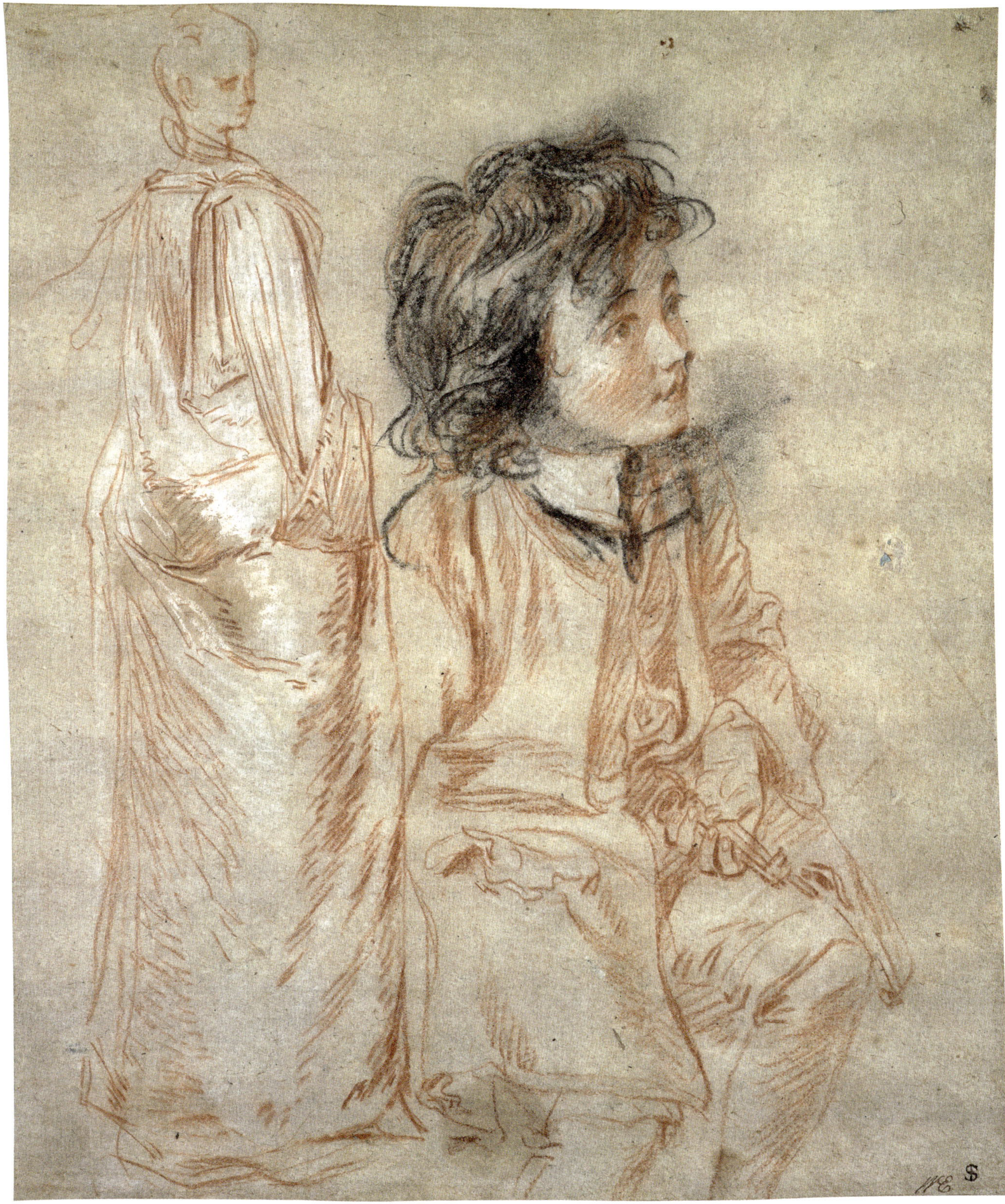

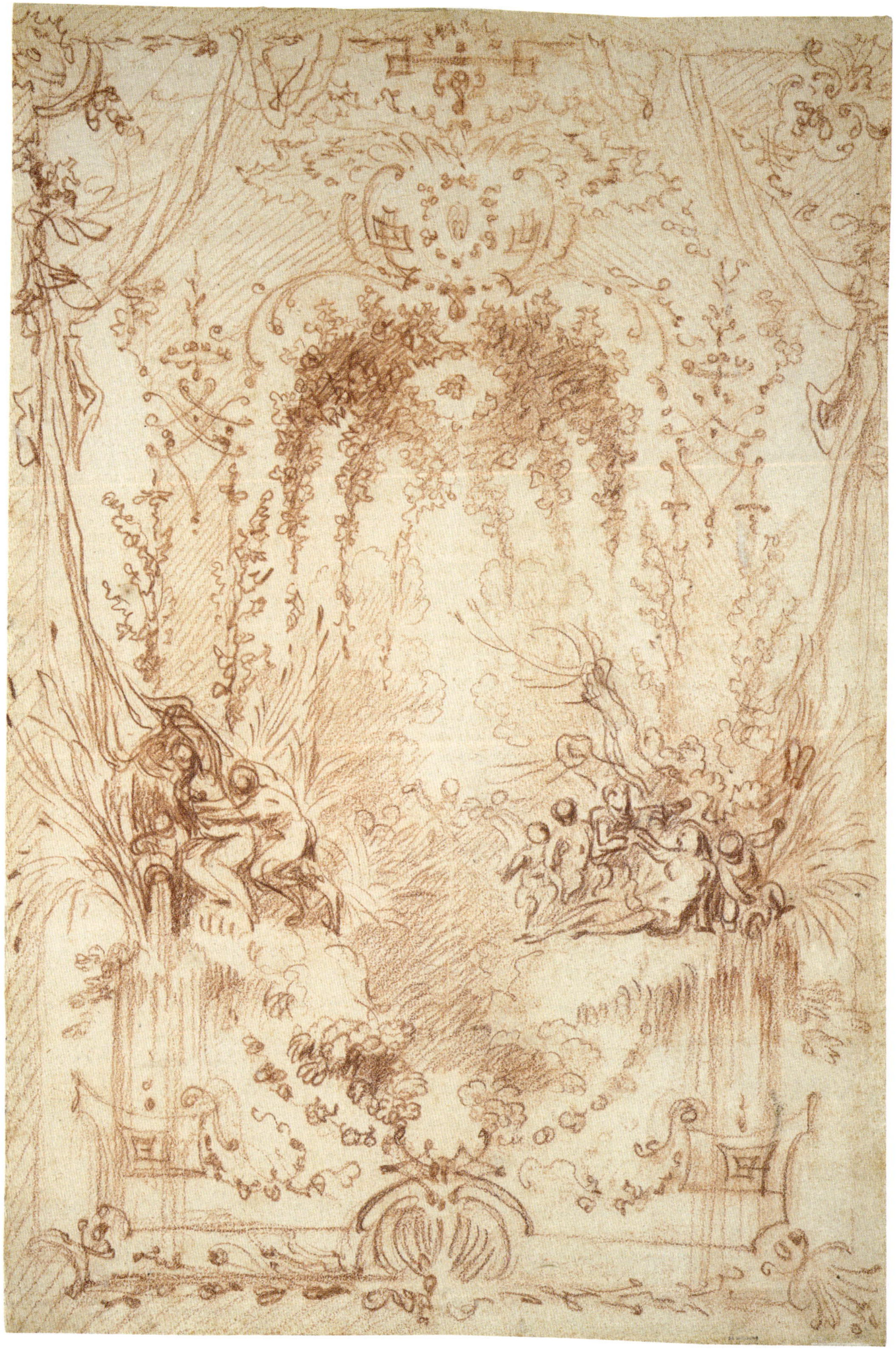

20

Arabesque Known as 'The Bower'

Red chalk on paper, 402 x 268 mm

National Gallery of Art, Washington DC, Ailsa Mellon Bruce Fund, 1982, inv. 1982.72.1

PROVENANCE: PM 192; RP 234; New York 1999, no. 9 (Alan Wintermute); Washington 2009, no. 39 (Margaret Morgan Grasselli)
LITERATURE: PM 192; RP 234; Grasselli 2001, p. 332, note 5; Edwards 2006, pp. 54, 58, and see p. 176, plate 14; Sheriff 2006, p. 18

This red chalk drawing, Watteau's finest arabesque, has recently been studied very closely by Margaret Morgan Grasselli (2009–10). It owes its title *The Bower* to the engraving made by Gabriel Huquier (1695–1772) for the *Recueil Jullienne*. In 1996 we suggested a date of *c.* 1714, although Margaret Morgan Grasselli prefers *c.* 1716. She has been able to show that Watteau first drew the left-hand side of the page and then folded it over the right-hand side in order to obtain a counter-proof (the vertical fold can clearly be seen in the centre). In a second phase he returned to work on the composition as a whole, completing it with two bacchanalian scenes that he then swiftly removed.

Although the influence on Watteau's development of the decorative work of Claude Gillot and Claude Audran III was very important, it is not perceptible here. Above and beyond the art of decoration, whose rules the artist has mastered perfectly, Watteau creates a highly spontaneous page in which imagination and fantasy mingle. PR

21

Head of Henry IV and Amor Seen in Half-length, after Rubens

Red chalk on paper, 141 x 188 mm; counter-proof; damage at lower left

Carolyne Roehm, New York

PROVENANCE: unknown; Galerie Ratton-Ladrière, Paris, in 1992; Mrs Carolyne Roehm, Paris
LITERATURE: not mentioned in PM; RP 244

This counter-proof, dating from *c.* 1714, was taken from a drawing of a detail of *Henri IV Receives the Portrait of Marie de Médicis* (fig. 16). In this third work in Rubens's series of 24 paintings narrating the life of Marie de Médicis, formerly in the Palais du Luxembourg and now in the Musée du Louvre, Amor shows the king a portrait of his future queen.

Watteau regularly copied Rubens. He was allowed access to the Palais du Luxembourg thanks to its 'concierge' (today we would say curator), Claude Audran III, with whom the artist worked in 1708–09. To RP 175, RP 349 and RP 342 we must now add a figure of abundance from the painting *The Happiness of the Regency*, sold in Paris by Artcurial on 21 June 2010. PR

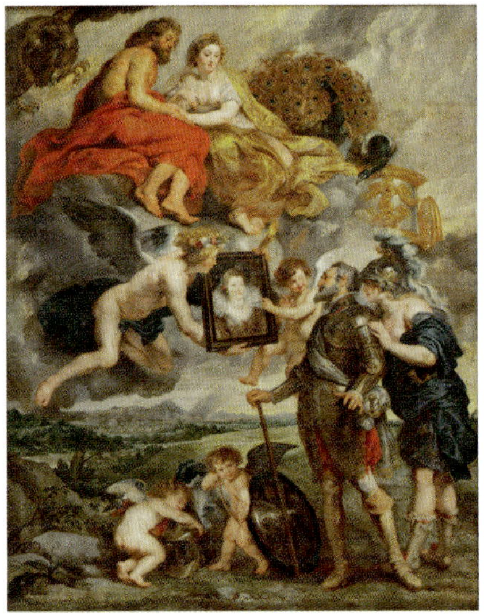

Fig. 16
Peter Paul Rubens, *Henri IV Receives the Portrait of Marie de Médicis*, 1621–25. Oil on canvas, 394 x 295 cm. Musée du Louvre, Paris

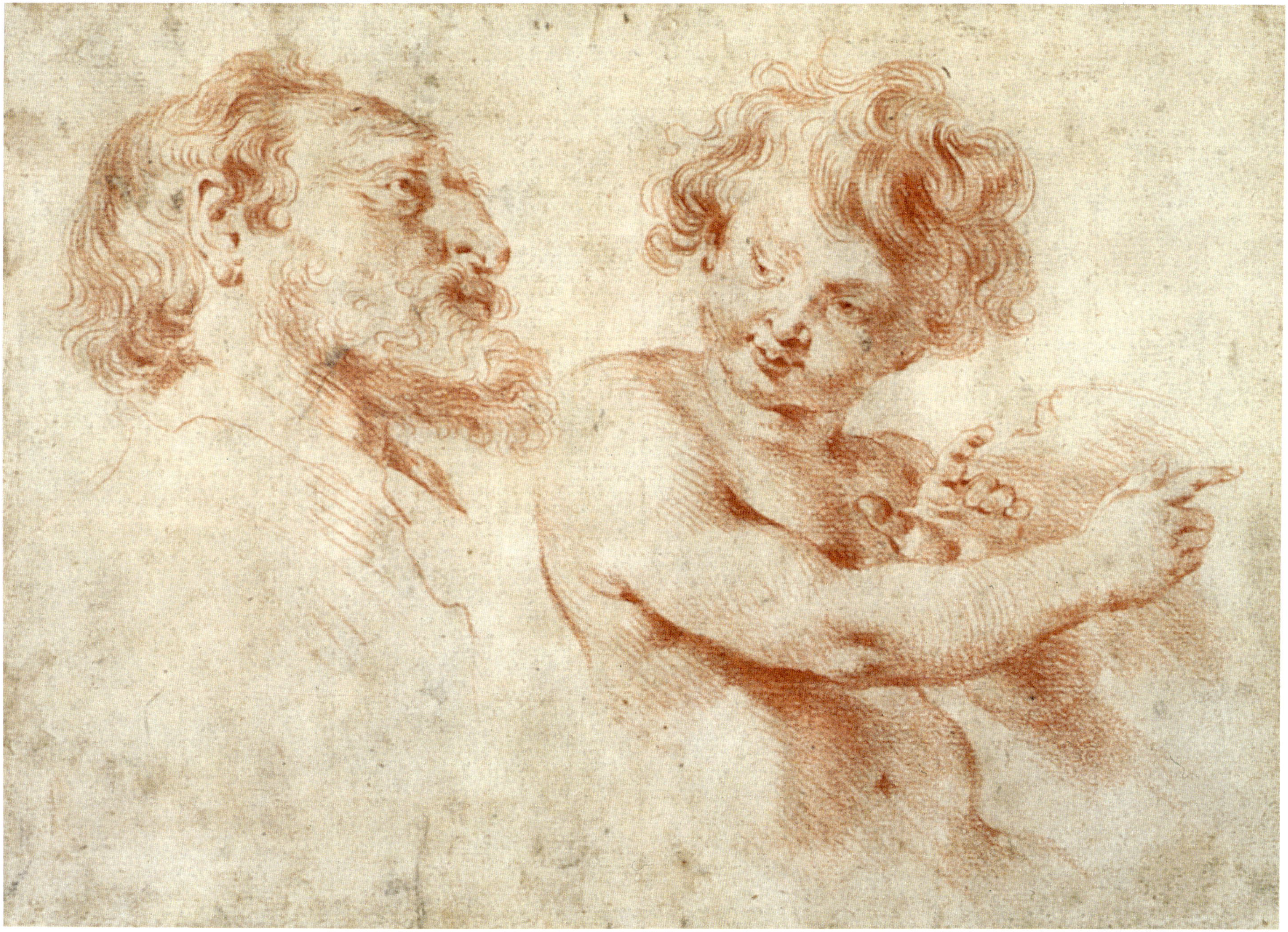

Red chalk on cream paper, 217 x 157 mm; arched frame line with ears at the top of the drawing Inscriptions in pen and red ink on the mount *Wataue*, and in pen and brown ink on the reverse side *D No 58*

Museum Boijmans Van Beuningen, Rotterdam, Koenigs Collection, inv. F.I. 17

PROVENANCE, EXHIBITED: PM 908; RP 263
LITERATURE: PM 908; RP 263

22

Study for an Arched Decorative Panel with Hunting Dogs and Dead Game

Doubt has sometimes been cast on the attribution to Watteau of this somewhat surprising drawing, unreasonably in our view: the liberty and confidence of the execution argue strongly in favour of the artist. All that is needed to convince the viewer is a comparison of the hunting dog seen in profile with the dogs in the arabesque representing *The Temple of Diana* in the Pierpont Morgan Library, New York (RP 233). It is this comparison that allows us to suggest a date of *c.* 1714–15.

What was the intended purpose of this drawing? Its arched composition with ears might make one think that, rather than a copy of an Old Master painting (perhaps Nordic?), it was part of an unrealised project for a painted panel to decorate a dining room or a hunting lodge. It seems that Watteau remembered the still-life with game on the right of the page for his *Meeting of the Hunt* (Wallace Collection, London) as well as for his *Return from the Hunt* (whereabouts unknown; DV 19). PR

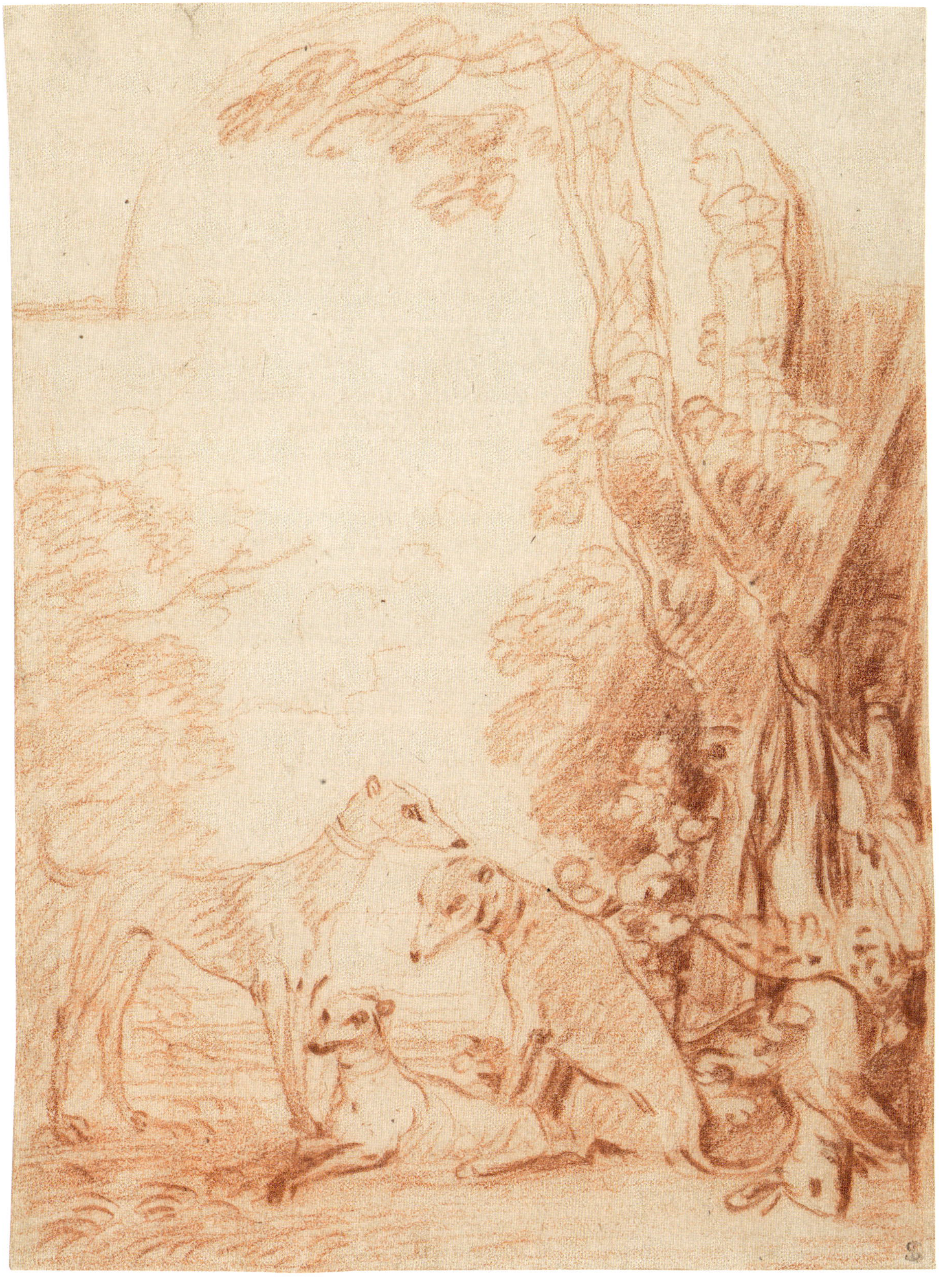

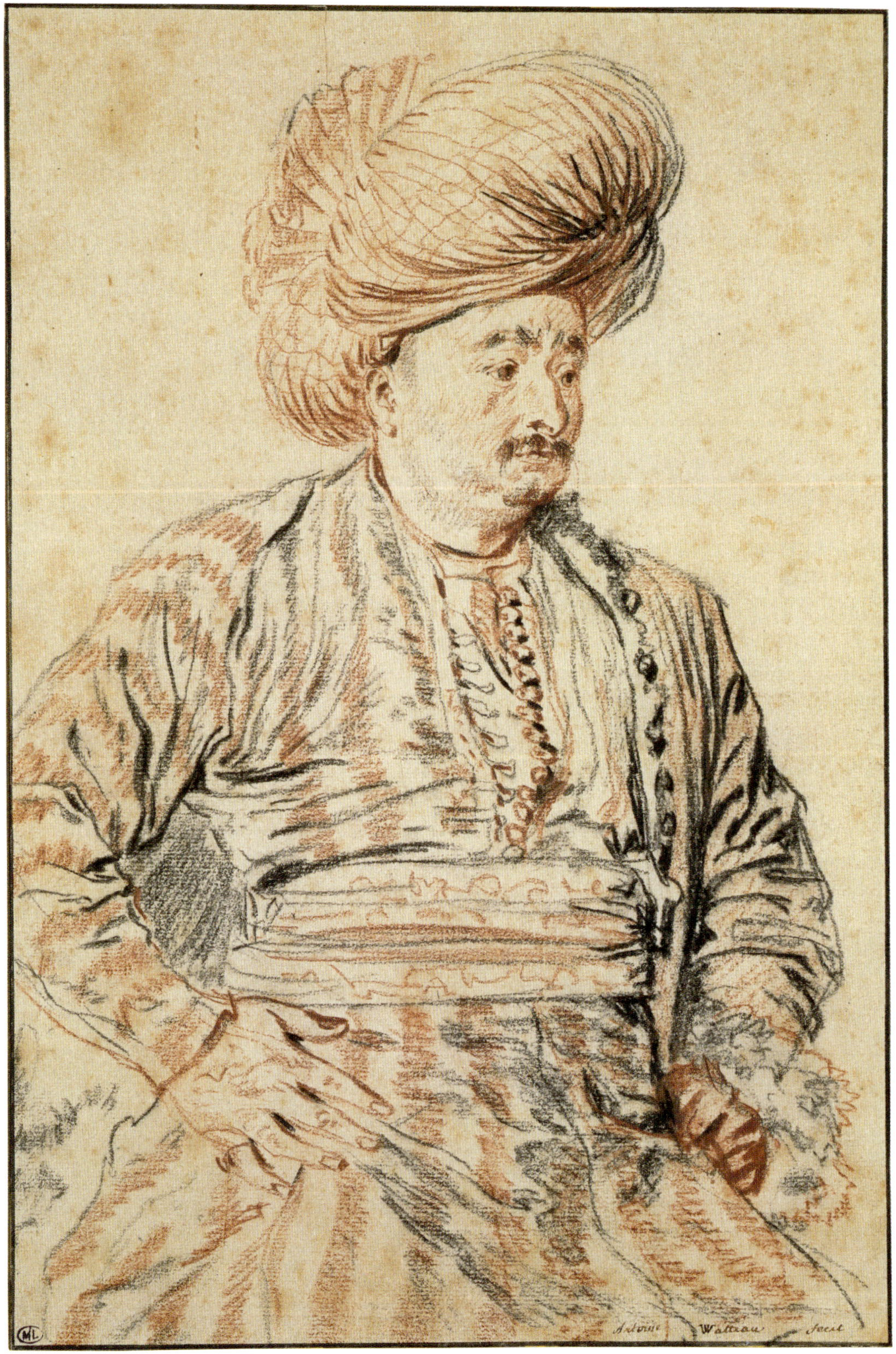
Watteau
fecit

Red and black chalk on cream paper, 301 x 197 mm; frame line drawn in pen and brown ink
Inscription in pen and brown ink at lower right *Antoine Watteau fecit*; on the back, inscription in pen and brown ink *portrait de L'ambassadeur de perse Mehemet Riza Beg / intendant de la province d'Erivan / qui fit son entré aparis le 7 février 1715 / Dessiné d'après nature par antoine Vateau / il est gravé d'ans Lœuvre* [*sic*] *de ce Maître*

Musée du Louvre, Paris, Département des Arts graphiques, inv. R.F. 36735

PROVENANCE, EXHIBITED: PM 790; RP 281; Musée du Louvre mark L. 1886a at lower left; Paris 1997, no. 306 (Pierrette Jean-Richard); Milan 2003, no. 281
LITERATURE: PM 790; RP 281; Roland Michel 1998, pp. 753–54; Alan Wintermute in New York 1999, p. 27, fig. 14; Arikha 2001, pp. 49–50; Rosenberg 2001, pp. 33, 35, fig. 36; Prat 2003, pp. 26–76, fig. 8; Temperini 2005, p. 13, rep.

23

Seated Persian Wearing a Turban

The arrival in Paris of a delegation from Persia on 7 February 1715 caused a sensation. Louis XIV, who was nearing his death (which occurred on 1 September), received the ambassadors at an audience at Versailles on 19 February. They took leave of the King on 13 August and left Paris on 30 August.

Watteau would have had plenty of opportunities to see them: nine drawings refer to the visit of this legation (RP 281–89; RP 287 appeared at auction quite recently, see New York 2008, no. 16). The majority are drawn with black and red chalk, and six of them were engraved, five by François Boucher (1703–1770) for the *Figures de différents caractères*. Four are exhibited here, including the present sheet, which was acquired by the Musée du Louvre in 1978. The work comes, as does cat. 25, from the mysterious collection of Andrew James, one of the largest holdings of drawings by Watteau ever made, dispersed at Christie's, London, on 22–23 June 1891 after the death of his daughter Sarah Ann.

Although the date of the drawing poses no problem – the delegation's visit provides one of the few secure anchor points in Watteau's challenging chronology – the identity of the model remains a mystery: contrary to indications on the back of the drawing, the subject does not seem to be the leader of the delegation, Mehemet or Mohamed Reza (who was known, or said, to be bearded).

Marianne Roland Michel (1997) has been able to prove that Watteau first drew his model in red chalk alone, that at that moment in his work he (or someone) made a counter-proof of his drawing and that at a second stage he returned to the drawing and worked over it with black chalk.

The model's costume attracts the attention most of all, particularly his voluminous turban, whose elegant complexity the artist took pleasure in capturing. Nor does he neglect the anxious face of the model, who appears to be on the defensive. PR

24

Seated Persian Wearing a Fur Hat

Red and black chalk on cream paper, 250 x 212 mm; frame line drawn in pen and black ink; fully glued to backing

Teylers Museum, Haarlem, inv. M21a

PROVENANCE, EXHIBITED: PM 791; RP 282; Paris 2001, no. 34
LITERATURE: PM 791; RP 282; Arikha 2001, p. 49; Edwards 2006, p. 48

This drawing's origins remain shrouded in mystery. The entry to cat. 23 explains its date (1715), and the circumstances of its execution.

Watteau emphasises the determined attitude of his corpulent model, who is represented with unaccustomed realism. Although he draws the profile, the hook-nosed face and the fur hat with delicacy, he uses very energetic, almost brutal strokes in red as well as black chalk for the hands and the costume, which scarcely allow us to judge whether or not the model is oriental.

The artist gives unprecedented space, rare in his work, to psychological analysis – surprising in comparison with the Persian in the Louvre (cat. 23). PR

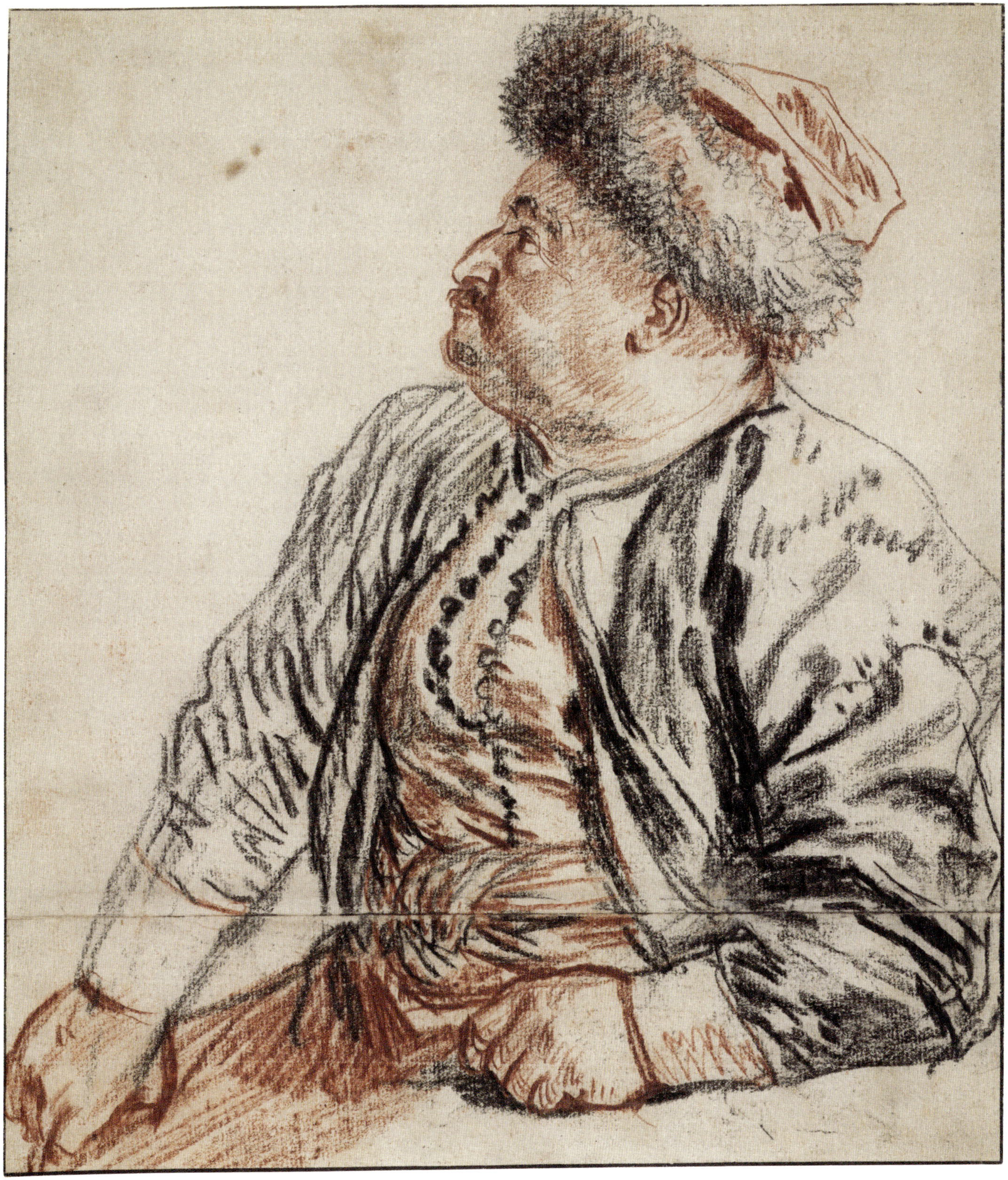

Red and black chalk on paper, 203 x 102 mm; frame line drawn in pen and black ink

The Trustees of the British Museum, London, inv. 1891-7-13-14

PROVENANCE: PM 793; RP 288
LITERATURE: PM 793; RP 288

25

Persian Servant Carrying a Plate

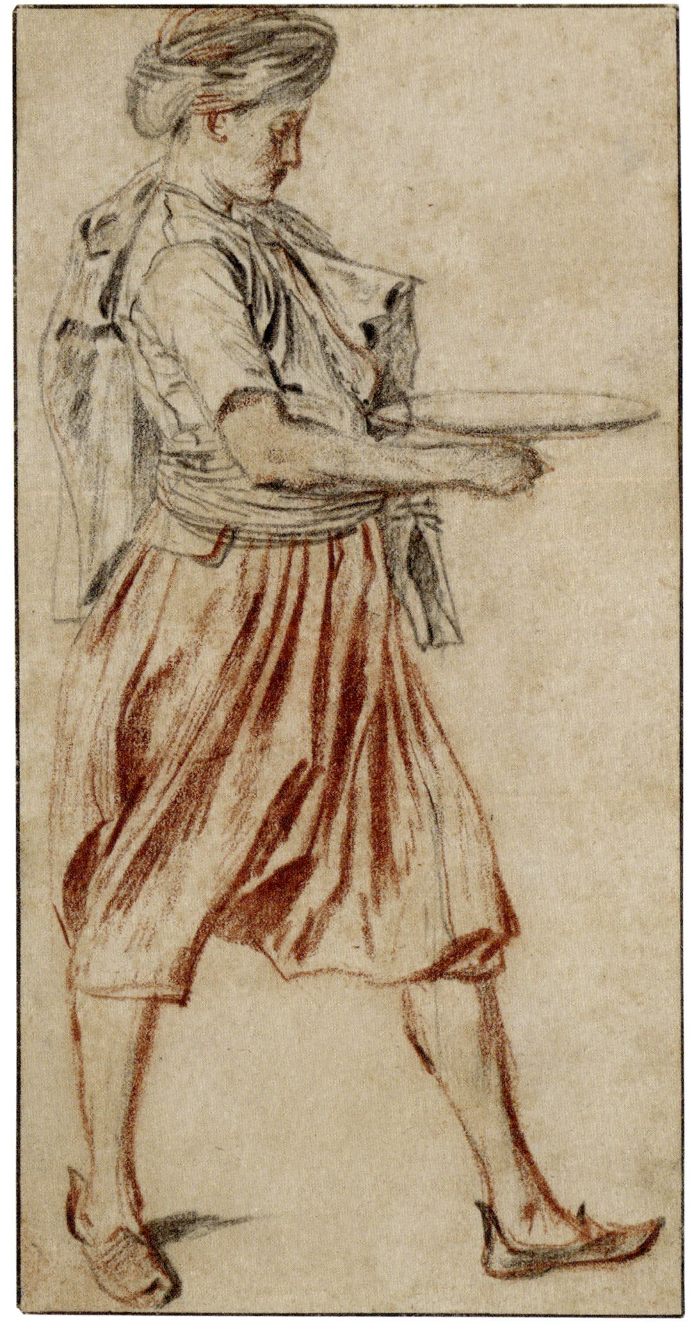

The date of this drawing and the historical circumstances surrounding its execution are explained in the entry to cat. 23.

Like the *Seated Persian Wearing a Turban* in the Musée du Louvre (cat. 23), this sheet belonged to Andrew James. When his celebrated collection was dispersed in 1891 the drawing was acquired by the British Museum for 33 guineas (the Louvre's *Seated Persian* sold for 38 guineas).

Watteau was most interested here in the servant's 'exotic' clothing, his turban, sash and trousers, 'sarouel' according to experts, and slippers. He is depicted carrying a dish and moving determinedly towards the right.

The model, seen in profile, is drawn in black chalk as far as the waist. The rest of his body is in red chalk. With the aid of some touches of black chalk (the slippers) and red chalk (the face and ears), skilfully placed, Watteau enriches his composition, making it livelier and more immediate. PR

26

Persian Servant Carrying a Plate, Seen in Profile

Red and black chalk on paper, 251 x 158 mm; frame line drawn in pen and black ink; fully glued to backing
On the back, inscription in pen and brown ink (damaged and made illegible during restoration) *Dessin que m'a laissé Watteau / a moy son ami / Caylus*

Teylers Museum, Haarlem, inv. M21

PROVENANCE, EXHIBITED: PM 794; RP 289
LITERATURE: PM 794; RP 289; Arikha 2001, p. 50; Rosenberg and Barthélémy 2011

The date of this drawing and the historical circumstances surrounding its execution are explained in the entry to cat. 23; see also cat. 25.

The drawing belonged to two major figures in eighteenth-century France, on the one hand the Comte de Caylus, the eminent archaeologist and friend of Watteau (as is recalled in the note on the reverse of the drawing) and on the other Pierre-Jean Mariette, the greatest collector of drawings of the century. The figure was drawn twice by Gabriel de Saint-Aubin (1724–1780), first in the margin of his copy of the catalogue to the Mariette sale then, shortly afterwards, in the margin of the catalogue to the Fournelle sale. Sold for 25 *livres* at the first sale, the sheet made only 20 at the second. The circumstances of its entry into the Teylers Museum in Haarlem are unknown.

We do not consider that the model for the present drawing is the same as for the previous one, even though these two Persian servants must have been drawn at the same sitting. This one has no moustache, wears no sash and looks obviously younger. Watteau shows him in repose rather than walking, attentive to what is going on and ready to intervene.
PR

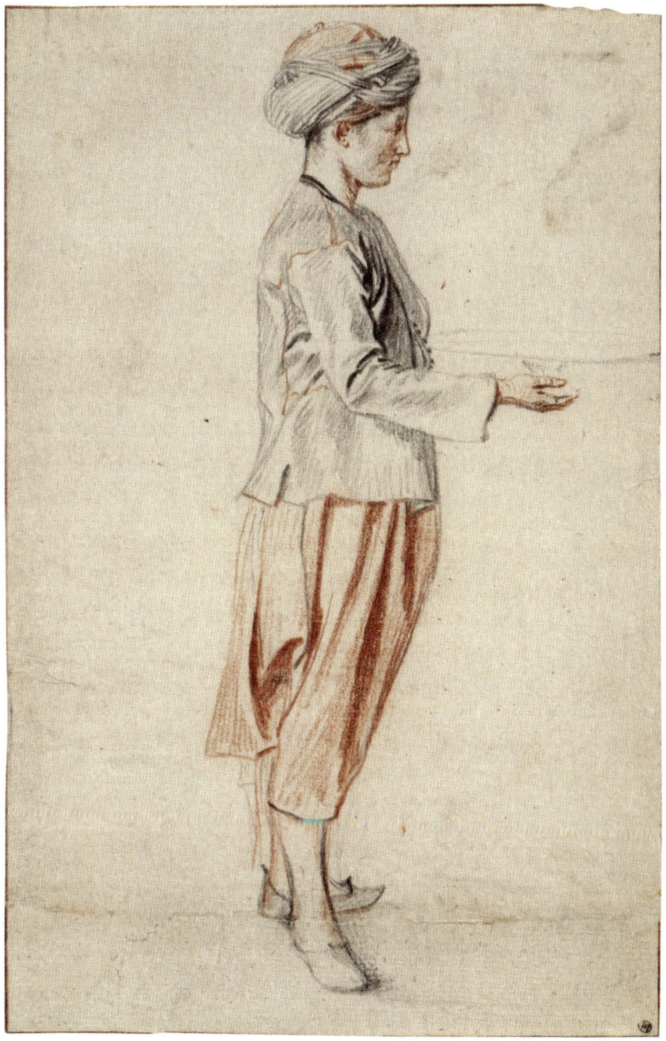

27

Standing Savoyard

Red chalk, brush and grey wash and red and black chalk stumping on paper, 359 x 221 mm; a band 32 mm wide added to the base, completed by Watteau; the drawing is reinforced at the upper corners with tabs

The Art Institute of Chicago, Helen Regenstein Collection, inv. 1964.74

PROVENANCE, EXHIBITED: PM 492; RP 290; New York 1999, no. 14 (Alan Wintermute)
LITERATURE: PM 492; RP 290; Roland Michel in Cambridge 1998, p. 67, fig. 23; Temperini 2005, p. 15, rep.; Edwards 2006, pp. 46, 48, 59, and see p. 174, plate 12; Sheriff 2006, p. 25

This drawing – which contains a good deal more red than black chalk – very probably dates from 1715 and is part of a series of five 'Savoyards' (for the date of these drawings, see the next entry). Since the case worn on a strap under his left arm is certainly a marmot case, the function of the object carried on his back has been questioned. Is it a basket (RP) or a curiosity box (Alan Wintermute in New York 1999)? By contrast, too few questions have been asked about the model, with his broad hat and emaciated fingers. In our opinion, if he is not a dwarf, he is at least a man of restricted growth whose smile helps him to triumph over his poverty.

The sheet is without doubt one of Watteau's most successful pieces. Like Rembrandt or Le Nain (whom Watteau was to copy), the artist removes none of the model's dignity. The disillusioned, possibly rather anxious smile is neither desperate nor pathetic, as it is in the red chalk drawing in the Musée Bonnat, Bayonne (RP 293). The Savoyard fixes us with his gaze, without blinking, without fear, and in the same way as the painting *Pierrot*, called *Gilles* in the Musée du Louvre (fig. 17), whose monumentality this work foreshadows, he seems to be examining us. The drawing's emotional power lies in the mute dialogue between model and spectator. PR

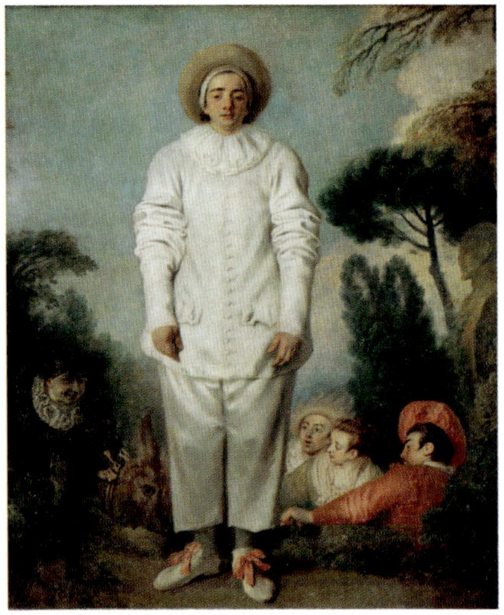

Fig. 17
Pierrot, called *Gilles*, 1718–19.
Oil on canvas, 184 x 149 cm.
Musée du Louvre, Paris

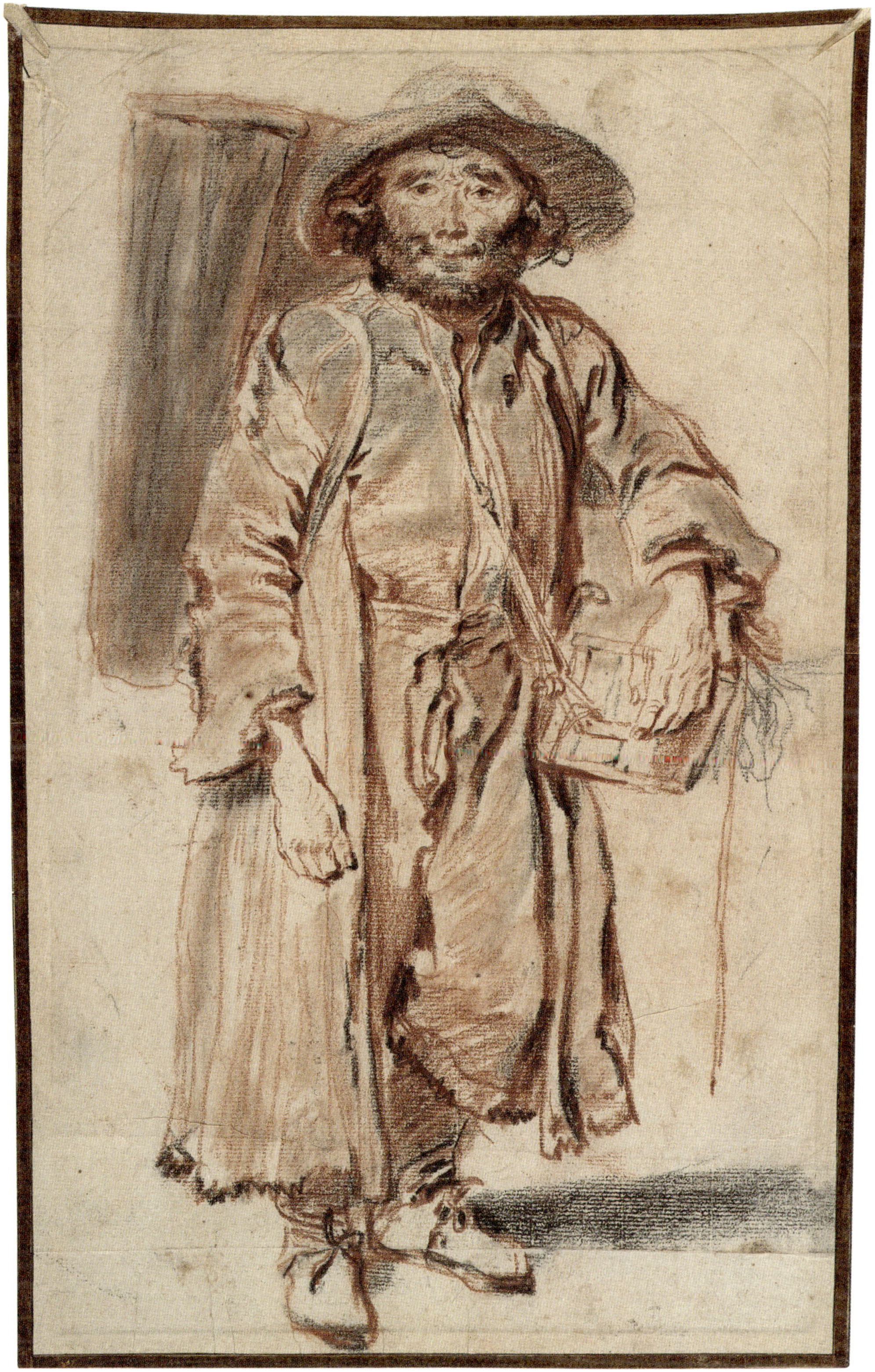

28

Seated Savoyard, His Left Elbow Resting on His Curiosity Box

Red and black chalk, red chalk stumping and wash on paper, 225 x 152 mm; frame line drawn with pen and black ink
Inscriptions in black chalk at lower left *8* and *Vatteau*; on the back, fragment of a letter crossed out with a red chalk line, elements of which can be found on the reverse side of RP 299 (Metropolitan Museum of Art, New York) and RP 200 (whereabouts unknown); the letter is partially covered by a fragment of lining paper and is almost completely illegible

Istituti museali della Soprintendenza Speciale per il Polo Museale Fiorentino

PROVENANCE, EXHIBITED: PM 493; RP 292
LITERATURE: PM 493; RP 292; Börsch-Supan 2000, p. 107, rep.; Grasselli 2001, p. 333, note 24

Watteau drew the same Savoyard five times: the present drawing, cat. 27, RP 291 (Museum Boijmans Van Beuningen, Rotterdam), RP 293 (Musée Bonnat, Bayonne) and a lost drawing, known via an engraving made by Boucher for the *Figures de différents caractères* (RP G52). These five sheets can be dated to 1715 for two reasons. During his stay in Paris in June 1715, Count Carl Gustav Tessin (1695–1790) bought a parcel of drawings by Watteau, including a counter-proof of the present seated Savoyard (this counter-proof is now in the Nationalmuseum, Stockholm). It is very probable that Etienne Jeaurat (1699–1789) also engraved the drawing for his *Figures françoises et comiques* in 1715.

The Savoyards generally hailed from Savoie, an extremely poor region that was attached to Piedmont at the time and from which they took their name. They carried out various street trades in the winter months, working as knife grinders, chimney sweeps and bootblacks (cat. 30) and begging while exhibiting their marmots.

In the present drawing the Savoyard is seated, his marmot case on his knees and his elbow on his curiosity box. Like their owners, the marmots came from Savoie. They entertained the children of Paris. The curiosity boxes were attached to the Savoyards' backs with straps that can be easily seen in the foreground of the Florence drawing. They contained various kinds of entertainments, among them magic lanterns, dioramas of various kinds and peepshows.

Watteau depicted his model as he was – badly dressed, with an untidy beard, left foot turned in and a lost expression; but he does not caricature him or remove his human dignity.

According to Margaret Morgan Grasselli (2001) the red wash is probably 'added'. We have unfortunately been unable to obtain a photograph of the letter on the reverse of the drawing; see cat. 31. PR

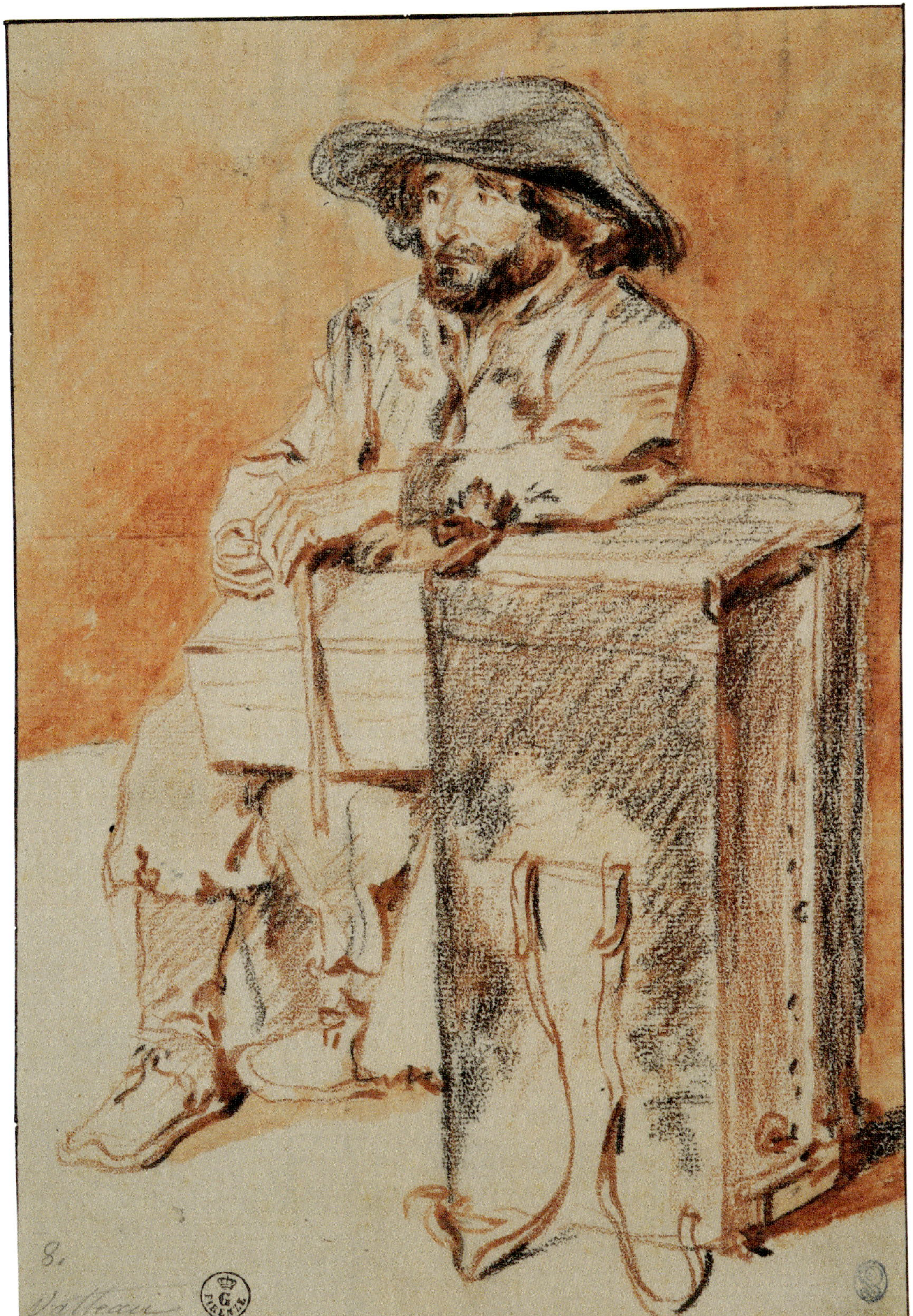

Red chalk and touches of black chalk on paper, 298 x 187 mm

Statens Museum for Kunst, Copenhagen, inv. 10207/1927

PROVENANCE: PM 491; RP 295
LITERATURE: PM 491; RP 295

29

Young Savoyard Holding an Oboe, with a Marmot Case Slung across His Shoulder

This drawing is little known and seldom exhibited. It very probably dates, for the reasons given above (cat. 28) from 1715. It represents a Savoyard, still a teenager, his marmot case slung across his shoulder (on this animal and its owner, see cat. 28) and holding an oboe in his hand.

The present sheet has been compared with a slightly larger sheet now in the Musée du Petit Palais, Paris (RP 294), which depicts a young Savoyard – definitely not the same model – with an oboe and a marmot case, but in that work the animal is lying for all to see on top of its case. Unlike the drawing in the Petit Palais, which was engraved by Boucher and used by Watteau for his painting of the same subject now in the State Hermitage Museum, St Petersburg, this Copenhagen page has retained its original freshness.

Note the hasty addition of a landscape in the background, simply a decorative device. PR

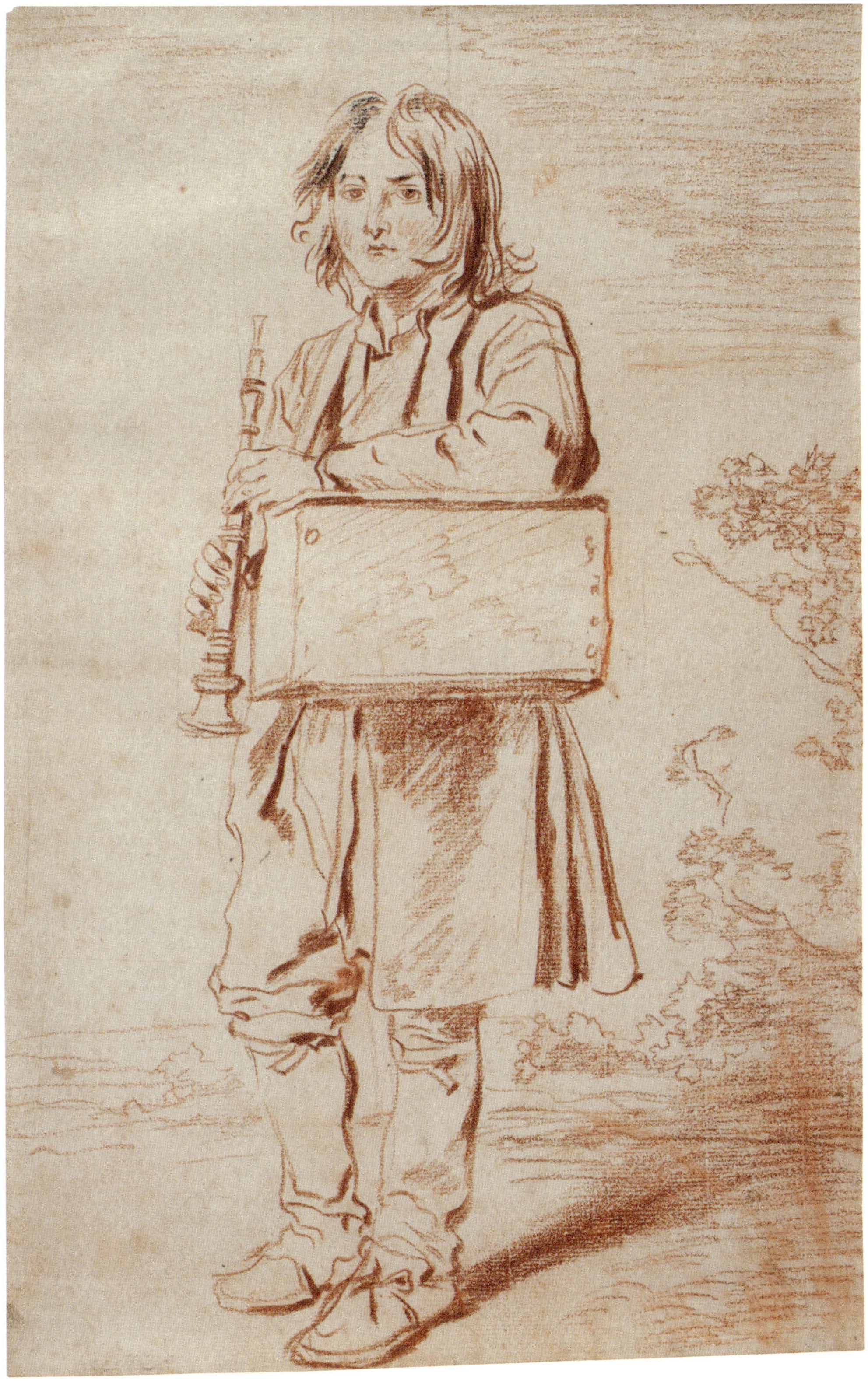

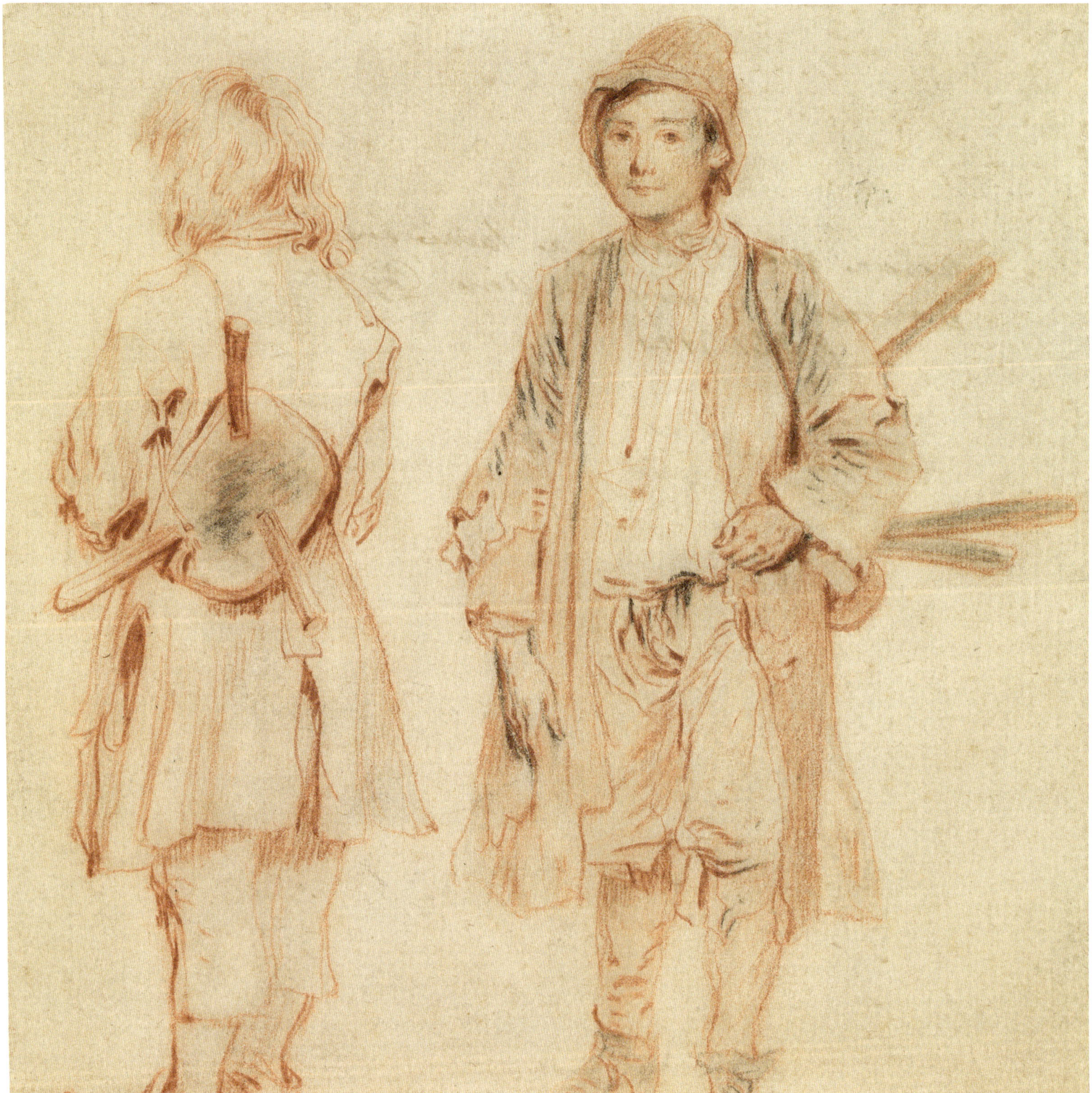

30

Two Shoeshine Boys, One Seen from the Back, the Other from the Front, Each with a Stool Slung across the Shoulder

Red and black chalk and wash on yellowed paper, 223 x 217 mm; the drawing has been lengthened at the base by a different hand (232 x 225 mm with the addition), and the shoes of both figures have been completed by this same hand; the enlargement is edged with a first frame line in pen and brown ink; second frame line in pen and brown ink
On the back, partially hidden by the mount, inscription in pen and brown ink *dessin que Wateau a laissé / en mourant a moy son ami / Caylus / Juillet 1721*

Museum Boijmans Van Beuningen, Rotterdam, Koenigs Collection, inv. F.I. 68

PROVENANCE, EXHIBITED: PM 499; RP 297
LITERATURE: PM 499; RP 297; Fumaroli 1996, p. 43, fig. 20

This drawing depicts two young shoeshine boys or, more probably, to be precise, two small bootblacks. Such boys used to scrape the mud off the boots of passers-by in the street. Did they sit on the three-legged stools seen in the drawing, slung over their shoulders on a strap, or were these for the use of customers who would stand and place their boots on them?

If we believe the handwritten inscription on the back (as in cat. 26), which is visible through the paper, Watteau, at the moment of his death, gave the drawing to the Comte de Caylus. The owner of the drawing is the same Caylus who wrote the biography of Watteau (and others); he was also an eminent archaeologist, the re-inventor of encaustic painting, even a novelist, but also an amateur engraver, who wished to engrave the two boys for the *Figures de différents caractères* (see cat. 4). Although his first print, taken from the boy seen from behind, appears in the celebrated volume, the second was refused (probably by Jean de Jullienne, publisher of *Figures de différents caractères*) for being too weak; it was replaced by an engraving by Pierre-Charles Trémolières. Interestingly, both prints, by Caylus and by Trémolières, depict the boy holding a scraper, which confirms the activity he was engaged in.

Executed almost entirely in red chalk, the drawing probably dates from 1715. It belongs to the group of popular figures produced by Watteau, whose sympathy with his models is manifest. PR

31

Seated Savoyard Woman

Two tones of red chalk and black chalk on paper, 308 x 199 mm
On the back, inscription in pen and brown ink *Monsieur / Jay receu aujourd'huÿ au matin vos deux Lestres Ense[mble] / qui ont autant donné de peines au facteur qu'elles m'[ont] Causée de surprise*… (on this inscription, attributed to Watteau and the subject of much discussion, see cat. 28 and the Savoyarde in the Metropolitan Museum of Art, New York (RP 299), whose reverse bears an inscription that the British Museum drawing partially repeats

The Trustees of the British Museum, London, inv. 1891-7-13-5

PROVENANCE, EXHIBITED: PM 457; RP 300
LITERATURE: PM 457; RP 300; Mary Taverner Holmes in New York 1999, p. 6, fig. 3.1

This drawing comes from the collection of Andrew James and was sold in 1891 on the death of his daughter Sarah Ann, when it was acquired by the British Museum. It may have belonged previously to Jean de Jullienne, then to Pierre-Jean Mariette.

It depicts a Savoyarde with her marmot case on her knee. Watteau drew the same old woman at least twice, probably during the same sitting (in the drawing in the Metropolitan Museum of Art, New York [RP 299] she stands, leaning heavily on a staff with her marmot case slung over her shoulder).

A third Savoyarde used to exist. Unfortunately the drawing is lost but the composition is known through an engraving by Caylus (fig. 18). She is seated, as here, but seen in a three-quarter view.

Like the male Savoyards, these women came from Savoie and lived by begging. They showed their marmots to passers-by for a small sum.

Watteau had no hesitation in depicting, with cruel truth, this squat old woman, probably rickety, at any rate physically diminished. She is passive and resigned, her look absent yet anxious. The artist has managed to interest us in this image of human distress without seeking to arouse our pity. Unlike so many eighteenth-century artists, writers as well as painters, Watteau does not ignore the poor, who as we know were so numerous during his lifetime.

Small strokes in red chalk can be seen at the lower edge of the sheet. Watteau was making sure that the point of his red chalk was perfectly sharpened. PR

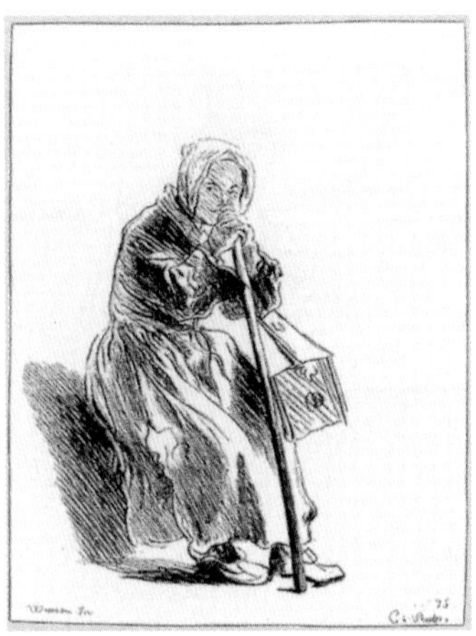

Fig. 18
Seated Savoyard Woman, engraved by the Comte de Caylus for the *Figures de différents caractères*, 1726–28 (RP G11)

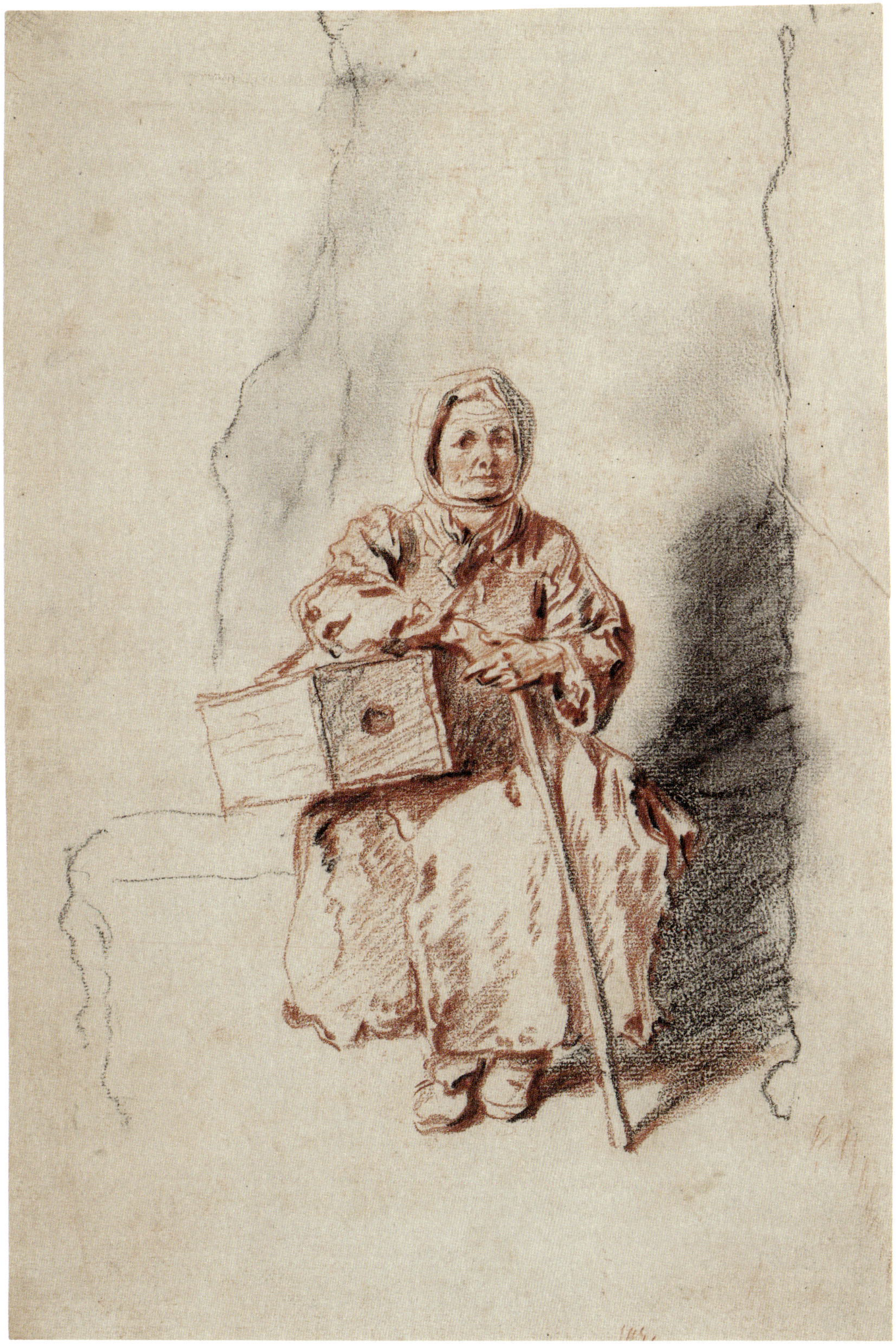

32

An Old Woman Seated Beside an Infant in a Cradle

Red, black and white chalks on paper, 164 x 215 mm

Louis-Antoine and Véronique Prat Collection, Paris

PROVENANCE, EXHIBITED: PM 498; RP 301; Los Angeles 2004, no. 26; Barcelona 2007, no. 26 (Pierre Rosenberg)
LITERATURE: PM 498; RP 301; Grasselli 2001, p. 314; Christie's, New York, auction catalogue, 28 January 2009, under no. 89; Paris 2010, no. 89 (Marie-Catherine Sahut)

To date we know of six drawings used by Watteau to paint his *Equipment Convoy*, engraved by Laurent Cars for the *Recueil Jullienne* (fig. 19). The painting has just been rediscovered (it appeared at Christie's, New York, 28 January 2009, no. 89). They are mainly red chalk sketches of soldiers (see cats 4, 14) datable to *c.* 1712–13. The present page, probably executed in 1715, successfully combines red and black chalk with some white highlights with perfect visual intelligence.

The old woman, seen kneeling on the ground, watches over a baby in a wooden cradle. It would be good to think she was the baby's grandmother. She looks at us with a tired smile, watching the draughtsman towards whom the suckling turns its gaze. There is no social criticism, no sentimentality, but dignified complicity and mutual respect between Watteau and his model. PR

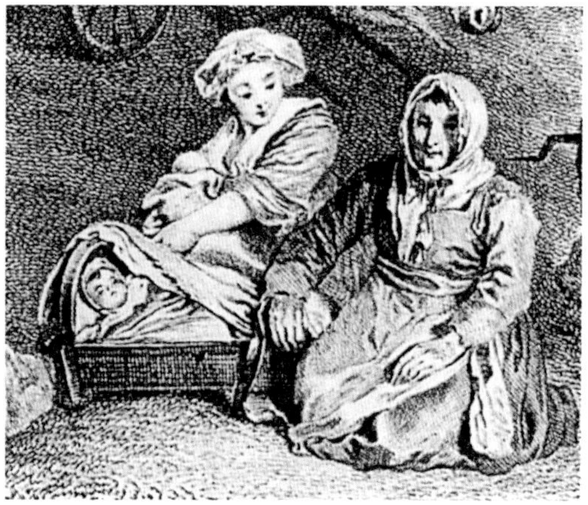

Fig. 19
Detail of *Equipment Convoy*, engraved by Laurent Cars for the *Recueil Jullienne*, 1735. British Museum, London (RP 301a)

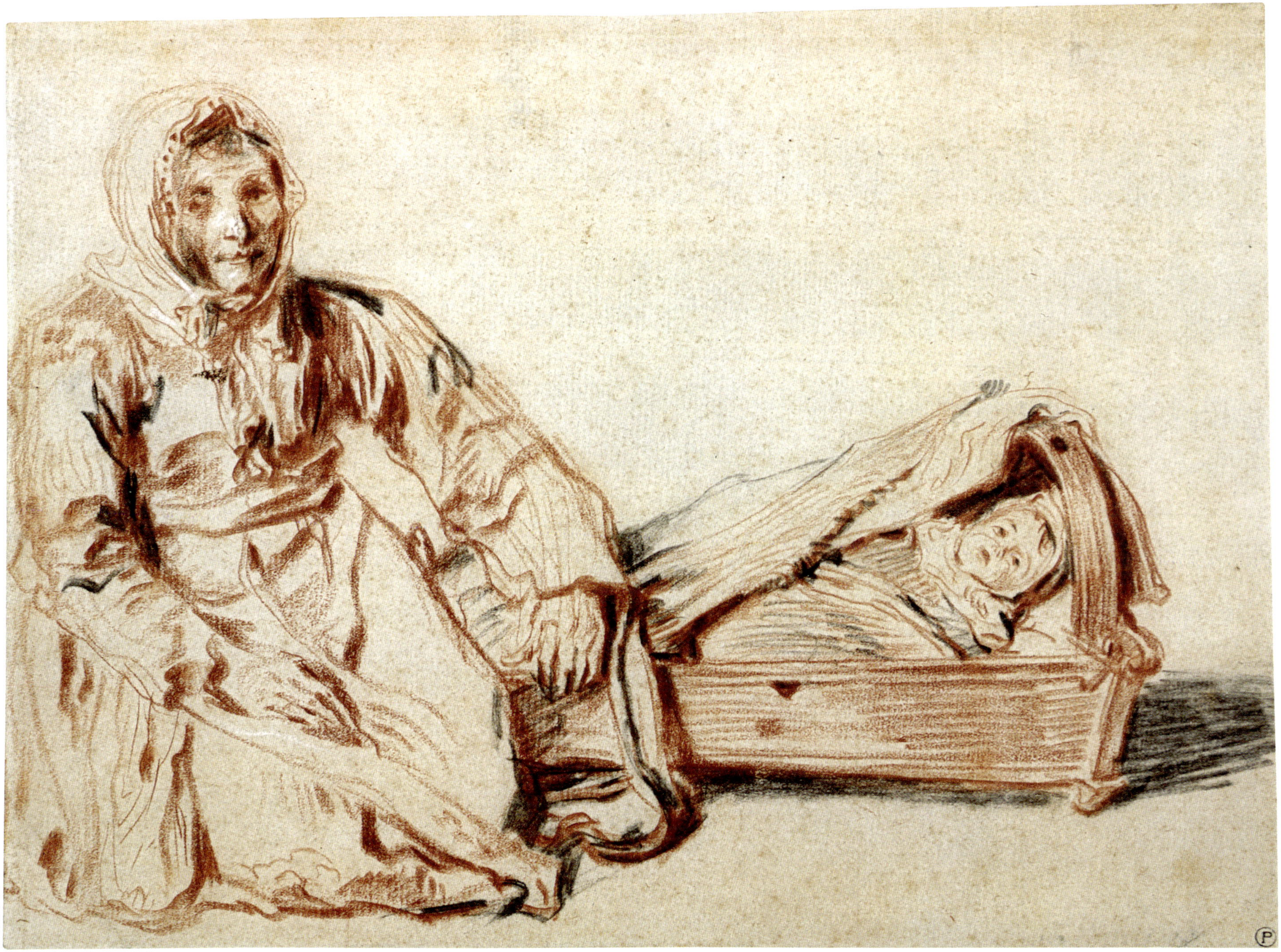

33

Woman on a Swing, Seen from the Back

Red and black chalks and graphite on paper, 167 x 130 mm

Private collection

PROVENANCE: PM 540; RP 310
LITERATURE: PM 540; RP 310

This drawing, convincingly dated to *c.* 1715, was engraved by Boucher for the *Figures de différents caractères.* Watteau uses it in two of his paintings, *The Shepherds* (Schloss Charlottenburg, Berlin) and *Pastoral Pleasures* (Musée Condé, Chantilly), the latter engraved by Nicolas-Henri Tardieu for the *Recueil Jullienne* (DV 209).

This image is one of the most seductive of all Watteau's graphic output. The page is almost entirely executed in black chalk, mixed with a few silvery highlights of graphite. Only the ropes of the swing and the hands and ears of the young woman are drawn in red chalk – plus the nape of her neck; one of those napes of which Watteau is the unrivalled master.

Seen from behind, beyond time, the elegant young woman hangs in a void. Is she flying away or replacing her feet on the ground? Who has pushed her? What does she dream of? This recalls Fragonard's *The Swing* (fig. 20). PR

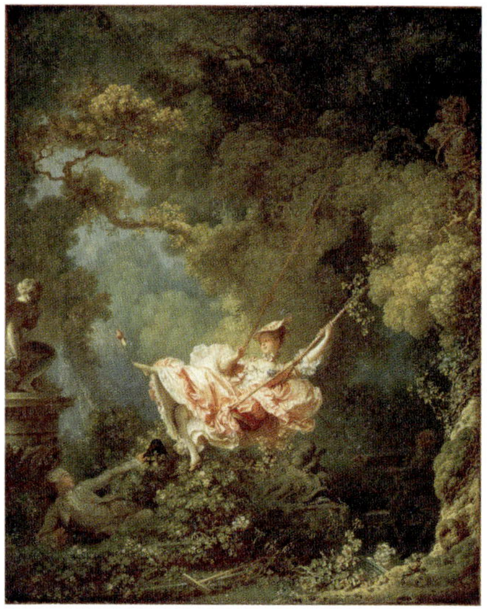

Fig. 20
Jean-Honoré Fragonard,
The Swing, 1767.
Oil on canvas, 81 x 64.2 cm.
The Wallace Collection, London

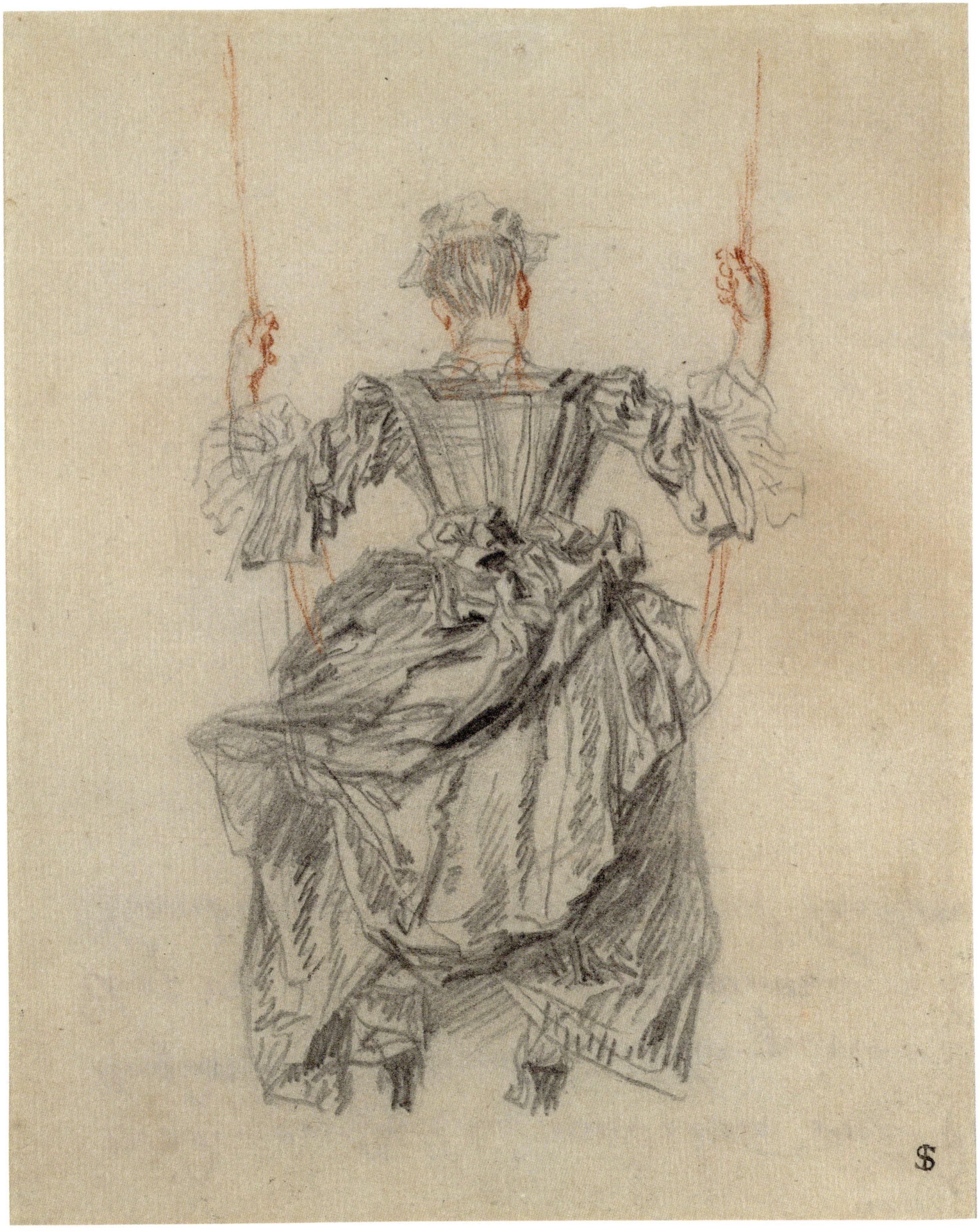

34

Portrait of Antoine de La Roque

Red chalk on beige paper, 228 x 169 mm; a band of paper measuring 14 mm has been added at the top of the sheet; slightly enlarged at left and right

Fitzwilliam Museum, Cambridge, inv. 2266

PROVENANCE, EXHIBITED: PM 912; RP 317
LITERATURE: PM 912; RP 317; Moureau 2001, p. 349; Rosenberg 2001, p. 32, fig. 30

This drawing, usually dated to 1715, very probably depicts Antoine de La Roque (1672–1744), whose portrait Watteau also painted (fig. 21).

La Roque (for more on the model, see Moureau 2001) had his leg shattered by a bullet at the Battle of Malplaquet (1709), a 'frightful butchery'; it had to be amputated above the knee. La Roque wrote the earliest biographical essay on Watteau and a number of opera librettos, and was Editor of the *Mercure de France* from 1721 until his death.

Watteau depicts him standing, leaning with his right hand on a stick. His crutch can be spied under his left arm. La Roque fixes us with his gaze. His pose evidently costs him a lot of effort, but Watteau wanted to draw him as a friend, not as an invalid. PR

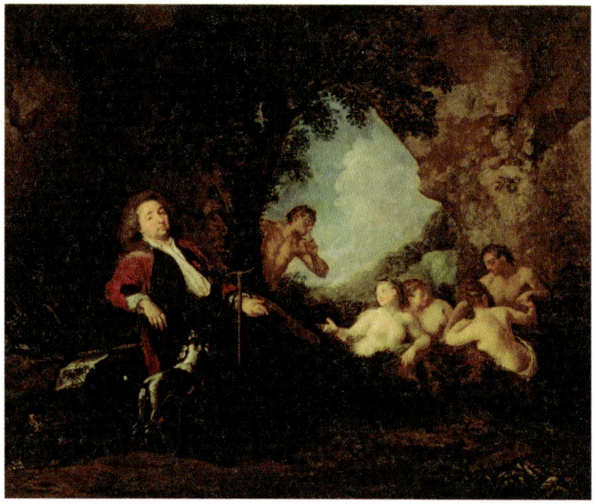

Fig. 21
Portrait of Antoine de La Roque, 1715. Oil on canvas, 46 x 54.5 cm. Fuji Museum, Tokyo

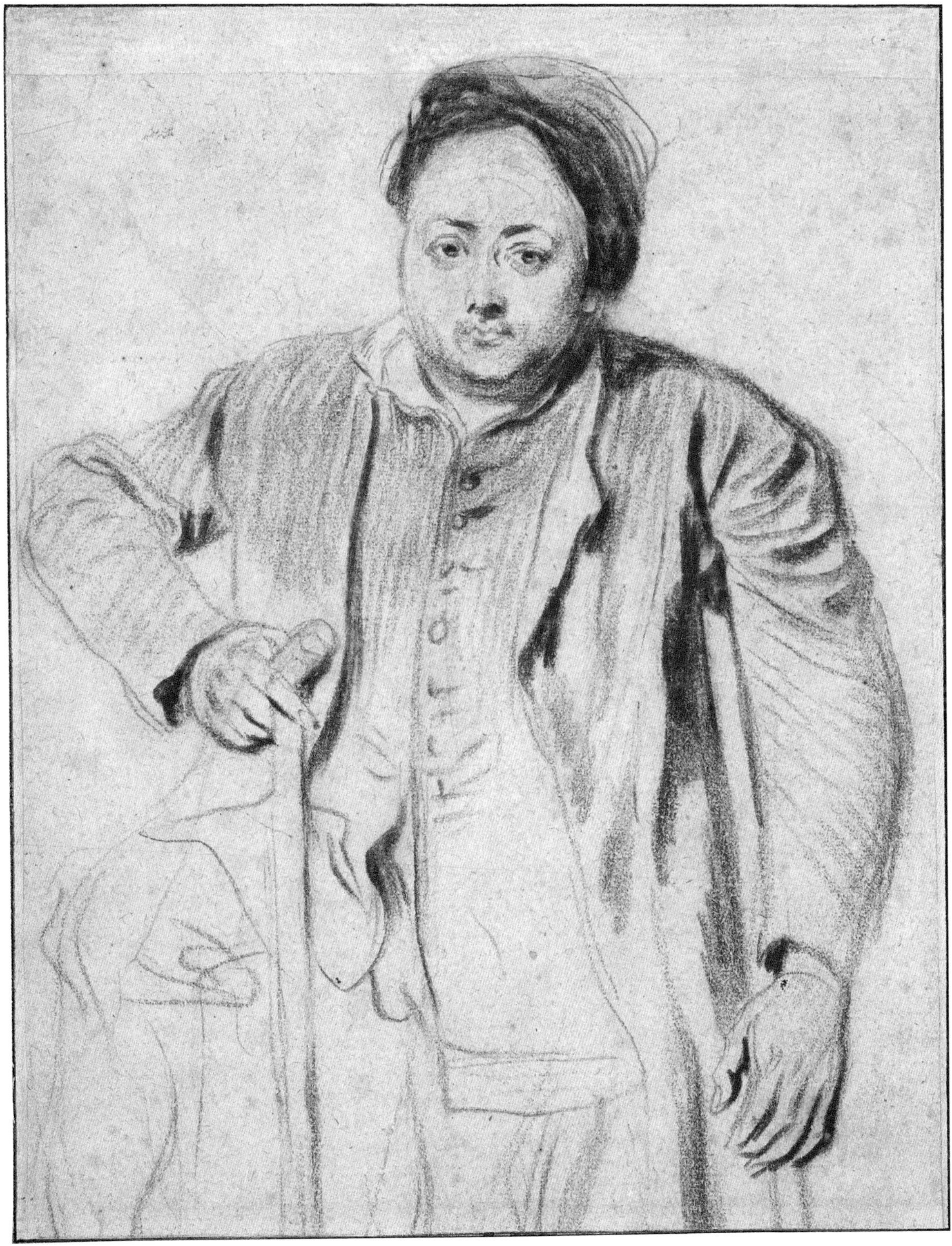

35

Two Crouching Youths in a Landscape, after Domenico Campagnola

Red chalk on paper, 235 x 232 mm; frame line drawn with pen and brown ink

Musée du Louvre, Paris, Département des Arts graphiques, inv. 33374

PROVENANCE: PM 438; RP 342; Musée du Louvre mark L. 1886 at lower left
LITERATURE: PM 438; RP 342; Rosenberg 2001, pp. 61 and 60, fig. 73; Rosenberg 2005, p. 120, pl. LVI, fig. 44

Although Watteau almost never left Paris, except occasionally to return to his birthplace of Valenciennes and a short visit to England, he regretted never having been able to visit Italy. His second place in the Prix de Rome competition in 1709 made him hope for such a trip.

Although he hardly travelled, he wanted to be familiar with the work of the Old Masters and copied their paintings as well as their drawings frequently throughout his life: Rubens and Van Dyck, plus various seventeenth-century French artists, including Mellan and Le Nain, but he was most interested in the sixteenth-century Venetian painters, with whom he felt a special bond.

The present red chalk drawing is a copy of a pen-and-ink drawing, formerly attributed to Titian and now ascribed to Domenico Campagnola (*c.* 1500–1564), which now belongs to the collection of the Albertina in Vienna (fig. 22). Both drawings, which may have been glued to the same mount in the eighteenth century, seem to have belonged to Pierre Crozat before entering the Mariette collection. Gabriel de Saint-Aubin drew one of the two in the margin of his copy of the sale catalogue (fig. 23).

Watteau's copy is faithful to the original except in one detail: he opted for red chalk whereas the Venetian original was in pen and ink, a medium never used by Watteau.

The subject of Campagnola's drawing, and of the copy, has given rise to all sorts of interpretations, some convincing, some less so. PR

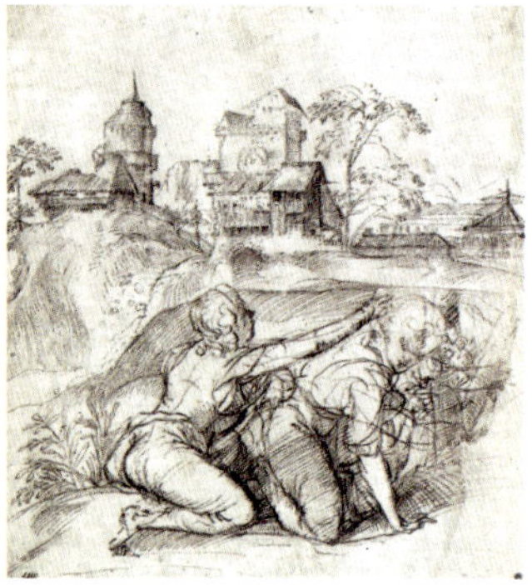

Fig. 22
Domenico Campagnola, *Two Young People Crouching in a Landscape*. Pen and brown ink, 236 x 213 mm. Albertina, Vienna

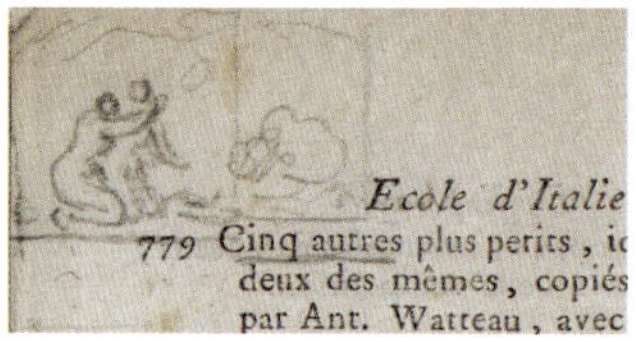

Fig. 23
Gabriel de Saint-Aubin, Sketch in the margin of the artist's copy of the catalogue of Pierre-Jean Mariette's sale, 15 November 1775 – 30 January 1776. Museum of Fine Arts, Boston. Bequest of William A. Sargent

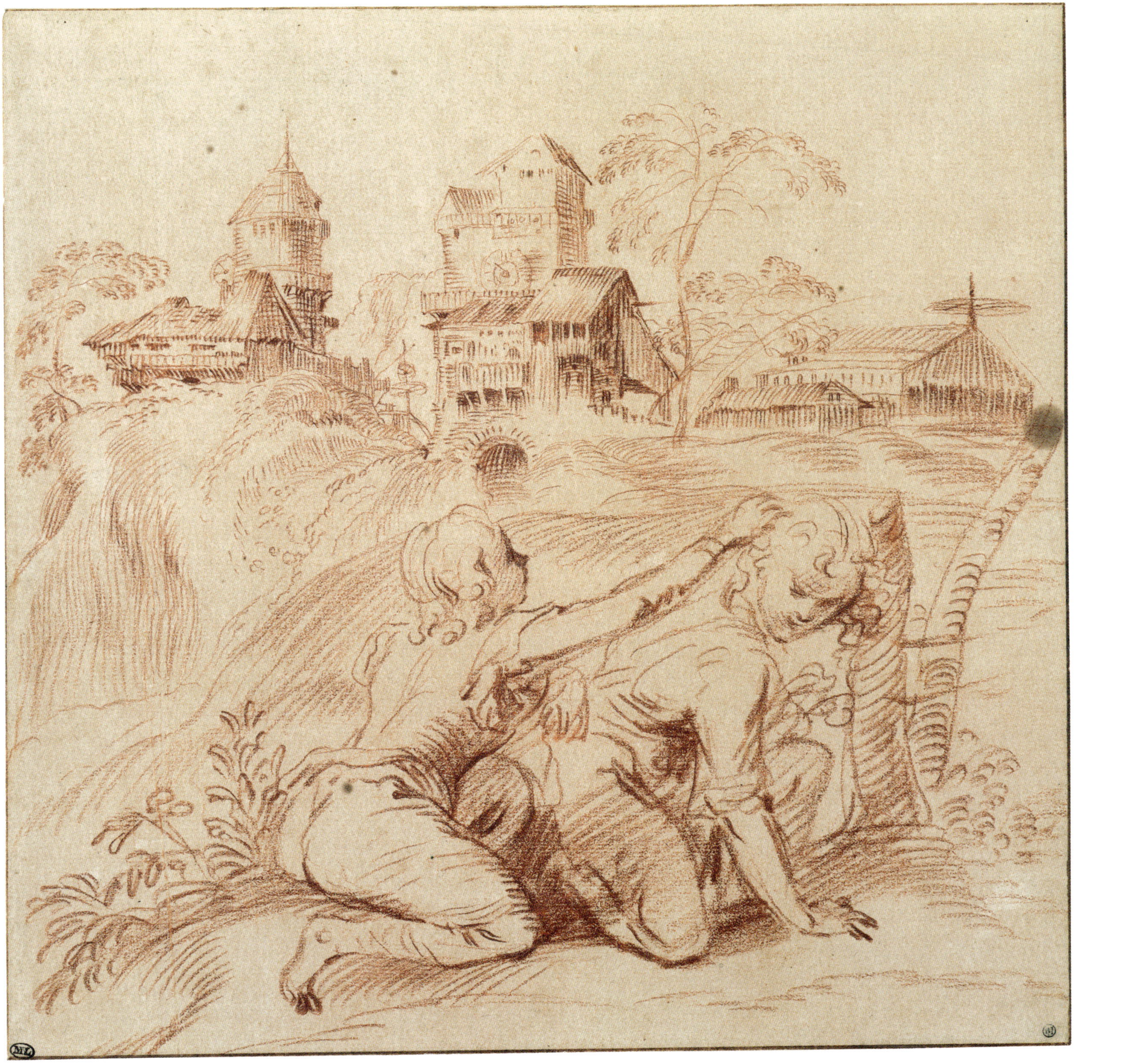

36

Standing Friar

Red and black chalk on paper, 332 x 230 mm

The Samuel Courtauld Trust, The Courtauld Gallery, London, inv. PG 220

PROVENANCE: PM 503; RP 368
LITERATURE: PM 503; RP 368; Roland Michel 1998, p. 752; Grasselli 2001, p. 333, note 24

This portrait of a Carmelite friar has an ironical, mocking undertone unusual in Watteau's work. The model, certainly drawn from life, lowers his eyes and purses his lips. His baby face, with its falsely serious look, contrasts with the large size of his hat.

The date proposed by us in 1996 (1715–16) failed to convince. Marianne Roland Michel (1997) would have preferred the drawing to appear at the end of the first volume of our catalogue raisonné rather than among the first illustrations of the second volume. In addition, the background does not appear in Boucher's engraving from the drawing, which appears in *Figures de différents caractères.*

Before Count Seilern presented it to the Courtauld Institute in 1978, the drawing, with many of Watteau's other great works, belonged to Andrew James. PR

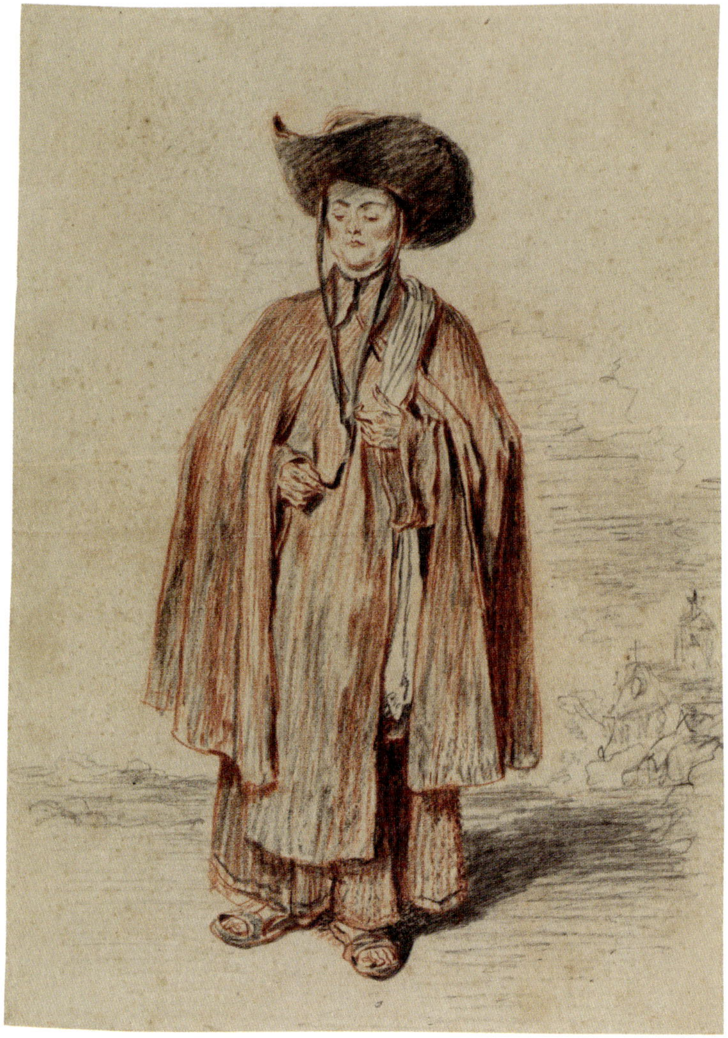

Red chalk on cream paper, 202 x 340 mm

Rijksmuseum, Amsterdam, inv. 1953:181. This drawing was recovered from Germany after the Second World War

PROVENANCE, EXHIBITED: PM 636; RP 399; Paris 2003, no. 8 (R. J. A. te Rijdt)
LITERATURE: PM 636; RP 399; Roland Michel 1998, p. 752 and fig. 45

37

Two Studies of a Woman Seated on the Ground

As was his habit, Watteau used this drawing in several of his paintings: *The Scale of Love* (National Gallery, London), *The Embarrassing Proposal* (State Hermitage Museum, St Petersburg) and *Pleasures of the Dance* (Dulwich Picture Gallery, London). In his 1748 lecture on the artist, Caylus informs us: 'When the fancy took him to do a painting, he had recourse to his anthology (the "bound volumes" in which he used to draw). He chose the figures that suited him best at that moment. He formed groups with them, most often according to a background landscape which he had devised or prepared. It was very unusual for him to do otherwise.' This information could apply to many of Watteau's drawings shown here (for the complete text of Caylus's lecture, see Rosenberg 1984, pp. 53–89).

Watteau has drawn in red chalk the same model in two positions and at different distances. He lingers over every fold of her dress and over the young girl's face, which he depicts with authority and tenderness. PR

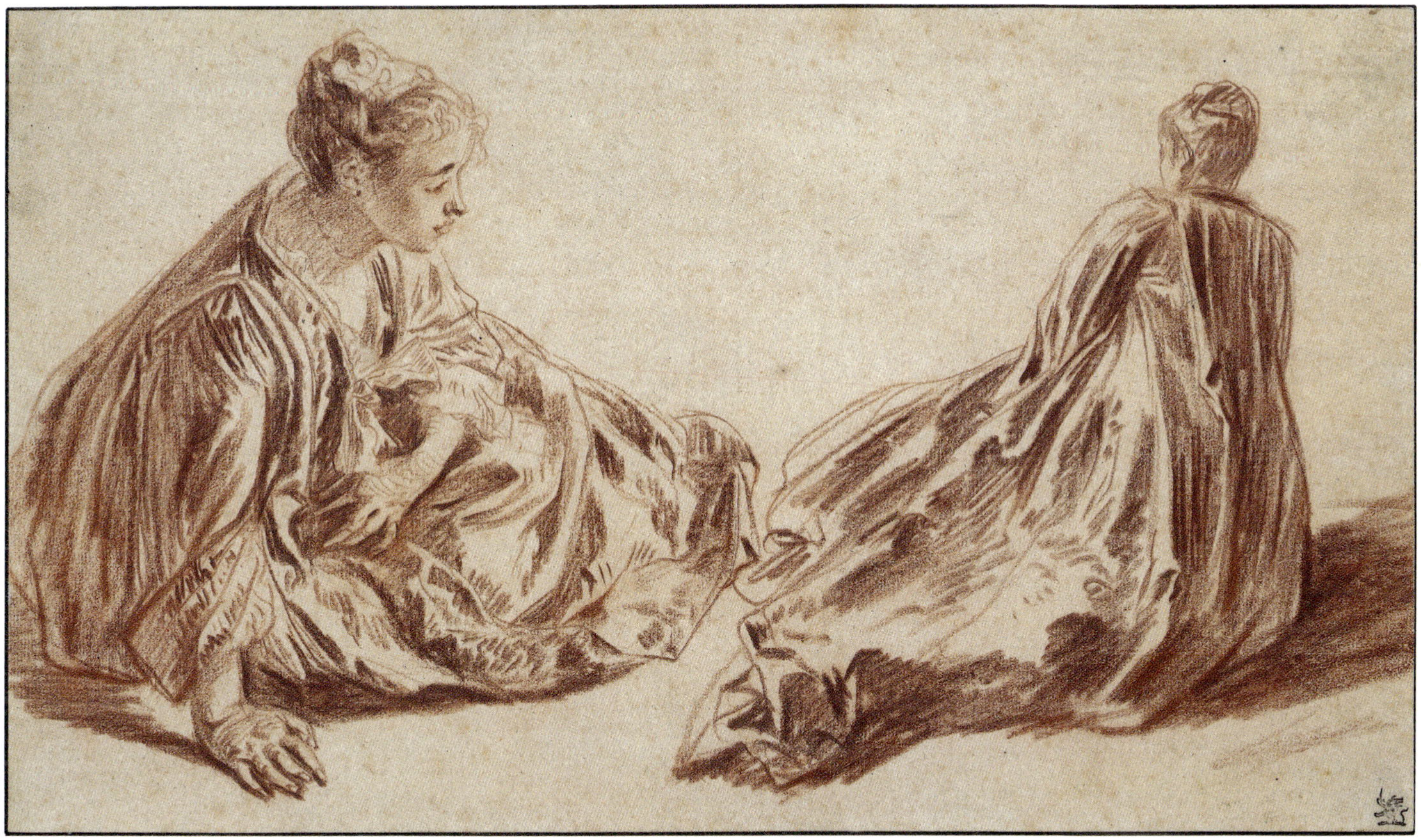

Red, black and white chalks on beige paper, 326 x 283 mm
Inscription in chalk at lower right *283*

Musée du Louvre, Paris, Département des Arts graphiques, inv. R.F. 4111

PROVENANCE, EXHIBITED: PM 513; RP 370; Budapest 2008, no. 40
LITERATURE: PM 513; RP 370; Grasselli 2001, p. 312; Hattori 2001, p. 64, note 13; Edwards 2006, pp. 52–54, fig. 9; Conisbee 2009, p. 471, note 14

38

Seated Young Woman Holding a Basket in Her Left Hand

On the death of Charles de La Fosse on 13 December 1716, the wealthy banker Pierre Crozat (1665–1740), who had commissioned from de La Fosse four oval paintings on the subject of the *Seasons* to decorate the dining room of his residence in the Rue de Richelieu, turned to Watteau and asked him to execute them in de La Fosse's place. One of these paintings, *Summer*, belongs to the National Gallery of Art, Washington. *Spring* had only just been located (1964) when it was burned in a fire. The other two ovals remain to be found, but their compositions are known through the engravings made from them (fig. 24).

Six drawings by Watteau related to this commission are known today (four are exhibited here, cats 38–41). They should be dated *c.* 1717 (see Hattori 2001), and not '*c.* 1715–17' as we suggested in our 1996 catalogue raisonné.

The present drawing, a famous study for the main figure in *Spring*, came from the collection of the Goncourt brothers (Jules made an engraving from it); its state of conservation is not perfect. Watteau uses the three-chalk technique with which his name is regularly associated. In just a few months, Watteau had acquired perfect mastery of the treatment of light (and of the female nude). The face of *Spring*, lit from below, combines all three techniques; it is both energetic and elegant, and the composition on the page, with its seductive interplay of arms and legs, is particularly successful. PR

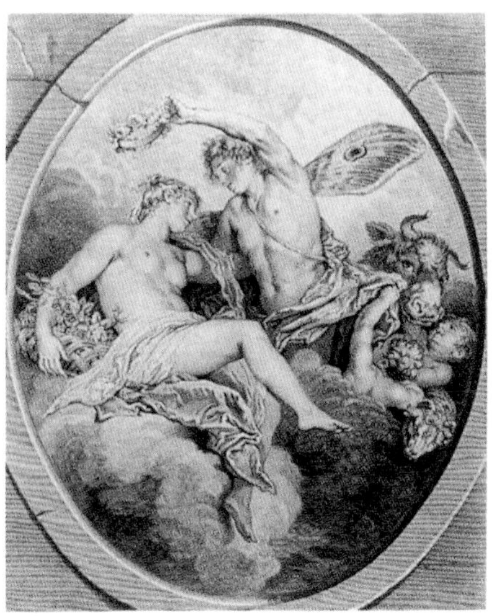

Fig. 24
Spring, from Crozat's *Seasons*, engraved by Louis Desplaces for the *Recueil Jullienne*, 1738. British Museum, London (RP 301a)

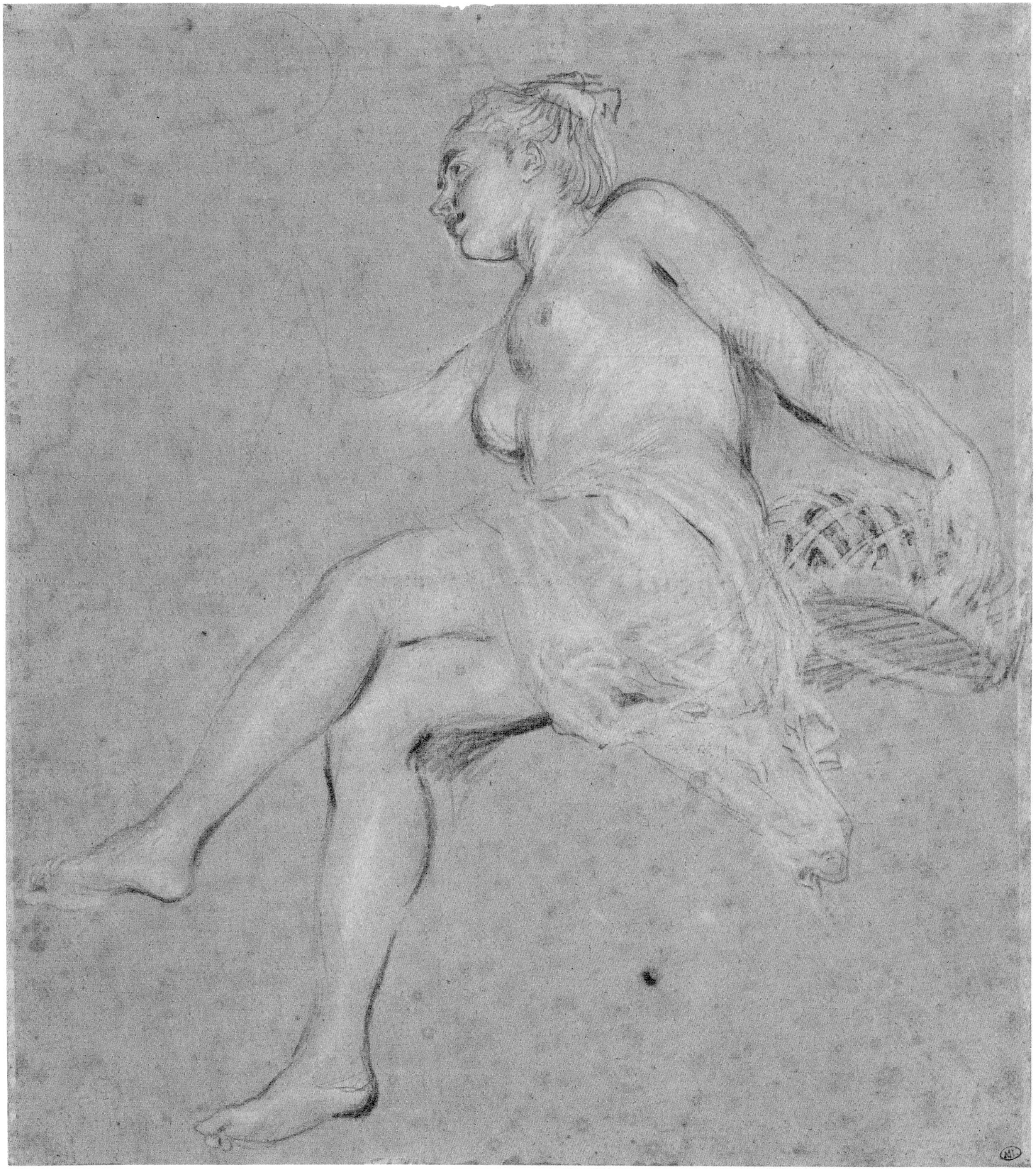

39

Semi-nude Man, Seen in Three-quarter View and Turned to the Left, Lifting a Glass (Bacchus)

Red, black and white chalks on beige paper, 280 x 204 mm; small strip of paper added at lower edge; frame line drawn in pen and black ink

Musée du Louvre, Paris, Département des Arts graphiques, inv. R.F. 28980

PROVENANCE, EXHIBITIONS: PM 511; RP 371; Musée du Louvre mark L. 1886a at lower right
LITERATURE: PM 511; RP 371; Hattori 2001, pp. 57, 64, note 13 and p. 61, fig. 9; Grasselli 2001, p. 312; Conisbee 2009, p. 471, note 14

The entry for cat. 38 explains the circumstances of the commission and the date of this work, which also comes from the collection of the Goncourt brothers (Edmond made an engraving from it). The sheet was bequeathed to the Louvre in 1938 by the American collector Walter Gay, whereas cat. 38 was presented by Isaac de Camondo in 1911. The present work is a preparatory study for the central figure in *Autumn*, a painting that is now lost but for which other preparatory studies survive, in the Musée Cognacq-Jay, Paris (RP 372), and the Courtauld Institute, London (cat. 41). However, it is easy to recognise Bacchus in the composition with his coronet of vine shoots and his glass of wine; in the Louvre drawing, Watteau simply produced a male academic nude (which has nothing academic about it, nonetheless). He neglects the face, preferring to concentrate on the model's torso and long legs, using strong white highlights to emphasise both face and legs.

The relaxed elegance of the pose is remarkable. PR

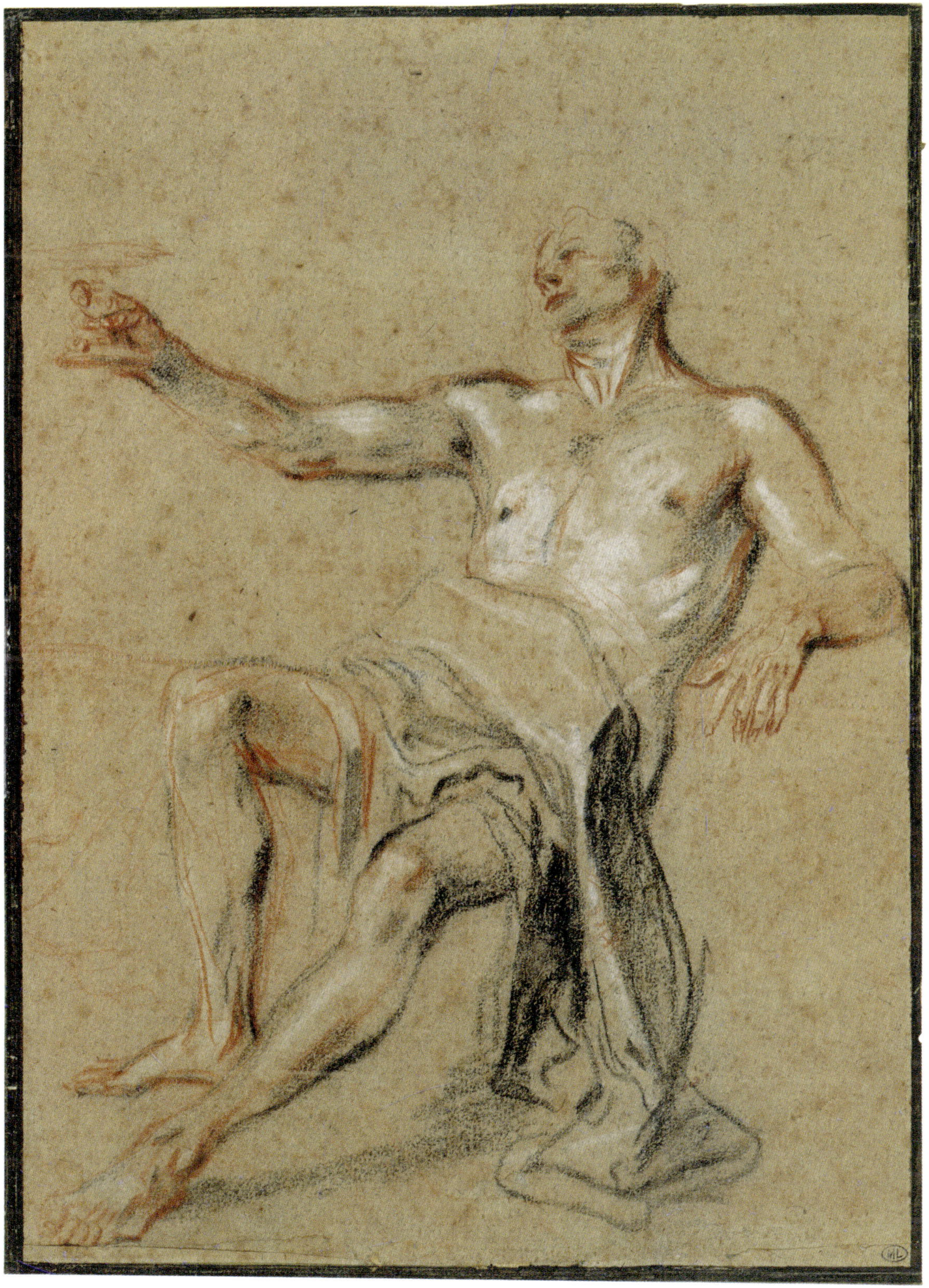

40

Nude Man Holding a Bottle in Each Hand

Red and black chalks and faint white highlights on two joined sheets of cream paper, 277 x 226 mm; frame line drawn in pen and brown ink; fully glued to backing

The Metropolitan Museum of Art, New York. Bequest of Walter C. Baker, 1971, inv. 1972.118.238

PROVENANCE, EXHIBITED: PM 518; RP 373; New York 1999, no. 44 (Mary Taverner Holmes)
LITERATURE: PM 518; RP 373; Hattori 2001, p. 64, note 13; Grasselli 2001, p. 312; Conisbee 2009, p. 471, note 14

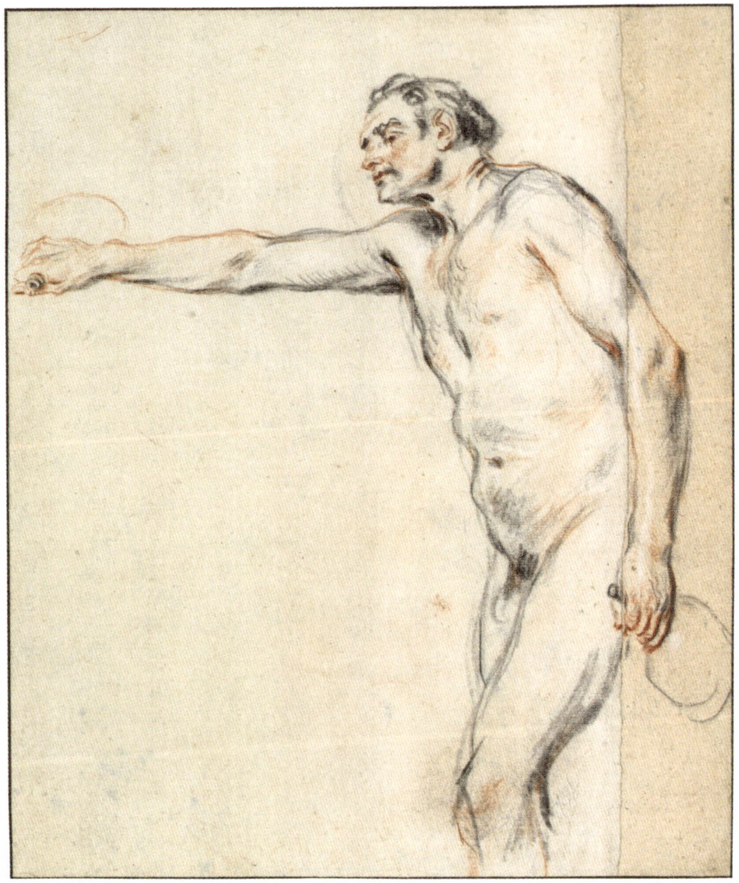

The circumstances of the commission and the date of the drawing are discussed in the entry for cat. 38.

Watteau painted four ovals on the subject of the *Seasons* for Crozat. *Autumn* is lost but, in addition to the engraving taken from the vanished canvas (fig. 25), four drawings directly related to the painting are known. The present page, a very fine academic male nude, reveals some important variations from the man standing pouring wine in the background in the composition, in fact a satyr standing in as Bacchus's cup-bearer. This must undoubtedly have been an initial idea, abandoned by Watteau in favour of the Courtauld Institute drawing (cat. 41). On the latter page, the features of the model are much closer to those of the satyr in the final composition, whereas here the artist presents a far more realistic image.

In front of a drawing like this, Caylus's observation (see Rosenberg 1984, p. 72), made at the lecture on Watteau read out by him to the Académie Royale de Peinture et de Sculpture on 13 February 1748, cannot fail to amaze us: '[Watteau], having no knowledge of anatomy, and having almost never drawn a nude, could neither read one nor express one.' PR

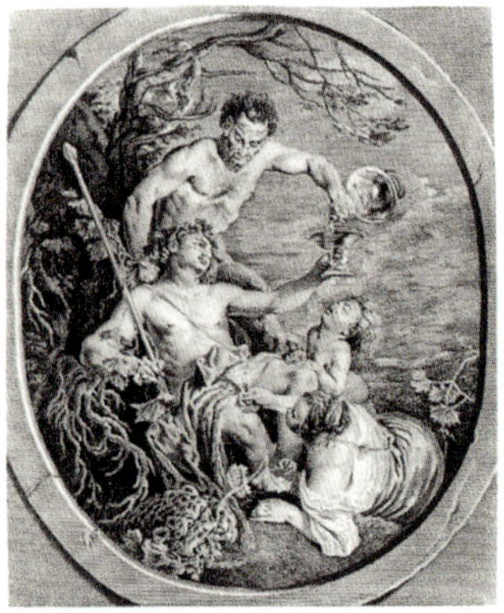

Fig. 25
Autumn, from Crozat's *Seasons*, engraved by Etienne Fessard for the *Recueil Jullienne*, 1735. British Museum, London (RP 301a)

Red, black and white chalks on paper, framed in pen and brown ink, 285 x 211 mm

The Samuel Courtauld Trust, The Courtauld Gallery, London, inv. PG 221

PROVENANCE: PM 521; RP 374
LITERATURE: PM 521; RP 374; Hattori 2001, p. 64, note 13; Grasselli 2001, p. 312; Conisbee 2009, p. 471, note 14

41

Satyr Holding a Bottle in Each Hand

The entry to cat. 38 explains the circumstances of this commission and the date of the drawing.

One of four studies recovered to date for *Autumn*, one of the Crozat *Seasons*, now lost (see cats 39 and 40 and RP 372), this is the preparatory drawing for the satyr who serves Bacchus with wine, a figure not modified for the painting in any way. In the engraving, and therefore in the painting, Bacchus's head hides the satyr's left hand, as well as his legs and genitals, which Watteau sketches in only lightly.

The rapidity of execution, accuracy of line and absence of hesitation are greatly to be admired. PR

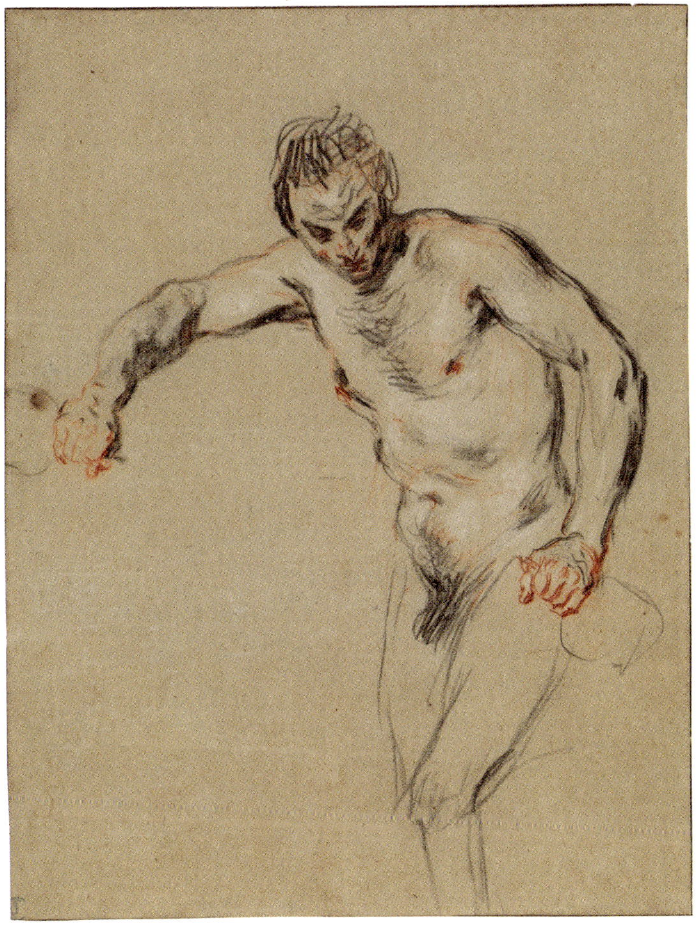

Red, black and white chalks, wash and graphite on beige paper, 244 x 297 mm; frame line drawn in pen and brown ink

Musée du Louvre, Paris, Département des Arts graphiques, inv. 33360

PROVENANCE, EXHIBITED: PM 515; RP 375; Musée du Louvre mark L. 1886a at lower right and L. 2207 at lower centre; Paris 2000B, no. 1 (Laura Angelucci); Budapest 2008, no. 39

LITERATURE: PM 515; RP 375; Fumaroli 1996, p. 38, fig. 5; Alan Wintermute in New York 1999, p. 44, fig. 42; Colin B. Bailey in New York 2009B (French edition), pp. 35 and 190, fig. 4.2

42

Nude Man Kneeling, Holding Fabric in His Right Hand

This drawing, which must date from 1717 and not from 1715–16, is one of Watteau's extant preparatory studies for *Jupiter and Antiope* (fig. 26; a painting presented to the Musée du Louvre by Dr La Caze, one of the discoverers of Watteau, in 1869). The second drawing, which belongs to the Fondation Custodia in Paris, has practically no variations from the satyr in the painting. Jupiter, as will be remembered, disguised himself as a satyr in order to take advantage of Antiope (twins were born of their union, Amphion and Zetios).

Thanks to his perfect mastery of the use of black and red chalk with white highlights, and to the power of his execution, Watteau makes us feel the violence of the god-satyr's gesture as he uncovers the nymph in preparation for possessing her.

This drawing, like many of the preceding ones, in particular the studies for the Crozat *Seasons* which also date from *c.* 1717, was executed from the model and drawn from life. PR

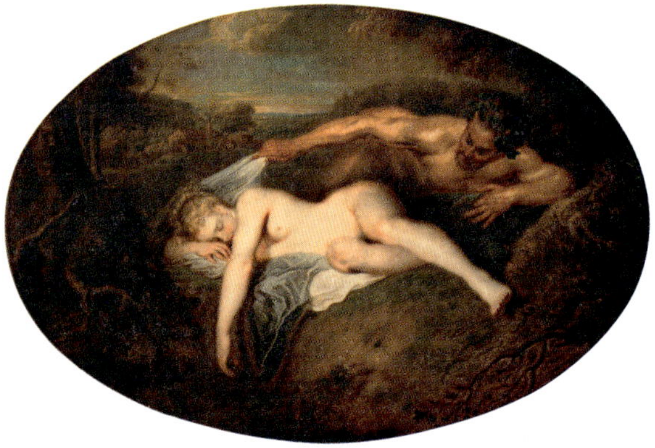

Fig. 26
Jupiter and Antiope, 1715.
Oil on canvas, 73.5 x 107.5 cm.
Musée du Louvre, Paris

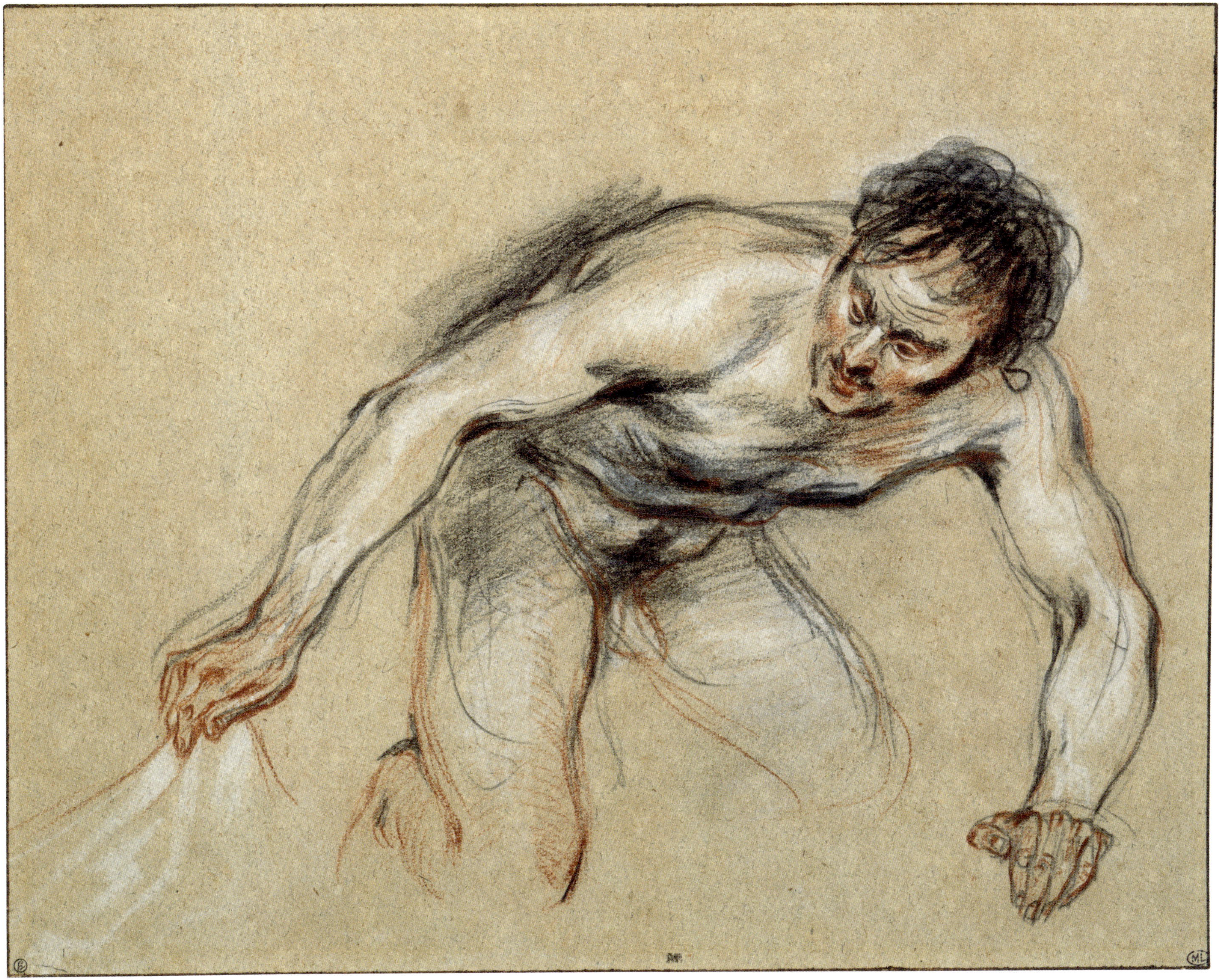

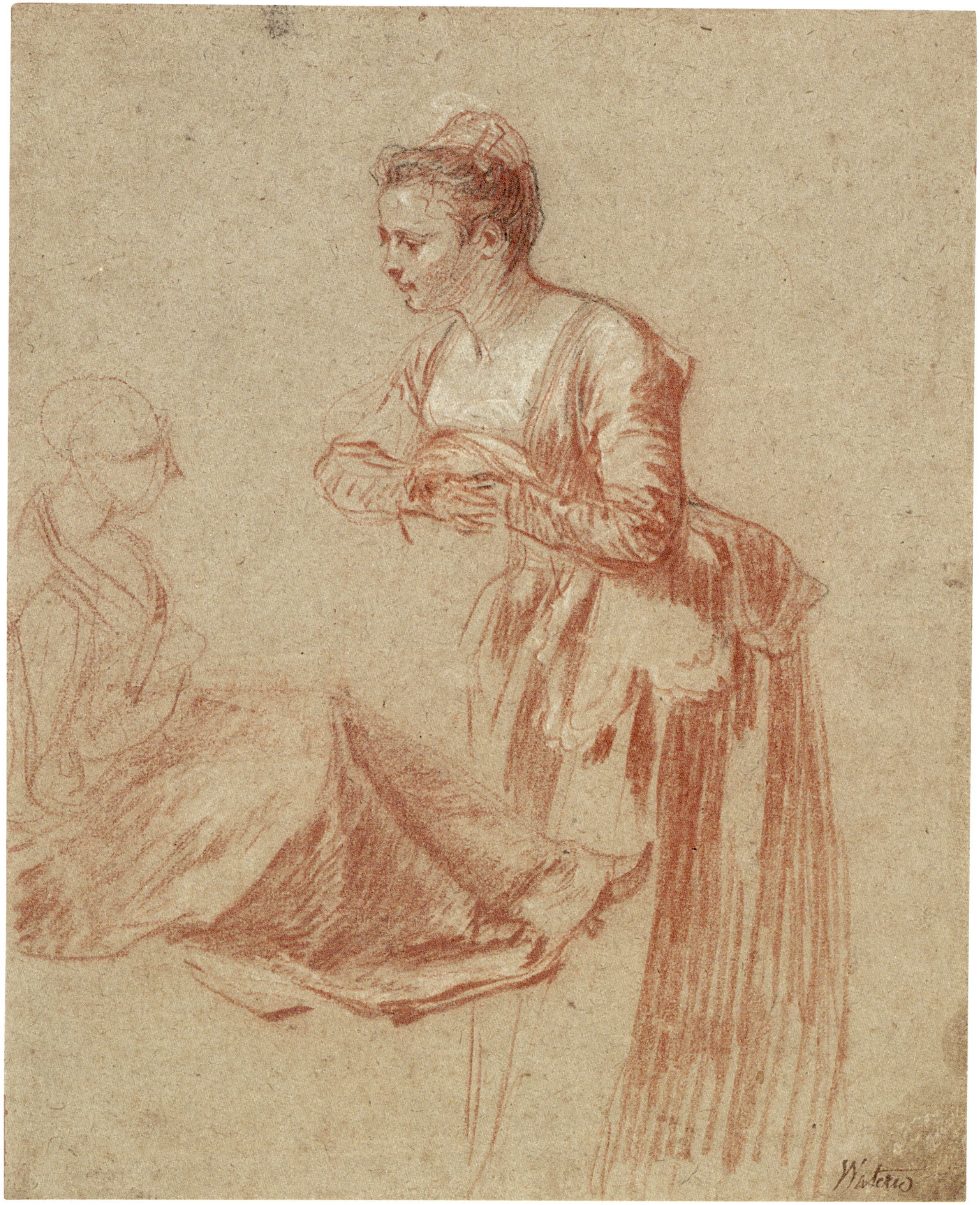

Red, black and white chalks on brownish paper, 269 x 214 mm; fully glued to backing
Inscription in pen and brown ink at lower right *Wateau*

Albertina, Vienna, inv. 12.009

PROVENANCE: PM 560; RP 397
LITERATURE: PM 560; RP 397; Roland Michel 1998, pp. 753–54, fig. 47

43

Two Studies, One of a Young Woman Leaning Forward, the Other of a Woman Seated on the Ground

This drawing from Vienna makes one wonder about Watteau's working methods. He presents two studies of women, one seated, one standing (holding her wrist onto which she seems to be slipping a bracelet). The red chalk used by Watteau for these two drawings is of two different shades. In our view in 1996 the left-hand drawing, more detailed in its execution, was earlier in date (1715–16) than the right-hand drawing (1717), which was technically more accomplished. In 1998 Marianne Roland Michel pointed out that the left-hand study partially covered the gown of the standing woman, and that as a consequence both drawings belonged to the same date and thus the order of our suggestion should be reversed.

In our opinion, the woman seated on the left was executed first. Watteau, who used to draw in 'bound volumes' that he kept close at hand, liked to add new drawings to pages that were partially empty. It seems to us that this is what he has done here. He completed the page with the drawing of the standing woman but, hindered by the skirt and foot of the seated woman, interrupted his drawing where they occurred.

The beautiful, pensive face of the standing young woman is particularly memorable. PR

Red, black and white chalks on beige paper, 297 x 173 mm; numerous small brownish pinholes; fully glued to backing Inscriptions in pen and brown ink: at lower left *79* and at lower right *Vateau*; on the back, inscription in pen and brown ink *portraist de rebel*

Musée des Beaux-Arts, Rennes, inv. 794.1.2593

PROVENANCE, LITERATURE: PM 846; RP 403, col.; Edwards 2006, pp. 48–49, and see p. 182, plate 20

44

Seated Violinist Tuning His Instrument

Although Ingres portrayed only a few of his violinist friends with their instruments (Panseron, Paganini, Baillot), his predecessor Watteau devoted many sheets to violin players, indispensable protagonists of his imaginary *fêtes galantes* as of the private concerts he frequently attended. The figure of the violinist was essential to the gatherings he depicted in his earliest paintings, but appears only occasionally in his youthful drawings: on the right-hand side of a page of studies of three men (RP 100), or seated and seen playing from behind with a cape over his shoulder (RP 265); at this period, pictures of guitarists or players of other more popular instruments are much more numerous.

After 1715–16, a plausible date for the present drawing, when Watteau's habit of using three differently coloured chalks began (although some commentators, not including us, maintain that the white chalk on the figure's right hand is a later addition), guitarists outnumber violinists once again; Watteau portrays one more, however, also wearing a cape and seen in profile in an attractive drawing in the British Museum, London (RP 510), then two more, in the act of playing (RP 539), to be seen in *The Quadrille* (in the former Stirling Post Collection; DV 177). The subject of a red chalk drawing (RP 593), now lost, may have been the painter and amateur violinist Nicolas Vleughels; he is shown tuning his instrument, as are the two figures wearing berets in a sheet of studies in Washington (RP 594). The two final portraits of professional violinists belong to a later date: the *Portrait of a Young Violinist in Profile* (fig. 27), a masterpiece now in the National Gallery of Ireland, Dublin, used as the cover for the museum's inventory of drawings; it shows the musician with the violin under his arm, eyes staring blankly as he listens attentively to the string he is trying to tune. The likeness of the violinist Giovanni Antonio Guido (RP 668), a musician in the employ of the Duc d'Orléans, is as striking for the absence of any instrument as it is for his curious spectacles; strangest of all, however, is the pallid light cast on his white powdered face by a row of Argand oil lamps on a dais.

Watteau is known to have been acquainted with a number of violinists, including Guido, who was well known at the time. Rebel, named in an inscription on the reverse of the Rennes drawing, was Jean-Féry Rebel (1666–1747), a violinist at the Paris Opéra and one of the Twenty-four Violinists to the King. He was later appointed Master of Music at the Académie Royale, and from 1718 was composer to the Chambre du Roi. The earliest date for this drawing would make him forty-nine, however, which is clearly implausible for this very youthful figure. Watteau made a drawing of Rebel in the act of composing, now in a very bad state of conservation (Musée Magnin, Dijon; RP 658); we chose it for the catalogue raisonné in preference to a better-preserved but less well executed drawing (RP R418). L-AP

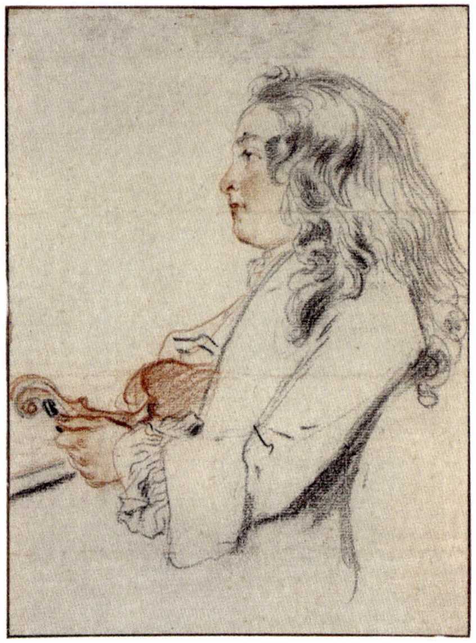

Fig. 27
Portrait of a Young Violinist in Profile, c. 1718–19. Red and black chalk with stumping, 205 x 152 mm. National Gallery of Ireland, Dublin

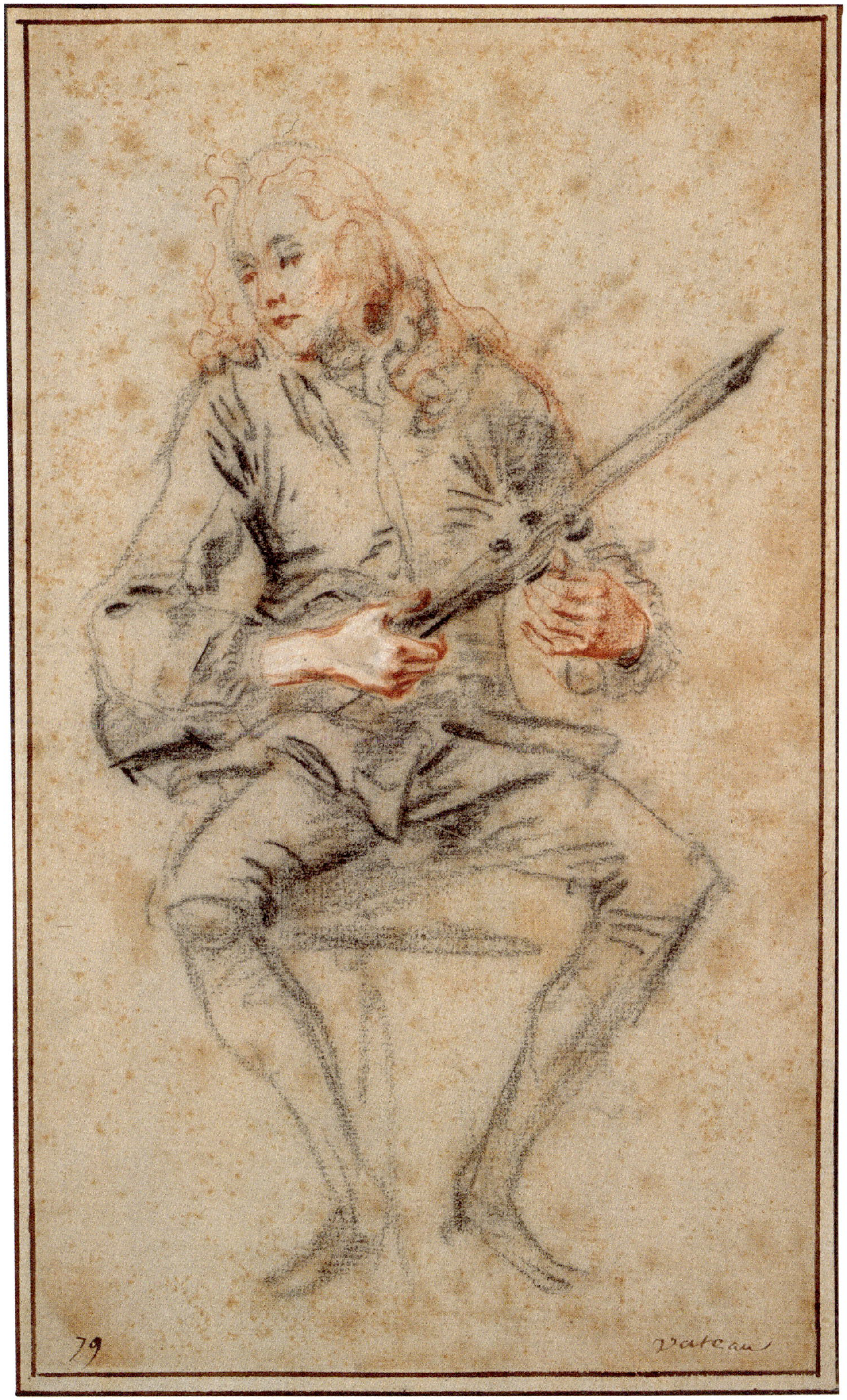

Red chalk and white highlights (two figures and arm), black chalk and white highlights (vines) on paper, 227 x 368 mm; frame line drawn in pen and black ink; fully glued to backing

Petit Palais, Musée des Beaux-Arts de la Ville de Paris, inv. D. Dutuit 1039

PROVENANCE, EXHIBITED: PM 666; RP 407; Valenciennes 2004, no. 4, col.
LITERATURE: PM 666; RP 407, col.; Bailey 1997, p. 48; Roland Michel 1998, p. 751, fig. 44
ENGRAVINGS, COPIES: RP 407

45

Studies of a Man Stretched out on the Ground; a Seated Man Dressed as a Gardener Holding a Blade of Grass; Vine Branches; and of a Hand Holding the Train of a Dress

Our suggestion of *c.* 1715–16 as a date for this page in our catalogue raisonné was based on our linking of the two male figures with three paintings belonging to slightly later dates: *The Enchanted Isle* (1717; private collection) for the left-hand figure, *The Awaited Proposal* (1716; Musée d'Angers) and *The Shy Lover* (1718; Palacio Real, Madrid) for the figure on the right. In the two latter paintings the young lover seems to be plucking the petals from a flower that he contemplates in brooding fashion.

An interesting problem is the presence of the vine shoots, whose execution with sharpened black chalk seems unusual for Watteau. Since similar (but not identical) vegetation appears in the engravings of the two figure drawings executed by François Boucher in the *Figures de différents caractères* (nos 153 and 282), it could be surmised that the foliage had been added to the drawing at a later date, in imitation of these two engravings. However, in her review of our catalogue raisonné, Marianne Roland Michel hypothesised that the vine shoots must be in Watteau's hand; she compares them with the few studies of vegetation generally attributed to him, usually to be found on the reverse side of his figure drawings (RP 136 verso and RP 138 verso). It seems to us, nevertheless, that the foliage here is much more jagged-edged. Margaret Morgan Grasselli has put forward the hypothesis that the white highlights may have been added by one of the Dutuit brothers, but in fact the drawing was not acquired until after their death, as arrears on the Dutuit bequest to the Petit Palais, Paris. Finally, Colin B. Bailey supports our position, considering 'these weakly drawn vine leaves [...] suspect'. Worthy of note, however, is the fact that the chalk highlights, although placed on the figures with discernment, are added somewhat erratically when it comes to the foliage. L-AP

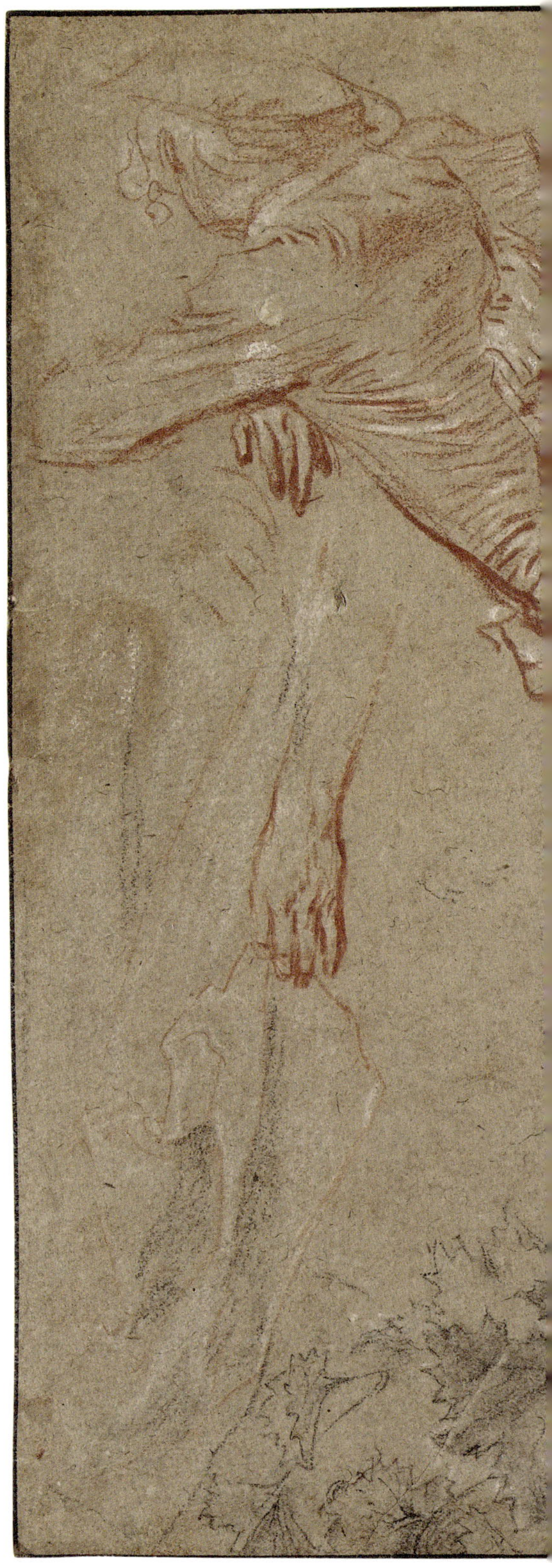

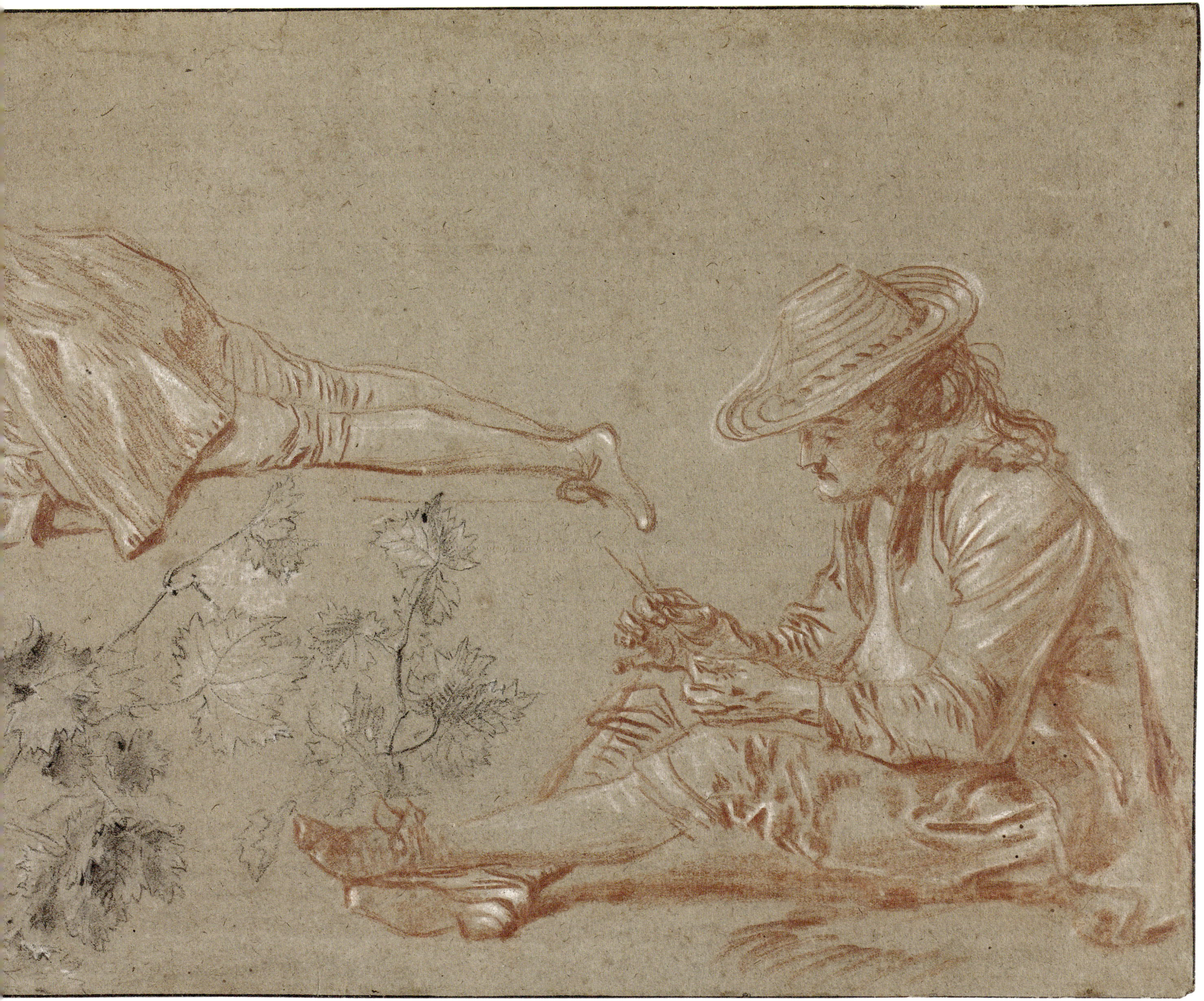

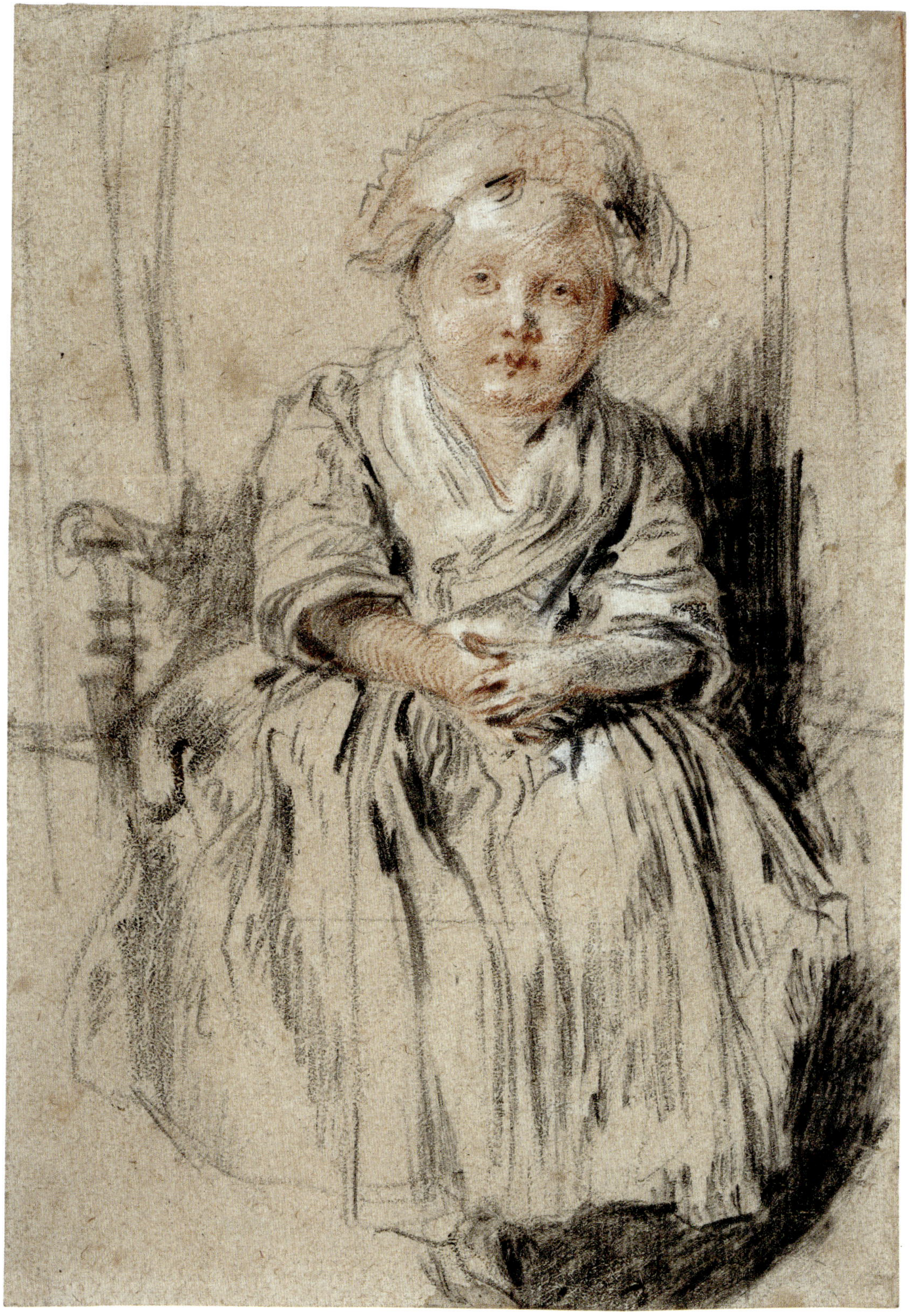

46

Child Seated in a Chair

Red, black and white chalks on cream paper, 177 x 122 mm

Rijksmuseum, Amsterdam, inv. 1953: 185. This drawing was recovered from Germany after the Second World War

PROVENANCE, EXHIBITED: RP 410; Paris 2003, no. 9
LITERATURE: PM 698; RP 410, col.

This is one of Watteau's most successful drawings of children; the disproportion between the small model and the large armchair recalls another well-known image, the 1818 drawing by Ingres of little Charles Lethière lost in a large armchair (see Hans Naef, *Die Bildniszeichnungen von J. A. D. Ingres*, Bern, 1977–80, vol. 4, no. 232, rep.). It is difficult to decide whether this child is a boy or a girl, as at this period very young boys were dressed like girls.

The large stroke of black chalk, similar to those to be seen in the Savoyards series of drawings and the 'Persians', suggests a date for this page in the region of 1715–16; it was never re-used or engraved. L-AP

Two shades of red chalk, black chalk and white highlights on cream paper, 222 x 217 mm

Harvard Art Museum, Fogg Museum, Cambridge, Mass. Bequest of Meta and Paul J. Sachs, inv. 1965.336

PROVENANCE, EXHIBITED: RP 413; New York 1999, no. 21, col. rep.
LITERATURE: PM 712; RP 413, rep.; Grasselli 2001, p. 313
COPY: PM 712; RP 413

47

Two Studies of a Child's Head and Four Studies of Women's Heads

Although this drawing is in the Fogg Art Museum, it is not from the Winthrop Collection but from the collection of Meta and Paul J. Sachs and can therefore be allowed out on loan. It must be one of the earliest pages of studies of heads in which the heads co-ordinate with one another within a restricted space, encouraging the relationship between them – even though this may not always be obvious at first sight.

Opinions are somewhat divided about the date of this drawing. Margaret Morgan Grasselli assigned it to 1713, then 1714, and Martin Eidelberg to a later date. In the catalogue raisonné we suggested a date of 1715–16 for the four women's heads and surmised that the two heads of children, one of which (the upper one) reappears in the late painting *Iris, It's Early to Be Thinking of Dancing* (*c.* 1719; Staatliche Museen, Berlin), were perhaps placed on the page after the others in the space remaining on the left. Grasselli returned to the subject in 2001, reiterating that, in her opinion, the Fogg studies of heads and those in a Louvre drawing that uses the same female model (RP 414) must have been executed before the nude studies in red, black and white chalks relating to the Crozat *Seasons*, usually dated *c.* 1715–16, but which according to Cordélia Hattori (2001) must have been studied by Watteau at the beginning of 1717, after the death in December 1716 of Charles de La Fosse who had received the original commission; she finds the three-crayon technique used here much more sophisticated. Alan Wintermute (New York 1999) has suggested a date 'around 1715'.

Although the combined use of the three colours may not yet have achieved its later perfection, and although it seems evident that the women's heads were sketched using only red chalk before being enhanced with darker tones and heightened with white chalk, the monumentality of the faces and the intense psychological characterisation seem to suggest that this is a mature work, even if it is an early one. In fact, Watteau acquired mastery of the three-colour technique in 1715 and also achieved new assurance in his portrayal of faces and expressions; the execution of this page, at least of the four faces in the centre and on the right, should undoubtedly be assigned to this date. The same model, wearing the strange beret, a straw hat, a larger beret or bareheaded, appears in at least five other studies (RP 414 in the Louvre, mentioned above, and also RP 415, RP 458, RP 482 and RP 484). L-AP

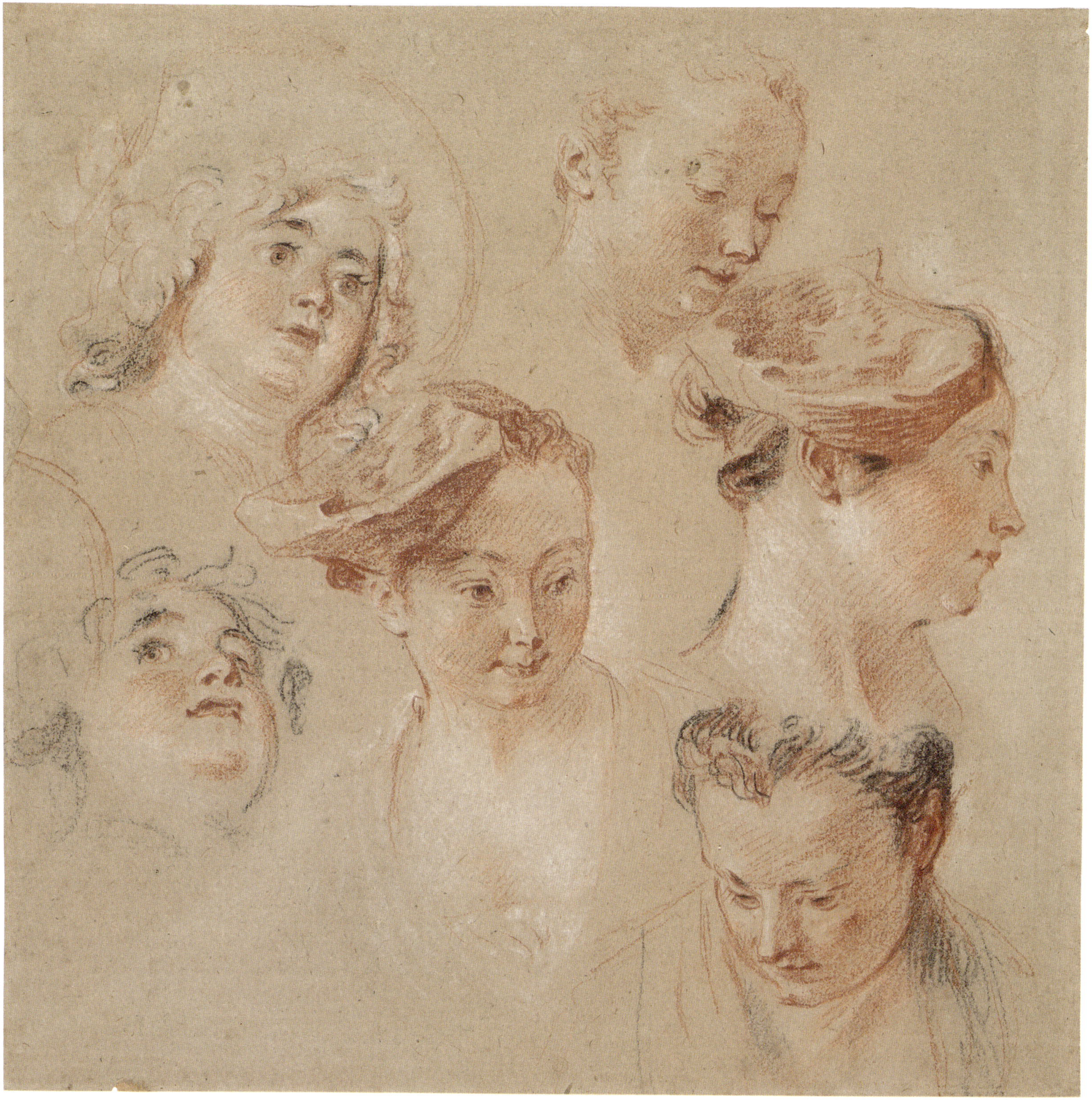

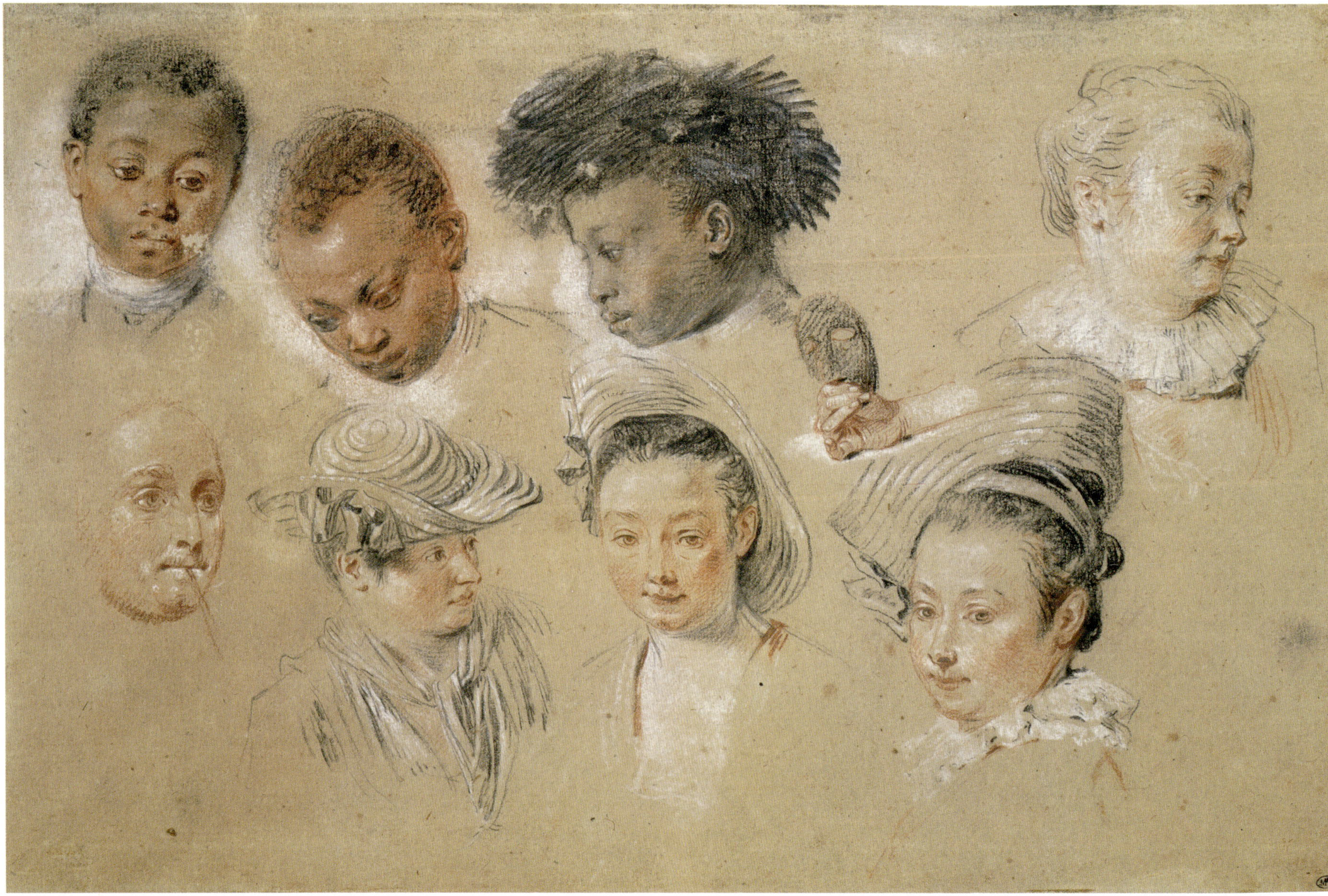

Red, black and white chalks, pastel highlights and wash on beige paper, 265 x 397 mm

Musée du Louvre, Paris, Département des Arts graphiques, inv. 33383

PROVENANCE, EXHIBITED: PM 729
LITERATURE: PM 729; RP 415, col.; Grasselli 2001, p. 315, fig. 2; Edwards 2006, pp. 48–49, and see p. 171, plate 9
COPIES: PM 729; RP 415

48

Studies of Eight Heads and a Hand Holding a Mask

This page was for many years one of the Louvre's most celebrated possessions – until 1997, when on the occasion of the centenary of the Société des Amis du Louvre, another even more attractive page was acquired, slightly later in date but also displaying eight heads (cat. 74). The more recently acquired drawing also has perfect condition on its side, whereas the present page displays some worn patches and visible abrasions, for example on the cheek of the black man at the upper left and on the cap of the man in the centre.

The order in which the drawings appeared on the paper is quite difficult to establish, and plays an important part in deliberations over the work's date (1714 for Grasselli, 1717 for Roland Michel). The female model seems to be more or less the same age as she in the Fogg Museum's drawing (cat. 47), which suggests a date of *c.* 1715–16. The hand holding the mask is certainly earlier than the female study below it, as Watteau left the top of the hat unfinished in order to save that small study.

The musician standing alone on the far left may have been added later to fill a vacant space. Grasselli is critical of the connection made in our catalogue raisonné between some of the faces and various paintings by Watteau; in her opinion, this proves that in the present drawing Watteau repeated faces that had appeared earlier in paintings. We took the precaution of specifying that some of the connections appear to be more than purely hypothetical (the woman in the upper right and *The Foursome* (Fine Arts Museums of San Francisco) and that the dating of other paintings was subject to caution, for example *The Conversation* (private collection; DV 151), in which a very similar head of a black man can be found.

The chronology of Watteau's paintings, which are never signed or dated, is no more secure than that of his drawings, and nor are the artist's working practices any more reassuring – he did not hesitate to add to a drawing a figure used previously in a painting. Here, as in the theatre, the characters seem to be depicted 'in order of appearance', some more clearly than others, some lighter than others, some more finished than others. Despite some lapses (the white area used as a background to set off the black heads is not very successful), the page makes an impression thanks to its contrasts and also to the harmonious disposition of the heads. L-AP

Two tones of red chalk on paper, 176 x 254 mm

Private collection, Paris

PROVENANCE, LITERATURE:
PM 808; RP 416, col.

49

Ten Studies of a Left Hand

This drawing has never been exhibited before. The studies have always been in prestigious private collections in France (although the present page appeared in a saleroom in London in 1935, in the Fauchier-Magnan Collection) and are generally dated *c.* 1715–16. The hand and the shirtsleeve are typically masculine and, curiously enough, Watteau does not appear to have used any of these poses in a painting.

There is one intriguing detail, nevertheless: in 1984, Rosenberg suggested linking the hand at the bottom left with the hand of the standing female figure in *The Adventuress* (Musée des Beaux-Arts, Troyes); she holds a cane under the palm of her hand, and it is true that the tip of the standing figure's bent second finger touches the end of the cane. But the object evoked here by Watteau is much broader than the cane held by the young woman, and the ring finger and little finger in the painting are visible behind the stick.

The most attractive feature of this drawing is obviously its layout: it is organised in such a way as to give the spectator the feeling of being present at each movement of the model's hand, talking, arguing, holding a round box or leaning for a moment on the corner of a low wall. L-AP

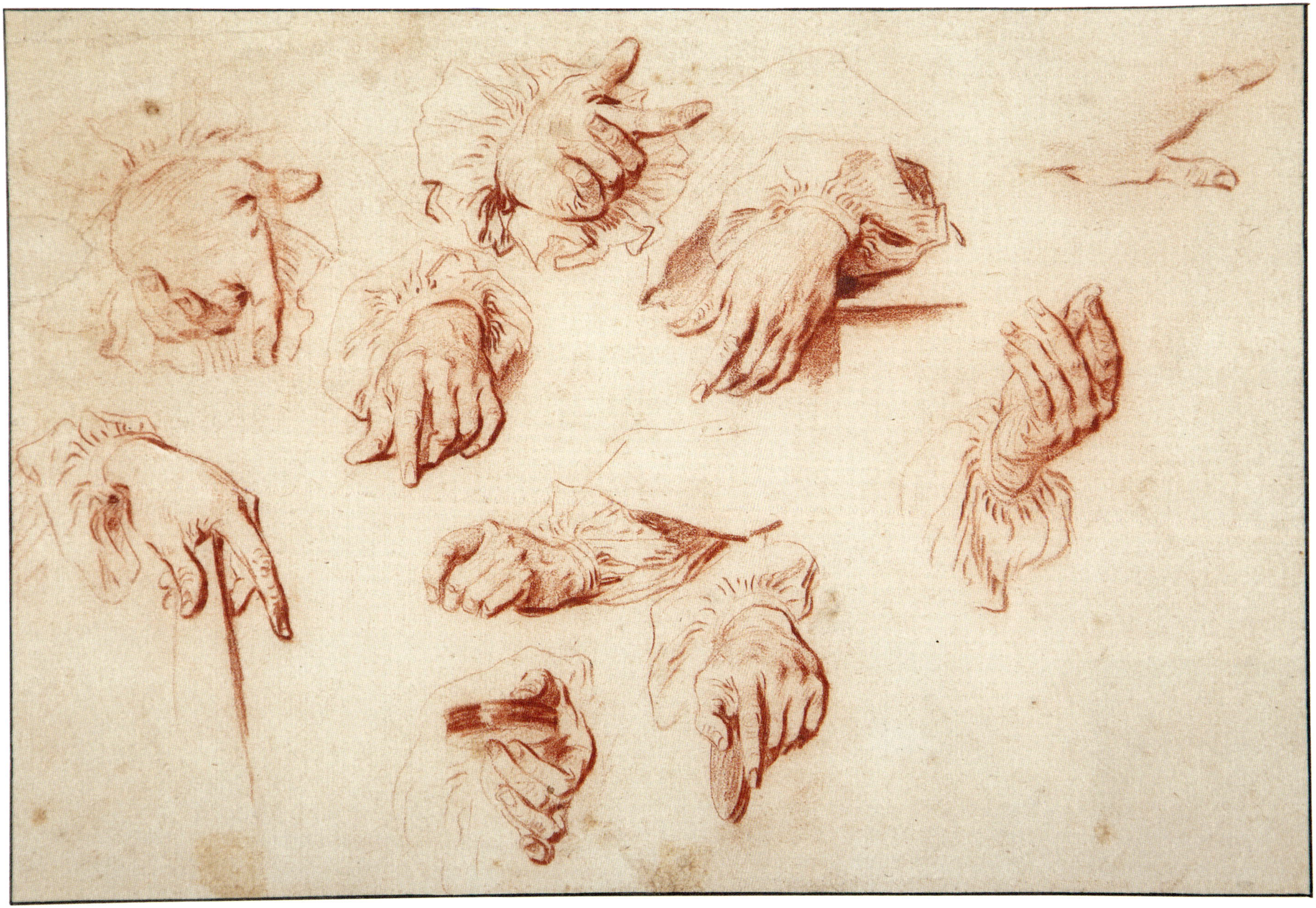

50

Sheet of Studies after Old Masters: Mystic Marriage of St Catherine, Holy Family

Red chalk on cream paper, 175 x 289 mm

The Samuel Courtauld Trust, The Courtauld Gallery, London, inv. PG 224

PROVENANCE, LITERATURE: PM 366; RP 422, col.

The manner in which Watteau copied the Old Masters did not develop over time. Although he sometimes copied with painstaking accuracy, as in some of the figures from Rubens in the Medici Gallery at the Musée du Louvre, he was also known to modify on occasion the coarseness of the original, for example in his celebrated copy of a drawing by Campagnola in the Musée du Louvre (cat. 35), in which he reproduces the figures much more delicately. In the present drawing, restraint gives way to a kind of relaxed lyricism, which allows the artist to use his red chalk with the fluidity of a paintbrush, particularly on the right-hand side.

It is not certain, in fact, that the right-hand part is copied from an Old Master, unlike the composition on the left, a Mystic Marriage of St Catherine, which can be compared with other paintings and drawings of the same subject by Paolo Veronese; some of Veronese's hallmarks can be spotted here, for instance the curly hair on the saint's head and the grouping of the three figures.

The sketch on the right, separated from the other by the palm frond held by St Catherine, has often been compared with a painting by Watteau of the Holy Family now in the State Hermitage Museum, St Petersburg (fig. 28). The variations are so considerable, however, that it is difficult to continue to support this opinion. It is amusing to note that the heads of the cherubs admiring the Holy Family appear directly above the palm frond held by the saint, further evidence of the separateness of the drawings; only a rapid glance might suggest that they had been produced at a single sitting.

One remarkable fact is that a composition close to the two appearing here appears among the paintings hanging in Gersaint's shop as depicted in *The Gersaint Shop Sign* (Schloss Charlottenburg, Berlin; fig. 4). Between the sales assistant behind the counter on the right and the young man inspecting the frame she presents to him, a painting is shown widthwise which, without any doubt, represents a Mystic Marriage of St Catherine. The composition could be the outcome of a kind of fusion between the two sides of the Courtauld Institute drawing. It has to be admitted, nevertheless, that there is more of the right-hand side of the drawing in the painting than of the left.

The liveliness of the line in this drawing suggests a date of *c.* 1715–16. L-AP

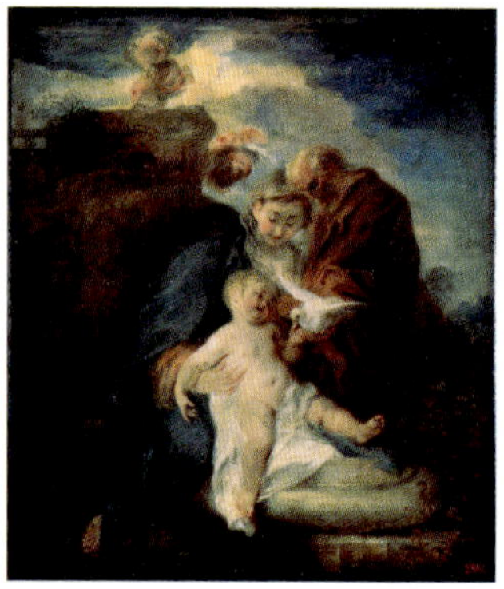

Fig. 28
The Holy Family (Rest on the Flight into Egypt), 1717–19. Oil on canvas, 129 x 97 cm. State Hermitage Museum, St Petersburg

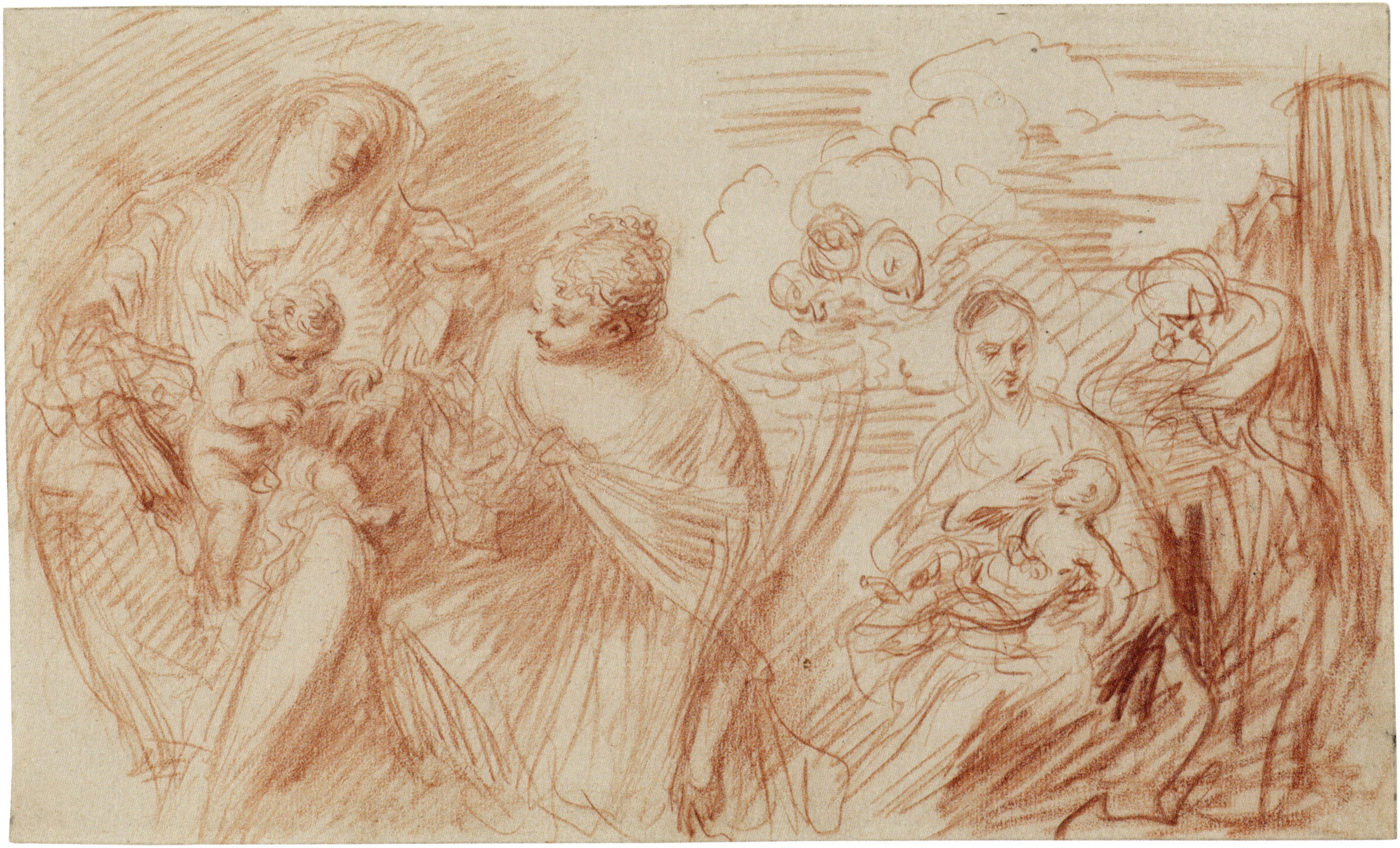

51

Brother Simon, after Zuccaro

Red and black chalks on paper, 242 x 185 mm
Inscription in pen and brown ink at lower right *Vataux fecit*; on the reverse side, inscription in black chalk *no 3205*

Musée Bonnat, Bayonne, inv. 83

PROVENANCE, EXHIBITED: PM 363; RP 423; Louvre mark (L. 1886a) at lower right; Paris 1997, no. 182
LITERATURE: PM 363; RP 423; Paris 1997, p. 174, no. 182 (Louis-Antoine Prat), col.

The earliest commentators interpreted this drawing as a depiction by Watteau of a person he had himself seen; at the Schwiter sale in 1883 the model was described as a fruit-seller, with the qualification that he was a Russian peasant. Edmond de Goncourt described him in the same terms in his 1875 catalogue of Watteau's works – without asking himself where and when Watteau might have met such a character!

In 1935 Pierre Lavallée, who admitted to having always considered the drawing to have been taken from life, identified the same model in a drawing by Federico Zuccaro (1540/41–1609) now in the Masson Collection at the Ecole des Beaux-Arts, Paris (fig. 29). This drawing is entitled *Portrait of Brother Simon*, and Zuccaro added on the reverse a long inscription describing the model: *Brother Simon, porter at (the Abbey of) Vallombrosa, with a dish of excellent Simian plums, on 24 August 1577*. Several other studies of peasants or clerics executed in 1577 by Zuccaro at Vallombrosa, a Benedictine house southeast of Florence, are known, but Watteau seems only to have copied this one, which he may have discovered among the Italian drawings brought back from Italy by Crozat in 1715. However, another drawing by Watteau after a *Self-portrait* by Zuccaro, using the same technique at the same date, now in a private collection in Paris (RP 424), is well known.

The confidence of the drawing and the monumentality of the treatment make it possible to connect this drawing chronologically with the series of Savoyards and Persians, *c.* 1715. This page is remarkable because of the use Watteau makes of red chalk, which subtly heightens the black chalk in the flesh tones; and there are powerfully drawn accents on the hand placed so firmly on the 'Simian plums'.

The genius of the artist is shown at its best in this involuntary experiment, so perfectly sustained; although he is copying a drawing one hundred and fifty years old, and of relatively inferior quality, the result is a great success. L-AP

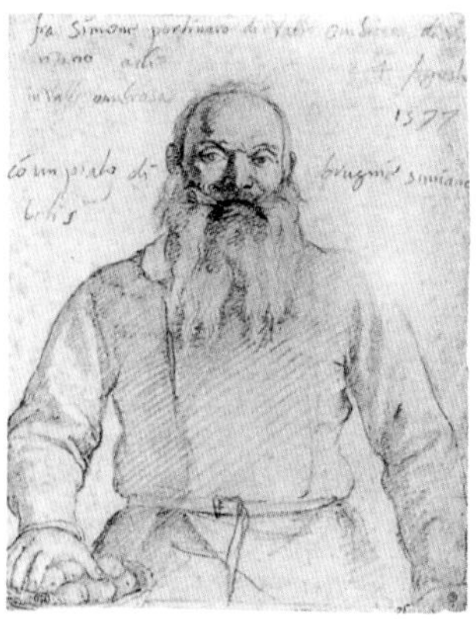

Fig. 29
Federico Zuccaro,
Portrait of Brother Simon, 1577.
Black and red chalk, 247 x 190 mm.
Ecole nationale supérieure des Beaux-Arts, Paris

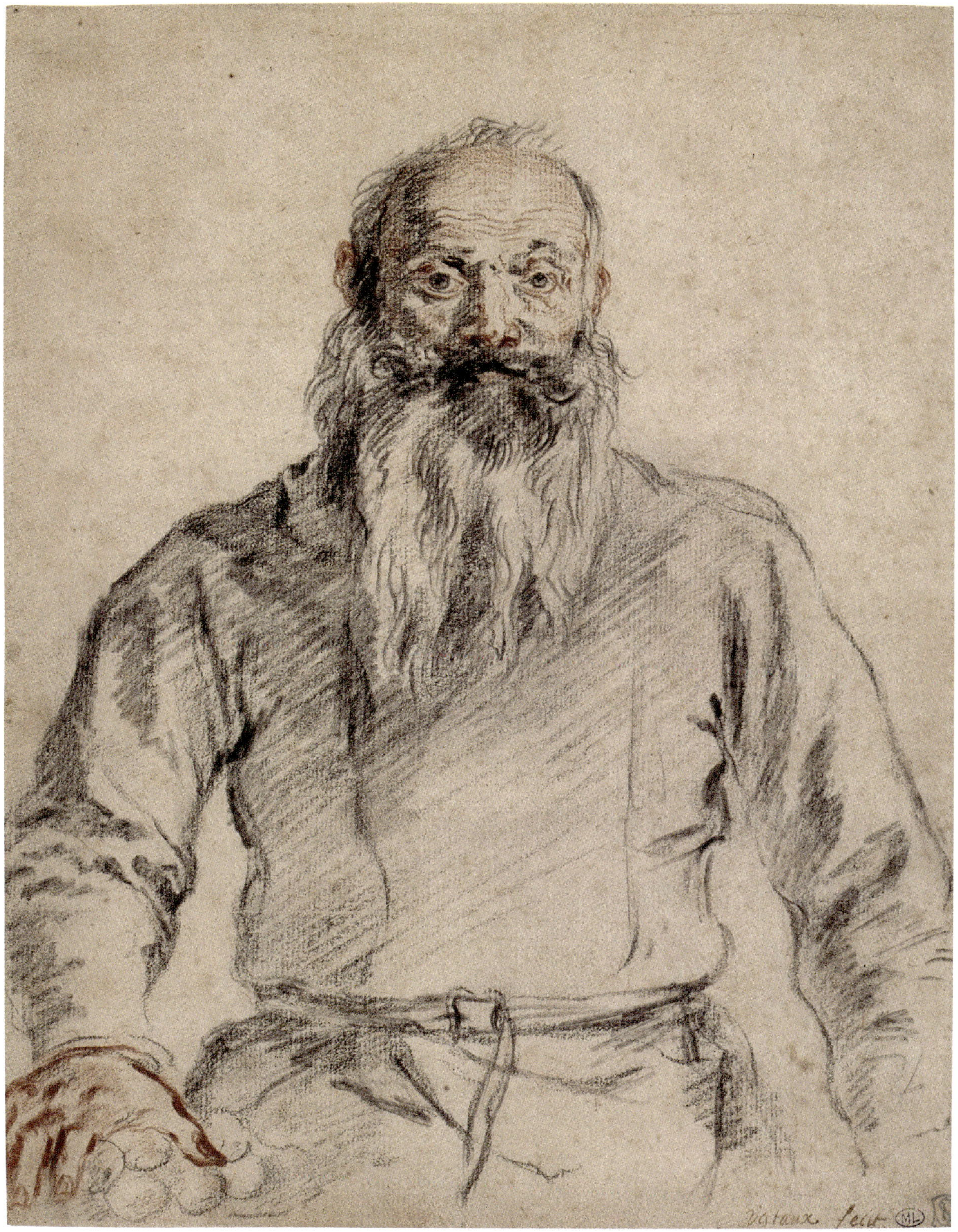

Red chalk and white heightening on grey-brown paper (recto); red chalk and white heightening on paper (verso), 220 x 252 mm; frame line drawn in pen and black ink

Private collection, New York

PROVENANCE, EXHIBITED: PM 343; RP 425, repr. recto and verso
ENGRAVINGS: PM 343; RP 425

52

Studies of Six Heads, after Le Nain, and a Head of a Bull, recto

Study of the Face of an Actor (Pierrot?) Leaning Forwards, verso

Watteau made copies of the paintings as well as the drawings of other artists. The homage he pays here to one of his predecessors is of another order, because it is taken from an artist who, to our certain knowledge, never drew. The Le Nain family, including Antoine, undoubtedly the author of the painting that inspired Watteau, seem never to have had recourse to preparatory drawings; we should remember that quite a number of great seventeenth-century artists – Velázquez, Vermeer, Caravaggio, Georges de La Tour – followed more or less the same practice.

Watteau cannot have been aware of this particularity when he decided to copy *Children's Dance* by Antoine Le Nain (fig. 30), of which there are several versions, the best and probably the original being now in a private collection in Switzerland (see Pierre Rosenberg, *Tout l'Œuvre peint des Le Nain*, Paris, 1993, no. 16, which also presents various derivations, including the present drawing, no. 16E).

One of the copies of this work was in England in the early eighteenth century, and the hypothesis has been voiced that the copy could have been made in 1720, when Watteau was in England. But the firm, contained style of the drawing suggests an earlier date – which one detail also confirms. The bull's head at the lower right can be compared with the head of Taurus in *Spring*, one of Crozat's *Seasons*. The preparatory drawings for this commission are now dated *c.* 1716–17, and thus this fine copy should probably date to the same period, executed from one of the versions of the painting that remained in France. Watteau depicted six of the eight figures in the painting, omitting the two farthest to the left. He has rendered the vivacity of the children most admirably and captured the more reflective quality of the old woman at the lower right.

On the reverse there appears a face that astonishingly seems to prefigure Watteau's *Pierrot*, called *Gilles* (fig. 17) in the Musée du Louvre. Here, however, the character (seen similarly from in front) is shown smiling rather hesitantly, and the unfinished nature of the face emphasises the fleeting nature of the smile. The actor leaning forward is reminiscent of the gesticulating figures to be found in Watteau's sketches for compositions, including a group of characters from the Commedia dell'Arte. The page from the Musée Jacquemart-André (cat. 82) is a striking example. L-AP

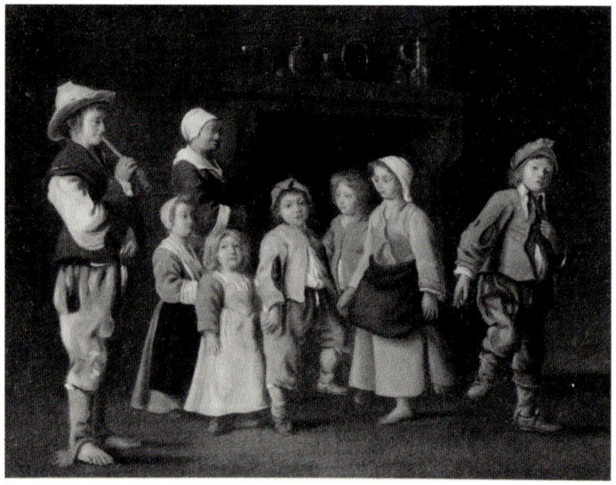

RIGHT
Fig. 30
Antoine Le Nain,
Children's Dance, 1643.
Oil on canvas, 33.4 x 40.2 cm.
Private collection, Switzerland

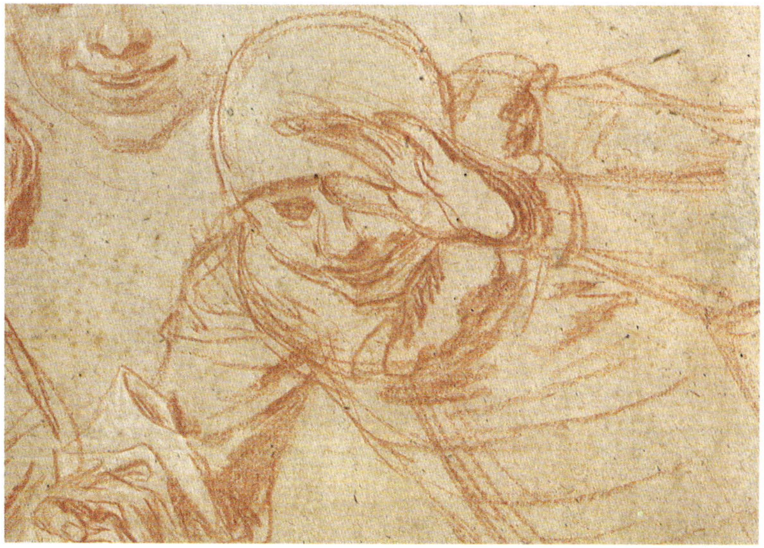

VERSO (DETAIL)

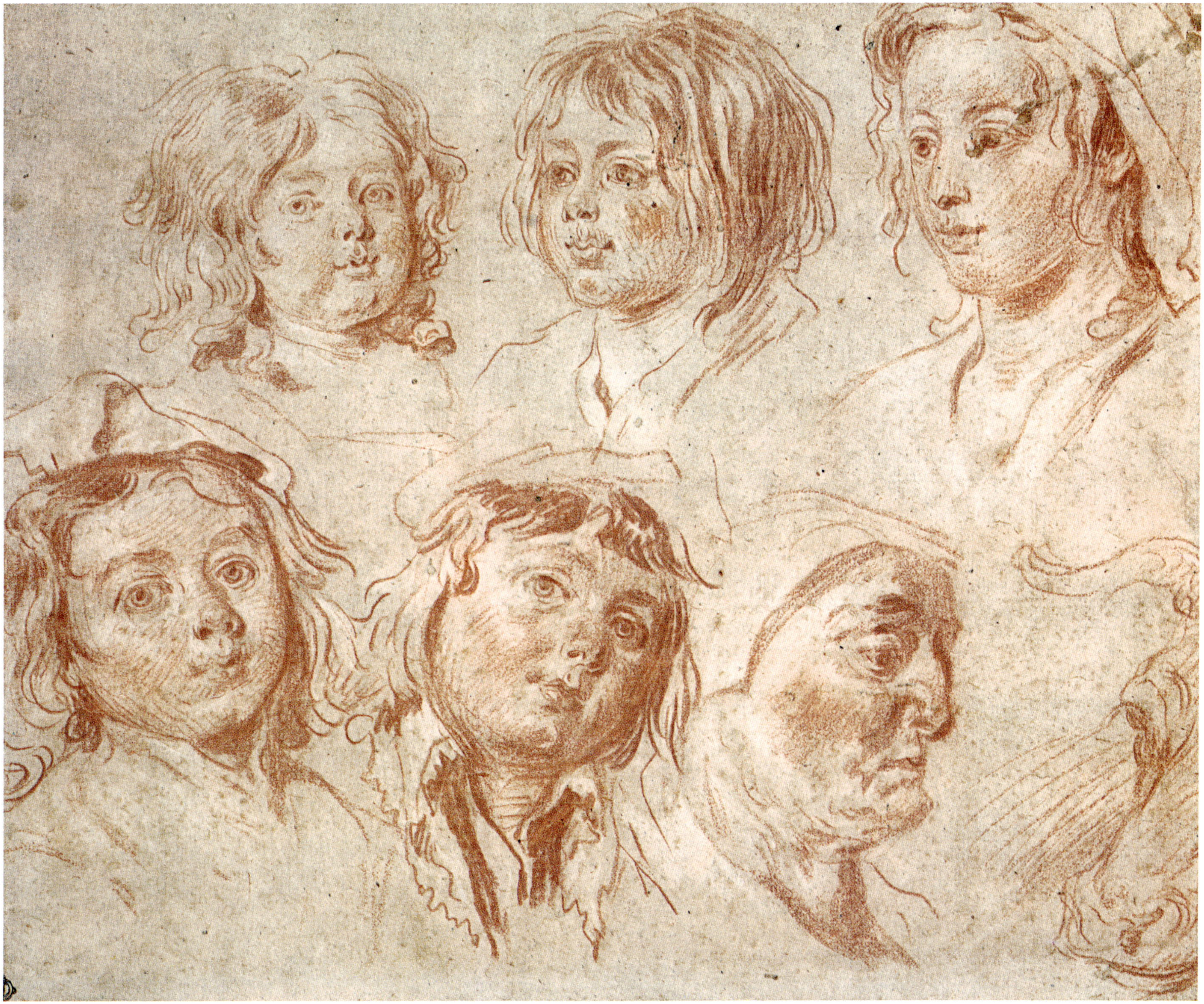

RECTO

53

Three Studies of a Young Girl Wearing a Hat

Red and black chalk, graphite on paper, 138 x 246 mm

Collection of Ann and Gordon Getty, San Francisco

PROVENANCE, LITERATURE:
PM 717; RP 438, col.; Bailey 1997, p. 46, figs 5, 48
COUNTER-PROOF, ENGRAVINGS:
PM 717; RP 438

Although it has never been exhibited before, this drawing fetched the highest price ever recorded for a drawing by Watteau when it came up for auction in the Gaines sale in 1986. And indeed, the inherent charm of the subject easily stands comparison with the high quality of the draughtsmanship. The page must have been even more seductive in its original state, when it included on the right – we know this by the existence of a more complete counter-proof (fig. 31) – a bust-length study of a young woman; this was detached from the rest and today is in a private collection (RP 439). The division must have taken place quite early on, as the bust-length study of the young woman bears the mark of Dominique Vivant Denon (d. 1825) and was engraved in his *Monuments des arts du dessin* (1829).

This is undoubtedly not the only intervention to which this magnificent drawing has been subjected, as the counter-proof indicates that the page used to be longer, above and below the three existing figures; the sheet bearing the separated female figure is 17 mm taller than this one. The deliberate reduction in size of the present sheet was very probably carried out in order to emphasise, by imposing a kind of physical concentration, the exceptional expressiveness of the three faces, or rather the three poses of the child – as Colin B. Bailey has rightly observed, these betray a mixture of timidity and curiosity. Also admirable is the rapidity of the treatment of the bonnets with an unusually firm black chalk, the delicacy of the flesh tones accentuated by small pencil strokes, and the vivacity of the three poses, which seem to anticipate the photographic snapshot.

The page can be dated with precision to around December 1716; this was when the Venetian painter Sebastiano Ricci was in Paris and made a copy after Watteau of the same child wearing the same hat. Ricci's drawing is now at Windsor Castle; it is known that Watteau also allowed Ricci to make copies of his other studies of children (private collection, New York, RP 440; Ricci's copies made from this page are also at Windsor). L-AP

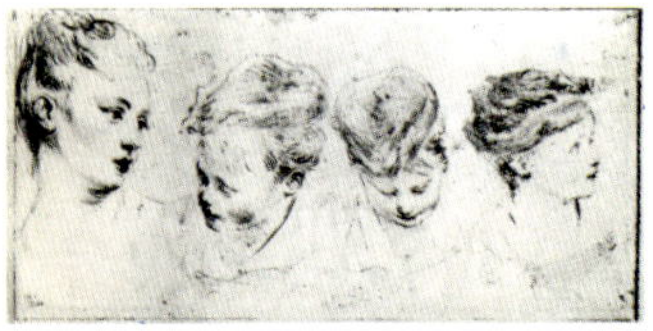

Fig. 31
Study of a Head of a Woman and Three of a Girl Wearing a Bonnet, counter-proof of RP 438.
170 x 325 mm. Whereabouts unknown

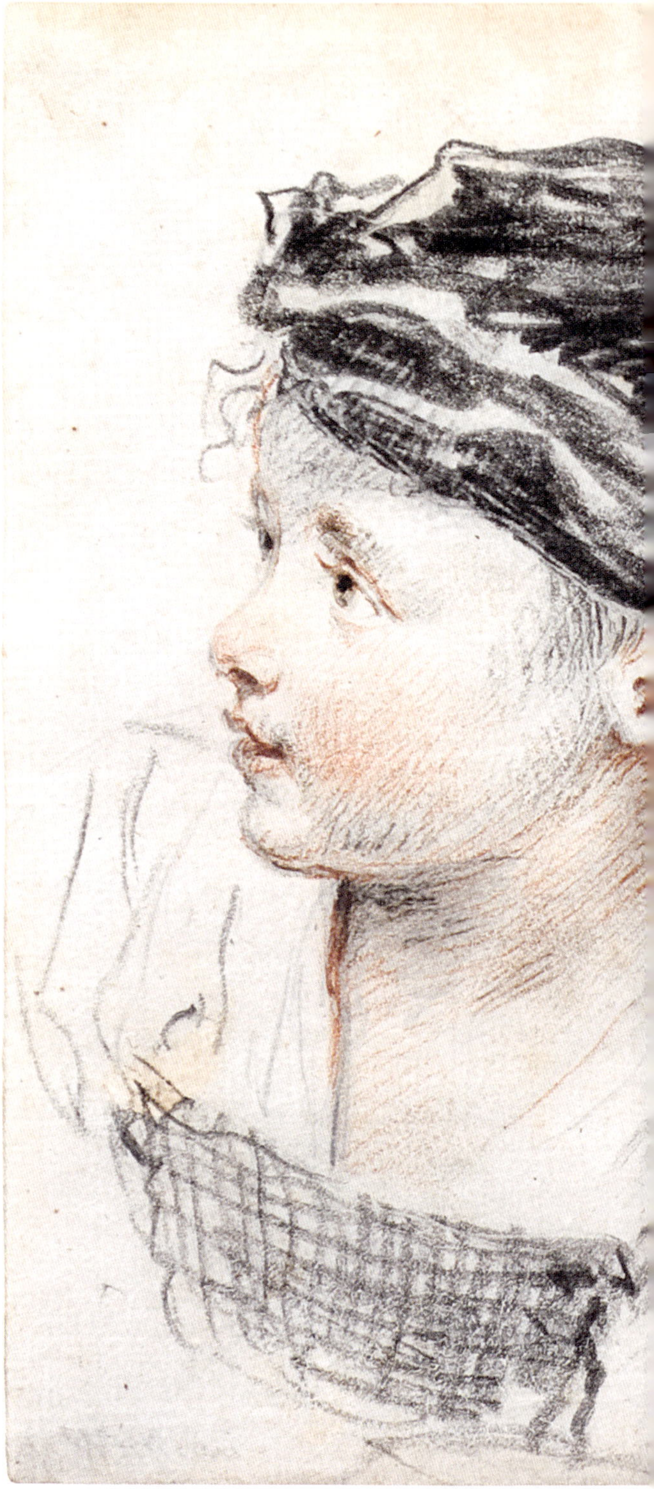

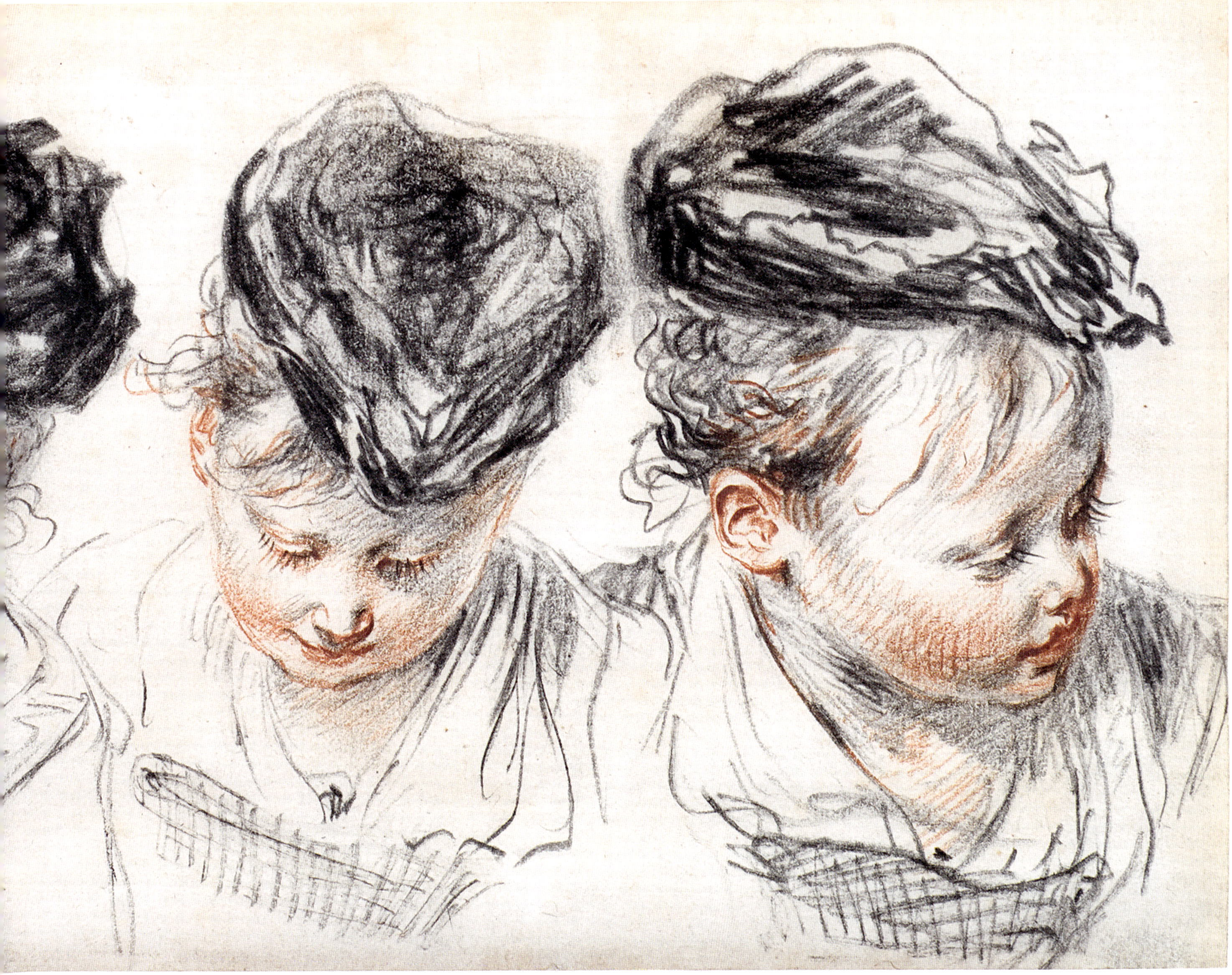

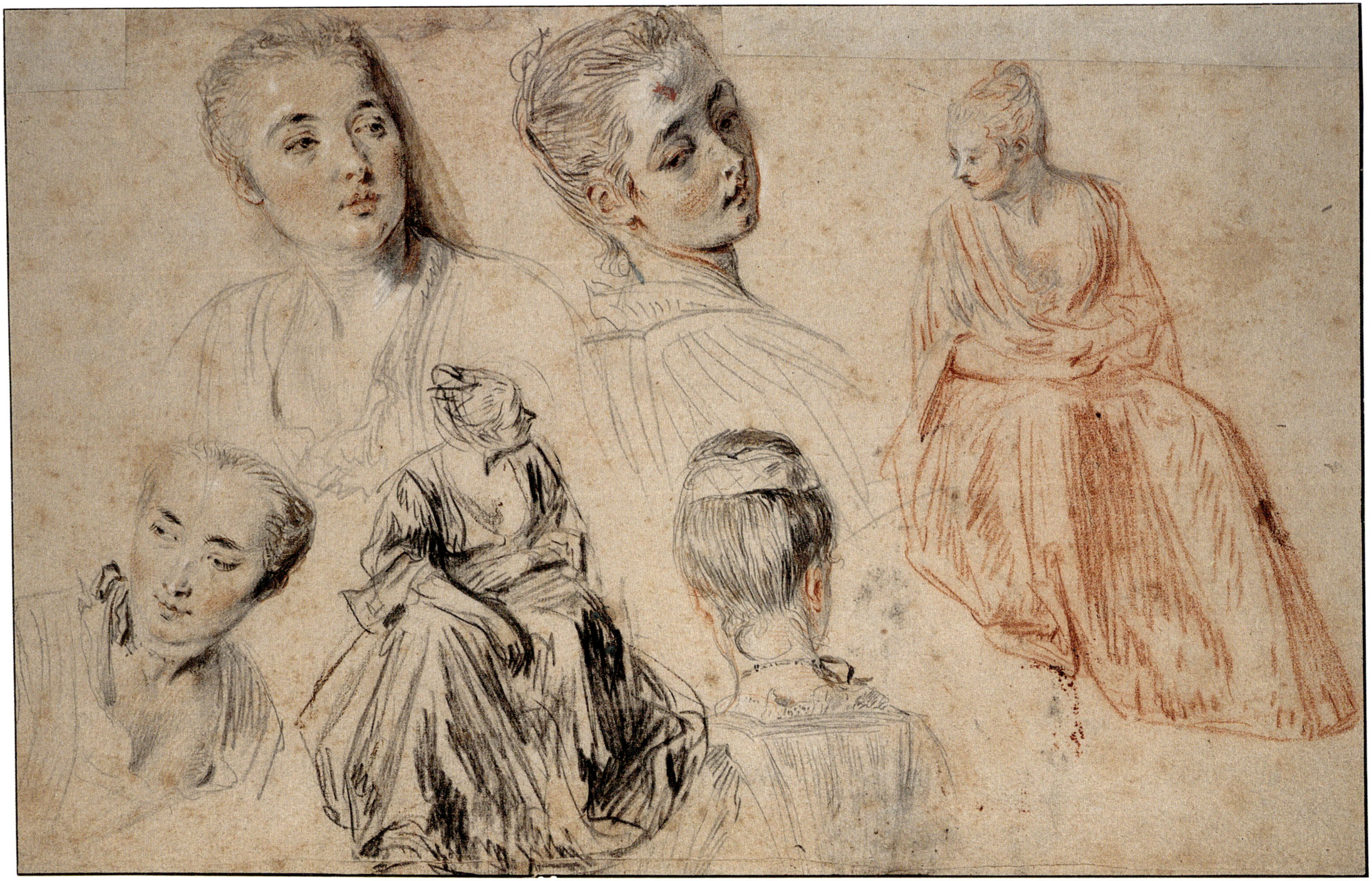

Red, black and white chalks, graphite, brush, brown wash and highlights using white gouache on cream paper, 230 x 353 mm; lacunae at left and top left; frame line drawn in pen and black ink

Rijksmuseum, Amsterdam, inv. 1953: 138. This drawing was recovered from Germany after the Second World War

PROVENANCE, EXHIBITED: PM 745; Paris 2003, no. 10, col.
LITERATURE: PM 745; RP 454, rep.; Temperini 2002, p. 19, col.
COPY: PM 745; RP 454

54

Four Studies of a Woman's Head and Two of a Seated Woman

The model who posed for these heads also appears in a drawing in the Teylers Museum, Haarlem (cat. 84), in which Watteau used similar highlights on brown wash, with the pigment heavily diluted with water. If the heads in the present sheet can be assigned to the years 1717–18, in our opinion the two studies of women that it also contains are earlier; Grasselli suggests a single date for the whole page (1717–18), whereas Roland Michel considers the heads to predate the full-length figures (1716 and 1718). This lack of certainty about dating is hardly surprising since we are looking at the work of an artist who neither signed nor dated his work and whose chronology is nothing if not imprecise. The study at the top left was used in *The Open-air Gathering* (Gemäldegalerie Alte Meister, Dresden; fig. 38), and the upper study in the centre in *Pleasures of Love* (Gemäldegalerie Alte Meister, Dresden).

The features of the young woman seated at lower left can be found almost identically – although drawn in a strongly synthetic style – on the face of a young woman on her knees, holding out her apron to gather up some flowers, in a drawing in the Musée de Valenciennes (RP 589); this image was also used again in *The Open-air Gathering*. L-AP

Red, black and white chalks on paper, 204 x 254 mm

Rijksmuseum, Amsterdam, inv. 1961: 96

PROVENANCE: PM 752; RP 455
EXHIBITED: Paris 2003, no. 11 (R. J. A. te Rijdt), col.
LITERATURE: PM 752; RP 455, col.

55

Crouching Child; Two Male Heads, One Wearing a Beret; Arms and Hands of a Recorder-player

The rich red of the chalk has survived miraculously well in this exquisite page of studies, which shows that Watteau was just as capable of producing a rapid, synthesising sketch (the child on the left) as he was of producing a delicate analysis of the gestures of a musician, or of expressing palpable empathy towards the two men whose heads alone can be seen, so perceptively described. The page was probably executed in two stages. The little girl (we assume), and the arms of the musician, which appear in the composition of *Woman Ogling* (whereabouts unknown; DV 13), can be ascribed to about 1716, and the heads probably to about 1718.

The page combines several of Watteau's favourite subjects – childhood, music and the theatre, as the face of the man seen at top right could well be that of an actor. L-AP

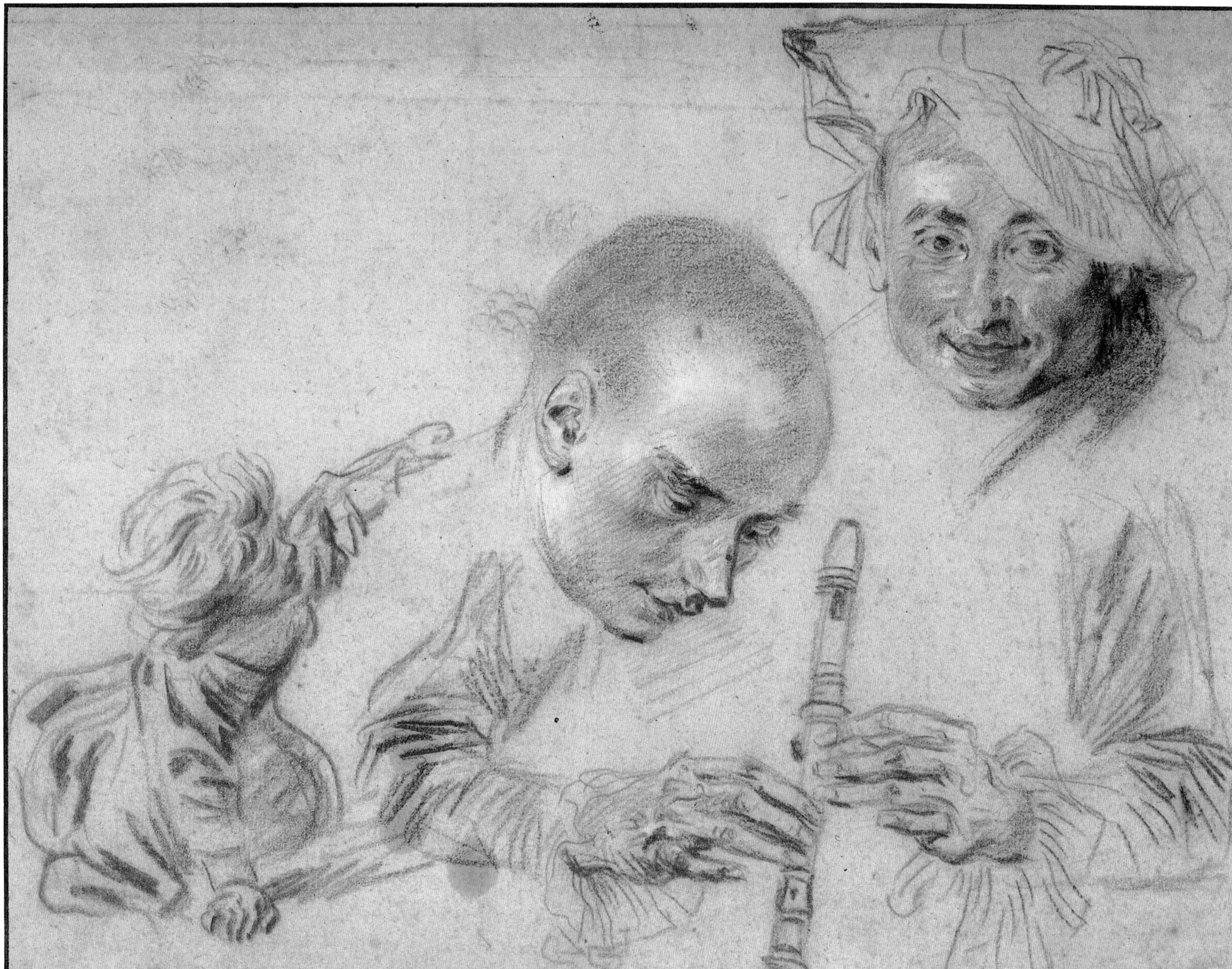

56

Seated Guitar-player

Red and black chalks, traces of graphite on paper, 264 x 203 mm

Musée du Louvre, Paris, Département des Arts graphiques, inv. RF 31370

PROVENANCE, EXHIBITED, LITERATURE: PM 839; RP 459, col.; Alan Wintermute in New York 1999, pp. 29, 30, fig. 18
COUNTER PROOF, ENGRAVINGS: PM 839; RP 459

The musician in this drawing faces in the same direction as the engraving in Dominique Vivant Denon's *Monuments des arts du dessin*, and it seems probable therefore that he owned it, although it does not bear his mark. We have one reservation, however: a counter-proof of the drawing exists in a private collection (RP 459a) and it could therefore be that Vivant Denon owned the counter-proof and had it engraved in the reverse direction. The page later entered the celebrated collection of Camille Groult, an unrivalled collection of drawings by Watteau that has now been completely dispersed.

The dazzling energy with which the red chalk is handled is slightly modified by the addition in black chalk of hatching along the body of the guitar, and subtle accents in the figure's hair; the graphite, which is finer, is reserved for the cuff from which the left hand emerges.

The model for this drawing reappears in many of Watteau's late drawings (RP 456, RP 461, RP 479, RP 484, RP 509, RP 591); his aquiline nose, pronounced eyebrows and dimples are easily recognisable.

As was his habit, Watteau used this drawing several times, placing the same guitar-player in *The Serenade* (Musée Condé, Chantilly), *The Surprise* (private collection; DV 31), which recently made a reappearance in the saleroom, and *The Open-air Gathering* (Gemäldegalerie Alte Meister, Dresden; fig. 38). In each case the costume and posture are identical and the position of the fingers painstakingly repeated. A date around 1715 could be suggested for this drawing, as the paintings in which the figure reappears belong either to this date (*The Serenade*) or to a later date (1716 for *The Surprise*, 1717–18 for the Dresden painting). The date of *c.* 1716 that we suggested in the catalogue raisonné was perhaps a year too late. L-AP

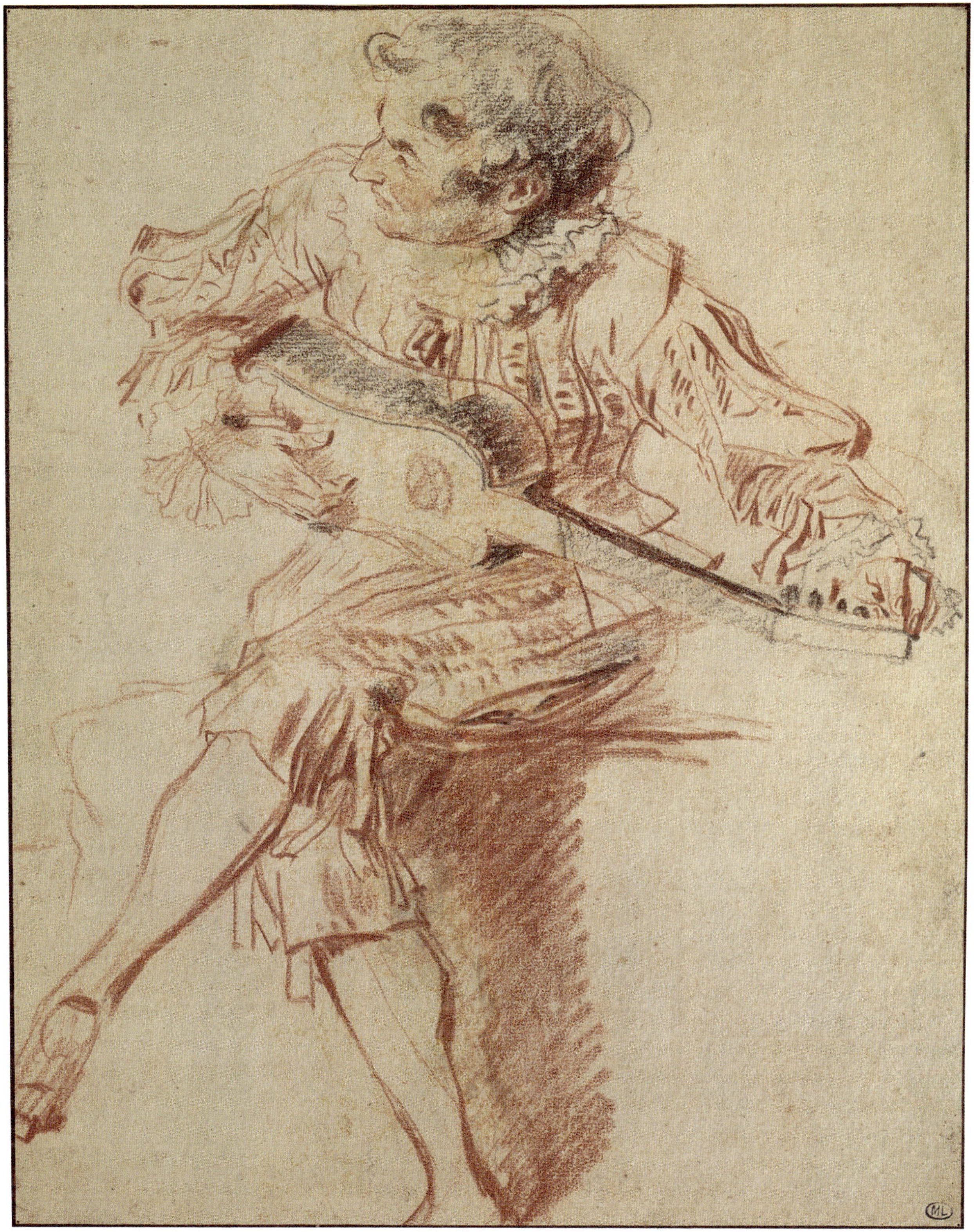

Red, black and white chalks with several tones of red chalk and graphite on beige-brown paper, 206 x 261 mm

Musée des Beaux-Arts, Rouen, inv. 822.1.76

PROVENANCE, EXHIBITED: PM 775; RP 461; Valenciennes 2004, no. 6
LITERATURE: PM 775; RP 461, col.; Temperini 2002, col. p. 19
COPY: PM 775; RP 461

57

Sheet of Studies with Five Male Heads, One Head of a Child, Two Hands Holding a Flute, and a Double Sketch of a Face at the Lower Right

Above the red chalk sketch of a face at the lower right (which has three eyes and two noses, as if Watteau had been uncertain where to place this rapidly abandoned head), it is just possible to make out a sketch of a costume on a half-length, headless figure. Several of the heads on this page, which is generally dated *c.* 1716, can be found in paintings. The Pierrot's head at the top left, the only head without any touches of black chalk, may possibly have been drawn slightly earlier than the others; it has often been linked with the *Outdoor Concert* (DV 72), although the hair of the figure in the engraving is much more luxuriant and his ruff is scalloped. The child at the lower left appears to be the same child as in the drawing of heads in the Fogg Museum (cat. 47). The man at the top right is used twice in engravings of paintings, *Indiscretion* (Museum Boijmans Van Beuningen, Rotterdam; DV 121) and *In the Dress of a Mezzetin* (Wallace Collection, London; DV 131), and the head in the lower centre appears in *Do You Want to Take Advantage of the Beauties?* (Wallace Collection, London; DV 84). Less certain (because the nose is less aquiline in the painting) is the link between the head on the right of the flute player's hands with the painting *Lesson in Love* (Nationalmuseum, Stockholm; DV 263); the hairstyle is very different and the hair longer. The intrusion of the flautist's hands into this series of faces adds a curious note to this collection of lively facial expressions – so dexterously laid out in relation to one another. L-AP

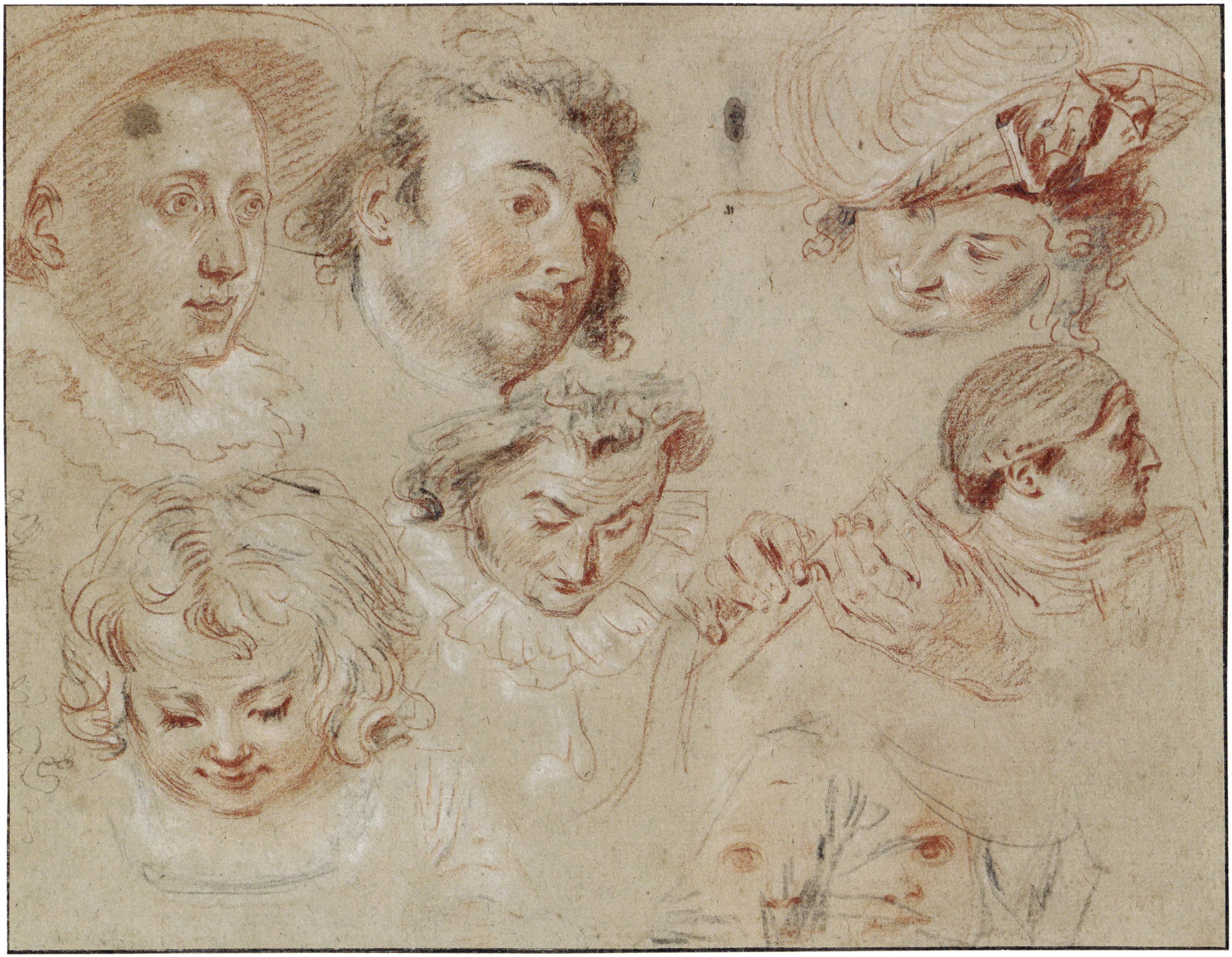

58

Seated Woman

58: lead and red chalk on paper, 155 x 94 mm; fully glued to backing

The Trustees of the British Museum, London, inv. 1895-9-15-935

PROVENANCE, EXHIBITED, LITERATURE: PM 601; RP 587, repr.
ENGRAVINGS: PM 601; RP 587

59

Woman Seen from the Back Seated on the Ground, Leaning Forward

59: red and black chalk, wash and graphite on paper, 145 x 182 mm; fully glued to backing

The Trustees of the British Museum, London, inv. 1895-9-15-936

PROVENANCE, EXHIBITED, LITERATURE: PM 610; RP 467, col.
ENGRAVINGS: PM 610; RP 467

These two drawings mounted together were acquired with the Malcolm Collection in 1895. One is much more famous than the other, but Marianne Roland Michel wonders whether they may originally have been part of the same sheet. Although they are similar in technique, the precision of the second contrasts with the character of the first, which has a certain fluidity and a quality of evanescence, and is less painstakingly drawn. The relationship between the black chalk, red chalk and graphite is different also, the gown of the female figure lying on the ground being scored with parallel, wavy lines drawn with obsessive care. The only connection between the two studies lies in the fact that both were engraved by the same artist, François Boucher, in *Figures de différents caractères*. We know that the young Boucher bagged the lion's share of this collection – Jean de Jullienne commissioned him to reproduce more than 100 drawings by Watteau (116 out of the 351 sheets).

The figure in cat. 59 was very obviously used (wearing a small *toque*) in *Pleasures of Love* (Gemäldegalerie Alte Meister, Dresden). It is also reproduced, much more discreetly, in *Rustic Entertainments* (Wallace Collection, London). The seated female figure can be found in the background of the same painting as well as in *The Charms of Life* (Wallace Collection, London; DV 183), in which she wears a pearl fillet on her head. Margaret Morgan Grasselli suggests a date of 1717–18 for the two drawings. In our catalogue raisonné we felt that the tidier of the two possibly belonged to a slightly earlier date. L-AP

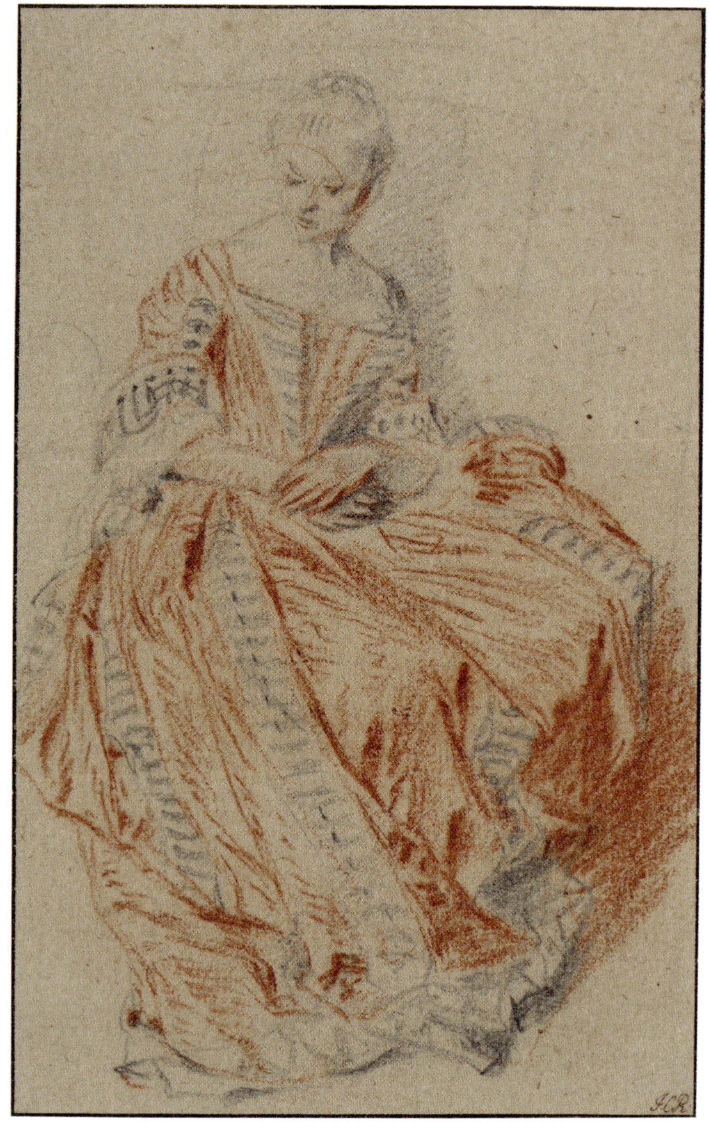

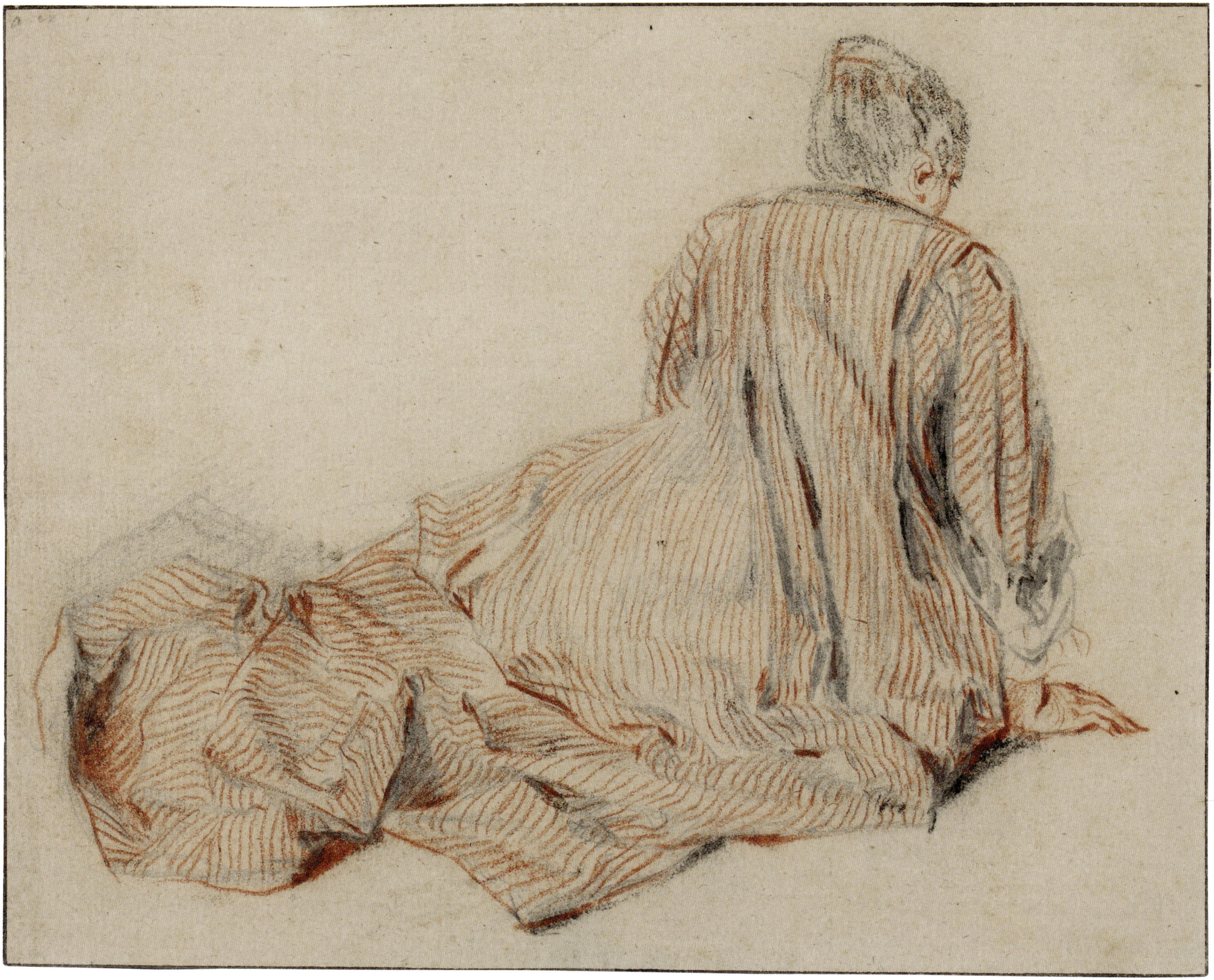

Red, black and white chalks on brownish paper, 231 x 264 mm; fully glued

Rijksmuseum, Amsterdam, inv. 1953: 186. This drawing was recovered from Germany after the Second World War

PROVENANCE, EXHIBITED, LITERATURE: PM 557; RP 476, col.; Paris 2003, no. 12 (R. J. A. te Rijdt), col. and detail on the cover
ENGRAVINGS: PM 557; RP 476

60

Studies of a Seated Woman and a Detail of Her Head and Shoulders

When Jean de Jullienne distributed Watteau's drawings to be engraved by a team of engravers for his two collections of *Figures de différents caractères* (1726–28), it seems very likely that he insisted that a single engraver take responsibility for reproducing with his graving tool the various figures that originally appeared on the same page; the present Amsterdam drawing is therefore one of the very rare cases in which two engravers, François Boucher and Laurent Cars, took on separately the two subjects on this outstanding page.

This drawing, whose authority and its intensive use of whites allow it to be dated *c.* 1716, has been linked to various paintings: *An Elegant Gathering* (DV 139), *Playful Conversation* (DV 95) and *The Family* (Rothschild Collection, Switzerland; DV 86). Since we know that the last-named painting portrayed the Le Bouc-Santussan family, it has been suggested that the drawing must depict Mme Le Bouc-Santussan, but in fact the comparison between the drawing and the painting is inconclusive. The work to which the figure in the drawing comes closest remains *An Elegant Gathering*: also in the drawing there is a rapid sketch in red chalk of the man who turns towards the young woman in the painting. L-AP

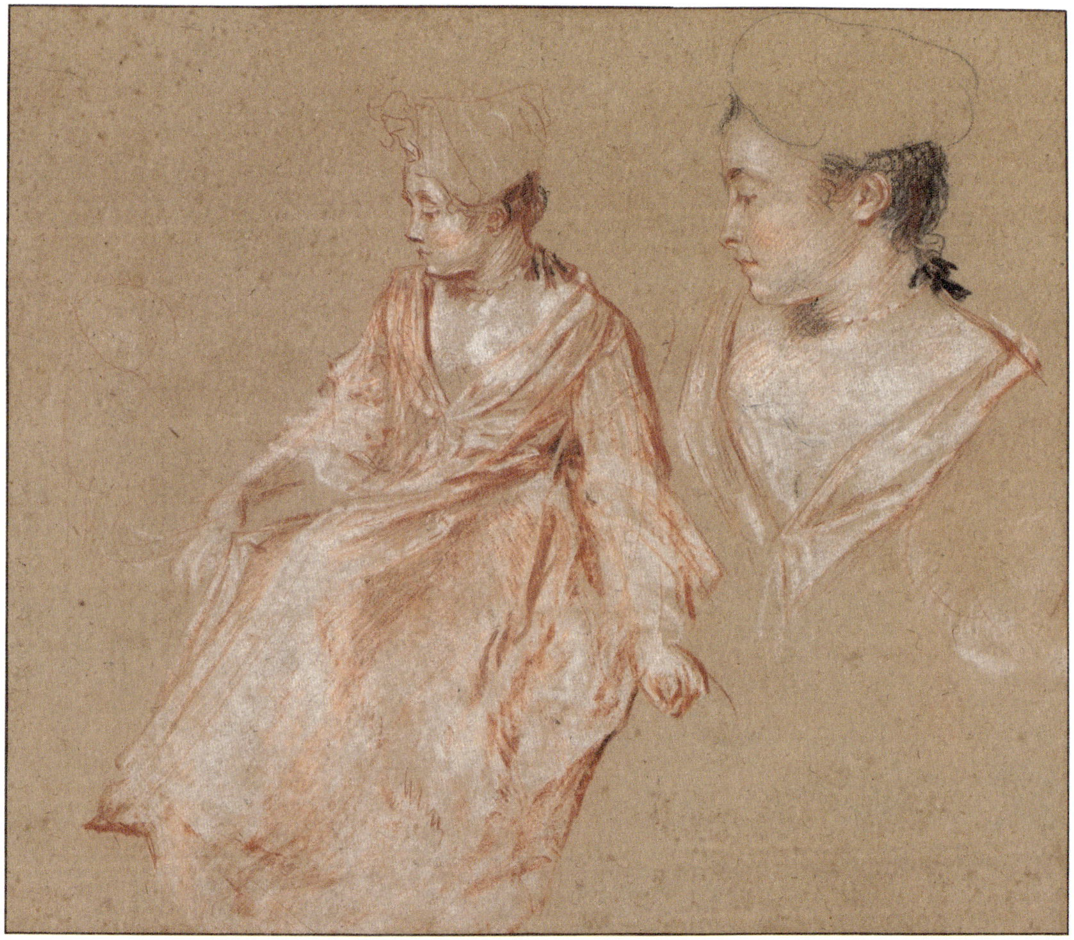

Red, black and white chalks on beige paper, 271 x 190 mm; pasted down

Museum Boijmans Van Beuningen, Rotterdam, Koenigs Collection, inv. F.I. 281

PROVENANCE, EXHIBITED, LITERATURE: PM 662; RP 477, col.
COPY: PM 662; RP 477

61

Standing Man Wearing a Cape, His Right Arm Extended

Like Grasselli, we have dated this drawing to *c.* 1716. The highly synthetic nature of the page is as striking as the manner in which the figure has been drawn. The impression is given that the cape was drawn on its own first, before the face and the arms and legs of the character were sketched in far more rapidly. The face appears to have been savagely treated, like a sort of mask lit by a theatrical spotlight, the light also spilling over onto the cape with its luminous white highlights. This figure has sometimes been linked to a celebrated but very small painting in the Musée du Louvre, *The Indifferent.* But both the posture and the cape are inverted in the painting, the left hand is hidden by the garment in the present drawing and the facial expressions of the two figures bear no relation to each other; that of the drawing is much calmer than that of the painting. L-AP

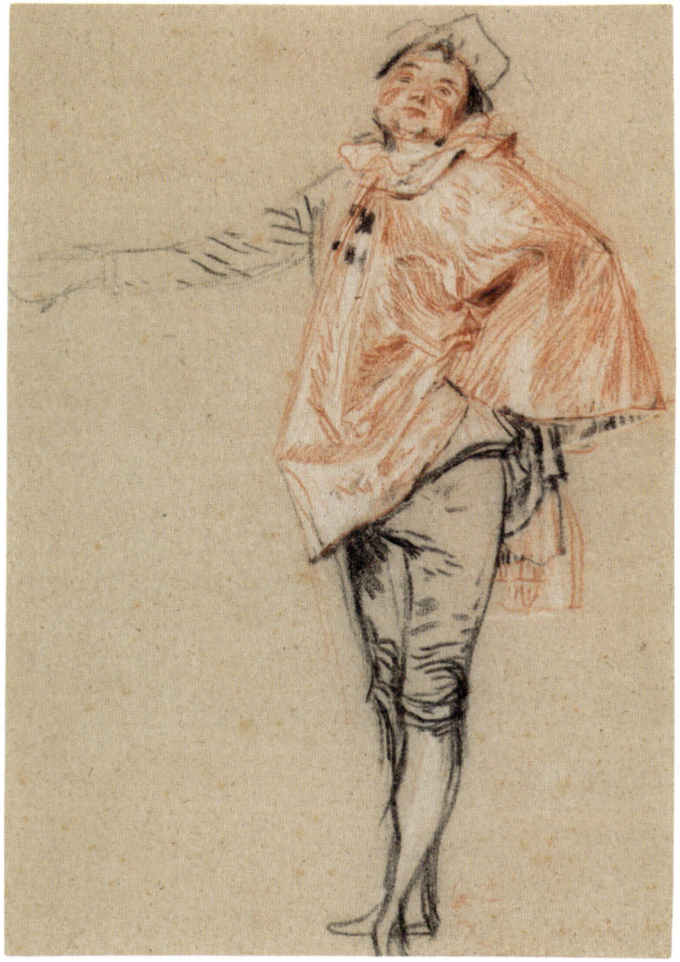

Red, black and white chalks on brown paper, 242 x 379 mm; one part missing (128 x 47 mm), restored at lower left

The Trustees of the British Museum, London, inv. 868-8-8-1275

PROVENANCE, EXHIBITED, LITERATURE: PM 830; RP 479, col.; Alan Wintermute in New York 1999, pp. 29, 30, fig. 20

62

Two Studies of a Guitar-player and One of a Figure, His Right Arm Outstretched

We date this sheet to *c.* 1716. The hand and outstretched arm were used in *The Prospect* (Museum of Fine Arts, Boston); they could also be compared with a page of studies of three hands, also in the British Museum (RP 507) and dated by us to *c.* 1716–17. The arm seems to have been drawn above the beret of the musician on the left, who is identifiable as one of Watteau's regular male models; the artist has emphasised his large, aquiline nose in numerous other studies. This figure was very probably drawn before the artist, standing back from the page, started on the full-length figure of the guitarist on the right-hand side of the page. This second figure was also used in *The Prospect*, without the beret – indeed, bare-headed.

The larger of the two studies has been used in various paintings: *The Scale of Love* (National Gallery, London; DV 199), *An Elegant Gathering* (DV 139) and *Elegant Pastimes* (Schloss Charlottenburg, Berlin). On each occasion the male character leans towards a young woman who appears to be charmed by his music. The beret is much flatter in *The Scale of Love* than in the other two compositions.

The accident visible at the lower left, which has permanently erased the end of the guitar, is to be deplored. But the concentration conveyed by the character, whose rough features contrast so markedly with the music he produces – one can almost hear its delicacy – contribute in no mean degree to the beauty of the page, such a rarity in portraying a male protagonist in action; it makes one wonder whether Watteau is simply depicting a model holding an instrument, or whether he has made a portrait of a genuine musician. L-AP

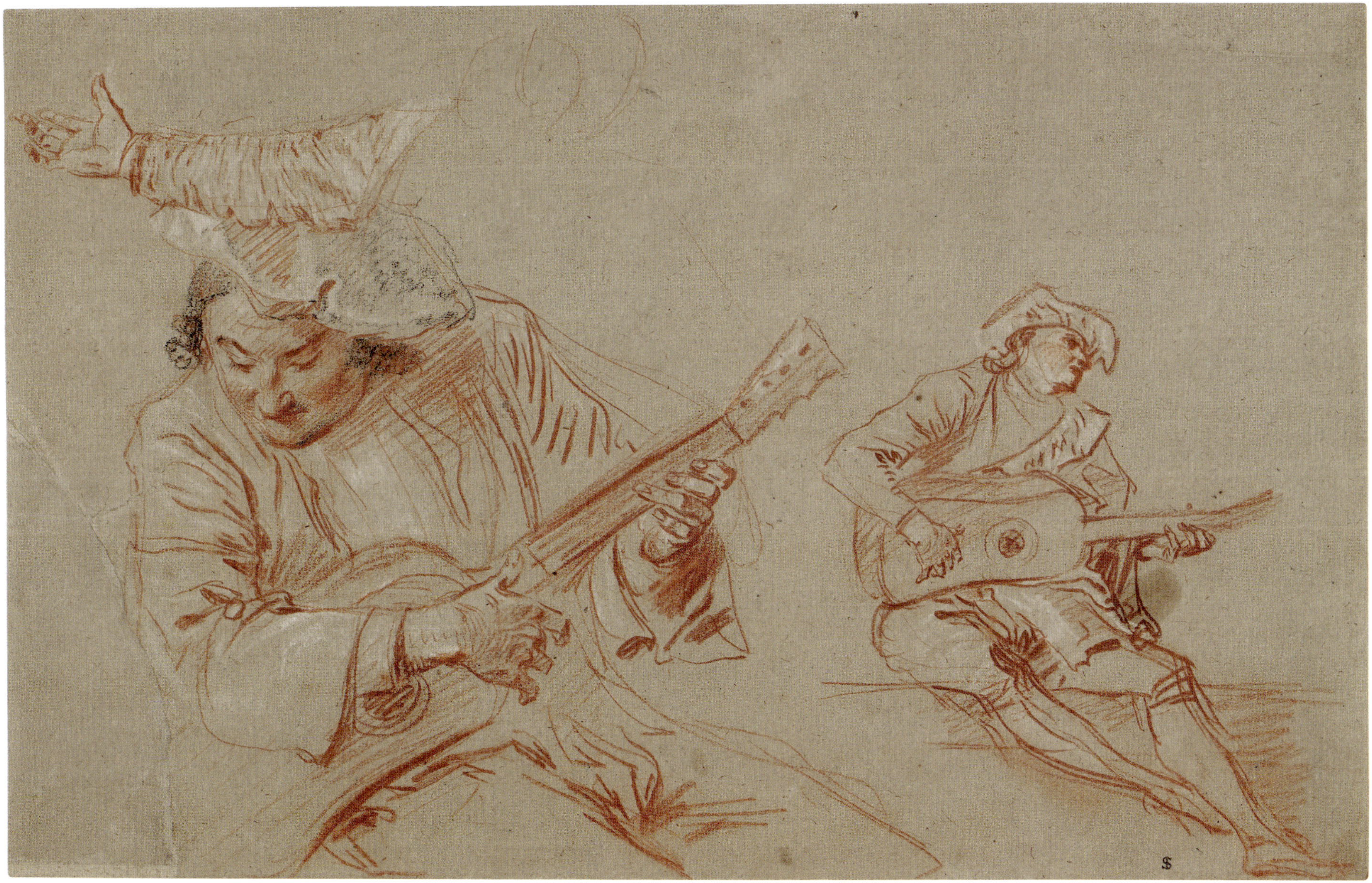

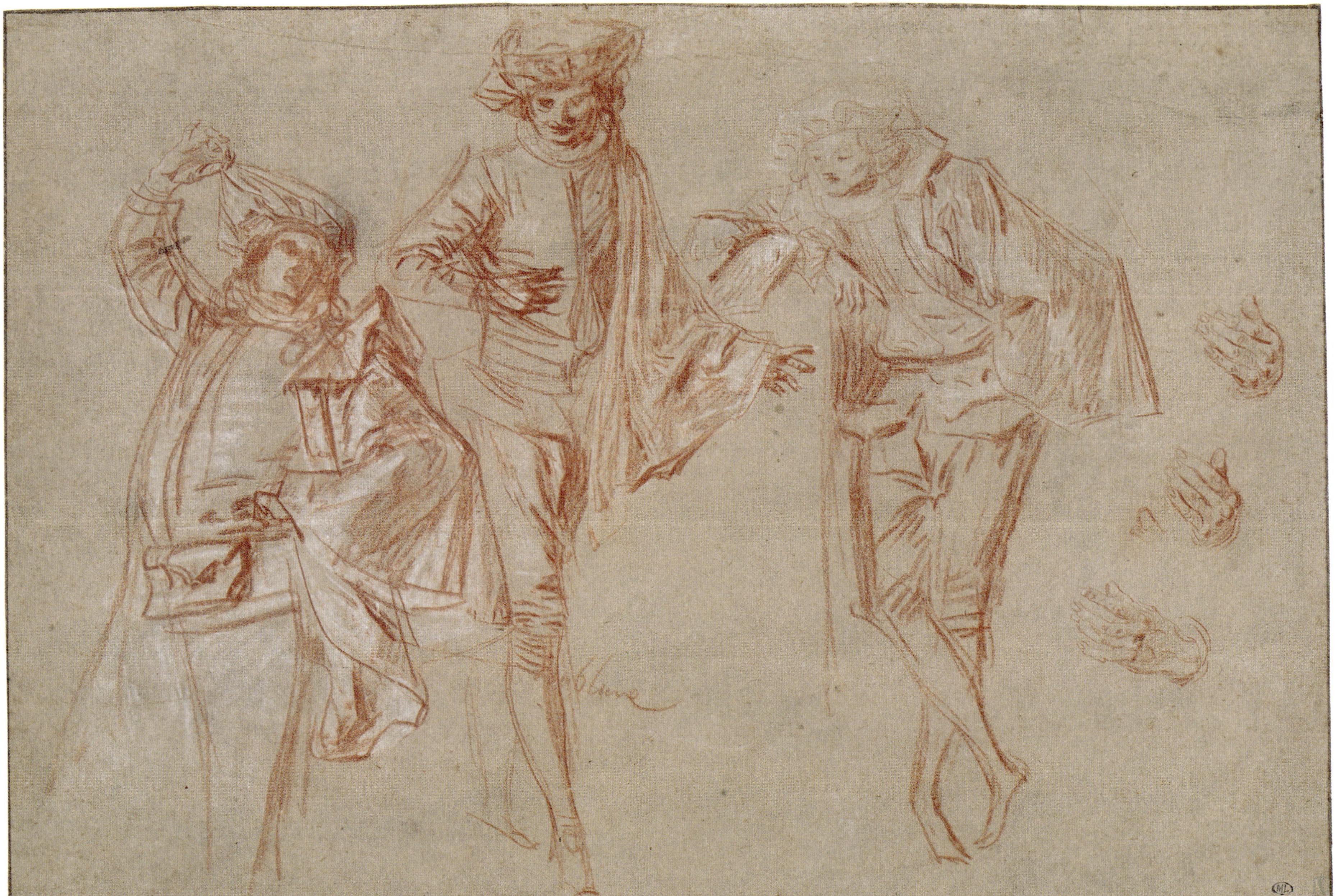

63

Three Studies of a Man Wearing a Beret and Three Studies of a Left Hand

Red chalk and white highlights on grey-brown paper, 264 x 387 mm

Musée du Louvre, Paris, Département des Arts graphiques, inv. RF 28979

PROVENANCE, EXHIBITED, LITERATURE: PM 670; RP 480, col.

With this drawing, we may be in the presence of a unique object, as the page bears a manuscript note that stands a good chance of being in Watteau's own hand. The word *doublure* (lining) inscribed in red chalk is prolonged leftwards by a faint straight line that appears to join a folded-back part of the cape of the figure on the left at the spot where a heavier line in red chalk must be intended to draw attention to the fact that the cape is turned back and that therefore its lining is revealed. A handwritten list of clothing, unfortunately curtailed, on the reverse side of a small sketch of a seated woman now in a private collection in New York (RP 275) is accompanied by a study of an arm and a left hand indisputably by Watteau; the list mentions nightshirts, cuffs and handkerchiefs. The handwriting looks as if it might be the same, but there is no absolute proof. Evidently the 'Watteau mystery' does not exist only in his paintings and drawings.

The most curious feature of this handsome drawing of the same model in various poses is that certain elements of it can be found, completely straightforwardly, in a painting that must belong to the same date, *The Pleasures of the Ball* (Dulwich Picture Gallery), in which we see a person leaning an elbow on a low entablature, although his cape is raised less high on the right; and also, and this is more unexpected and difficult to explain, in *The Village Sweetheart* (Sir John Soane's Museum, London; DV 116), which must date from 1715 at the latest. Margaret Morgan Grasselli has linked the latter composition with the three small studies of hands on the right of the present sheet.

The grace and freedom of the drawing style seem to suggest a date slightly later than 1715. Was the painting reworked at a later date? Or did Watteau make his model strike poses that he had already practised elsewhere? L-AP

64

The Remedy

Red, black and white chalks on brownish paper, 234 x 371 mm

The J. Paul Getty Museum, Los Angeles, inv. 86.GB.594

PROVENANCE, EXHIBITED: PM 865; RP 486; New York 1999, no. 24, col. and detail, p. 93
LITERATURE: PM 865; RP 486, col.

The Remedy seems more successfully finished than the majority of Watteau's drawings. The recumbent form of the naked young woman is depicted with unusual precision; the servant girl, who holds a clyster syringe prior to administering an enema, seems merely sketched in by comparison, and part of the figure is repeated over the existing image. Below the servant a preliminary study for the head of the naked young woman can be distinguished, turned round – or perhaps it belongs to another character, as it would have been unwise to begin the study of a recumbent figure on the right-hand side of the page.

In the case of the servant girl, another study of her exists, on the same page as two probably later studies of men's heads, in a drawing in the Musée du Louvre (fig. 32). Examination of the latter sheet makes it clear that the servant is kneeling rather than standing behind the bed; the present drawing, however, does not allow us to reach this conclusion.

The relationship between this drawing and a painting now in the Norton Simon Museum, Pasadena, *Naked Woman Lying Down*, which appears to have been cut off at the right, at the level of the naked young woman's knees, has often been noted. Both drawing and painting may be ascribed to *c.* 1716–17. L-AP

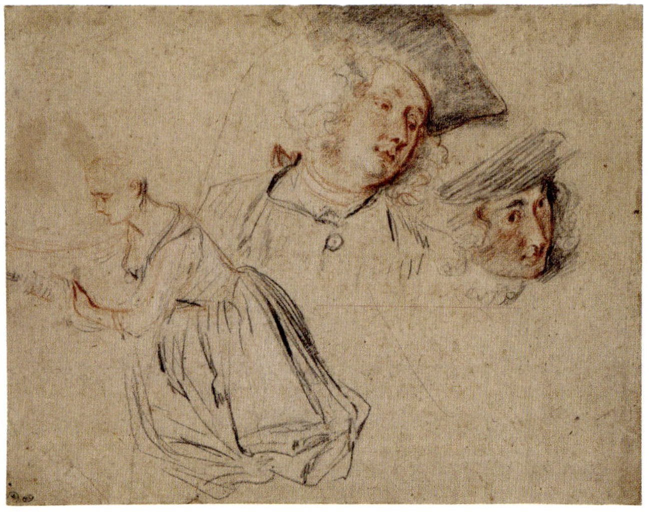

Fig. 32
Study of a Servant Girl Kneeling and Turning to the Left, Holding a Clyster Syringe; and Two Studies of Men's Heads Turning to the Right, 1716–17. Three chalks, 260 x 330 mm. Musée du Louvre, Paris

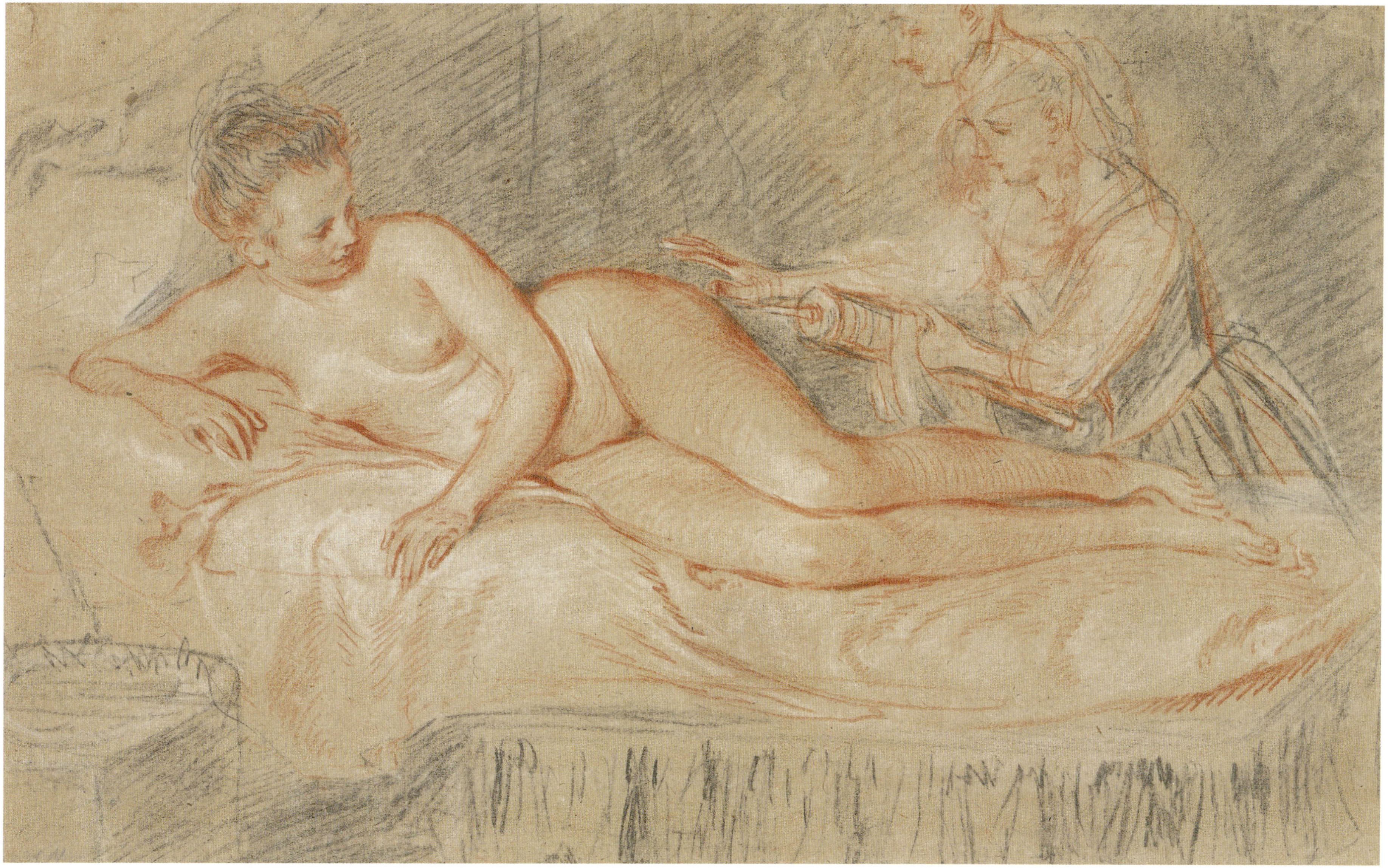

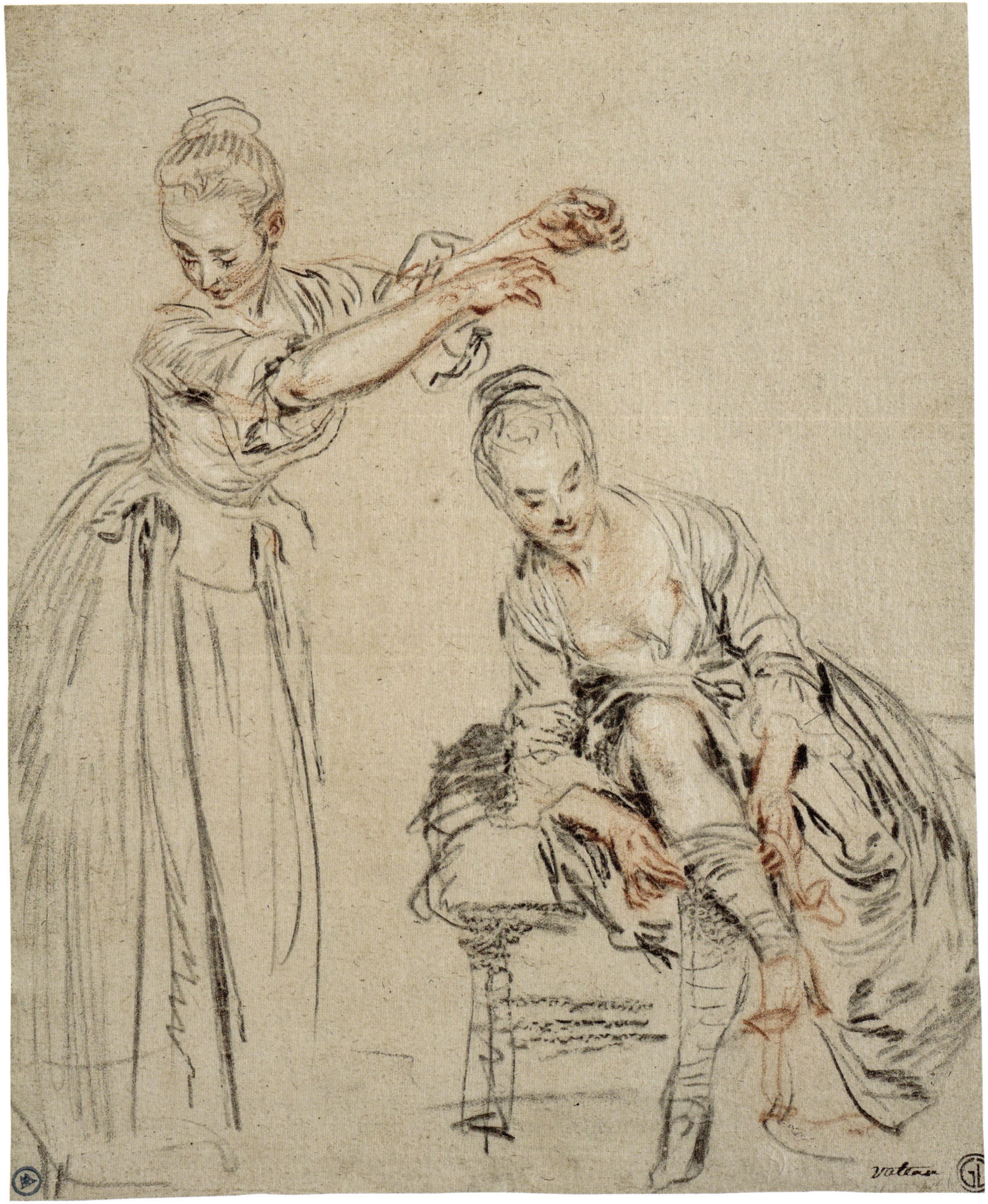

65

Two Studies of Women, the One on the Left with Arms Raised; the One on the Right Seated, Pulling up Her Stocking

Red, black and white chalks, black chalk and graphite on cream paper, 225 x 205 mm
Inscription in pen and brown ink at lower right *Vateau*

Nationalmuseum, Stockholm, inv. NM 280/1980

PROVENANCE, EXHIBITED, LITERATURE: PM 632; RP 488, col.

The two women in this drawing may not have posed at the same time, although both were drawn in *c.* 1716–17. The attitude of the woman on the left seems to have been posed with a very specific objective: in the two paintings in which she appears, *Lesson in Love* (Nationalmuseum, Stockholm; probably the reason for the museum's acquisition of the drawing in 1980) and *The Open-air Gathering* (Gemäldegalerie Alte Meister, Dresden; fig. 38), she is seen in the same position, distracted from her task of gathering flowers and looking down at another woman placed at a lower level.

The young woman on the right does not appear in any painting. She seems to be seated at one end of a sort of chaise longue or day-bed rather than on a stool; this detail makes it possible to compare her with the young models who posed, in a greater or lesser state of undress, stretched out on a seat of this type, in drawings made in 1717–18 (RP 578 to RP 583 and RP 585). As in the drawing now in the Fondation Custodia, Paris (RP 585), the model's nipples are marked with a light pencil stroke at the very edge of her bodice. L-AP

66

Two Dancers

Red, black and white chalks on cream paper, 269 x 229 mm; a fragment of paper (105 x 23 mm) has been added at upper right; frame line drawn in pen and brown ink
Inscription at lower left in pen and brown ink *Watteau*; on the reverse side, inscription in black chalk *Auberge Watteau*

Klassik Stiftung, Weimar, inv. NR 1015

PROVENANCE, EXHIBITED: PM 545; RP 495, repr.; Eidelberg 2002, pp. 222, 224, fig. 8, p. 231, note 37; Weimar 2005, no. 40 (Pierre Rosenberg), col.
ENGRAVING: PM 545; RP 495

Whether Goethe acquired this drawing from the dealer Johann Gottlieb Simmel (1766–1836) in 1814, or from another dealer, Carl Gustav Boerner (1790–1855), in 1828 is not clear. Either way, the page is one of the finest pieces in his collection of drawings, now in Weimar. It juxtaposes two figures, only one of which, the figure on the right, was engraved by Benoît Audran as no. 74 in the *Figures de différents caractères*; in the print, the dancer appears with her hat on her head, whereas in the painting in which she appears later, *Venetian Festivities* (National Gallery of Scotland, Edinburgh), she is bareheaded, with a slight alteration to her bodice on the left shoulder.

The man can be found in a painting now in private hands, *The Artist's Dream*, which, despite Martin Eidelberg's claims in 2002, is still challenged by some; other figures from drawings by Watteau are juxtaposed with this one in a composition whose subject is an extremely unexpected one for the period, and some still consider it a nineteenth-century pastiche. Our catalogue raisonné puts the date of the present drawing at 1715–16, whereas Margaret Morgan Grasselli hesitates in her publications between our date and 1716–17. The three chalk colours are used here with consummate skill and ease. L-AP

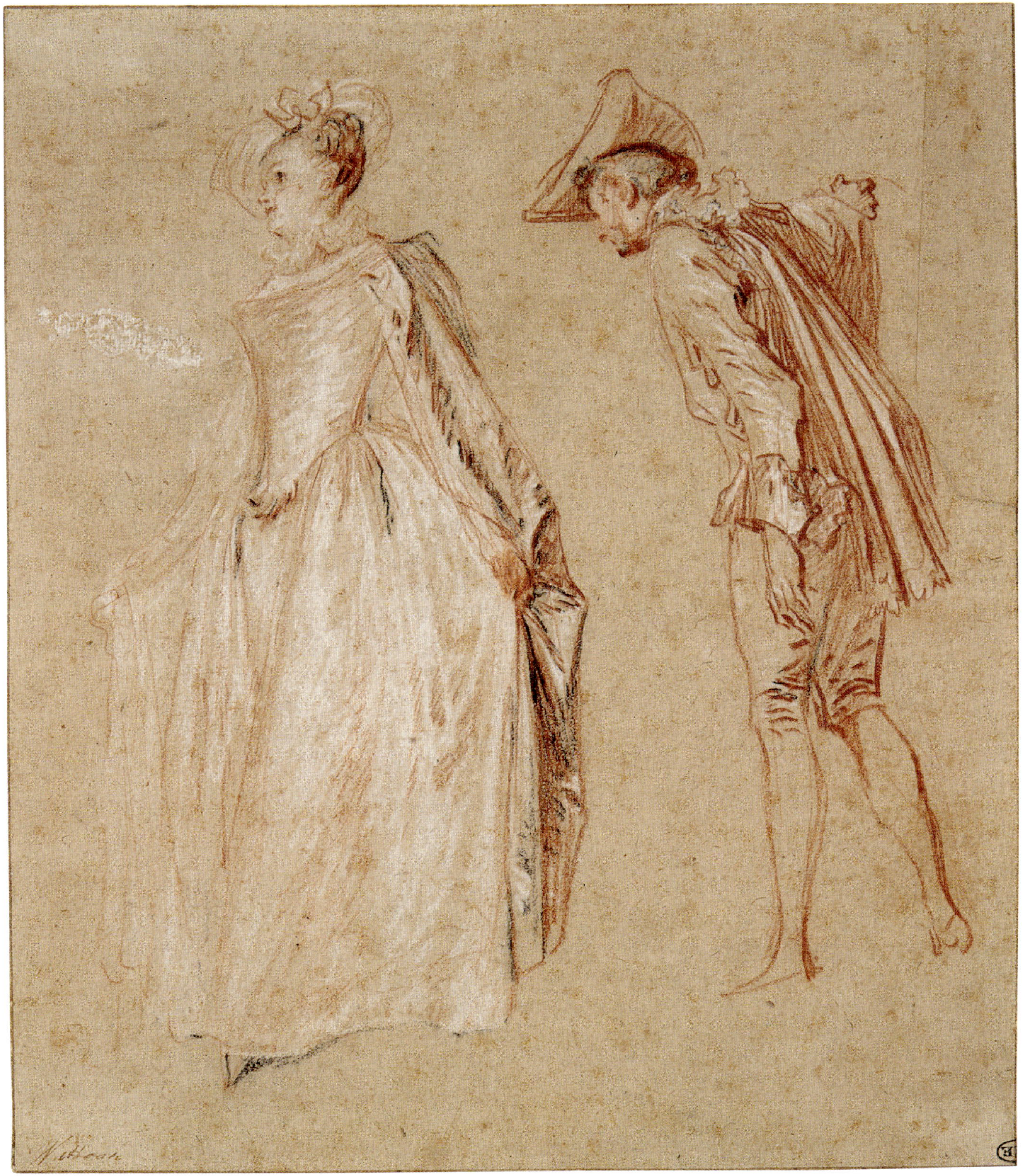

67

Four Studies of a Woman's Head

Red, black and white chalks on beige paper, 258 x 235 mm
Inscription in graphite at lower right *Watteau*

Private collection, New York

PROVENANCE, EXHIBITED, LITERATURE: PM 783; RP 520, col.
COUNTER-PROOFS, ENGRAVINGS, COPIES: PM 783; RP 520

This masterpiece left France at the beginning of the 1980s, before its evident historical importance was recognised. One of the earliest (*c.* 1716–17) large pages combining several women's heads – to the exclusion of male models (RP 521 to RP 523, then RP 634, RP 635 and RP 659) – it has unfortunately been slightly cut down to both left and right. The same model, with her pointed, slightly *retroussé* nose, appears in the British Museum drawing (cat. 68), which must have been executed at the same sitting; in fact Watteau used the features of this young woman on many other occasions (RP 226, for the latest part of that drawing, executed in two stages with an interval of several years, RP 522 and RP 571). According to Margaret Morgan Grasselli, the British Museum drawing was probably made first, then the young woman changed her headgear twice, adopting successively, as seen here in the lower part of the page, a beret then a hat with an upturned brim adorned with a red ribbon. It is difficult to be sure about the two loops she wears in the upper register, or how they are fixed: perhaps they are the corners of a kerchief tied around her chignon? The beauty of the layout is further enhanced here by the incredible accuracy of the drawing and the delicate mixing of the various coloured chalks. L-AP

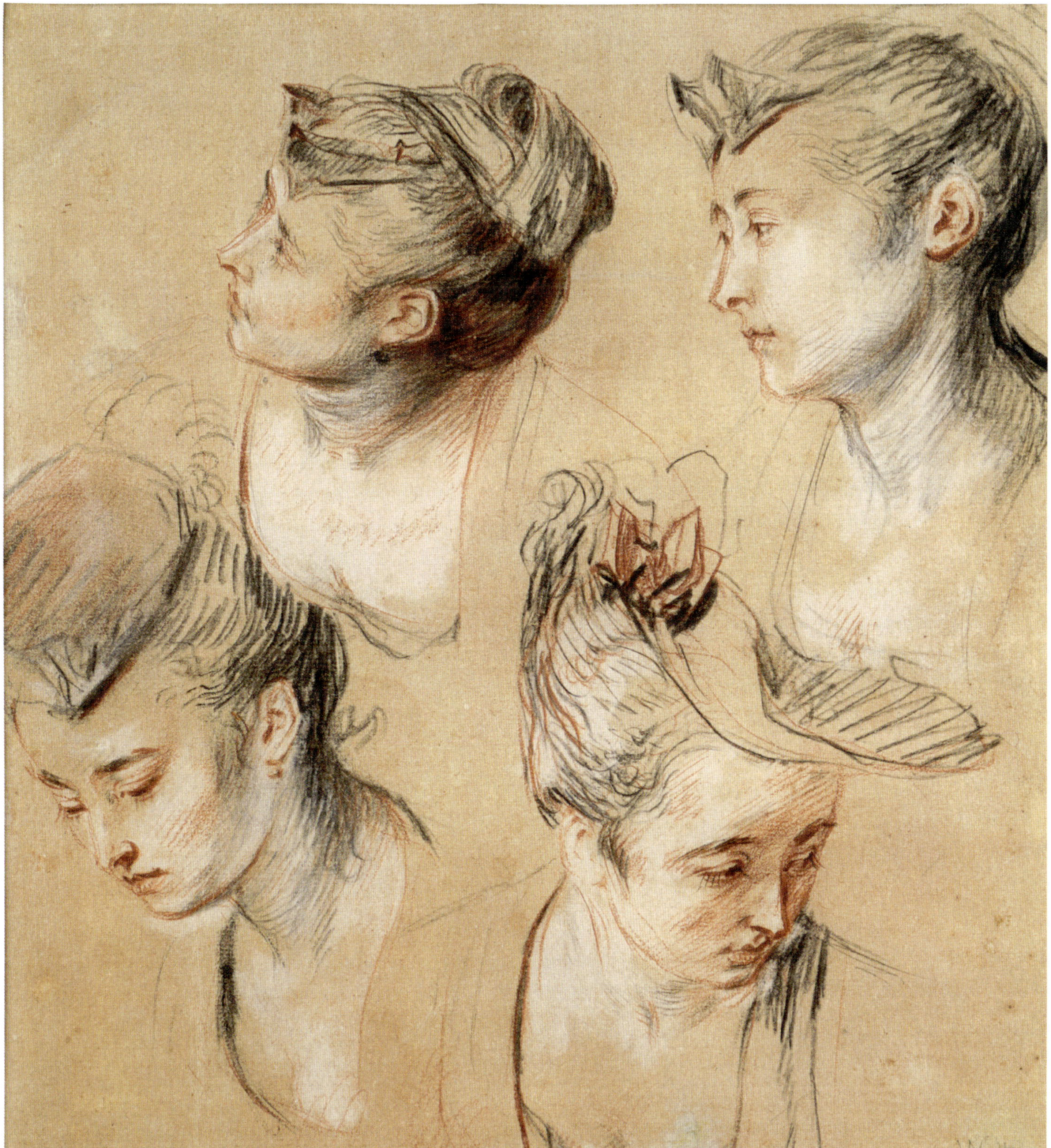

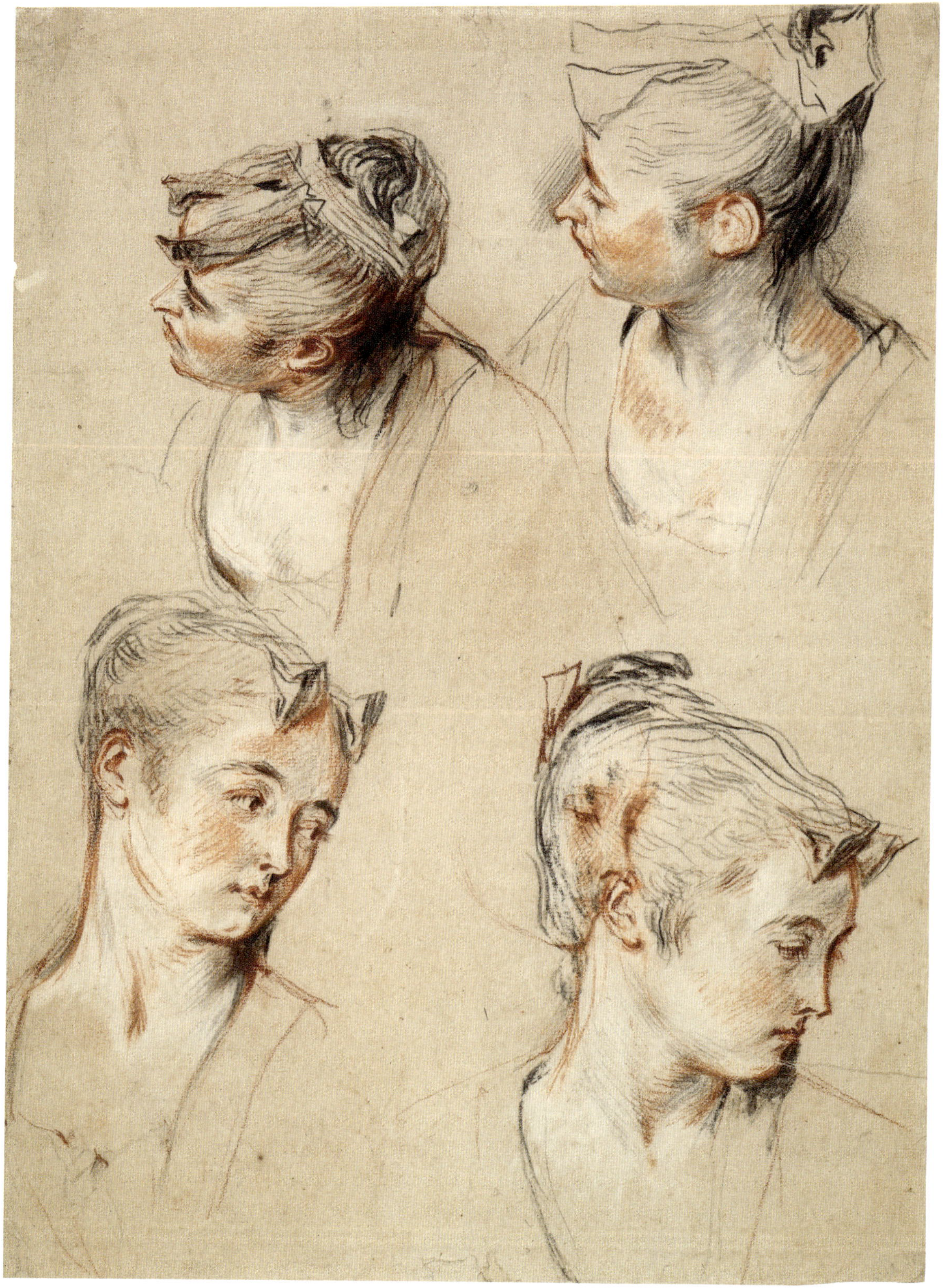

68

Five Studies of a Woman's Head

Red, black and white chalks with two tones of red chalk, red wash and highlights using white gouache on cream paper, 329 x 238 mm

The Trustees of the British Museum, London, inv. 1895-9-15-941

PROVENANCE, EXHIBITED, LITERATURE: PM 788; RP 521, col.; Bailey 1997, p. 46, figs 4, 48

In the same area of the previous drawing (cat. 67), high up on the left, one finds a head turned to the left in an almost identical pose. However, not only does the British Museum page look more technically complex and larger in size, Watteau having used a longer (or less brutally amputated) sheet of paper, but some hesitancies are revealed in a drawing that would otherwise seem as perfectly successful and serene as the New York work. A fifth woman's head, soon abandoned and drawn over, can be made out under the back of the head of the young woman at lower right; this fleetingly glimpsed profile is almost the same as the one on the face superimposed over it, and it must simply have been his desire for a perfectly balanced page that induced Watteau to move the head to the right and to repeat it slightly lower down the sheet; the sketch that can just be made out under the hair in black chalk also seems beautifully observed. This poetry in pencil contributes more than it detracts from the pleasure to be obtained by examining this masterpiece. L-AP

69

Four Bust-length Studies of a Woman; One, Barely Sketched, Holding a Fan in Her Right Hand

Red, black and white chalks on cream paper, 341 x 241 mm
Inscription in pen and brown ink at lower left *Vataux fec.*

Museum of Fine Arts, Boston. Bequest of Forsyth Wickes. The Forsyth Wickes Collection, inv. 65.2610

PROVENANCE, EXHIBITED: PM 786; RP 522; New York 1999, no. 29, col.
LITERATURE: PM 786; RP 522, col.
COUNTER-PROOFS: PM 786; RP 522

This drawing uses the same model as the two preceding works (cats 67–68); she can also be found in some drawings in the Metropolitan Museum of Art, New York (cat. 18) and the Clark Art Institute, Williamstown (RP 571). The evident proximity of the sittings suggests that these works are of the same date. Although two counter-proofs were taken from the present page (frequent in the case of red chalk drawings by Jean-Baptiste Greuze or Hubert Robert, but much more unusual for drawings by Watteau), one of which is now in the British Museum, it remains luminous in aspect and delightfully fresh.

The figure on the left at the top can be found in two paintings, *The Scale of Love* (National Gallery, London) and *Elegant Pastimes* (Gemäldegalerie, Berlin); in both instances she is much less elegant than she is here, as if the transfer from drawing to painting had dulled her. L-AP

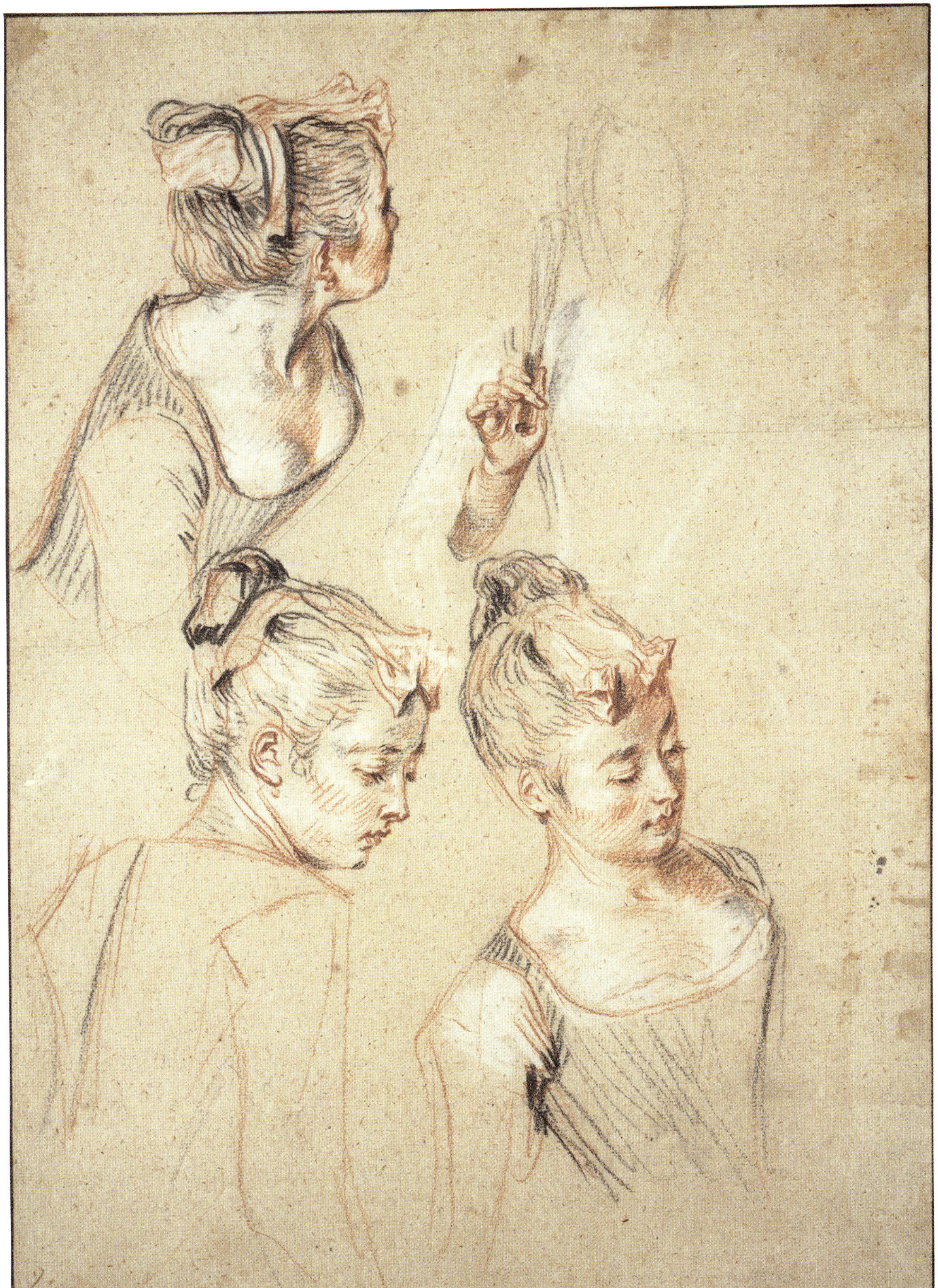

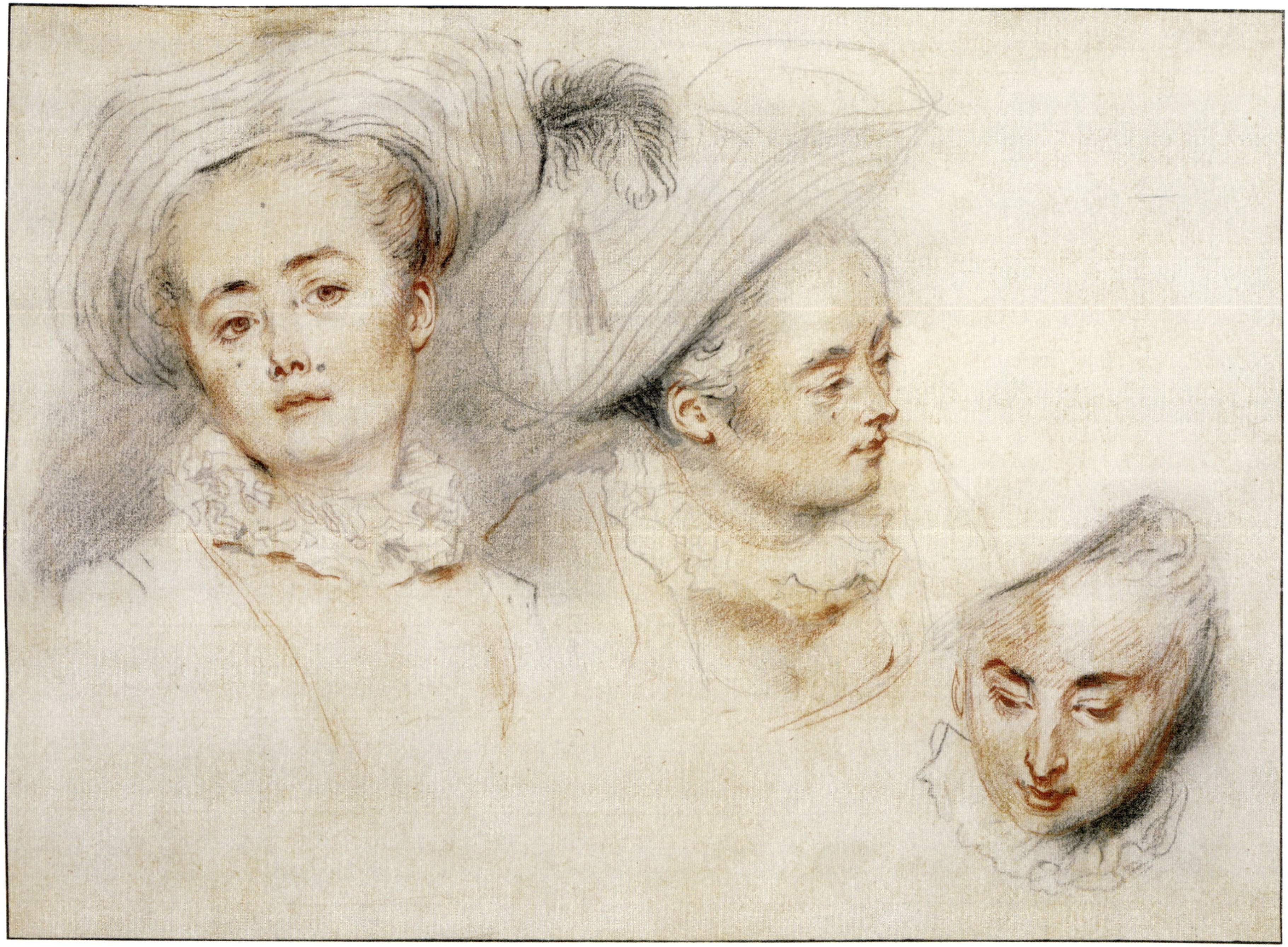

70

Three Studies of a Woman Wearing a Feathered Hat

Red, black and white chalks and stumping on paper, 232 x 310 mm; frame line drawn in pen and brown ink

Calouste Gulbenkian Museum, Lisbon, inv. 2.300

PROVENANCE, EXHIBITED, LITERATURE: PM 777; RP 523, repr.

This sheet was probably executed at the same period as the heads in cats 67–68, in *c.* 1716–17. The young woman's face is morphologically quite close to the preceding faces, with just as sharp a nose and cheeks that are slightly fuller.

Calouste Gulbenkian collected very little graphic art and was really only interested in drawings by the great French masters. Undoubtedly they reminded him of the century from which he had assembled an unrivalled series of paintings and works of decorative art.

The red chalk is rather faded in this drawing, except on the right-hand head, and shading plays a crucial role in securing the transition between the two main figures. L-AP

71

Nude Woman with Her Arm Raised

Red and black chalks on yellowed and bleached cream paper, 281 x 232 mm; darker vertical band ten millimetres wide at the extreme left; at lower right, very faint trace of an erased figure (see entry); frame line drawn with pen and brown ink

Musée du Louvre, Paris, Département des Arts graphiques, inv. 33361

PROVENANCE, EXHIBITED, LITERATURE: PM 522; RP 540, repr.; Fumaroli 1996, pp. 41, 42, fig. 17; Bailey 1997, p. 46, figs 3, 48
COUNTER-PROOF: PM 522; RP 540

This page has for a long time been linked to the character studies connected with Crozat's *Seasons* (although the present figure is nowhere to be seen in these), and to slightly later drawings depicting a young model in varying stages of undress posing on a day-bed. Its date hovers between 1717 and 1718–19, but it remains in fact undatable; it must have been executed in one of the 'chambers' in which Caylus informs us that he drew the model in the company of Watteau: 'Where he settled most easily was in the rooms I had in different *quartiers* of Paris which were used only for sittings with models, for painting and drawing.'

The drawing bears two unusual characteristics, both of which reduce its value. Firstly, having entered the Musée du Louvre following the distraint of the Saint-Morys collection in 1793, it was considered important enough to be hung continuously, from Year Five of the Revolution and throughout the first quarter of the nineteenth century, in the Galerie d'Apollon; this meant that, along with many other drawings in the Louvre that enjoyed similar celebrity, it suffered from exposure to natural light. The paper is yellowed by sunlight, probably irremediably.

Secondly, a much less common occurrence, one of its owners before the Revolution, thinking to improve the drawing, simply rubbed out the figure of a seated (and clothed) woman in the lower right-hand part of the page. This figure, now hardly visible to the naked eye, is known via the counter-proof of the drawing (fig. 33), now in the Wallraf-Richartz Museum, Cologne, which was taken before the figure had been erased. Although we cannot see her face, it is possible that the erased drawing represented the same model, as the clothed young woman in the counter-proof wears a bracelet identical to the one worn by the nude model.
L-AP

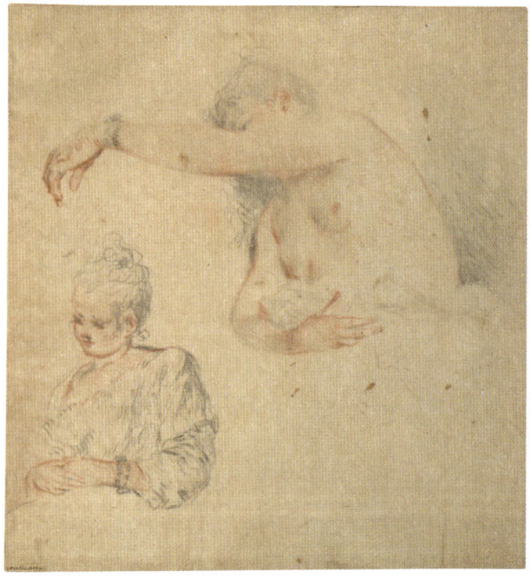

Fig. 33
Bust of a Nude Woman with Her Arm Raised to the Left; Bust of a Young Woman, Her Hands Clasped, counter-proof, 1717. Black and red chalks, 259 x 236 mm. Wallraf-Richartz Museum and Fondation Corboud, Cologne

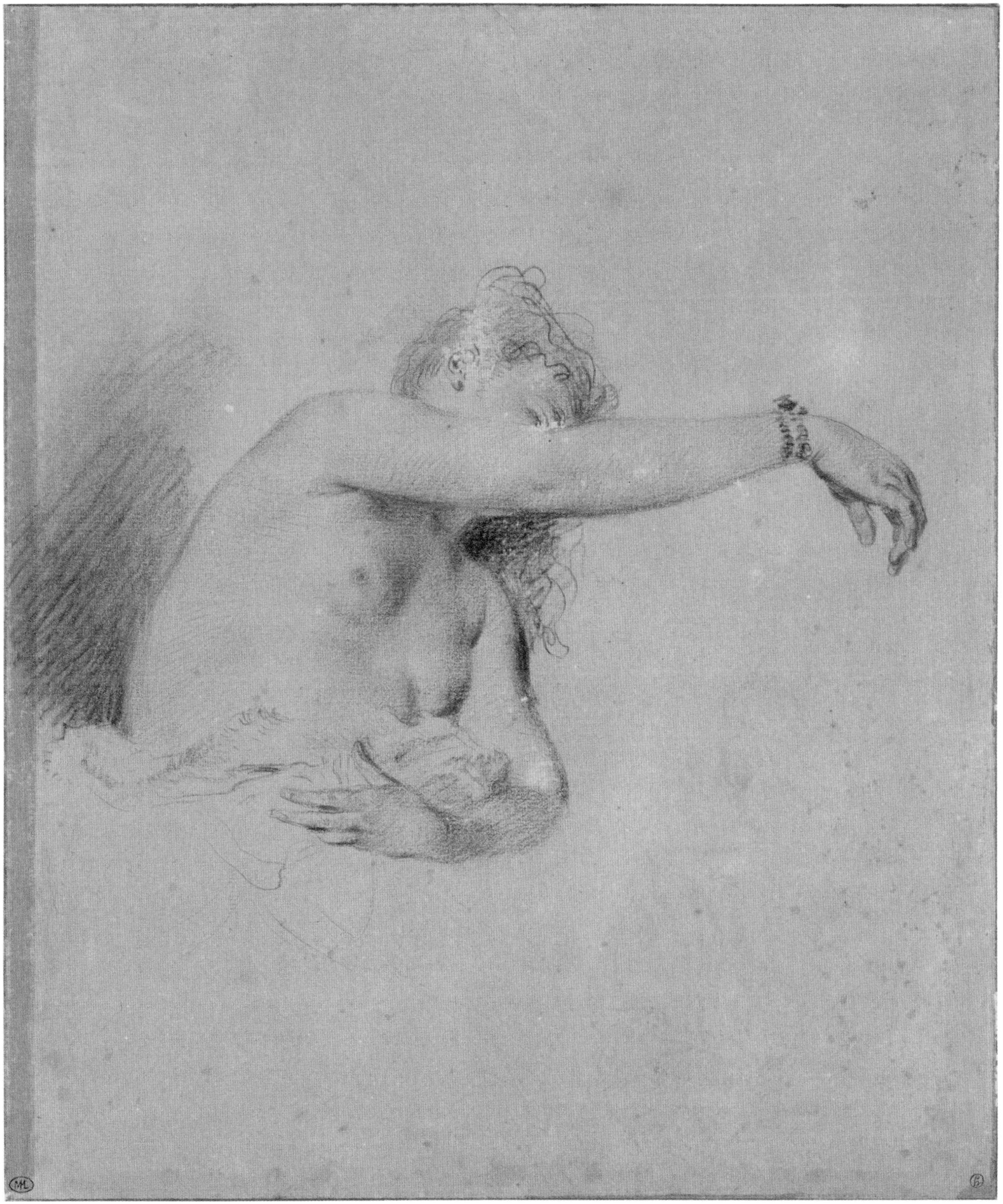

Red and black chalks on paper, 208 x 148 mm; oil stain in the centre

The Trustees of the British Museum, London, inv. 1846-11-14-23

PROVENANCE, EXHIBITED, LITERATURE: PM 551; RP 545, col. COUNTER-PROOF: PM 551; RP 545

72

Two Studies of a Woman, One Holding Out Her Apron, the Other in Half-length, Turned to Her Right

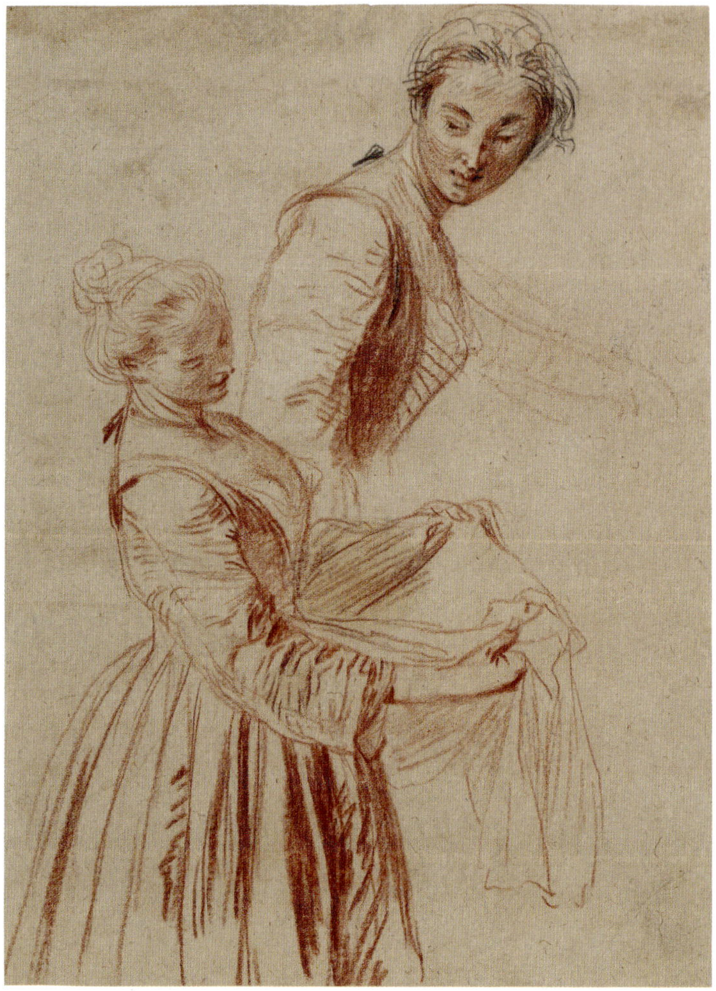

The British Museum acquired this fine drawing along with two others by the artist in 1846, well before the 'rediscovery' of Watteau by the Goncourt brothers. The features of the young woman at the top are recognisable from a page of studies of heads now in the Fondation Custodia, Paris (RP 557), ascribed in our catalogue raisonné to *c.* 1717 and by Margaret Morgan Grasselli to 1717–18. The second face in the upper register of the latter drawing is seen almost from the same angle as this one. The upper figure in the present drawing does not seem to have been used in any known painting.

By contrast, the young woman holding out her apron can be found in two important mature works, *Pilgrimage to the Isle of Cythera* (Schloss Charlottenburg, Berlin), and *Rustic Entertainments* (private collection; DV 126). Another young woman, similar in pose and making the same gesture, can be seen in the middle ground of *The Open-air Gathering* (Gemäldegalerie Alte Meister, Dresden; fig. 38) and is linked with *Lesson in Love* (Nationalmuseum, Stockholm), which is based on the drawing in the National Museum, Stockholm (cat. 65).

The dense, darkish tone of the red chalk in the upper figure goes perfectly with the black accents used exclusively in the hair and the small bow at the back of the neck. L-AP

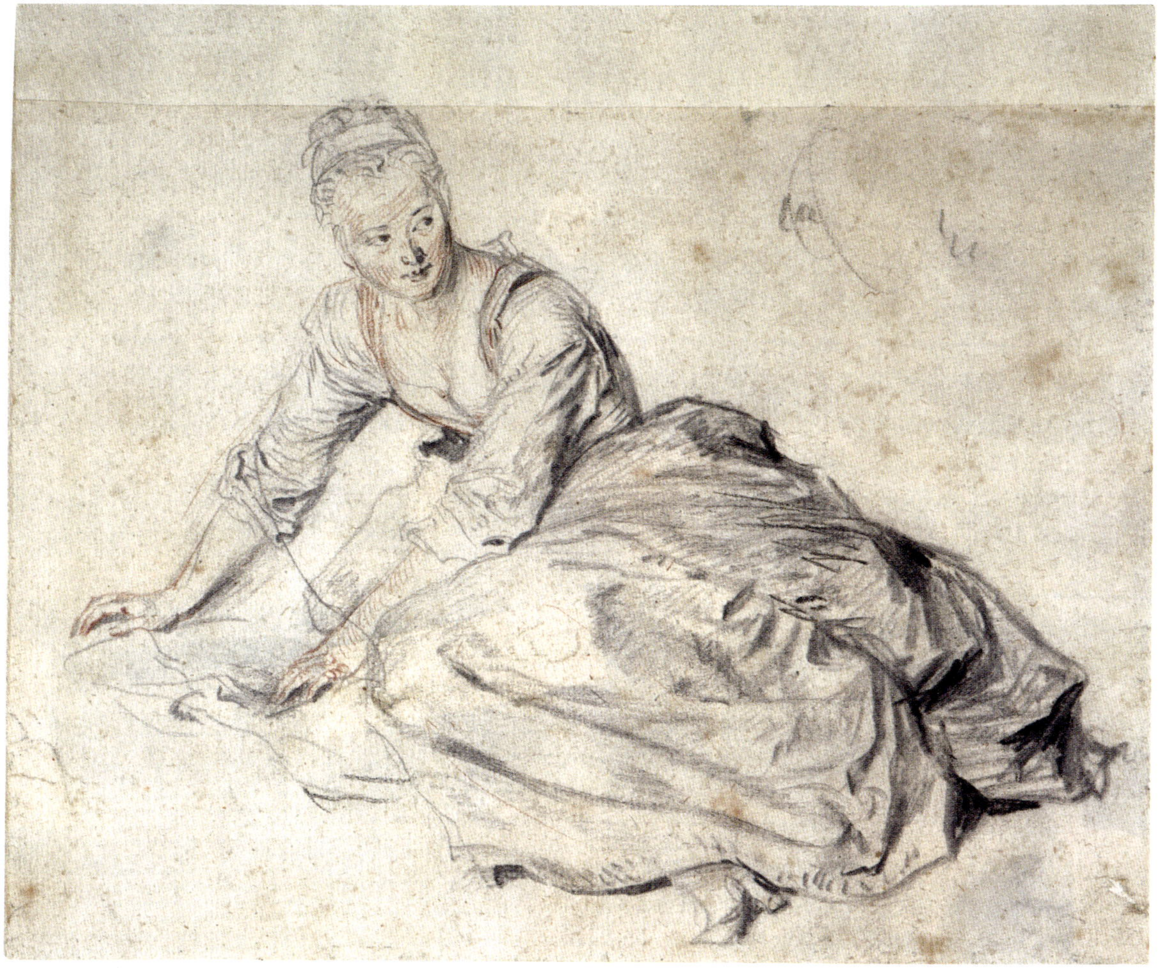

Red and black chalks, graphite on paper, 177 x 205 mm; piece added near centre and repaired hole

Musée Cognacq-Jay, Paris, inv. J. 191

PROVENANCE, LITERATURE:
PM 594; RP 549, rep.

73

Young Woman Seated on the Ground

In this drawing, which dates from about 1717, red chalk is employed more sparingly than usual. Indeed it is used only to suggest the skin tones of the seated figure; the facial features and hairstyle are drawn in black chalk and accentuated with touches of graphite. Unusual for Watteau, this approach emphasises the figure's elegance and precision. Oddly enough it is not to be found in any known painting, despite being so successful – it could easily have appeared in any of Watteau's series of *fêtes galantes*.

Of the eleven drawings by Watteau owned by Ernest Cognacq, all now in the Musée Cognacq-Jay, Paris (one of them, RP 200, disappeared from the collection at an unknown date), this example could be considered the most important, although the most moving undoubtedly remains the drawing of the men packing a crate (cat. 88), highlight of the present show.

The band of paper at the top of this page was probably added by someone else; very light finishing touches have been made to the hairstyle. The young woman's movement, caught dramatically just as she turns, her gaze towards the extreme left, contrasts nicely with the delightful detail of her foot in its elegant high-heeled shoe, extended yet apparently flat on the ground. L-AP

74

Six Studies of Women's Heads and Two of a Boy

Red, black and white chalks with several tones of red chalk, traces of red wash and white gouache on cream paper, 225 x 348 mm

Musée du Louvre, Paris, Département des Arts graphiques, inv. RF 51760

PROVENANCE: PM 743; RP 562, then, instead of 'Private collection, Paris' stated in 1996, Comte Charles de Ganay, Paris; acquired by the Société des Amis du Louvre in 1997 on the occasion of their centenary and donated to the museum (museum mark Louvre L.1886a at lower right)
EXHIBITED: PM 743; RP 562; then Paris 2000A, no. 203, col.
LITERATURE: PM 743; RP 562; Feinberg and Zuccari 1997, pp. 243, 244, fig. 18; Viatte 1997A; Viatte 1997B; Roland Michel 1998, p. 752; Rosenberg 2000, rep. on the cover and p. 28, fig. 26; Temperini 2002, col. p. 25
COUNTER-PROOFS, ENGRAVINGS, COPIES: PM 743; RP 562; this counter-proof reappeared on the art market in 2001

In our catalogue raisonné we quoted Eugène Féral, the appraiser at the Josse sale at which this drawing came up for auction in May 1894, who declared: 'We believe that nothing finer than this exists.' A year after publication of our catalogue the drawing was given by the Société des Amis du Louvre to the museum they support to celebrate their centenary.

In 1996, when our catalogue raisonné was published, we were unaware of a photograph of an interior in the home of H. H. A. Josse, which was later published in the catalogue of an auction (Christie's, New York, 24 November 1998, lot 25) in which a chest of drawers belonging to the collector was to be sold. In the photograph, noted in the catalogue as having been taken in about 1926 but in fact certainly earlier, it is easy to spot Watteau's drawing, hanging with others to the left of a mirror. The chest of drawers was acquired by the Comtesse de Béhaigne at the same Josse sale as the Watteau drawing, on 28–29 May 1894.

The sheet of studies is extremely well known for its beauty, for the perfection of its layout and for that 'extra something' added by the head sketched low down, almost in the centre of the lower register. The six female faces all seem to belong to the same model; the boy's features are known to us via another drawing in the J. Paul Getty Museum, Los Angeles (cat. 75), in which he appears to the left of a flute player. In our catalogue raisonné we also linked it with two later sketches for which the boy may have been the model, but this is not certain. Watteau must have known him quite well, because he represented him, standing this time but also in profile (as in the upper register of our drawing), in a page now lost but known through an engraving by Caylus in *Figures de différents caractères* (fig. 34). L-AP

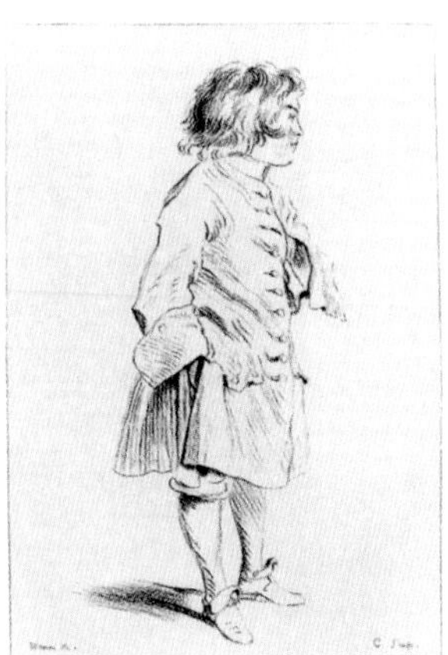

Fig. 34
Profile of Young Boy Standing, Turned to the Right, engraved by the Comte de Caylus after Watteau, 1726

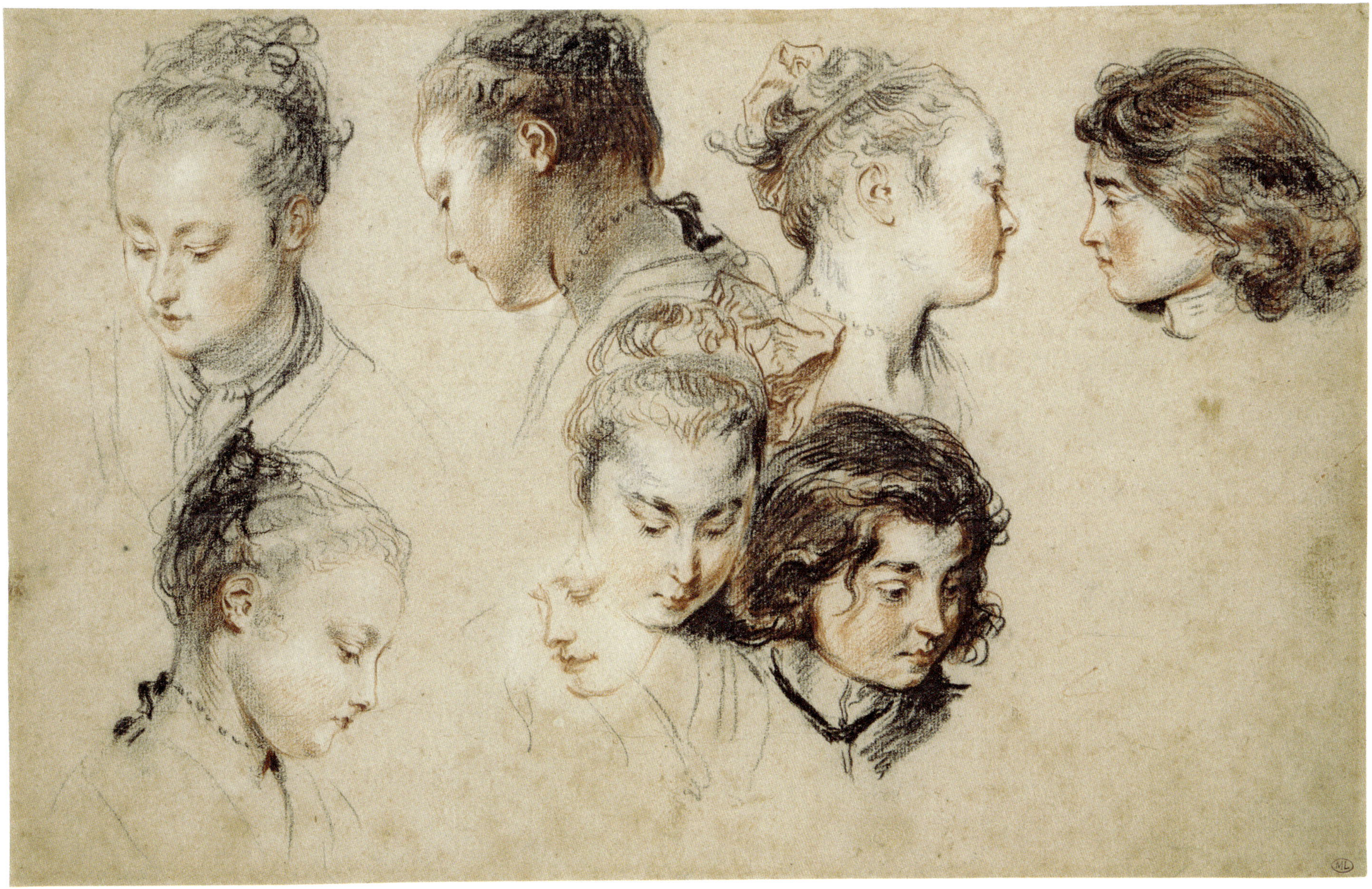

Red, black and white chalks on buff-coloured paper, 214 x 336 mm; damage to upper part and at lower left

The J. Paul Getty Museum, Los Angeles, inv. 88.GB.3

PROVENANCE, EXHIBITED, LITERATURE: PM 837; RP 576; New York 1999, no. 35, col.
ENGRAVINGS: PM 837; RP 576

75

Head of a Boy and Two Half-length Studies of a Flute-player

The age of the small boy seems to be the same as in the Louvre drawing (cat. 74), in which he appears twice; this allows us to date this fine drawing to *c.* 1717. It is not certain whether the same musician playing the flute appears both times; the character on the left seems older than the one on the right, whose nose is definitely straight, not aquiline. The careful balancing of the poses of the two figures gives the illusion of musicians playing together, swaying to the rhythm of the music. The small boy was almost certainly added to the page at a later date; he has the air of an intruder, attracted by the music.

The flautist on the right can be found in *In Perfect Tune* (private collection; DV 23), a painting dated *c.* 1719 in which, according to the leading specialist in the representation of music in painting, A. P. de Mirimonde, he is hardly worthy to be called a flautist as the position of his fingers on the flute is incorrect. L-AP

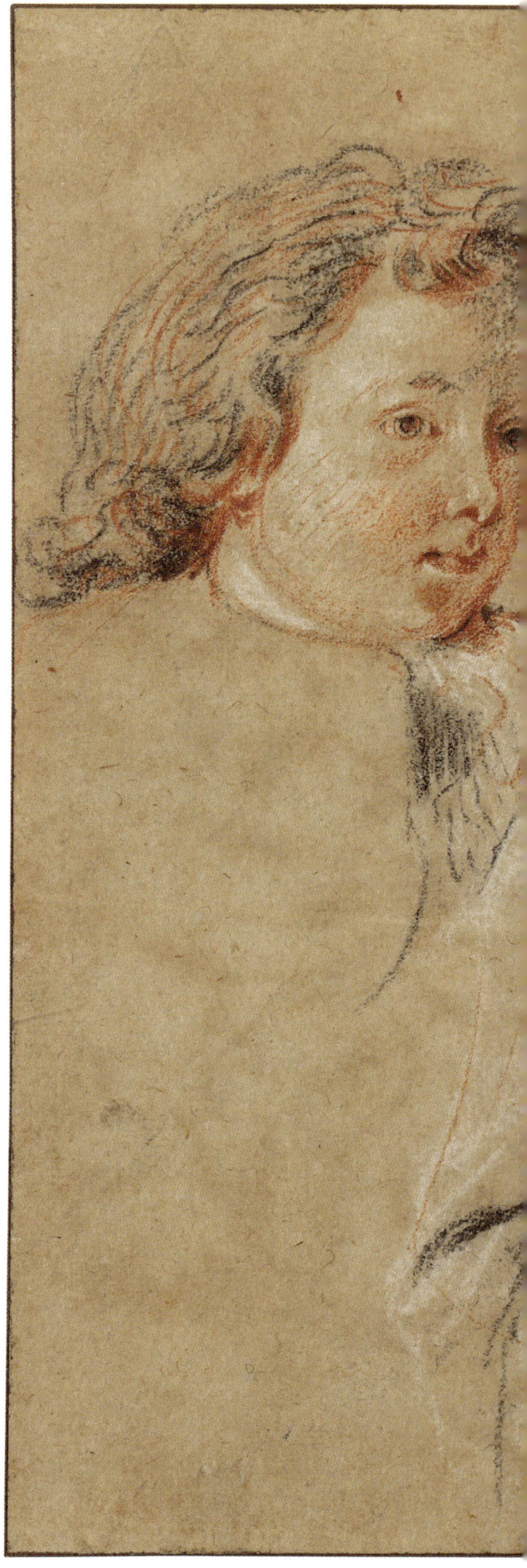

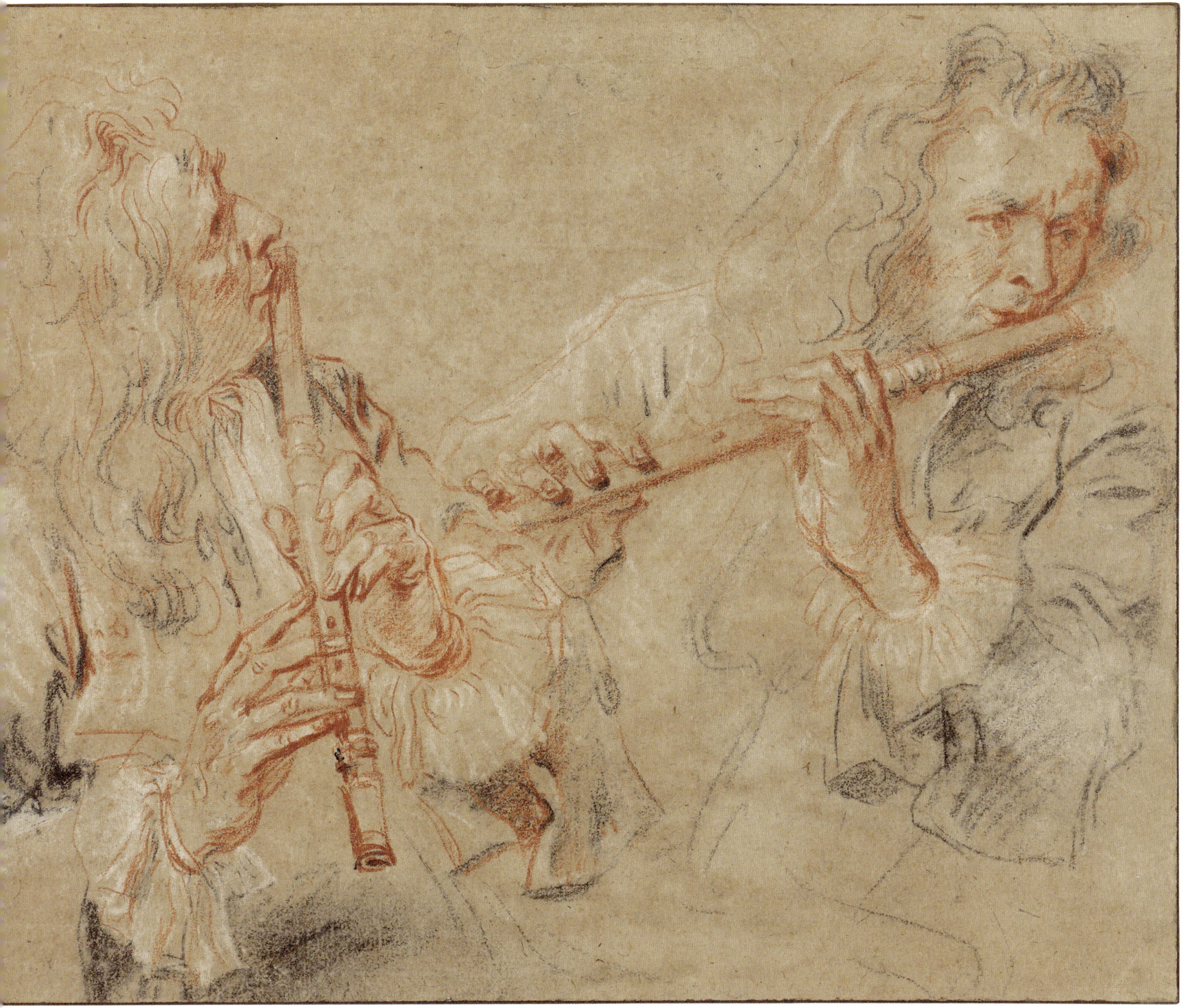

76

Semi-nude Woman, Seated on a Day-bed Holding Her Left Foot in Her Hands

Red, black and white chalks on greyish paper, 339 x 221 mm
Inscription in black chalk at lower left *Watteau* (in Jullienne's handwriting, according to Parker, 1931)

The Trustees of the British Museum, London, inv. 1860-6-16-136

PROVENANCE, EXHIBITED, LITERATURE: PM 526; RP 581, rep.

This drawing is part of a small group of studies of young women in various states of undress, usually seated or lying on a kind of chaise longue or day-bed, behind which Watteau sometimes places a curtain or hanging. The drawing in the Louvre (cat. 71) could perhaps be considered as part of this group, but it may be slightly earlier than the others.

The series has been variously dated: 1716–17 by Donald Posner, 1716–18 by Marianne Roland Michel, 1717–18 by us in the 1996 catalogue raisonné and by Margaret Morgan Grasselli. A number of the drawings were acquired by the Swedish diplomat Count Carl Gustav Tessin while he was ambassador to France between 1718 and 1719, and this provides us with a *terminus ante quem* for the dating. Although the story may have been passed from one to another, early biographers of Watteau tell us repeatedly that, at the end of his life, the artist destroyed any *risqué* drawings he had produced; this series of drawings (RP 578–85) appears to constitute the only evidence of a 'private academy', of the kind illustrated shortly afterwards by Gabriel de Saint-Aubin in his celebrated engraving of that name: in it, a young man draws a naked woman voluptuously stretched out on a sofa in a small room with a large fireplace.

The present drawing is the only one in the series in which the garment recently removed by the model lies beside her, placed on a closed basket that she perhaps carries from sitting to sitting. She seems to be holding a kind of spatula in her left hand, sketched in very lightly, enabling her to reach the toenails of her left foot. Watteau has used the stump less freely than in the other drawings in the series, and the distinction between the red chalk (for flesh) and the black is clearly made. Unfortunately the page has been counter-proofed (the counter-proof has not reappeared) and is not in perfect condition. It is attractive nevertheless, thanks to its confident realism, tinged with a feeling of empathy for the young woman. She, with the freedom of a professional life model, relaxes in front of the artist, displaying the same lack of inhibition as the models who later posed for the pastels of Edgar Degas. L-AP

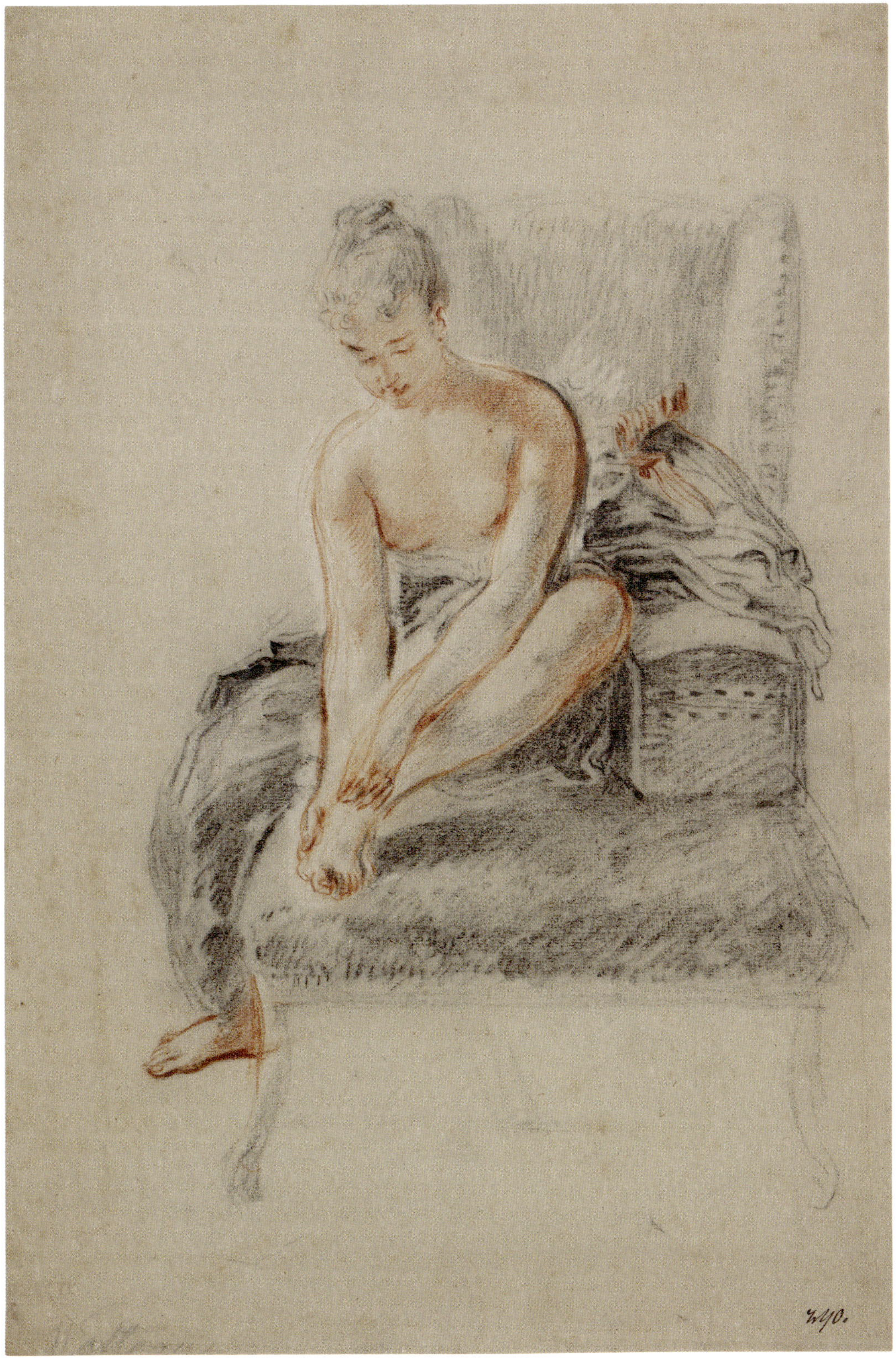
270.

Red, black and white chalks and graphite on cream paper, 225 x 294 mm

Musée du Louvre, Paris, Département des Arts graphiques, inv. RF 774

PROVENANCE, EXHIBITED, LITERATURE: PM 825; RP 596, col. ENGRAVINGS, COPIES: PM 825; RP 596

77

Three Studies of a Seated Woman, in Two of Which She Plays the Guitar

The three figures were all engraved by the same artist, Benoît Audran, for the *Figures de différents caractères*, but Jean de Jullienne suggested that the engraver isolate the figure on the left for one image and show the two on the right together in another; in the latter engraving, Audran had to invent the back panel of the guitar-player's gown as Watteau had not had the space to draw it on the page. Like Watteau's many other studies of musicians, this example should probably be dated to *c.* 1717–18. The use of red chalk is kept to a minimum: the hands of the young woman on the right (the only hands visible) and her facial features, also delineated in red chalk. Watteau has chosen to use red to emphasise the shadows on the faces of the two women musicians (she is the same woman seen from different angles). In another beautiful and famous page of studies of a female musician and two other women, now in the Art Institute of Chicago (*c.* 1717; RP 538), black chalk also predominates, with red chalk occupying a secondary role and a few strokes of what appears to be graphite for emphasis.

The figure here on the left appears in a painting in the Wallace Collection, *The Charms of Life.* The guitar-player on the right also used to appear, before she was transformed into something else at a later date, as an X-ray examination of the painting has revealed. She can also be found in *The Embarrassing Proposal* (State Hermitage Museum, St Petersburg) and, with her head held slightly higher and her eyes wide open, in *Harlequin, Pierrot and Scapin* (whereabouts unknown; DV 274). L-AP

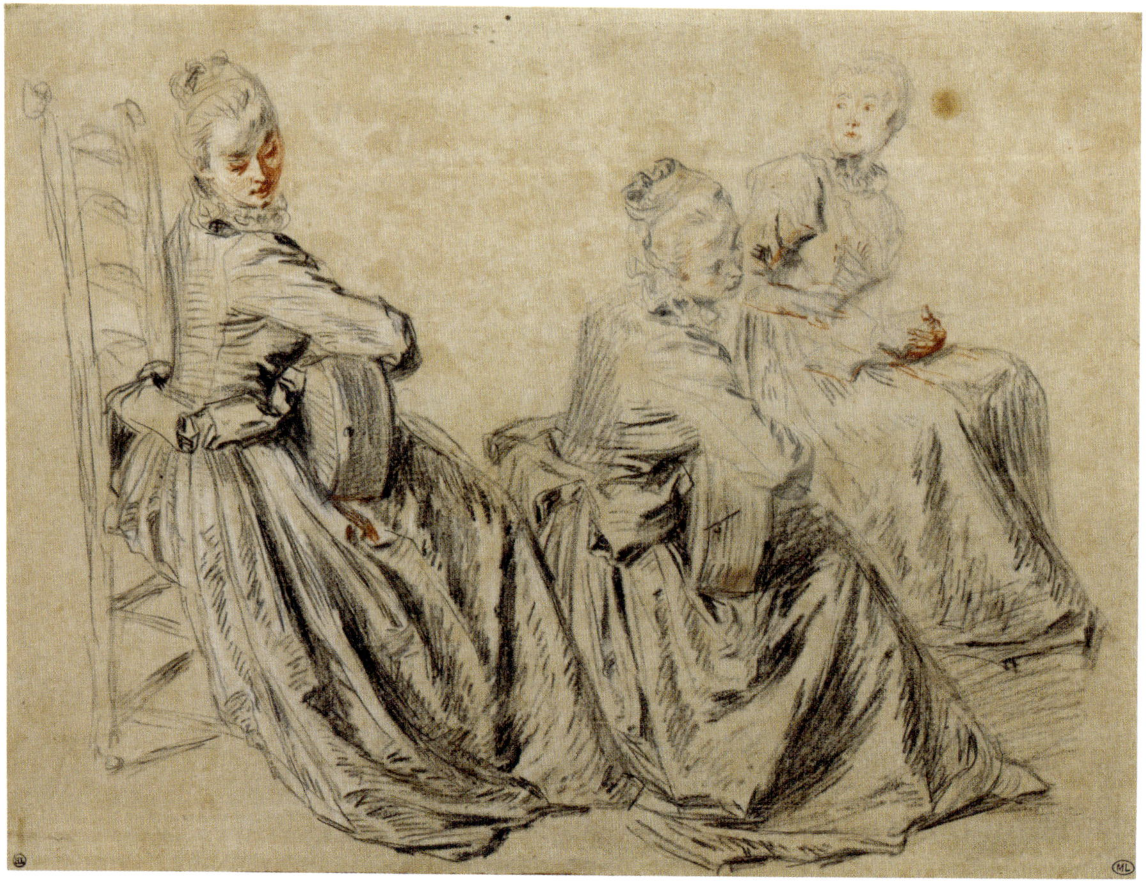

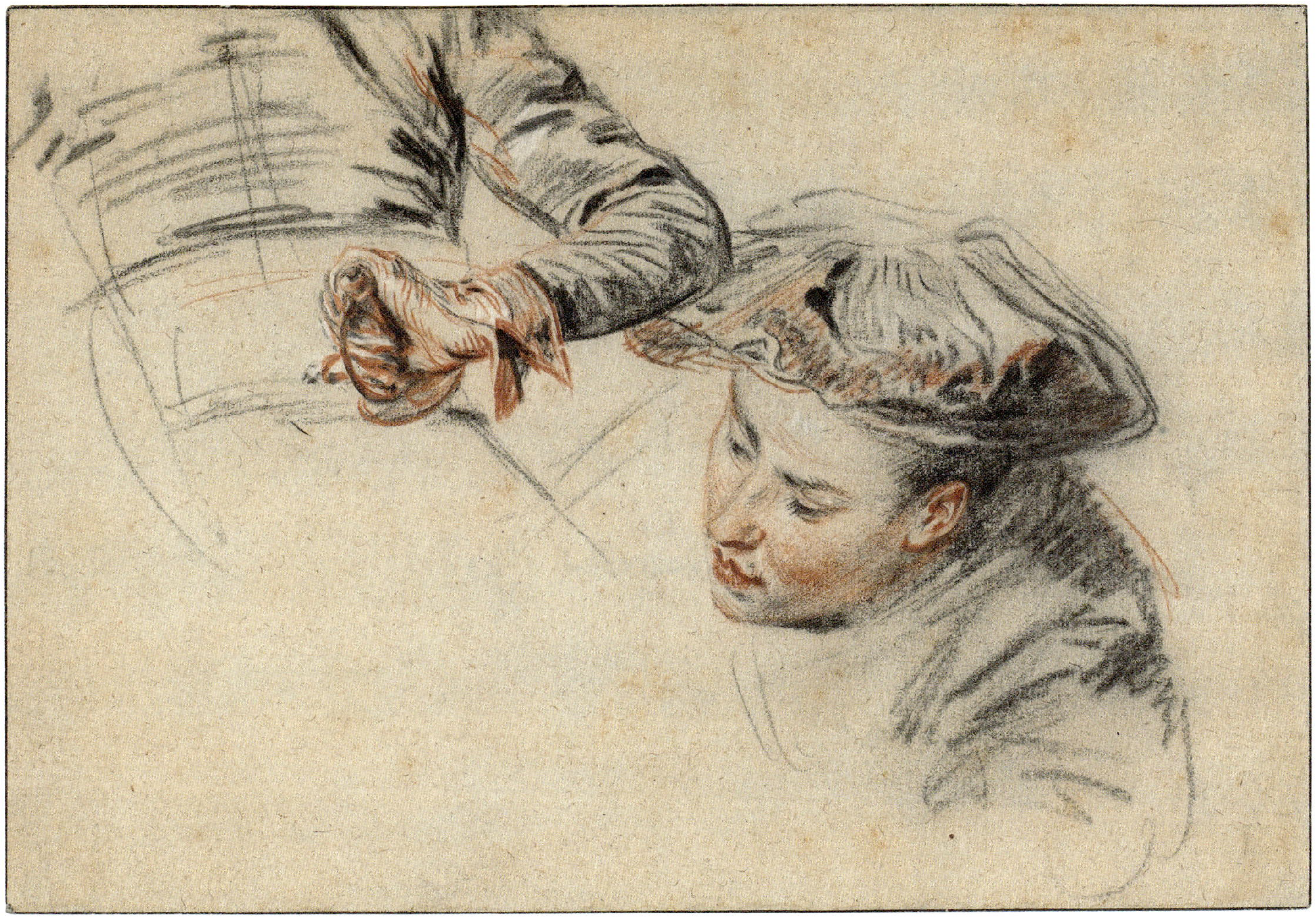

78

Bust of a Man, His Sword in His Left hand; Head of a Man Wearing a Large Beret

Red, black and white chalks on cream paper, 179 x 255 mm
On the back, inscriptions in pen and brown ink at lower left *B 120* and in graphite, at upper right *No 30 H*

Rijksmuseum, Amsterdam, inv. 1953: 188. This drawing was recovered from Germany after the Second World War

PROVENANCE, EXHIBITED: PM 684; RP 602; Paris 2003, no. 14, col.
LITERATURE: PM 684; RP 602, col.

Watteau drew the arm holding the sword first, then, in a second phase, the head of a man wearing a beret which he did not have space to finish. Worthy of admiration are the artist's unerring touch and the dynamic impression made by the drawing, datable to *c.* 1717. The hand on the sword can also be found in *Harlequin, Pierrot and Scapin* (whereabouts unknown; DV 274), a painting engraved by L. Suruge during Watteau's lifetime, in 1719 at the latest, which provides a *terminus ante quem* for dating the drawing. Margaret Morgan Grasselli has suggested a comparison between this head and that of one of the male figures in *Pleasures of Love* (Gemäldegalerie Alte Meister, Dresden), which is tilted at the same angle but not wearing a beret; the date of this drawing confirms this, as the painting is generally dated 1717. L-AP

Red and black chalks, dark red chalk, stumping, white highlights and grey wash on cream paper, 243 x 270 mm; slight damage at upper right; frame line drawn in pen and brown ink

Musée du Louvre, Paris, Département des Arts graphiques, inv. RF 28721

PROVENANCE, EXHIBITED, LITERATURE: PM 730; RP 608, col.; Alan Wintermute in New York 1999, p. 33, fig. 25; Temperini 2002, col., p. 25
COUNTER-PROOF: PM 730; RP 608

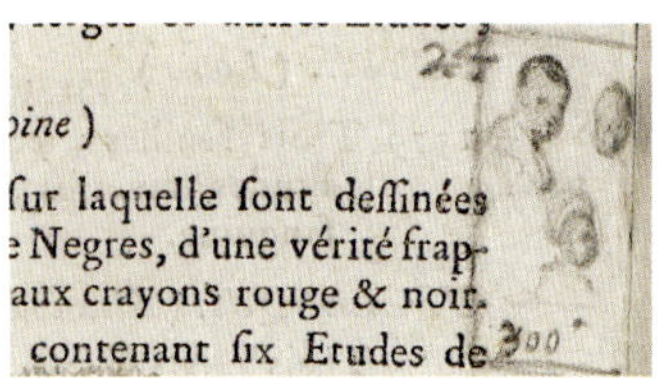

Fig. 35
Gabriel de Saint-Aubin, Sketch in the margin of the artist's copy of the catalogue of Pierre-Jean Mariette's sale, 15 November 1775 – 30 January 1776. Museum of Fine Arts, Boston. Bequest of William A. Sargent

79

Three Studies of the Bust of a Black Boy

One of Watteau's most celebrated and most frequently reproduced drawings, *Three Studies of the Bust of a Black Boy* was described in the catalogue to the Mariette sale in 1775–76 as being 'strikingly realistic'; the sheet's importance did not escape Gabriel de Saint-Aubin, who sketched it to one side of this comment in his copy of the sale catalogue (fig. 35), a valuable document now in the Museum of Fine Arts, Boston.

Two other drawings of heads of black males (RP R206 and RP R207), more monumental but somewhat expressionless, were catalogued as being by Watteau by Parker and Mathey in 1957; Jean-Pierre Cuzin has since been able to demonstrate that in fact they were by Charles de La Fosse, a friend of Watteau, who used the faces without any great spiritual depth in his painting *The Adoration of the Magi* now in the Louvre.

Watteau drew young black males on only two other occasions: on a great sheet of heads now in the Louvre (cat. 48), in which the young African wearing a feathered headdress could be the same model; and in a drawing in Rotterdam (RP 630) where the black man is placed beside the study of a woman, both fragments having been separated for years, at least since 1857, and having been recently reunited. Again, this could be the same model.

We are familiar with the presence of the little black servants in paintings of *fêtes galantes* or portraits of women, as could be found in the domestic life of the period. Well before Watteau's day, their flesh tones and the power of their strongly etched features attracted the attention of artists concerned with their particular brand of expressiveness, among them Veronese, Rubens and Van Dyck. The artist's particularly subtle combination of various chalks and the light accents of wash that underlie them has enabled him to convey brilliantly the play of light on a dark skin.

The young black boy at the top right appears again in *Outdoor Concert* (whereabouts unknown; DV 72) and, with minor variations, in *The Charms of Life* (Wallace Collection, London). Although reversed, the pose of the boy at the top left is close to a character in the centre of *Flirtatious Girls to an Assignation to Meet Young Men…* (State Hermitage Museum, St Petersburg; DV 36). L-AP

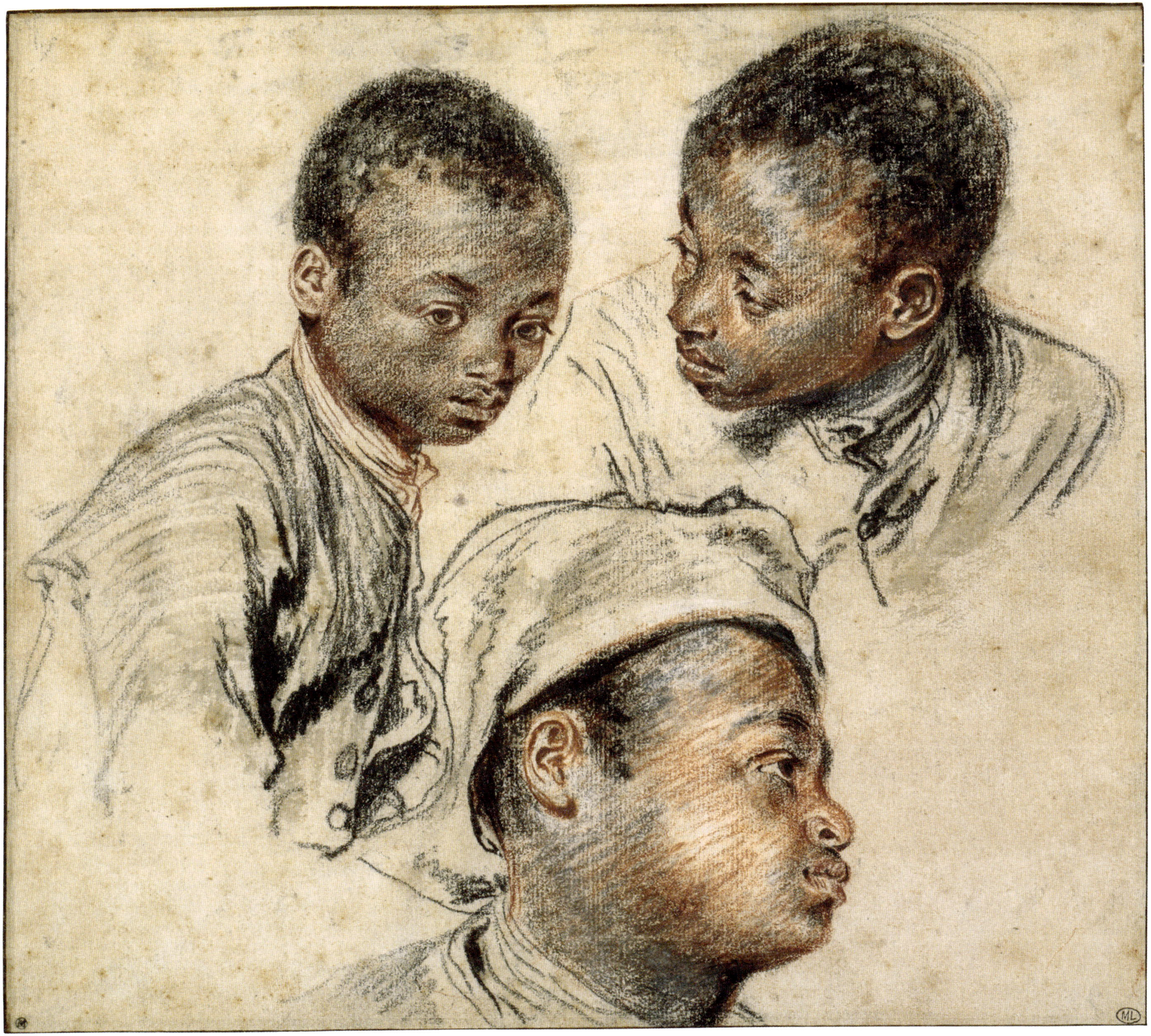

Head of a Man Wearing a Skullcap: Three Studies of Hands; Two Studies of Kittens

Red, black and white chalks and graphite on brownish paper, 200 x 181 mm; horizontal band of paper ten millimetres wide added at the top

Musée du Louvre, Paris, Département des Arts graphiques, inv. 33358

PROVENANCE, EXHIBITED, LITERATURE: PM 889; RP 614, repr.

The band of paper added to the top of this sheet, which has no drawing on it, must have been placed there to increase the dimensions of the page, allowing the various subjects to breathe more freely. We know that Pierre-Jean Mariette, one of the owners of this most attractive drawing, which probably dates from *c.* 1718, was familiar with this kind of operation, particularly when a sketch seemed to him to come too close to the edge of any page in his collection. In this case as well, the drawing caught the attention of Gabriel de Saint-Aubin, who reproduced it in a quick, allusive sketch in his copy of the catalogue to the Mariette sale (Museum of Fine Arts, Boston).

Four studies of a much older, stouter cat can be found in a page of red chalk drawings, evidently earlier in date (*c.* 1715?), now in Bayonne (RP 315); there is a fine drawing of a tabby cat, mistaken for many years for a leopard, in the Musée Cognacq-Jay, Paris (RP 554). The kitten depicted here is probably the same animal that appears – also in duplicate – in a delightful page of studies now in a private collection (RP 613), which can be ascribed to the same date as the present drawing.

The two hands in red chalk in the upper register pose an intriguing problem. Watteau reused them in *The Pleasures of Summer* (private collection; DV 102) (see fig. 36); the problem resides in their proximity, as in the painting these two hands belong to two separate people, a man and a woman shown facing each other. The man, seen from behind, extends his hands with fingers stretched apart towards a young woman who makes a gesture of rejection with her fan; the two hands are seen in the same position as in the drawing, which need not cause surprise, but also virtually in the same relationship one to the other, which makes us wonder what Watteau had in mind when he placed them thus on the sheet of paper. L-AP

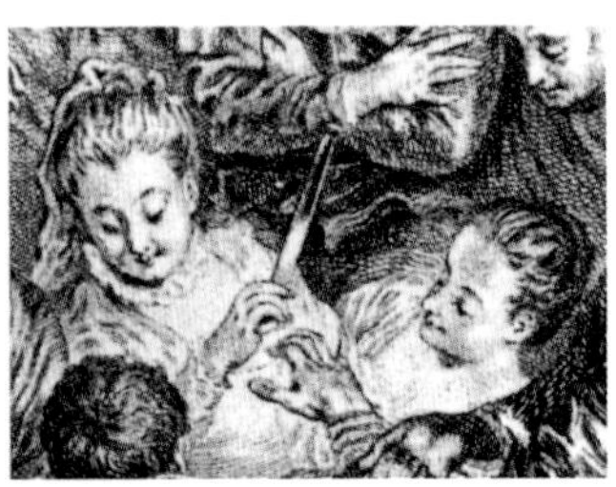

Fig. 36
Detail of *The Pleasures of Summer*, engraved by J. de Favannes, 1731

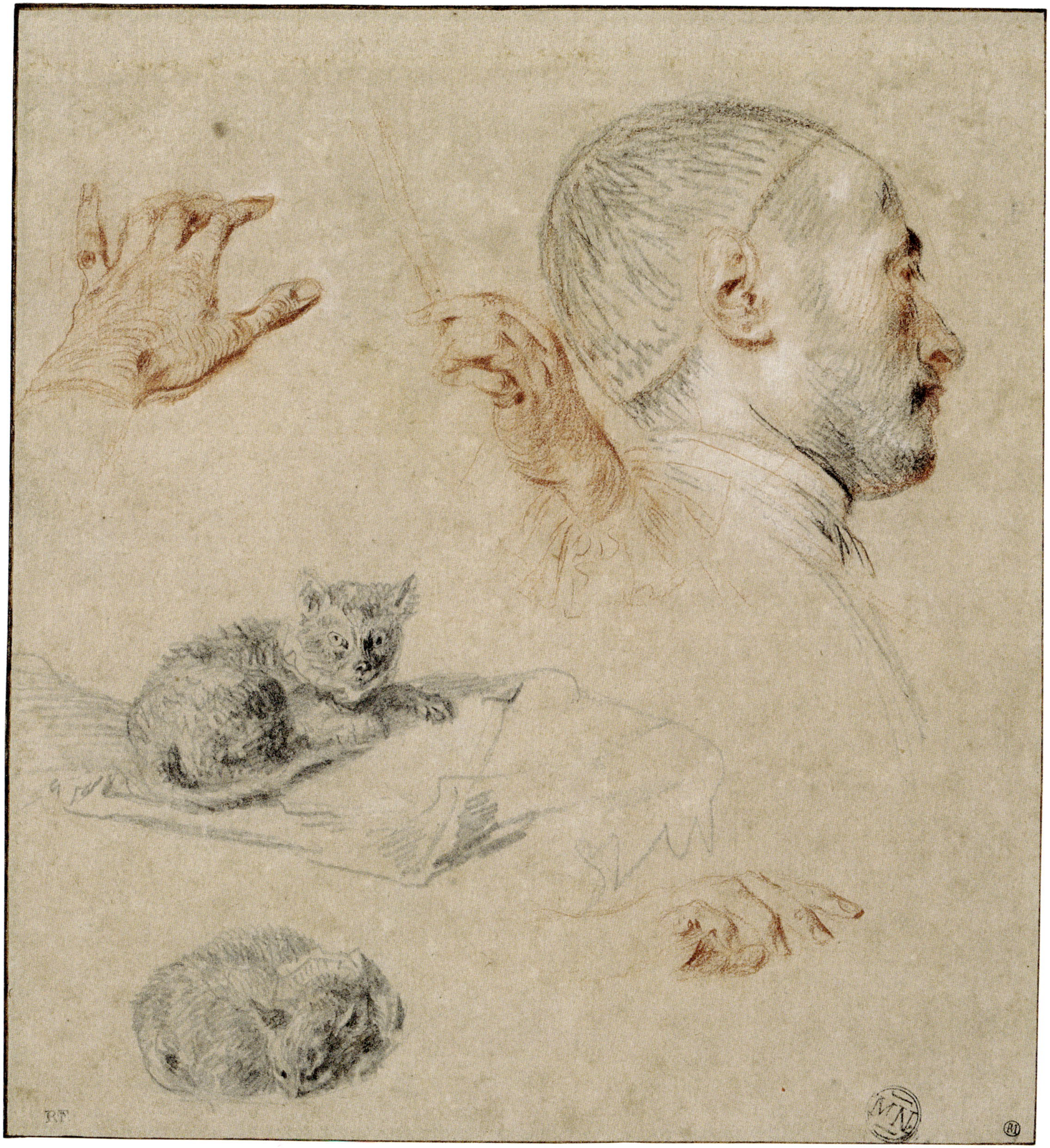

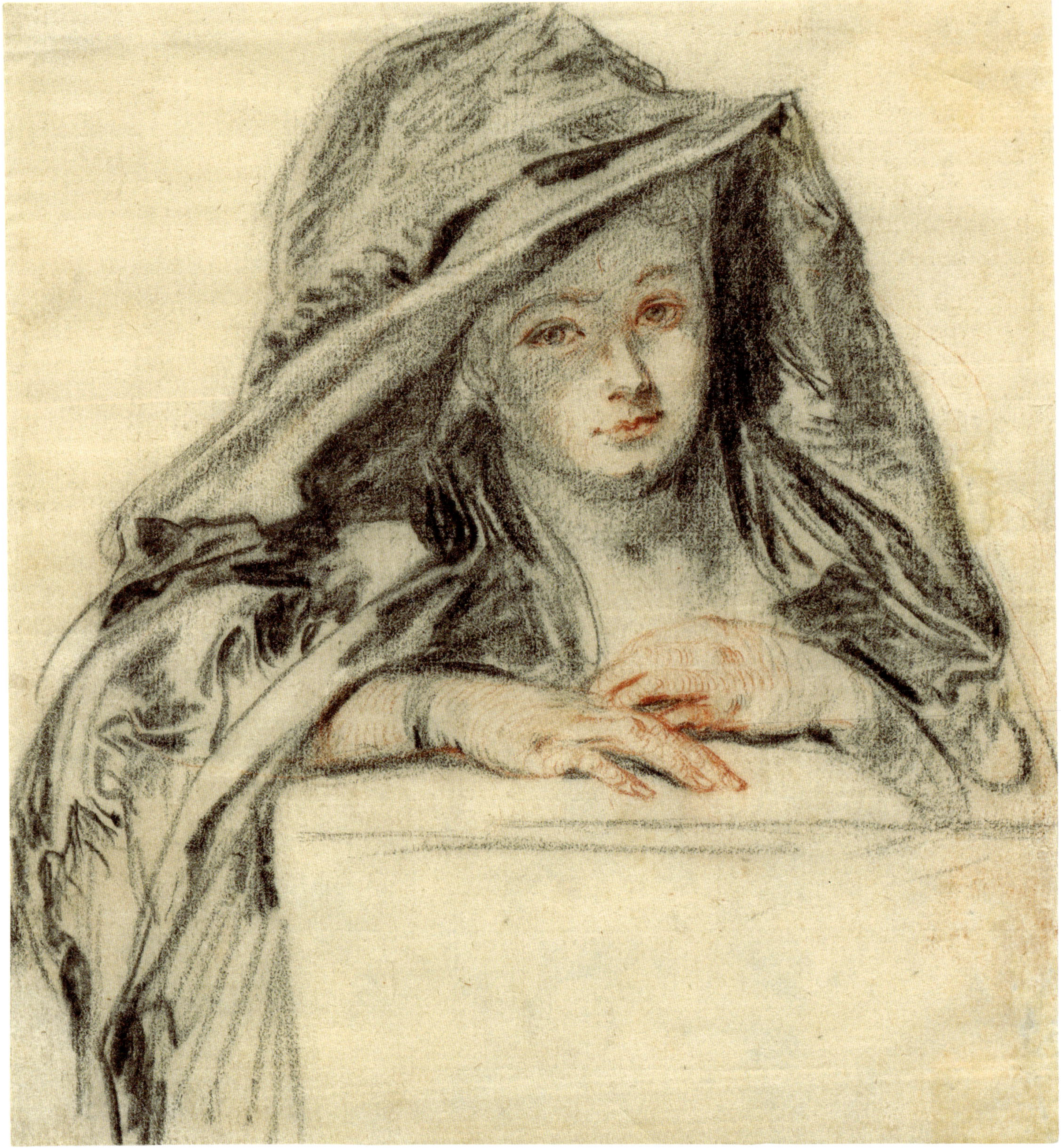

81

Woman Wearing a Mantle over Her Head and Shoulders

Red and black chalks and graphite on paper, 197 x 179 mm

Sterling and Francine Clark Art Institute, Williamstown, inv. 1831

PROVENANCE, EXHIBITED: PM 618; RP 619; New York 1999, no. 41, col.
LITERATURE, ENGRAVINGS: PM 618; RP 619, rep.

Watteau had already drawn twice, in *c.* 1717, a young woman wearing a large mantilla on her head, depicted to the waist in the two drawings now in two museums in Amsterdam (RP 567 and RP 568). Boucher engraved the second of these two pages in *Figures de différents caractères*, as he did the present drawing. The same woman, seated on the ground and wearing a dark cape, can also be found in two less delicate drawings, executed with less finesse, one in the Courtauld Institute, London (*c.* 1716?; RP 451), and the other in the Musée Condé, Chantilly (*c.* 1718; RP 600).

Watteau seems to have returned to this subject a few months later in this character study, which has a monumental feel despite its small dimensions; in our catalogue raisonné we suggested a date of *c.* 1718, whereas Margaret Morgan Grasselli leans towards 1718–19.

The artist must have felt the need to depict female figures draped in this manner to alternate with the graceful bare heads of so many of the women who appear in the paintings of *fêtes galantes*. Here, however, we should consider the almost funereal nature of a figure entirely framed in black, leaning against a coping that could be that of a tomb, and whose gaze expresses sorrow or at least regret. The touches of red chalk around the left eye give the impression that the eyes are damp and the gaze somewhat veiled. Watteau rarely dramatised female figures as he has here, concentrating just as intently on the hands, which are striking because they appear almost not to belong to the figure – as if they had been placed there at a later stage. L-AP

Red chalk and light stumping on paper, 145 x 179 mm
Inscription in red chalk at upper right: *4* (according to the 1994 catalogue)

Institut de France, Musée Jacquemart-André, Paris, inv. 1592

PROVENANCE, EXHIBITED, LITERATURE: PM 873; *Dessins français de la collection Chennevières*, exh. cat., Musée Jacquemart-André, Paris, 1994, no. 15; RP 621, col.

Group of Comedians near a Fountain with a Nymph Leaning Against a Dolphin

Group studies for a composition are very seldom found in Watteau's work, so seldom in fact that we have only been able to exhibit one example. The celebrated drawing from the Art Institute of Chicago (RP 599; fig. 37) is connected with the painting *Pleasures of Love* (Gemäldegalerie Alte Meister, Dresden). The rarity of such group studies should be measured against the yardstick of Caylus's famous words from his *Life* of Watteau, read out at the Académie des Beaux-Arts in 1748: 'I repeat that ordinarily he would draw without any purpose. He never made any sketches or outlines for any of his paintings, however light or unfinished these might have been.'

The only painting to which any sustained or painstaking sketches can be attached – to the extent that they could be qualified as preparatory drawings (RP 552, RP 622 and RP 179 verso) – seems to be *The Italian Players* (National Gallery of Art, Washington). The same grouping has also been attached to another painting, *The French Players* (Metropolitan Museum of Art, New York), in which a Crispin appears who resembles the one emerging here on the far right. The two paintings are generally dated to *c.* 1720, and the page of drawings here slightly earlier, to 1718–19.

The New York painting contains on the left-hand side a study of a fountain with a naiad seen from behind, her elbows resting on a dolphin. This combination can be found in the *The Open-air Gathering* (Gemäldegalerie Alte Meister, Dresden; fig. 38), although this contains no actors. Perhaps this drawing brings together two different designs, or is it possible that the page is not really a preliminary sketch for a composition as it is generally understood?

Noteworthy in this sheet is the appearance of the actors on a slightly raised stage, a stage into which the fountain on the left is integrated. We know that Watteau always enjoyed juxtaposing human figures with stone figures in his paintings, as for example in his composition entitled *French Performance*, which is known from an engraving (DV 294).

Here the arrangement of the figures is handled particularly successfully, but nevertheless it leaves us with a question that needs answering. The fake agitation of the naiad on the left, and the genuine agitation of Crispin on the right contrast sharply with the hieratic attitude of the Pierrot, who reminds us irresistibly of the celebrated painted figure in the Louvre (fig. 17). L-AP

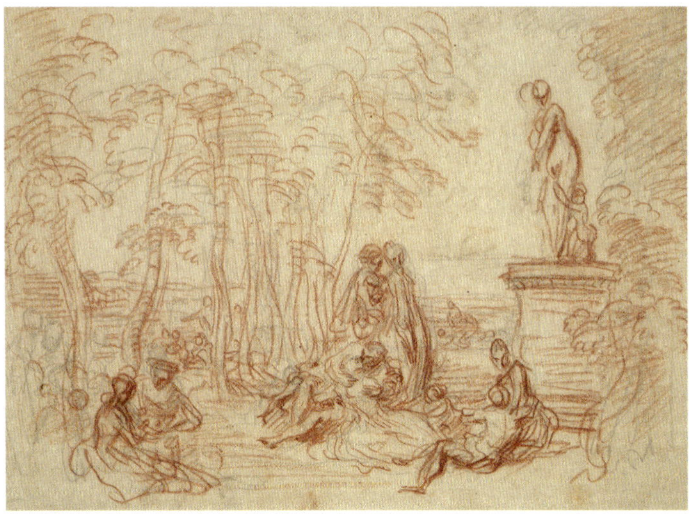

RIGHT
Fig. 37
Study for Pleasures of Love, 1717–18. Red chalk and graphite, 196 x 265 mm. Helen Regenstein Collection; Mrs Henry C. Woods and Wirt D. Walker Fund Endowments, The Art Institute of Chicago, inv. 1975.343

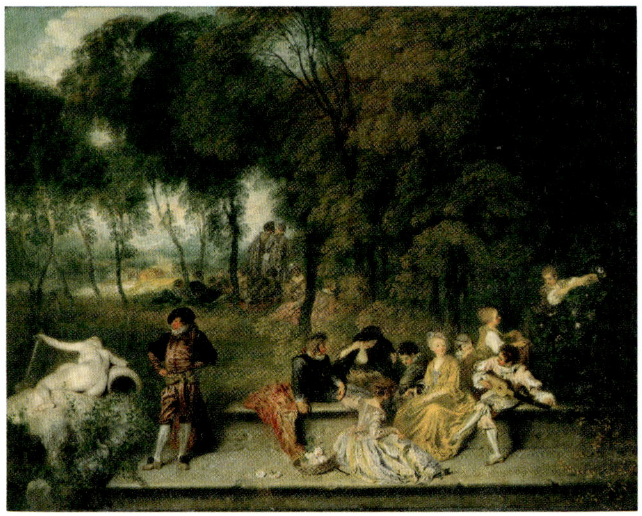

FAR RIGHT
Fig. 38
The Open-air Gathering, *c.* 1717–18. Oil on canvas, 60 x 75 cm. Gemäldegalerie Alte Meister, Dresden

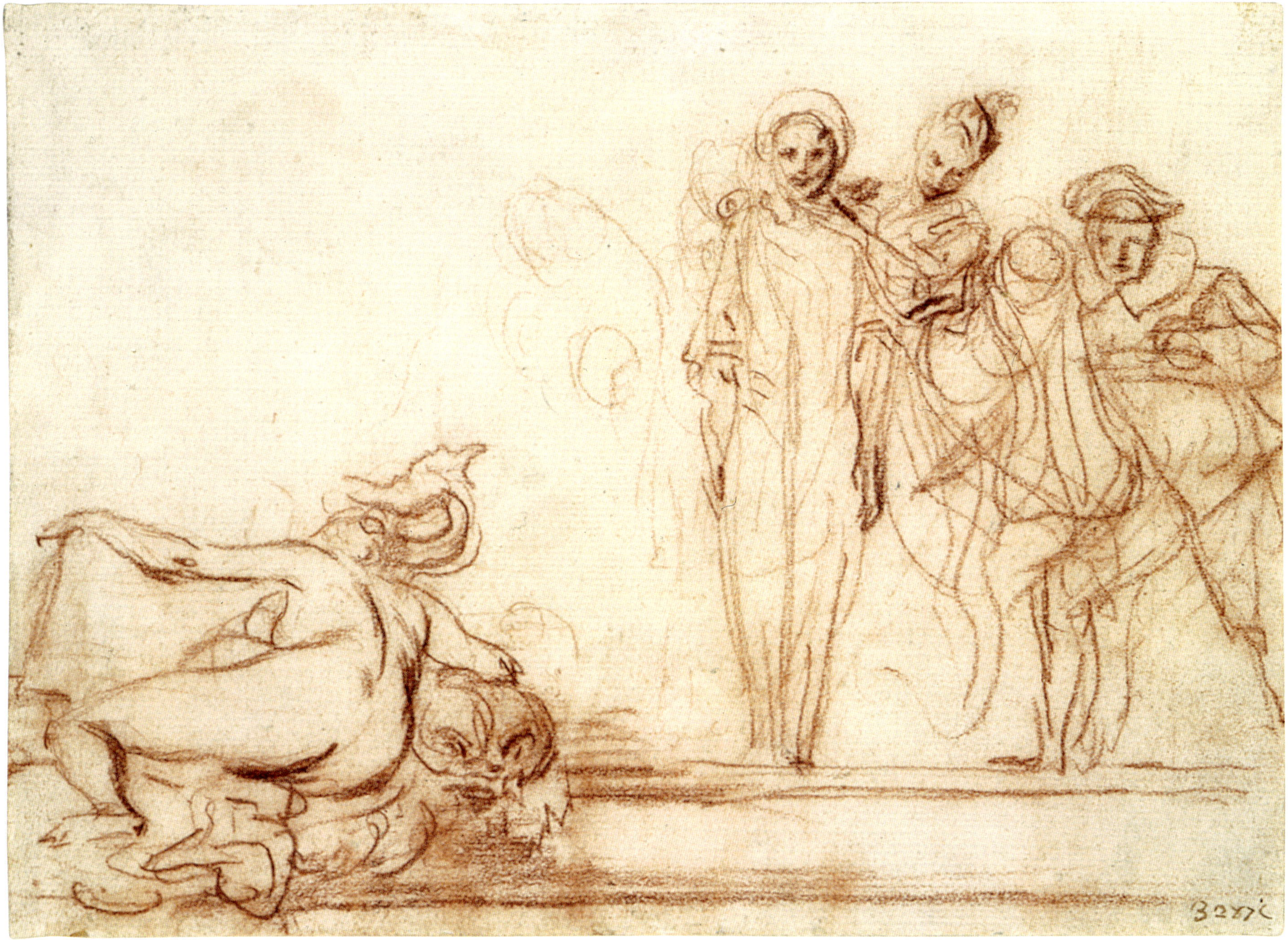

83

Two Bust-length Studies of Young Women (Portraits of the Daughters of Pierre Sirois)

Red and black chalks, stumping on paper, 189 x 125 mm; frame line drawn in pen with black ink

The Trustees of the British Museum, London, inv. 1895-9-15-942

PROVENANCE, EXHIBITED, LITERATURE: PM 925; RP 627, col. COPY: PM 925; RP 627

Pierre Sirois (1665–1726) was an art dealer and a friend of Watteau. He was also his first client, and purchased his first painting of a military subject, subsequently inviting him to his house in 1718; Watteau probably drew a portrait of him in 1718–19 (RP 626). This is still in a private collection, having appeared at auction in Paris on the occasion of one of the final dispersals of Watteau's work from the Groult collection.

Watteau used this drawing for his painting *In the Dress of a Mezzetin* (Wallace Collection, London), a composition portraying Sirois, his two daughters and two other unidentified figures. Sirois had a daughter from his first marriage, then three boys and three girls from his second. Two of the later daughters are depicted here, in poses repeated, but with very different hairstyles (these have the effect of turning the girls into characters from the Commedia dell'Arte), in the painting in the Wallace Collection. Here Watteau has depicted them in their normal outfits, one wearing a hairband and the other a mobcap.

The identification of these two young women has been the source of some argument. Emile Dacier and Albert Vuaflart, the specialists in engravings after Watteau, claim that above is Marie-Anne-Elisabeth, born in 1697, and below Anne-Elisabeth, born in 1692. Margaret Morgan Grasselli and Marianne Roland Michel on the other hand consider the second figure to be a third daughter, Marie-Louise, born in 1695, who in 1718 was to marry another art dealer and friend of Watteau, Edme-François Gersaint (1694–1750), who was immortalised by his shop sign, Au Grand Monarque, situated on the Pont Notre-Dame and painted by Watteau at the end of his life (see cat. 88, fig. 4).

The faces of the young girls are depicted more flatteringly in the British Museum drawing than in the painting in the Wallace Collection, and the artist's empathy with his models, so evident here, is much less pronounced in the painting. The lower portrait must have been made first: in order to perfect the upper portrait Watteau has added, in red chalk, along the first model's temple, a serpentine line which terminates the shoulder of the younger sister. L-AP

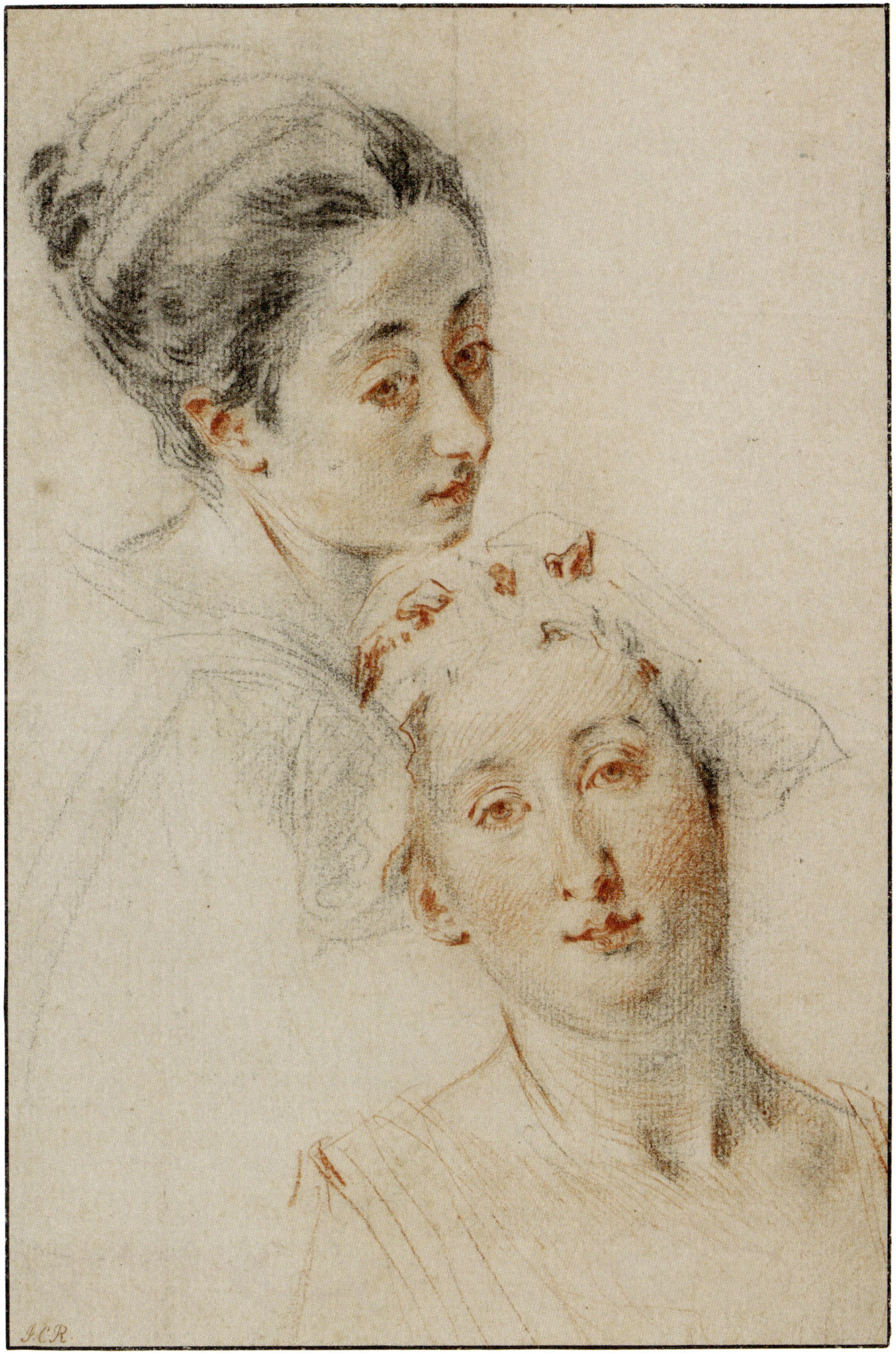

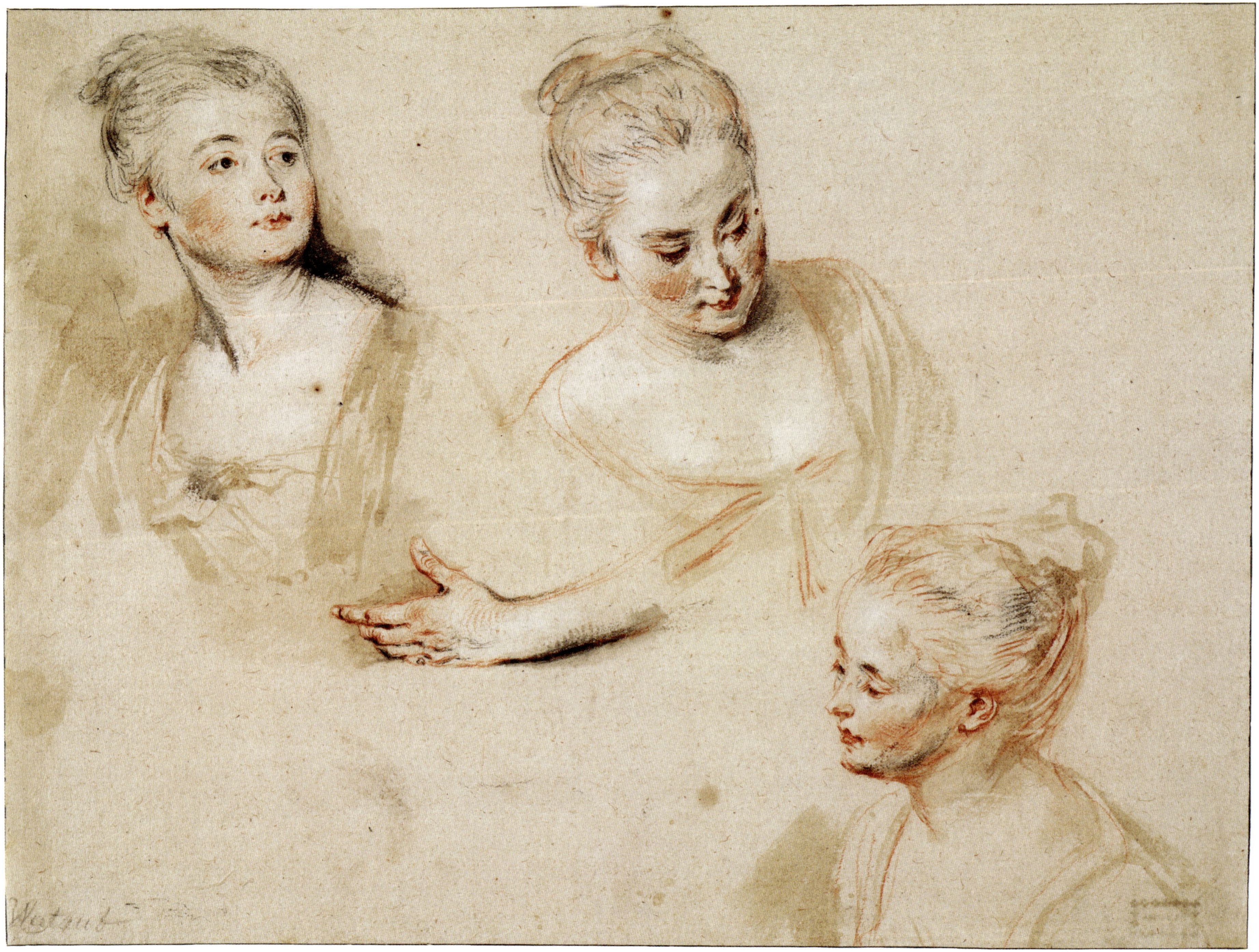

Red, black and white chalks, brush, brown, grey and red wash on beige paper, 265 x 346 mm
Inscription in black chalk at lower left *Wataut*

Teylers Museum, Haarlem, inv. M14

PROVENANCE, EXHIBITED, LITERATURE: PM 779; RP 634, col.

84

Three Bust-length Studies of Women; Study of a Left Forearm

The female model here is certainly the same as the model for the Amsterdam drawing (cat. 54), which contains studies of a seated woman, undoubtedly earlier (*c.* 1716?), and women's heads, two of which are heightened (as here) with a light brown wash. The studies of heads should, in our opinion, be dated to 1718–19 (1717–18 for Margaret Morgan Grasselli).

The brown wash here is much more remarkable, and it is used in a manner unusual for Watteau, who employs it to construct the bodice of the woman on the left, the bust of the woman in the centre and to suggest the chignon of the woman on the right. Much diluted and applied very delicately, it contrasts admirably with the strong, confident accents of red chalk and the highlights, generally quite short, of black chalk.
L-AP

Red and black chalks, stumping and brush, grey wash on cream paper, 202 x 146 mm; traces of frame line drawn in pen and brown ink at lower edge

Private collection, New York

PROVENANCE, LITERATURE: PM 784; RP 646, repr.
ENGRAVING: PM 784; RP 646

85

Bust of a Young Woman Wearing a Bonnet, Her Head in Profile

Watteau's stay in London lasted from the end of September 1719 to June or July 1720; he was hoping to regain his health, but neither the ministrations of Dr Mead, who is possibly though not very probably portrayed in a drawing in the Pébereau Collection (RP 636; fig. 39) (see Paris 2009, no. 21), nor those of a charlatan, Dr John Misaubin, produced any improvement. In addition came the worry of the crash caused by John Law's system (a radical restructuring of French public finances), in which Watteau seems to have lost large sums of money; Jullienne was able to save 6,000 *livres* for him, returning the money to him when he arrived back in Paris.

Few drawings can with any certitude be assigned confidently to Watteau's English visit. In fact only two are known, this page and another now in the British Museum (RP 645; fig. 11), which depicts the same model twice. The latter sheet is drawn on a page bearing as a watermark the arms of the City of London; it is almost certain that it dates from Watteau's cross-channel visit. The same young woman, very simply attired, with roundish cheeks, probably appears in both drawings; she is turned towards the left in each. In this case Watteau very delicately paints the shadows with a light wash, which softens the forms and adds subtlety to the light. L-AP

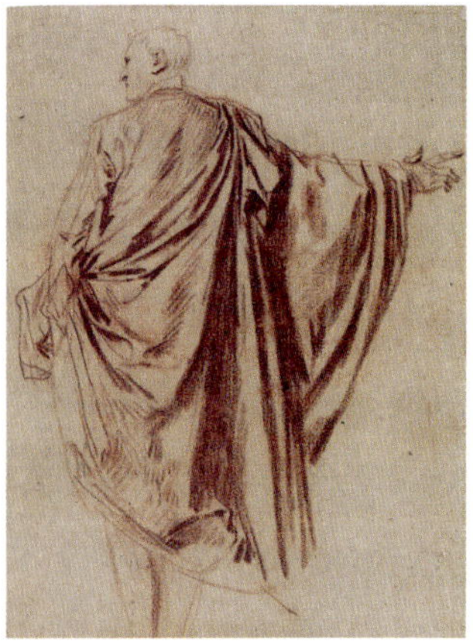

Fig. 39
Standing Man in a Gown, Seen from Behind, His Head Turned to the Left, His Right Arm Raised, c. 1720. Red chalk, 172 x 126 mm. Collection Pébereau, Paris

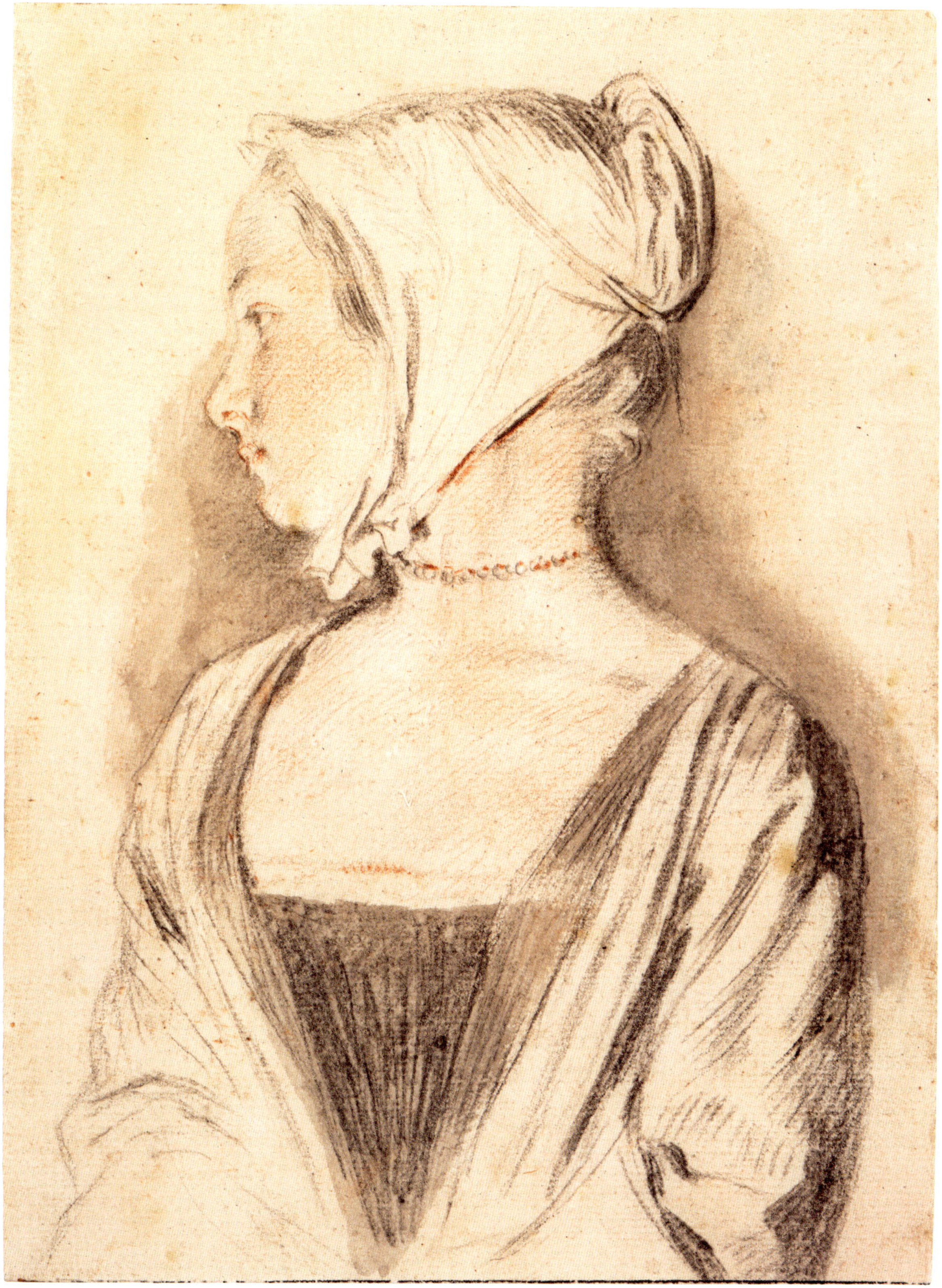

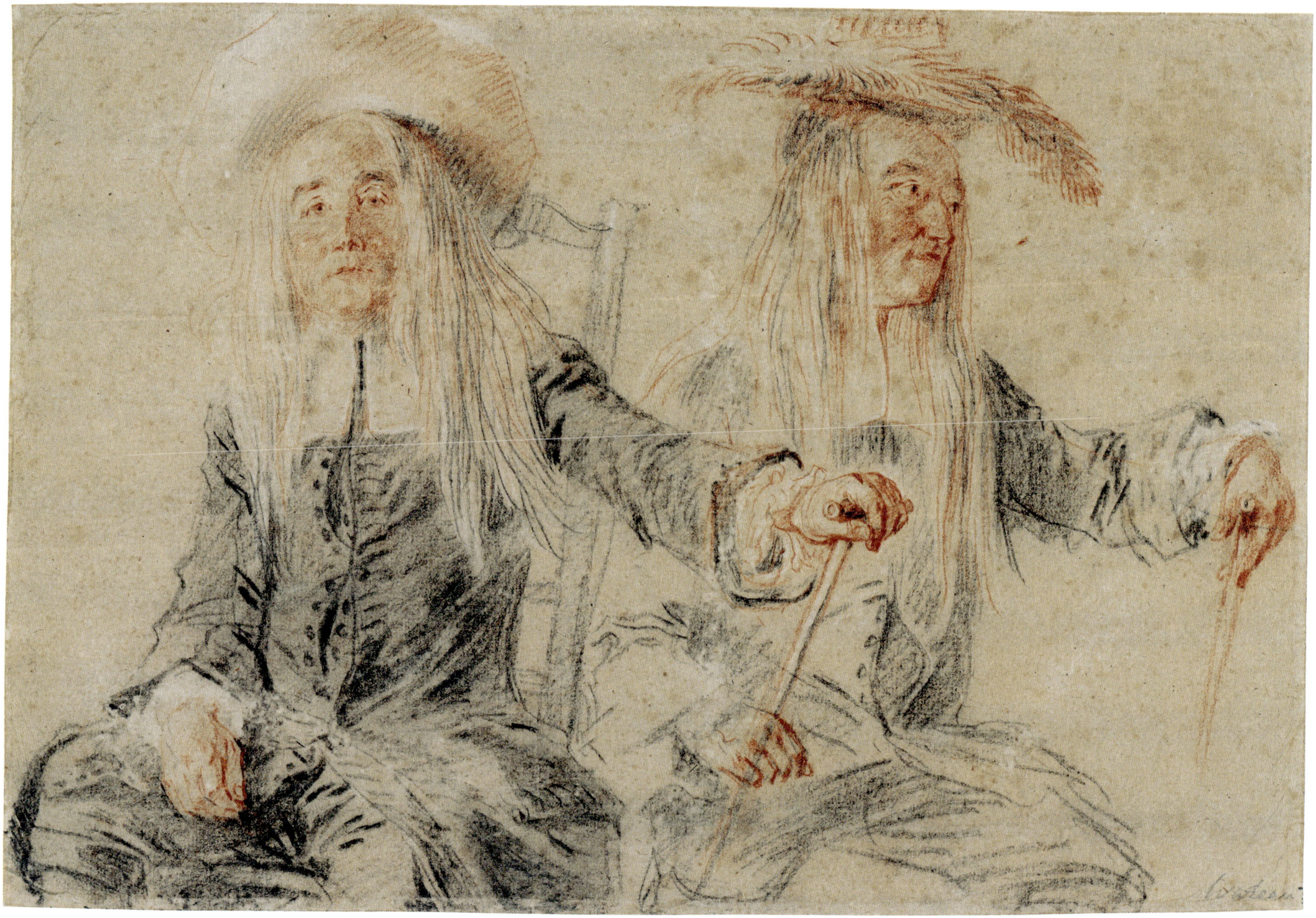

Red, black and white chalks on cream paper, 365 x 257 mm; fully glued to backing
Inscription in graphite at lower right *Wateau*

Staatliche Museen zu Berlin, Kupferstichkabinett, inv. KdZ 2319

PROVENANCE, EXHIBITED: PM 914; RP 653, col.; Rosenberg 2000, p. 31, fig. 29; Temperini 2002, col. p. 27
ENGRAVINGS, COPY: PM 914; RP 653

86

Double Portrait of Canon Haranger, His Left Hand Resting on a Cane

The curious character depicted here – curious as much for his good-natured look as for the strange plumed headdress he wears on the right, which seems to have been added later in a spirit of mockery – was one of Watteau's close friends. It is almost certain today that he is Canon Haranger (d. 1735), but for a long time the drawing was thought to portray an actor by the name of Pierre La Thorillière; some of Boucher's engravings taken from this drawing and published in various copies of *Figures de différents caractères* bear his surname. However, the copy of the same anthology now in the Bibliothèque de l'Arsenal in Paris names the model as Haranger 'chanoine st Germain l'auxerrois ami de Watteau' (Canon of Saint-Germain l'Auxerrois and friend of Watteau). In addition, the copy of the Jullienne sale catalogue annotated by Mariette, also in the Bibliothèque de l'Arsenal, names Haranger as the model for both studies.

Watteau seems to have walked around his model as the Canon posed in a chair with his left hand on his thigh and his right on the knob of his walking stick. Why do we get the impression that the character on the right is quite a bit fatter, and also a little older? Is it because Boucher gave him another headdress, the skullcap to be seen in his engraving? Boucher does not reproduce the unsuitable plumed hat. It is impossible not to feel somewhat surprised by this celebrated page, and the feeling of malaise is increased by a desire to place this drawing accurately in Watteau's chronology; other pages, produced earlier or later in the artist's career (RP 75, RP 130, RP 135, RP 460), are known which depict an (old?) man with equally long hair. At the time of the 1984 Watteau retrospective (see Washington 1984), Margaret Morgan Grasselli thought the work should be assigned to *c.* 1716; then in 1987 she reassigned it to the final months before Watteau's death. Marianne Roland Michel opted for 1716–17. In our catalogue raisonné we considered a date of *c.* 1720 to be plausible, taking into account the authority with which the two figures are placed on the page.

The Abbé Pierre-Maurice Haranger was linked to Watteau and according to Mariette possessed two paintings by him, *The Anxious Lady Love* (Musée Condé, Chantilly) and *Girl Dreaming* (private collection, New York). He is known above all for being one of the four friends among whom Watteau divided his drawings before he died, the three others being Gersaint, Jullienne and Nicolas Henin (other sources name Haranger as the sole heir to the drawings). At any rate, Haranger's estate inventory of 1735 mentions more than 1,000 drawings by Watteau, a huge number and far greater than the number we know today. L-AP

Red, black and white chalks on grey-brown paper, 340 x 245 mm; frame line drawn in pen and black ink

Nationalmuseum, Stockholm, inv. NM 2836/1863

PROVENANCE, EXHIBITED, LITERATURE: PM 787; RP 659, rep.; Rosenberg 2000, p. 35, fig. 35; Temperini 2002, col., p. 29

87

Four Studies of Women's Heads

As with many studies of heads, this page, which probably dates from about 1720 or just before, is divided into two registers, and the question we need to ask relates to the identity of the model or models, since the black corners of the headdress seen on the foreheads of the two women below do not appear on those above.

Agreement has been reached on the matter of the identity of these faces, if they belong to the same person – which we deem to be almost certain; they are either Marie-Anne-Elisabeth Sirois or her younger sister Marie-Louise, the future Mme Gersaint, both of whom we have already encountered in a study now in the British Museum (cat. 83). A woman considered to represent her, and whose expression is very similar to the expression of the woman at the top right here, can be found behind the counter in *The Gersaint Shop Sign* (Schloss Charlottenburg, Berlin; fig. 4), where we could expect to find her. L-AP

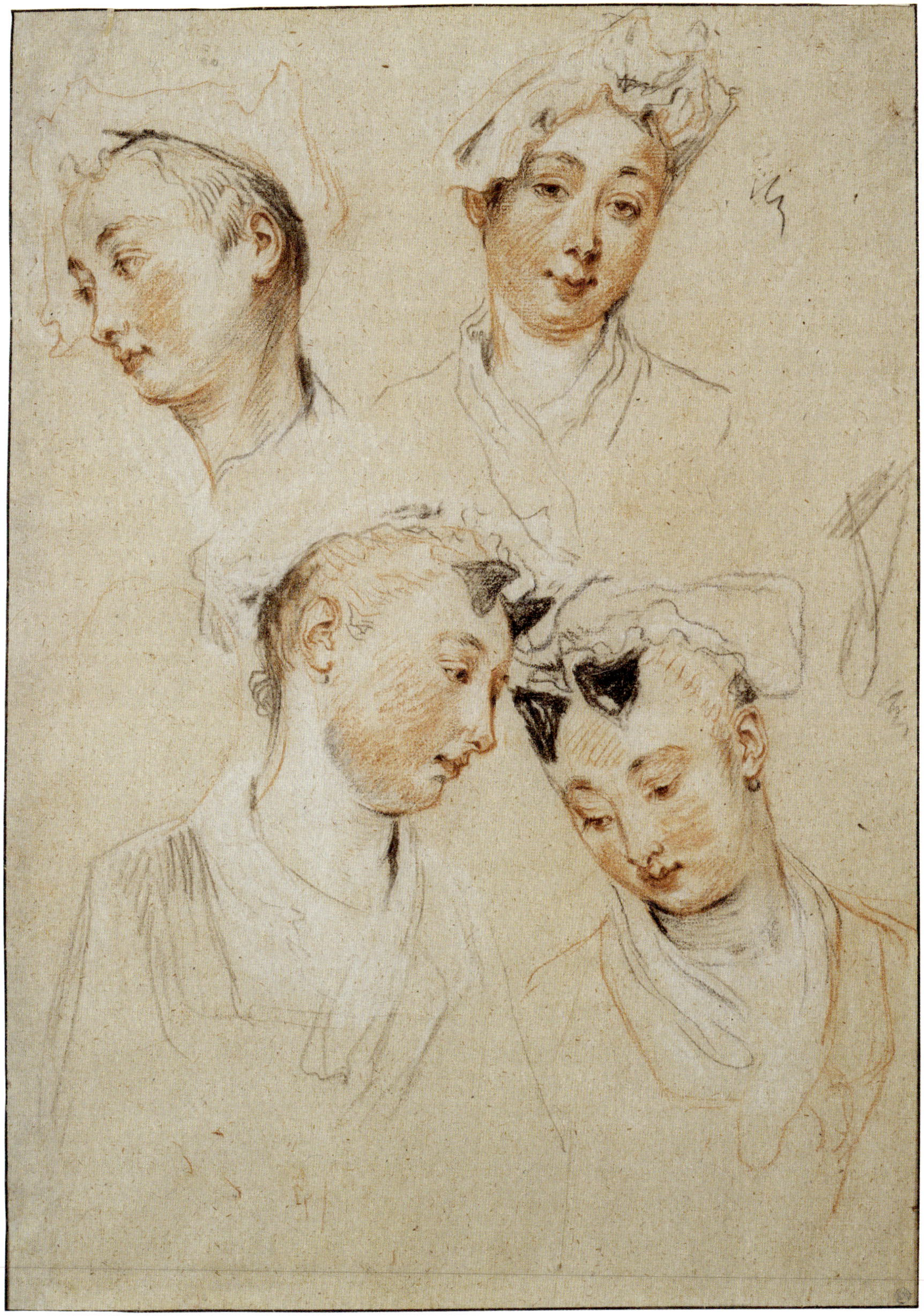

Red, black and white chalks on beige paper, 168 x 227 mm; frame line drawn in pen and brown ink

Musée Cognacq-Jay, Paris, inv. J. 195

PROVENANCE, EXHIBITED, LITERATURE: PM 688; RP 661, col.; Rosenberg 2000, p. 141, fig. 182; Temperini 2002, col. p. 27; Edwards 2006, pp. 54, 56–57, fig. 11; Vogtherr and Wenders de Calisse 2007, p. 302, fig. 9, p. 303

88

Two Men Packing a Crate, One Holding a Framed Picture, the Other a Mirror

We know that Watteau painted *The Gersaint Shop Sign* (fig. 4), depicting his friend's shop on the Pont Notre-Dame, on his return from England, probably between September 1720 and the first days of 1721, the year of his death. The present drawing is celebrated because of its relationship with this painting, but also because for a long time it seemed to be the only study that could genuinely be described as a preparatory study for the painting; the subjects are the two characters on the left of the composition, one handling a painted portrait of Louis XIV, which he places in a crate, the other a mirror frame.

In fact two other drawings can be linked to the painting: the first (RP 160) is a youthful work, a study of a young man standing, which Watteau repeated with some variations for the figure of the man seen standing in the centre; the second is a copy by Watteau of a figure by Bernard Picart (RP 203), also modified to become the old woman seen from behind, dressed in black, examining with her lorgnette a large oval composition standing on the floor.

Another, much earlier drawing can be connected with *The Gersaint Shop Sign*. Now in the Courtauld Institute, London (cat. 50), this is a copy in red chalk by Watteau, executed in about 1715–16, of two compositions by a sixteenth-century Venetian master, a Holy Family and a Mystic Marriage of St Catherine. The fusion of these two compositions resulted in the invention of a new painting, the one hanging on the right-hand wall of Gersaint's shop, just above the curved frame being displayed on the counter by the young woman (Mme Gersaint or, more probably, one of her daughters; see cat. 87). Many authors believe that this curved frame contains a mirror, but it would not be surprising – considering that three people, two men and a woman, are looking at it from three different points of view – if it were instead a small painting, probably Northern European, possibly painted on copper.

The most obvious question remains: did Watteau draw the two men with his painting in mind, or did he draw them – as Caylus maintains – with no particular aim? At all events the page, with its somewhat jagged lines and the accents that suggest more than they emphasise, can be assigned to a fairly late date. A query also hangs over the choice of red chalk heightened with white for the right-hand figure, and black chalk enhanced with a little red for the flesh of the left-hand figure; it is also worth noting that, at some stage between the drawing and the painting, each character has taken the place of the other. L-AP

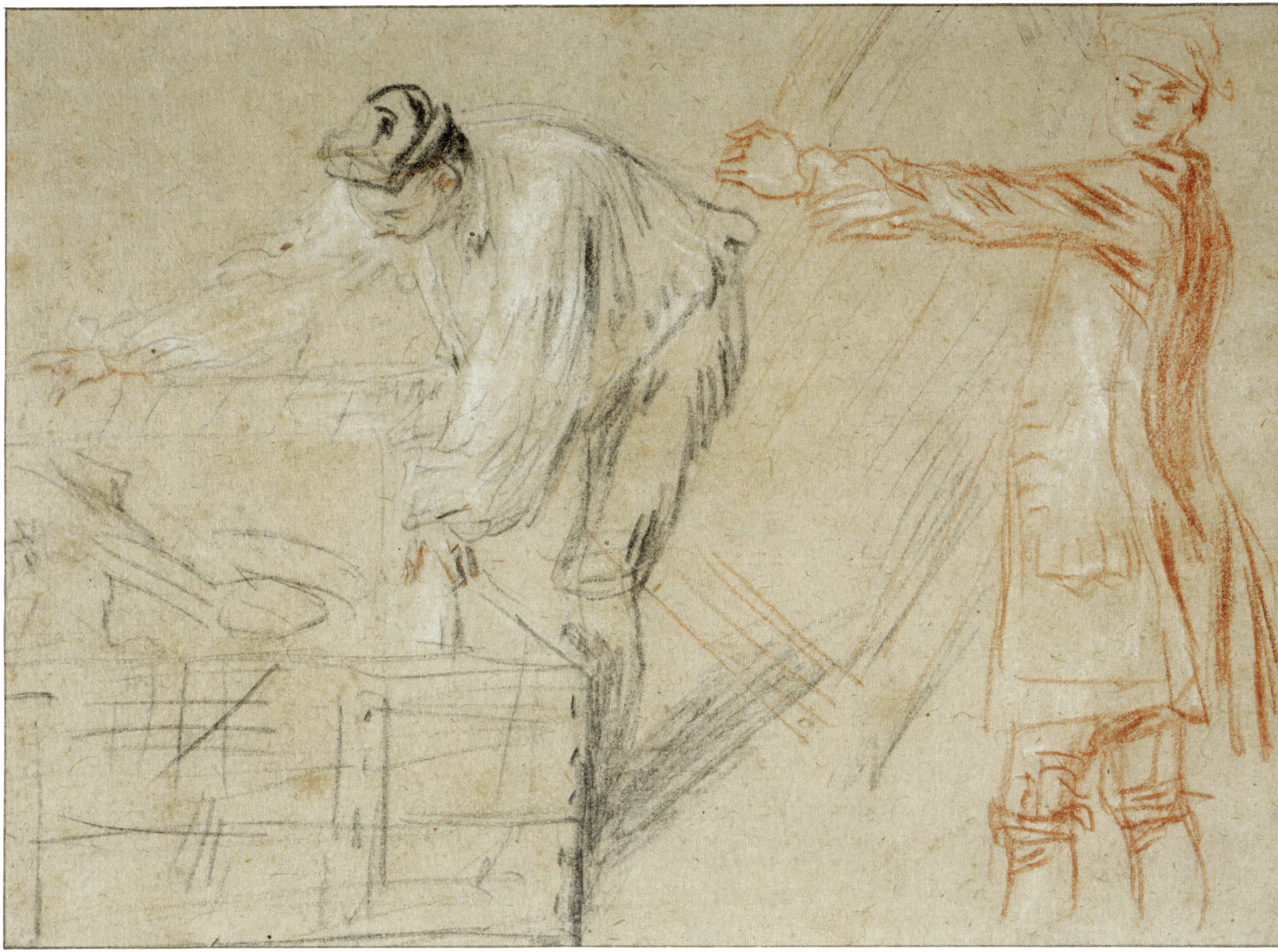

Bibliography and Sources

Arikha 2001
Avigdor Arikha, 'Note à propos des dessins de Watteau', in *Mélanges en hommage à Pierre Rosenberg: peintures et dessins en France et en Italie, XVIIe–XVIIIe siècles*, Paris, 2001

Bailey 1997
Colin B. Bailey, 'Books in Review: Antoine Watteau 1684–1721: catalogue raisonné des dessins', *On Paper*, 1, 5, May–June 1997, pp. 45–48

Barcelona 2007
Pasión por el dibujo: de Poussin a Cézanne; obras maestras de la Colección Prat, exh. cat., Fundación 'La Caixa', Barcelona, 2007

Börsch-Supan 2000
Helmut Börsch-Supan, *Antoine Watteau, 1684–1721*, Cologne, 2000

Braunschweig 2005
Andreas W. Vetter, *Antoine Watteau – 'Venezianische Feste'*, exh. cat., Herzog-Anton-Ulrich-Museum, Braunschweig, 2005

Brugerolles 1984
Emmanuelle Brugerolles, *Les Dessins de la Collection Armand-Valton: la donation d'un grand collectionneur du XIXe siècle à l'Ecole des Beaux-Arts; inventaire général*, Paris, 1984

Budapest 2008
Poussintől Davidig: francia mesterrajzok a Louvre gyűjteményéből / From Poussin to David: French Master Drawings from the Louvre, exh. cat., Szépművészeti Múzeum, Budapest, 2008

Burollet 2008
Thérèse Burollet, *Pastels et dessins, Musée Cognacq-Jay. Musée du XVIIIe siècle de la Ville de Paris*, Paris, 2008

Cambridge 1998
Mastery and Elegance: Two Centuries of French Drawings from the Collection of Jeffrey E. Horvitz, exh. cat., Arthur M. Sackler Museum, Harvard University, Cambridge, Mass.; Art Gallery of Ontario, Toronto; Musée Jacquemart-André, Paris; National Gallery of Scotland, Edinburgh; National Academy Museum and School of Fine Arts, New York; Los Angeles County Museum of Art, 1998–2000

Camesasca 1983
Ettore Camesasca, *Tout l'œuvre peint de Watteau*, Paris, 1983

Camesasca and Sunderland 1968
Ettore Camesasca and John Sunderland, *The Complete Paintings of Watteau*, New York, 1968

Chantilly 1996
Pierre Rosenberg, *Watteau et son cercle dans les collections de l'Institut de France*, exh. cat., Musée Condé, Chantilly, 1996–97

Chicago 1974
Harold Joachim, *The Regenstein Collection of European Drawings*, exh. cat., The Art Institute of Chicago, 1974

Conisbee 2009
Philip Conisbee (ed.), *French Paintings of the Fifteenth through the Eighteenth Century*, National Gallery of Art Systematic Catalogue, Princeton, 2009

Cordellier, Rosenberg and Märker 2007
Dominique Cordellier, Pierre Rosenberg and Peter Märker, *Dessins français du musée de Darmstadt: XVIe, XVIIe et XVIIIe siècles*, Paris, 2007

Dacier and Vuaflart 1922
Emile Dacier and Albert Vuaflart, *Jean de Jullienne et la gravure de Watteau au XVIIIème siècle*, Paris, 1922

Edwards 2001
JoLynn Edwards, 'John Law and His Painting Collection: Connoisseur or Dupe?', in *Art and Culture in the Eighteenth Century: New Dimensions and Multiple Perspectives*, Newark, 2001, pp. 59–75

Edwards 2006
JoLynn Edwards, 'Watteau Drawings: Artful and Natural', in Sheriff 2006, pp. 41–62

Eidelberg 1977
Martin Eidelberg, *Watteau's Drawings, Their Uses and Significance*, PhD dissertation, Princeton University, 1977

Eidelberg 2002
Martin Eidelberg, 'Watteau's "Rêve de l'artiste" Unveiled', *Gazette des Beaux-Arts*, October 2002, pp. 217–32

Eidelberg 2003
Martin Eidelberg, 'How Watteau Designed His Arabesques', *Cleveland Studies in the History of Art*, August 2003, pp. 68–79

Feinberg and Zuccari 1997
Larry J. Feinberg and Frank Zuccari, 'A Rediscovered "Fête Champêtre" by Watteau in the Art Institute of Chicago', *Burlington Magazine*, 139, 1129, April 1997, pp. 236–47

Fumaroli 1996
Marc Fumaroli, 'Une Amitié paradoxale: Antoine Watteau et le comte de Caylus (1712–1719)', *Revue de l'Art*, 114, 1, 1996, pp. 34–47

Geneva 2006
Suite française: dessins de la collection Jean Bonna, exh. cat., Musée d'Art et d'Histoire, Geneva, 2006 (see also Paris 2006 for a variant edition)

Goncourt 1875
Edmond de Goncourt, *Catalogue raisonné de l'œuvre peint, dessiné, et gravé d'Antoine Watteau*, Paris, 1875

Grasselli 2000
Margaret Morgan Grasselli, 'Following in Watteau's Line: Some Drawings by Jean-Baptiste Pater', *Master Drawings*, 2000, 38, 2, pp. 159–67

Grasselli 2001
Margaret Morgan Grasselli, 'Reviews: Pierre Rosenberg and Louis-Antoine Prat, "Antoine Watteau 1684–1721, Catalogue raisonné des dessins"', *Master Drawings*, 39, 3, Autumn 2001, pp. 310–34

Hattori 2001
Cordélia Hattori, 'De La Fosse à Watteau, Les saisons Crozat', *Revue du Louvre*, April 2001, 2, pp. 56–65

Henriot 1928
Gabriel Henriot (ed.), *Collection David-Weill*, vol. 3, Paris, 1928

Huyghe and Adhémar 1950
René Huyghe and Hélène Adhémar, *Watteau: sa vie, son œuvre*, Paris, 1950

Los Angeles 2004
Passion for Drawing: Poussin to Cézanne, Works from the Prat Collection, exh. cat., Los Angeles County Museum of Art, Toledo Museum of Art, Naples Museum of Art, Florida, Philadelphia Museum of Art, 2004–05

Mathey 1959
Jacques Mathey, *Antoine Watteau, peintures réapparues*, Paris, 1959

Méjanès 1999
Jean-François Méjanès, 'L'Album Groult, Nouvelles Acquisitions', *La Revue du Louvre*, 1999, 1, p. 88

Milan 2003
Il gran teatro del mondo. L'anima e il volto del Settecento, exh. cat., Palazzo Reale, Milan, 2003–04

Monreau and Grasselli 1987
François Monreau and Margaret Morgan Grasselli (eds), *Antoine Watteau (1684–1721): The Painter, His Age and His Legend*, Paris and Geneva, 1987

Moureau 2001
François Moureau, 'De Watteau à Chardin: Antoine de la Roque, journaliste et collectionneur', in *Mélanges en hommage à Pierre Rosenberg: peintures et dessins en France et en Italie, XVIIe–XVIIIe siècles*, Paris, 2001, pp. 349–55

New York 1993
Cara D. Denison, *French Master Drawings from the Pierpont Morgan Library*, exh. cat., Musée du Louvre, Paris; Pierpont Morgan Library, New York, 1993–94

New York 1999
Alan Wintermute, Colin B. Bailey and Pierre Rosenberg, *Watteau and His World: French Drawing from 1700 to 1750*, exh. cat., Frick Collection, New York; National Gallery of Canada, Ottawa, 1999–2000

New York 2007
Untitled exhibition, exh. cat., Mark Brady Gallery, New York, 2007

New York 2008
Untitled exhibition, exh. cat., Mark Brady Gallery, New York, 2008

New York 2009A
Katharine Baetjer (ed.), *Watteau, Music and Theater*, exh. cat., The Metropolitan Museum of Art, New York, 2009

New York 2009B
Watteau to Degas: French Drawings from the Frits Lugt Collection, exh. cat., Frick Collection, New York, 2009

Ottawa 2003
Colin B. Bailey, Philip Conisbee and Thomas W. Gaehtgens, *The Age of Watteau, Chardin, and Fragonard: Masterpieces of French Genre Painting*, exh. cat. National Gallery of Canada, Ottawa; National Gallery of Art, Washington DC; Staaliche Museen zu Berlin, 2003–04

Oxford 1994
Drawings by Contemporaries of Voltaire: Eighteenth-century French Drawings from the Print Room of the Ashmolean, exh. cat., Ashmolean Museum, Oxford, 1994

Paris 1997
La Donation Jacques Petithory au Musée Bonnat, Bayonne: objets d'art, sculptures, peintures, dessins, exh. cat., Musée du Luxembourg, Paris, 1997–98

Paris 2000A
Louis-Antoine Prat, *L'Empire du temps, mythes et créations*, exh. cat., Musée du Louvre, Paris, 2000

Paris 2000B
Posséder et détruire: stratégies sexuelles dans l'art d'occident, exh. cat., Musée du Louvre, Paris, 2000

Paris 2001
Collectionner, passionnément: les collectionneurs hollandais de dessins au XVIIIe siècle, exh. cat., Fondation Custodia, Institut Néerlandais, Paris, 2001

Paris 2003
R. J. A. te Rijdt, *De Watteau à Ingres: dessins français du XVIIIe siècle du Rijksmuseum Amsterdam*, exh. cat., Fondation Custodia, Institut Néerlandais, Paris, 2003

Paris 2006
Suite française: dessins de la collection Jean Bonna, exh. cat., Ecole nationale supérieure des Beaux-Arts, Paris, 2006 (see also Geneva 2006 for a variant edition)

Paris 2009
Maîtres du dessin européen du XVIe au XXe siècle, la collection Georges Pébereau, exh. cat., Musée du Louvre, Paris, 2009–10

Paris 2010
Marie-Catherine Sahut, *Antoine Watteau et l'art de l'estampe*, exh. cat., Musée du Louvre, Paris, 2010

Parker 1931
Karl Theodor Parker, *The Drawings of Antoine Watteau*, London, 1931

Parker and Mathey 1957
Karl Theodor Parker and Jacques Mathey, *Antoine Watteau: catalogue complet de son œuvre dessiné*, Paris, 1957

Plax 2000
Julie-Anne Plax, *Watteau and the Cultural Politics of Eighteenth-century France*, Cambridge, New York and Melbourne, 2000

Posner 1984
Donald Posner, *Antoine Watteau*, Ithaca, 1984

Prat 2003
Louis-Antoine Prat, 'Philippe de Chennevières, Nélie Jacquemart-André et Jeffrey E. Horvitz: trois collections de dessins d'artistes français', in *Dessins français aux XVIIe et XVIIIe siècles, Rencontres de l'Ecole du Louvre*, Paris, 2003

Roland Michel 1984
Marianne Roland Michel, *Watteau: An Artist of the Eighteenth Century*, London, 1984

Roland Michel 1998
Marianne Roland Michel, 'The Rosenberg-Prat Catalogue of Watteau's Drawings', *The Burlington Magazine*, 140, 1148, November 1998, pp. 749–54

Rosenberg 1984
Pierre Rosenberg (ed.), *Vies anciennes de Watteau*, Paris, 1984 (Italian edition: *Le Vite antiche*, Bologna, 1991)

Rosenberg 1990
Pierre Rosenberg, 'Un Chef d'œuvre entre au Louvre: *Les Deux Cousines* de Watteau', *Revue du Louvre et des Musées de France*, 1990, pp. 259–62

Rosenberg 2000
Pierre Rosenberg, *From Drawing to Painting: Poussin, Watteau, Fragonard, David and Ingres*, Princeton, 2000 (see Rosenberg 2001 for French edition)

Rosenberg 2001
Pierre Rosenberg, *Du Dessin au tableau: Poussin, Watteau, Fragonard, David et Ingres*, Flammarion, Paris, 2001 (the French edition of Rosenberg 2000)

Rosenberg 2003
Pierre Rosenberg, 'L'album Groult, dit aussi album Lepeltier', in *Preußen: die Kunst und das Individuum*, Berlin, 2003, pp. 29–39

Rosenberg 2005
Pierre Rosenberg, *De Raphaël à la Révolution: les relations artistiques entre la France et l'Italie*, Paris, 2005

Rosenberg and Barthélémy 2011
Pierre Rosenberg and Laure Barthélémy, *La Collection Mariette: les dessins français*, Paris, 2011

Rosenberg and Prat 1996
Pierre Rosenberg and Louis-Antoine Prat, *Antoine Watteau, 1684–1721: catalogue raisonné des dessins*, 3 vols, Milan, 1996

Sarasota 2006
Suzanne Boorsch and John Marciari (eds), *Master Drawings from the Yale University Art Gallery*, exh. cat., The John and Mable Ringling Museum of Art, Sarasota, Florida; The Jack S. Blanton Museum of Art, Austin, Texas; Yale University Art Gallery, 2006–08

Sheriff 2006
Mary D. Sheriff (ed.), *Antoine Watteau: Perspectives on the Artist and the Culture of His Time*, Cranbury, New Jersey, 2006

Sydney 2003
The James Fairfax Collection: A Personal View of European Masterpieces, exh. cat., Art Gallery of New South Wales, Sydney, 2003

Sydney 2005
Emmanuelle Brugerolles, *Boucher, Watteau and the Origin of the Rococo*, exh. cat., Art Gallery of New South Wales, Sydney, 2005

Temperini 2002
Renaud Temperini, *Watteau*, Milan and Paris, 2002

Temperini 2005
Renaud Temperini, *Watteau*, Paris, 2005

Valenciennes 2004
Martin Eidelberg, *Watteau et la fête galante*, exh. cat., Musée des Beaux-Arts, Valenciennes, 2004

Viatte 1997A
Françoise Viatte, 'Un Dessin de Watteau (1684–1721) donné par la Société des Amis du Louvre au Département des Arts graphiques', *Revue du Louvre*, 1997, 4, pp. 24–26, rep.

Viatte 1997B
Françoise Viatte, 'A *Study of Heads* by Antoine Watteau at the Musée du Louvre', *Apollo*, November 1997, pp. 54–55, fig. col. 1, details fig. 2 and on the cover

Vidal 1992
Mary Vidal, *Watteau's Painted Conversations: Art, Literature and Talk in Seventeenth- and Eighteenth-century France*, London and New Haven, 1992

Vogtherr and Wenders de Calisse 2007
Christoph-Martin Vogtherr and Eva Wenders de Calisse, 'Watteau's "Shopsign": The Long Creation of a Masterpiece', *Burlington Magazine*, 149, 1250, May 2007, pp. 296–304

Washington 1984
Margaret Morgan Grasselli and Pierre Rosenberg, *Watteau 1684–1721*, exh. cat., National Gallery of Art, Washington DC; Galeries Nationales du Grand Palais, Paris; Schloss Charlottenburg, Berlin, 1984–85

Washington 2009
Renaissance to Revolution: French Drawings from the National Gallery of Art, 1500–1800, exh. cat., National Gallery of Art, Washington, 2009–10

Weimar 2005
David Mandrella, Hermann Mildenberger, Benjamin Peronnet and Pierre Rosenberg, *De Callot à Greuze: dessins français des XVIIe et XVIIIe siècles des musées de Weimar*, exh. cat., Stiftung Weimarer Klassik und Kunstsammlungen, Weimar; The Frick Collection, New York; Musée Jacquemart-André, Paris, 2005–06

Whiteley 2000
Jon Whiteley, *Ashmolean Museum: Catalogue of the Collection of Drawings, VII, French School*, 2 vols, Oxford, 2000

Wine 1997
Humphrey Wine, 'Book Reviews: "Watteau's Drawings"', *Apollo*, November 1997, pp. 59–60

List of Lenders to the Exhibition

Amsterdam
Rijksmuseum

Bayonne
Musée Bonnat

Berlin
Staatliche Museen zu Berlin, Kupferstichkabinett

Boston
Museum of Fine Arts

Cambridge
Fitzwilliam Museum

Cambridge, Mass.
Harvard Art Museum, Fogg Museum

Chicago
Art Institute of Chicago

Copenhagen
Statens Museum for Kunst

Darmstadt
Hessisches Landesmuseum

Dresden
Kupferstich-Kabinett, Staatliche Kunstsammlungen

Florence
Istituti museali della Soprintendenza Speciale per il Polo Museale Fiorentino

Geneva
Collection Jean Bonna

Haarlem
Teylers Museum

Lisbon
Calouste Gulbenkian Museum

London
British Museum
Courtauld Gallery

Los Angeles
J. Paul Getty Museum

New York
Metropolitan Museum of Art
Pierpont Morgan Library
Carolyne Roehm

Oxford
Ashmolean Museum

Paris
Ecole nationale supérieure des Beaux-Arts
Institut de France, Musée Jacquemart-André
Fondation Custodia
Louis-Antoine and Véronique Prat Collection
Musée Cognacq-Jay
Musée du Louvre
Petit Palais

Rennes
Musée des Beaux-Arts

Rotterdam
Museum Boijmans Van Beuningen

Rouen
Musée des Beaux-Arts

San Francisco
Collection of Ann and Gordon Getty

Stockholm
Nationalmuseum

Sydney
Art Gallery of New South Wales

Vienna
Albertina

Washington
National Gallery of Art

Weimar
Klassik Stiftung

Williamstown
Sterling and Francine Clark Art Institute

and others who wish to remain anonymous

Photographic Acknowledgements

All works of art are reproduced by kind permission of the owners. Every effort has been made to trace the photographers of works reproduced. Specific acknowledgements are as follows: .

Jörg P. Anders: cat. 86
© Jean-Gilles Berizzi: fig. 32
Boston, © 2011, Museum of Fine Arts: cat. 69
Herbert Boswank: cat. 11
Cambridge, © Fitzwilliam Museum: cat. 34
Cambridge, Mass., © President and Fellows of Harvard College/Allan Macintyre: cat. 47
Chicago, © The Art Institute of Chicago: cat. 27, figs 9, 37
Cologne, culture-images/Lebrecht: fig. 28
Cologne, Rheinisches Bildarchiv, rba_c017469: fig. 33
Darmstadt, © Hessisches Landesmuseum: cat. 9
Haarlem, © Teylers Museum: cats 10, 13, 24, 26, 84
London, © Agnew's: cat. 33
London, akg-images: figs 4, 20; Electa: fig. 2; Erich Lessing: figs 1, 3, 11, 14, 16, 17, 26, 38
London, © The Trustees of the British Museum: cats 25, 31, 59, 62, 68, 72, 76, 83, 58
Los Angeles, © J. Paul Getty Trust: cat. 64
New York, © 2010. Image copyright The Metropolitan Museum of Art/Art Resource/Scala, Florence: cats 18, 40
New York, © The Pierpont Morgan Library, 2008: cat. 1
Oxford, © Ashmolean Museum, University of Oxford: cats 3, 12
Paris, © The Bridgeman Art Library/Roger-Viollet: cats 45, 73, 88
Paris, © RMN: cat. 6; Michèle Bellot: cats 51, 79, 80, 39; Jean-Gilles Berizzi: cats 23, 48, 71; Gérard Blot: cats 63, 74; Christian Jean: cats 2, 35; Thierry Le Mage: cats 42, 56, 77; René-Gabriel Ojéda: fig. 30; Jean Schormans: cat. 38
Rouen, © Musées de la Ville de Rouen/M. Cavecin: cat. 57
Stockholm, © Nationalmuseum: cat. 87; Erik Cornelius: cat. 65
Tokyo, © Tokyo Fuji Art Museum/The Bridgeman Art Library: fig. 21
Washington, courtesy of the Board of Trustees, National Gallery of Art: cat. 20
Williamstown, Mass., © Sterling and Francine Clark Art Institute/Photo by Michael Agee: cat. 81

Index

All references are to page numbers.
Those in **bold** type indicate catalogue plates and those in *italic* type other illustrations.

Royal Academy Trust

Major Benefactors

The Trustees of the Royal Academy Trust are grateful to all its donors for their continued loyalty and generosity. They would like to extend their thanks to all those who have made a significant commitment, past and present, to the galleries, the exhibitions, the conservation of the Permanent Collection, the Library collections, the Royal Academy Schools, the education programme and other specific appeals.

HM The Queen
Her Majesty's Government
The 29th May 1961 Charitable Trust
Barclays Bank
BAT Industries plc
The late Tom Bendhem
The late Brenda M Benwell-Lejeune
British Telecom
John and Susan Burns
Mr Raymond M Burton CBE
Sir Trevor and Lady Chinn
The John S Cohen Foundation
Mr Adriaan de Mol van Otterloo
Sir Harry and Lady Djangoly
The Dulverton Trust
Alfred Dunhill Limited
The John Ellerman Foundation
The Eranda Foundation
Ernst & Young
Esso UK plc
Mr and Mrs Eugene V Fife
The Foundation for Sports and the Arts
Friends of the Royal Academy
John Frye Bourne
Jacqueline and Michael Gee
Glaxo Holdings plc
Diane and Guilford Glazer
Mr and Mrs Jack Goldhill
Maurice and Laurence Goldman
Mr and Mrs Jocelin Harris
The Philip and Pauline Harris Charitable Trust
The Charles Hayward Foundation
Robin Heller Moss
Heritage Lottery Fund
The Malcolm Hewitt Wiener Foundation
IBM United Kingdom Limited
The Idlewild Trust
Lord and Lady Jacobs
The JP Jacobs Charitable Trust
The Japan Foundation
Gabrielle Jungels-Winkler
Mr and Mrs Donald Kahn
Lillian Jean Kaplan Foundation
The Kresge Foundation
The Samuel H Kress Foundation
The Kirby Laing Foundation
The late Mr John S Latsis
The Leverhulme Trust
Lex Service plc
The Linbury Trust
Sir Sydney Lipworth QC and Lady Lipworth
John Lyons Charity
Ronald and Rita McAulay
McKinsey and Company Inc
John Madejski OBE DL
The Manifold Trust
Mr and Mrs John L Marion
Marks and Spencer
The Mercers' Company
The Monument Trust
The Henry Moore Foundation
The Moorgate Trust Fund
Mr and Mrs Minoru Mori
The Museums, Libraries and Archives Council
National Westminster Bank
Stavros S Niarchos
The Peacock Charitable Trust
The Pennycress Trust
PF Charitable Trust
The Pidem Fund
The Pilgrim Trust
The Edith and Ferdinand Porjes Trust
The Porter Foundation
John Porter Charitable Trust
Mr Gilberto Pozzi
Rio Tinto
John A Roberts FRIBA
Simon and Virginia Robertson
The Ronson Foundation
The Rose Foundation
Rothmans International plc
Dame Jillian Sackler DBE
Jillian and Arthur M Sackler
Mrs Jean Sainsbury
The Saison Foundation
The Basil Samuel Charitable Trust
Mrs Coral Samuel CBE
Sea Containers Ltd
Shell UK Limited
Miss Dasha Shenkman
William and Maureen Shenkman
The Archie Sherman Charitable Trust
Sir Paul Smith and Lady Pauline Denyer-Smith
Sir Hugh Sykes DL
Sir Anthony and Lady Tennant
Ware and Edythe Travelstead
The Trusthouse Charitable Foundation
The Douglas Turner Trust
Unilever plc
The Weldon UK Charitable Trust
The Welton Foundation
The Garfield Weston Foundation
The Maurice Wohl Charitable Foundation
The Wolfson Foundation
and others who wish to remain anonymous

Patrons

The Royal Academy is delighted to thank all its Patrons for generously supporting the following areas over the past year: exhibitions, education, the Royal Academy Schools, the Permanent Collection and Library, and Anglo-American initiatives; and for assisting in the general upkeep of the Academy.

Platinum
Mr and Mrs John Coombe
Mr and Mrs Patrick Doherty
Mrs Helena Frost
Mrs Nina Hirji Kheraj
Mr and Mrs David Shalit

Gold
His Excellency the American Ambassador
Mr and Mrs William Brake
Sir Ronald and Lady Cohen
Mr and Mrs Christopher Courage
Mrs Deanna Ibrahim
Mr and Mrs Ronald Lubner
Prof Anthony Mellows OBE TD and Mrs Mellows
Simon and Midge Palley
Lady Jane Rayne
Mrs Stella Shawzin
Mr and Dr Winkler
W Randall Work and Mandy Gray

Silver
Mrs Leslie Bacon
Mrs Gary Brass
Mrs Elie Brihi
Lady Brown
Sir Charles and Lady Chadwyck-Healey
Sir Trevor and Lady Chinn
Mrs Jennifer Cooke
The de Laszlo Foundation
Benita and Gerald Fogel
Mrs George Fokschaner
Mrs Anthony Foyle
Mr and Mrs Eric Franck
Jaqueline and Jonathan Gestetner
Michael and Morven Heller
Mr and Mrs Alan Hobart
Mr and Mrs Jon Hunt
S Isern-Feliu
Sir Martin and Lady Jacomb
Mr and Mrs S Kahan
Mr Nand Khemka and Princess Jeet Nabha Khemka
Mr D H Killick
Mr and Mrs James Kirkman
Mrs Aboudi Kosta
Lady Lever of Manchester
Sir Sydney Lipworth QC and Lady Lipworth CBE
Mr William Loschert
Mark and Liza Loveday
Mr Nicholas Maclean
Mr and Mrs Richard Martin
The Mulberry Trust
Mr and Mrs D J Peacock
Mr Basil Postan
The Lady Henrietta St George
Mr and Mrs Kevin Senior
Christina, The Countess of Shaftesbury
Mrs Lesley Silver
Richard and Veronica Simmons
Jane Spack
Mrs Elyane Stilling
Sir Hugh Sykes DL

Bronze
Lady Agnew
Miss H J C Anstruther
Edgar Astaire
Mrs Marina Atwater
Jane Barker
Stephen Barry Charitable Settlement
James M Bartos
Mrs Ginny Battcock
The Duke of Beaufort
Mrs J K M Bentley
Mrs Marcia Brocklebank
Mr and Mrs Charles H Brown
Mr Graham Brown
Jeremy Brown
Lord Browne of Madingley
Mr Raymond M Burton CBE
Mr F A A Carnwath CBE
Jean and Eric Cass
Mr and Mrs George Coelho
Denise Cohen Charitable Trust
Mark and Cathy Corbett
Mr and Mrs Sidney Corob
Julian Darley and Helga Sands
The Countess of Dartmouth
Lord and Lady Davies of Abersoch
Peter and Andrea De Haan
Mrs Norah de Vigier
Dr Anne Dornhorst
Lord Douro
Ms Noreen Doyle
Mr and Mrs Maurice Dwek
Lord and Lady Egremont
Mr and Mrs David Fenton
Bryan Ferry
Mr Sam Fogg
Mrs Kay Foster
Mrs Jocelyn Fox
Mr Monty Freedman
Arnold Fulton
The Lord Gavron CBE
Patricia and John Glasswell
Mark Glatman
Lady Gosling
Piers Gough
Mr Gavin Graham
Mr Louis Greig
Sir Ewan and Lady Harper
Mr Mark Hendriksen
Mr and Mrs Christoph Henkel
Ms Joanna Hewitt
Mr Patrick Holmes
Mrs Pauline Hyde
Mrs Raymonde Jay
Fiona Johnstone
Dr Elisabeth Kehoe
Mr Gerald Kidd
Norman A Kurland and Deborah A David
Joan H Lavender
Inez and George Lengvari
Mr Peter Lloyd
Mrs Diane Lockett
Miss R Lomax-Simpson
The Marquess of Lothian
Mr and Mrs Henry Lumley
Gillian McIntosh
Andrew and Judith McKinna
Sally and Donald Main
Mrs Sally Major
Mr and Mrs Eskandar Maleki
Mr Michael Manser RA and Mrs Jose Manser
Mr Marcus Margulies
Zvi and Ofra Meitar Family Fund
Mrs Alan Morgan
Mrs Joy Moss
Marion and Guy Naggar
Dr Ann Naylor
Ann Norman-Butler
North Street Trust
Mr Michael Palin
John H Pattisson
Mr Philip Perry
Mr David Pike
Mr and Mrs Anthony Pitt-Rivers
HRH Princess Marie-Chantal of Greece
Mrs Jasmin Prokop
John and Anne Raisman
Miss Myrna Rassam
Mrs Bianca Roden
Mrs Jenifer Rosenberg OBE
Lord Rothschild
Mr and Mrs K M Rubie
Ms Edwina Sassoon
H M Sassoon Charitable Trust
Carol Sellars
Dr Lewis Sevitt
Mr Robert N Shapiro
Victoria Sharp
Jonathan and Gillie Shaw
Mr James B Sherwood
Alan and Marianna Simpson
Brian D Smith
Mr Malcolm Smith
Mr J Sumption OBE
Mrs Kathryn Sumroy
Mrs D Susman
Lord Taylor of Holbeach and Lady Taylor
Mr Ian Taylor
Mr Anthony J Todd
Miss M L Ulfane
John and Carol Wates
Edna and Willard Weiss
Anthony and Rachel Williams
Mr William Winters
and others who wish to remain anonymous

Benefactor Patrons
Mary Fedden RA
Lord and Lady Foley
Mrs Mary Graves
Mrs Sue Hammerson
The Swan Trust
Sir Anthony and Lady Tennant

Benjamin West Patrons

Chairman
Lady Barbara Judge CBE

Platinum
William and Katherine Benz
Charles and Kaaren Hale

Gold
Lady Barbara Judge CBE

Silver
Lady J Lloyd Adamson
Mrs Spindrift Al Swaidi
Mrs Adrian Bowden
Mr and Mrs John R Olsen
Mr and Mrs Dave Williams

Bronze
Ms Ruth Anderson
Ms Sol Anitua
Mr Andy Ash
Mr Max Audley
Mr Stefano Aversa
Mr Mark Beith
Ms Michal Berkner
Ms Maryn Coker
Mr and Mrs Paul Collins
Mr Mark Dichter
Mr Jeffrey E Eldredge
Arthur Fabricant
Mr John Flynn
Cyril and Christine Freedman
Mr Metin Guvener
Mr Andrew Hawkins
Mr Brandon Hollihan
Mr and Mrs Marc Holtzman
Suzanne and Michael Johnson
Alistair Johnston and Christina Nijman
Mr and Mrs Kovacs
Mr and Mrs Wilson Lee
Charles G Lubar
Mrs Victoria Mills
Mr and Mrs Frank Moretti
Neil Osborn and Holly Smith
Lady Purves
Sylvia Scheuer
Mrs Sahim Sliwinski-Hong
Mr Adrian Smaus
Carl Stewart
Mrs Rola Tassabehji
Mrs Sayoko Teitelbaum
Lloyd Thomas
Mr and Mrs Julian Treger
Frederick and Kathryn Uhde
Mrs Yoon Ullmo
Prof Peter Whiteman QC
John and Amelia Winter
Mary Wolridge
Mrs Deborah Woodbury
and others who wish to remain anonymous

Schools Patrons

Chairman
Ms Clare Flanagan

Platinum
Mr Campbell Rigg
Matthew and Sian Westerman

Gold
Lord and Lady Myners
Mr James Stewart

Silver
Lord and Lady Aldington
Mr Sam Berwick
John Entwistle OBE

Bronze
Mrs Inge Borg Scott
Ian and Tessa Ferguson
Ms Clare Flanagan
Ken Howard OBE RA and Mrs Dora Howard
Mr Philip Marsden
Peter Rice Esq
Mr James Robinson
Anthony and Sally Salz
Mr Ray Treen
and others who wish to remain anonymous

Contemporary Circle

Chairman
Susie Allen

Patrons
Dr Jean Arundale
Mrs Jenny Borgerhoff Mulder
Viscountess Bridgeman
Dr Elaine C Buck
Ms Debra Burt
Jenny Christensson
Ms Maryn Coker
Helen and Colin David
Mr Peter d'Eugenio
Mrs Miel de Botton
Belinda de Gaudemar
Chris and Angie Drake
Mrs Wendy Ehst
Dr Barry Grimaldi
Caroline Hansberry
Mrs Susan Hayden
Margaret A Jackson
Ms Ina Kjellberg
Mr and Mrs Stephen Mather
Mr Andres Recoder and Mrs Isabelle Schiavi
Mrs Catherine Rees
Richard and Susan Shoylekov
Mrs Amy Jo Spitalier
Bob and Amy Stefanowski
Mr Robert Suss
John Tackaberry
Ms Inna Vainshtock
Cathy Wills
Manuela and Iwan Wirth
Mary Wolridge
and others who wish to remain anonymous

Trusts and Foundations
The Atlas Fund
The Ove Arup Foundation
The Peter Boizot Foundation
The Bomonty Charitable Trust
The Charlotte Bonham-Carter Charitable Trust
William Brake Charitable Trust
R M Burton 1998 Charitable Trust
C H K Charities Limited
P H G Cadbury Charitable Trust
The Carew Pole Charitable Trust
The Carlton House Charitable Trust
The Clore Duffield Foundation
John S Cohen Foundation
The Evan Cornish Foundation
The Sidney and Elizabeth Corob Charitable Trust
The Coutts Charitable Trust
Alan Cristea Gallery
The de Laszlo Foundation
The Dovehouse Trust
The Gilbert and Eileen Edgar Foundation
The Eranda Foundation
Lucy Mary Ewing Charitable Trust
The Margery Fish Charity
The Flow Foundation
Gatsby Charitable Foundation
The Great Britain Sasakawa Foundation
Sue Hammerson Charitable Trust
The Charles Hayward Foundation
The Hellenic Foundation
Heritage Lottery Fund
A D Hill 1985 Discretionary Settlement
The Harold Hyam Wingate Foundation
Institut für Auslandsbeziehungen e.V.
The Ironmongers' Company
The Japan Foundation
Stanley Thomas Johnson Foundation
The Emmanuel Kaye Foundation
The Kindersley Foundation
The Kobler Trust
The Samuel H Kress Foundation
The Lankelly Chase Foundation
Lapada Association of Art & Antique Dealers
The David Lean Foundation
The Leche Trust
A G Leventis Foundation
The Leverhulme Trust
The Lynn Foundation
The Maccabaeans
The McCorquodale Charitable Trust
Mactaggart Third Fund
The Simon Marks Charitable Trust
The Paul Mellon Centre for Studies in British Art
The Paul Mellon Estate

The Mercers' Company
Margaret and Richard Merrell Foundation
The Millichope Foundation
The Henry Moore Foundation
The Mulberry Trust
The J Y Nelson Charitable Trust
Newby Trust Limited
The Old Broad Street Charity Trust
The Peacock Charitable Trust
The Pennycress Trust
PF Charitable Trust
The Stanley Picker Charitable Trust
The Pidem Fund
The Edith and Ferdinand Porjes Charitable Trust
The Fletcher Priest Trust
Pro Helvetia
Mr and Mrs J A Pye's Charitable Settlement
The Radcliffe Trust
Rayne Foundation
The Reed Foundation
T Rippon & Sons (Holdings) Ltd
The Rootstein Hopkins Foundation
The Rose Foundation
The Rothschild Foundation
Schroder Charity Trust
The Sellars Charitable Trust
The Archie Sherman Charitable Trust
The South Square Trust
Spencer Charitable Trust
Stanley Foundation Limited
Oliver Stanley Charitable Trust
The Steel Charitable Trust
Peter Storrs Trust
Strand Parishes Trust
The Joseph Strong Frazer Trust
The Swan Trust
Swiss Cultural Fund in Britain
Thaw Charitable Trust
Sir Jules Thorn Charitable Trust
Tiffany & Co
Tillotson Bradbery Charitable Trust
The Albert Van den Bergh Charitable Trust
The Bruce Wake Charity
Celia Walker Art Foundation
Warburg Pincus Charitable Trust
The Wax Chandlers' Company
Weinstock Fund
The Garfield Weston Foundation
Wilkinson Eyre Architects
The Spencer Wills Trust
The Maurice Wohl Charitable Foundation
The Wolfson Foundation
The Hazel M Wood Charitable Trust
The Worshipful Company of Painter-Stainers
The Xander Foundation

American Associates of the Royal Academy Trust

Burlington House Trust
Mrs James C Slaughter
Benjamin West Society
Mr Francis Finlay
Mrs Deborah Loeb Brice
Mrs Nancy B Negley

Benefactors
Mrs Edmond J Safra
The Hon John C Whitehead

Sponsors
Mrs Drue Heinz HON DBE
David Hockney CH RA
Mr Arthur L Loeb
Mrs Lucy F McGrath
Mr and Mrs Hamish Maxwell
Diane A Nixon
Mr and Mrs Frederick B Whittemore
Dr and Mrs Robert D Wickham

Patrons
Mr and Mrs Steven Ausnit
Mr and Mrs E William Aylward
Mr Donald A Best
Mrs Mildred C Brinn
Mrs Benjamin Coates
Mr and Mrs Stanley De Forest Scott
Mrs June Dyson
Mr Jonathan Farkas
Mr and Mrs Lawrence S Friedland
Mr and Mrs Leslie Garfield
Dr Bruce C Horten
The Hon W Eugene Johnston and Mrs Johnston
Mr and Mrs Wilson Nolen
Lady Renwick
Mrs Mary Sharp Cronson
Mrs Frederick M Stafford
Ms Joan Stern
Ms Louisa Stude Sarofim
Martin J Sullivan OBE
Ms Britt Tidelius
Mr Robert W Wilson

Donors
Mr James C Armstrong
Mr Constantin R Boden
Dr and Mrs Robert Bookchin
Mrs Edgar H Brenner
Laura Christman and William Rothacker
Lois M Collier
Mr Richard C Colyear
Mr and Mrs Howard Davis
Ms Zita Davisson
Mr Robert H Enslow
Mrs Katherine D Findlay
Mr and Mrs Gordon P Getty
Mr and Mrs Gustave M Hauser
Mrs Judith Heath
Ms Elaine Kend
Mr and Mrs Nicholas L S Kirkbride
Mr and Mrs Gary Kraut
The Hon Samuel K Lessey Jr
Annette Lester
Mr Henry S Lynn Jr
Ms Clare E McKeon
Ms Christine Mainwaring-Samwell
Ms Barbara T Missett
Mrs Charles W Olson III
Cynthia Hazen Polsky and Leon B Polsky
Jane Richards
Mrs Martin Slifka
Mr Albert H Small
Mr Morton I Sosland

Corporate and Foundation Support
Annenberg Foundation
Bechtel Foundation
The Blackstone Charitable Foundation
The Brown Foundation
Fortnum & Mason
Gibson, Dunn & Crutcher
The Horace W Goldsmith Foundation
Leon Levy Foundation
Loeb Foundation
Henry Luce Foundation
Lynberg & Watkins
Northern Trust
Sony Corporation of America
Starr Foundation
Thaw Charitable Trust

Corporate Members of the Royal Academy

Launched in 1988, the Royal Academy's Corporate Membership Scheme has proved highly successful. Corporate membership offers benefits for staff, clients and community partners and access to the Academy's facilities and resources. The outstanding support we receive from companies via the scheme is vital to the continuing success of the Academy and we thank all members for their valuable support and continued enthusiasm.

Premier Level Members
A T Kearney Limited
The Arts Club
Barclays plc
BNY Mellon
CB Richard Ellis
Deutsche Bank AG
FTI Consulting
GlaxoSmithKline plc
Goldman Sachs International
Insight Investment
JTI
King Sturge
KPMG
LECG Ltd
Lombard Odier Darier Hentsch
Schroders plc
Smith and Williamson

Corporate Members
Abellio
All Nippon Airways
Aon
Apax Partners LLP
AXA Art Insurance & AXA Investment Managers
BNP Paribas
Booz & Co
The Boston Consulting Group UK LLP
Bovis Lend Lease Limited
British American Business Inc
British American Tobacco
Capital International Limited
Christie's
Clifford Chance LLP
Control Risks
Credit Agricole CIB
Ernst & Young
F & C Asset Management plc
GAM
Generation Investment Management LLP
Greenpark Capital
Heidrick & Struggles
HSBC
Jefferies International
John Lewis Partnership
JP Morgan
Lazard
Man Group plc
Mizuho International plc
Momart Limited
Morgan Stanley
Northern Trust
Panasonic Europe
Pentland Group plc
Rio Tinto
Royal Bank of Scotland
Royal Society of Chemistry
Slaughter and May
Société Générale
Tiffany & Co
Timothy Sammons Fine Art Agents
Trowers & Hamlins
UBS
Vision Capital Group
Weil, Gotshal & Manges

Supporters of Past Exhibitions

The President and Council of the Royal Academy would like to thank the following sponsors and benefactors for their generous support of major exhibitions in the last ten years:

2011
Modern British Sculpture
American Express Foundation
The Henry Moore Foundation
Hauser & Wirth
Art Mentor Foundation Lucerne
Sotheby's
Blain Southern
Tourism Partner: Welcome to Yorkshire

2010
GSK Contemporary – Aware: Art Fashion Identity
GlaxoSmithKline
Pioneering Painters: The Glasgow Boys 1880–1900
2009–2013 Season supported by JTI
Glasgow Museums
Treasures from Budapest: European Masterpieces from Leonardo to Schiele
OTP Bank
Villa Budapest
Daniel Katz Gallery, London
Travel Partner: Cox & Kings
Sargent and the Sea
2009–2013 Season supported by JTI
242nd Summer Exhibition
Insight Investment
Paul Sandby RA: Picturing Britain, A Bicentenary Exhibition
2009–2013 Season supported by JTI
The Real Van Gogh: The Artist and His Letters
BNY Mellon
Hiscox
Heath Lambert
Travel Partner: Cox & Kings
RA Outreach Programme
Deutsche Bank AG

2009
GSK Contemporary
GlaxoSmithKline
Wild Thing: Epstein, Gaudier-Brzeska, Gill
2009–2013 Season supported by JTI
BNP Paribas
The Henry Moore Foundation
Anish Kapoor
JTI
Richard Chang
Richard and Victoria Sharp
Louis Vuitton
The Henry Moore Foundation
J. W. Waterhouse: The Modern Pre-Raphaelite
2009–2013 Season supported by JTI
Champagne Perrier-Jouët
GasTerra
Gasunie
241st Summer Exhibition
Insight Investment
Kuniyoshi. From the Arthur R. Miller Collection
2009–2013 Season supported by JTI
Canon
Travel partner: Cox & Kings
Premiums and *RA Schools Show*
Mizuho International plc
RA Outreach Programme
Deutsche Bank AG

2008
GSK Contemporary
GlaxoSmithKline
Byzantium 330–1453
J F Costopoulos Foundation
A G Leventis Foundation
Stavros Niarchos Foundation
Travel Partner: Cox & Kings
Miró, Calder, Giacometti, Braque: Aimé Maeght and His Artists
BNP Paribas
Vilhelm Hammershøi: The Poetry of Silence
OAK Foundation Denmark
Novo Nordisk
240th Summer Exhibition
Insight Investment
Premiums and *RA Schools Show*
Mizuho International plc
RA Outreach Programme
Deutsche Bank AG
From Russia: French and Russian Master Paintings 1870–1925 from Moscow and St Petersburg
E.ON
2008 Season supported by Sotheby's

2007
Paul Mellon's Legacy: A Passion for British Art
The Bank of New York Mellon
Georg Baselitz
Eurohypo AG
239th Summer Exhibition
Insight Investment
Impressionists by the Sea
Farrow & Ball
Premiums and *RA Schools Show*
Mizuho International plc
RA Outreach Programme
Deutsche Bank AG
The Unknown Monet
Bank of America

2006
238th Summer Exhibition
Insight Investment
Chola: Sacred Bronzes of Southern India
Travel Partner: Cox & Kings
Premiums and *RA Schools Show*
Mizuho International plc
RA Outreach Programme
Deutsche Bank AG
Rodin
Ernst & Young

2005
China: The Three Emperors, 1662–1795
Goldman Sachs International
Impressionism Abroad: Boston and French Painting
Fidelity Foundation
Matisse, His Art and His Textiles: The Fabric of Dreams
Farrow & Ball
Premiums and *RA Schools Show*
The Guardian
Mizuho International plc
Turks: A Journey of a Thousand Years, 600–1600
Akkök Group of Companies
Aygaz
Corus
Garanti Bank
Lassa Tyres

2004
236th Summer Exhibition
A T Kearney
Ancient Art to Post-Impressionism: Masterpieces from the Ny Carlsberg Glyptotek, Copenhagen
Carlsberg UK Ltd
Danske Bank
Novo Nordisk
The Art of Philip Guston (1913–1980)
American Associates of the Royal Academy Trust
The Art of William Nicholson
RA Exhibition Patrons Group
Vuillard: From Post-Impressionist to Modern Master
RA Exhibition Patrons Group

2003
235th Summer Exhibition
A T Kearney
Ernst Ludwig Kirchner: The Dresden and Berlin Years
RA Exhibition Patrons Group
Giorgio Armani: A Retrospective
American Express
Mercedes-Benz
Illuminating the Renaissance: The Triumph of Flemish Manuscript Painting in Europe
American Associates of the Royal Academy Trust
Virginia and Simon Robertson
Masterpieces from Dresden
ABN AMRO
Classic FM
Premiums and *RA Schools Show*
Walker Morris
Pre-Raphaelite and Other Masters: The Andrew Lloyd Webber Collection
Christie's
Classic FM
UBS Wealth Management

2002
234th Summer Exhibition
A T Kearney
Aztecs
British American Tobacco
Mexico Tourism Board
Pemex
Virginia and Simon Robertson
Masters of Colour: Derain to Kandinsky. Masterpieces from The Merzbacher Collection
Classic FM
Premiums and *RA Schools Show*
Debenhams Retail plc
*RA Outreach Programme**
Yakult UK Ltd
Return of the Buddha: The Qingzhou Discoveries
RA Exhibition Patrons Group

* Recipients of a Pairing Scheme Award, managed by Arts + Business. Arts + Business is funded by the Arts Council of England and the Department for Culture, Media and Sport

Other Supporters

Sponsors of events, publications and other items in the past five years:

Carlisle Group plc
Castello di Reschio
Cecilia Chan
Country Life
Guy Dawson
Derwent Valley Holdings plc
Dresdner Kleinwort Wasserstein
Lucy Flemming McGrath
Fosters and Partners
Goldman Sachs International
Gome International
Gucci Group
Hines
IBJ International plc
John Doyle Construction
Harvey and Allison McGrath
Martin Krajewski
Marks & Spencer
Michael Hopkins & Partners
Morgan Stanley Dean Witter
The National Trust
Prada
Radisson Edwardian Hotels
Richard and Ruth Rogers
Rob van Helden
The Wine Studio